Praise for Sylvia, Queen of the Headhunters

'It is a brave man who keeps company with Sylvia Brooke, the extraordinary Ranee of Sarawak, but in Philip Eade this "most charming of despots" has met her match. He is a natural writer: percipient, sympathetic, amusing . . . and those who have never heard of Sylvia Brooke are in for a treat' Michael Holroyd

'Eade has uncovered a mine of marvellous material and handles it all with consummate wit and style. Indeed this is a dazzling debut, and I could not recommend it more highly as the perfect summer holiday read. Virtually every page contains a delicious anecdote, eccentric character or subtle aside to savour'
Hugh Massingberd, *Country Life*

'Philip Eade is eminently readable, with a detective's pertinacity at finding the clues to forgotten secrets and a raconteur's gift for sustaining his narrative interest . . . A rollicking good read'
Richard Davenport-Hines, *Sunday Telegraph*

'A thorough, fascinating and rather giddying book . . . sensational'
Lynne Truss, *Sunday Times*

'The unbelievable story of the outlandish last Ranee of Sarawak was the most gripping biography of 2007; stylish, funny, poignant, crammed with eccentrics, it may yet be a slow-burn bestseller'
Bartle Bull, Books of the Year, *Prospect*

'The kind of gift subject that biographers must dream of . . . Colourful anecdotes of eccentricity, lunacy and infidelity crowd every page' Christopher Hart, Books of the Year, *Sunday Times*

'Philip Eade brilliantly brings to life one of the 20th century's most exotic creatures. As astonishing an historical biography as you could ever hope to find' Justin Pollard

'An incredible story' *Daily Mail*

'Amazing and hilarious' Christopher Foyle, *Daily Express*

'Richly entertaining' *Irish Times*

'A scrupulous researcher . . . his prose is clear and his style pleasing: he writes with panache. This colourful book is his first, I am sure other fine volumes will follow'
Sara Wheeler, *Daily Telegraph*

'Philip Eade's stylish narrative never flags, nor his command of humour and irony. It is an altogether memorable work, the first I hope of many' Kenneth Rose

'There is no denying the technical accomplishment of his book – all the more remarkable because it is Eade's first'
Kathryn Hughes, *Guardian*

'Traces this tangled tale with diligence, humour and an easy style . . . For the true story read Philip Eade'
Christopher Esher, *Spectator*

'Luridly colourful . . . An entertaining peep-show view of the British ruling class at the end of the Imperial age'
Times Literary Supplement

'Eade adroitly handles both the tragic and the comic'
BBC History Magazine

'Outrage and eccentricity are things he does very well indeed'
Tablet

'Sylvia Brooke should have been an extra Mitford sister, such was the eccentricity and scandal of her life . . . it is a measure of his skill as much as the character of his subject that her remorseless *White Mischief*-style high-jinks don't pall . . . It's all highly entertaining'
First Post

Philip Eade was born in Shropshire, and read history at Bristol University. He was briefly a criminal barrister before turning to journalism. For several years he was on the staff of the *Daily Telegraph* as a writer and editor on its obituaries page. He lives in London and the Welsh Marches. This is his first book.

SYLVIA

Queen of the Headhunters

Philip Eade

PHOENIX

A PHOENIX PAPERBACK

First published in Great Britain in 2007
by Weidenfeld & Nicolson
This paperback edition published in 2008
by Phoenix,
an imprint of Orion Books Ltd,
Orion House, 5 Upper St Martin's Lane,
London WC2H 9EA

An Hachette Livre UK company

1 3 5 7 9 10 8 6 4 2

A CIP catalogue record for this book is available from the British Library.

ISBN 978-0-7538-2381-1

Typeset at The Spartan Press Ltd,
Lymington, Hants

Printed and bound at Mackays of Chatham plc,
Chatham, Kent

The Orion Publishing Group's policy is to use papers that are natural, renewable and recyclable products and made from wood grown in sustainable forests. The logging and manufacturing processes are expected to conform to the environmental regulations of the country of origin.

www.orionbooks.co.uk

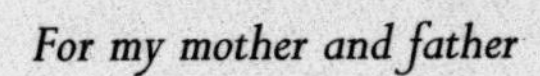

For my mother and father

Photographs are reproduced by kind permission of the Viscount Esher, Lord Tanlaw and other private collections with the following exceptions: James Brooke (*National Portrait Gallery*); Race Week (*Guildhall Library*); Vyner on the railway (*R. H. W. Reece*); Kayan dancing (*Guildhall Library*); installation group (*Sarawak Museum*); Sylvia at Garsington (*Adrian Goodman*); Dorothy Brett at Garsington (*National Portrait Gallery*); Dorothy at Taos (*National Portrait Gallery*); Dyak head feast (*Guildhall Library*); Sylvia in oriental creation (*Bodleian Library*); studio portrait of Sylvia (*National Portrait Gallery*); tea at the Astana (*Sarawak Museum*); Sylvia and Leonora poolside (*Guildhall Library*); Vyner and his Sarawak Rangers (*Guildhall Library*); Sylvia painting (*Bodleian Library*); oil painting of Leonora (*Lady Rosemary French*); press cuttings of Sylvia and her daughters (*Bodleian Library*); society tennis match (*Hulton Archive*); Sylvia, Elizabeth and Zena at Royal Academy (*Top Foto*); Vyner taking the salute (*R. H. W. Reece*); Leonora's wedding (*Ironwood Daily Globe*); Elizabeth and Harry Roy in the film *Rhythm Racketeer* (*Hulton Archive*); Sylvia with Blue Gifford (*Bodleian Library*); Sylvia with the Nawab of Pataudi (*Bodleian Library*); Vyner and Anthony Brooke (*Bodleian Library*); Sylvia and hairdresser (*Sarawak Museum*); Sylvia Cinema (*Borneo Literature Bureau*); Valerie and Bob Gregory (*Getty Images*); Princess Baba and her beachwear (*Getty Images*); the tribulations of Rajah Vyner (*Port Arthur News*); announcement of constitution (*R. H. W. Reece*); the Japanese surrender (*R. H. W. Reece*); Vyner receiving the Sword of State (*R. H. W. Reece*); signing the cession document (*Raymond Allas*); Anthony with his mother (*Anthony Brooke*); Anthony and Gita (*Anthony Brooke*); Sylvia with suitcases (*Bodleian Library*); Vyner in his lair (*Bodleian Library*); Sylvia with Frank de Buono (*Bodleian Library*); Elizabeth, Leonora and Valerie (*Lady Rosemary French*).

CONTENTS

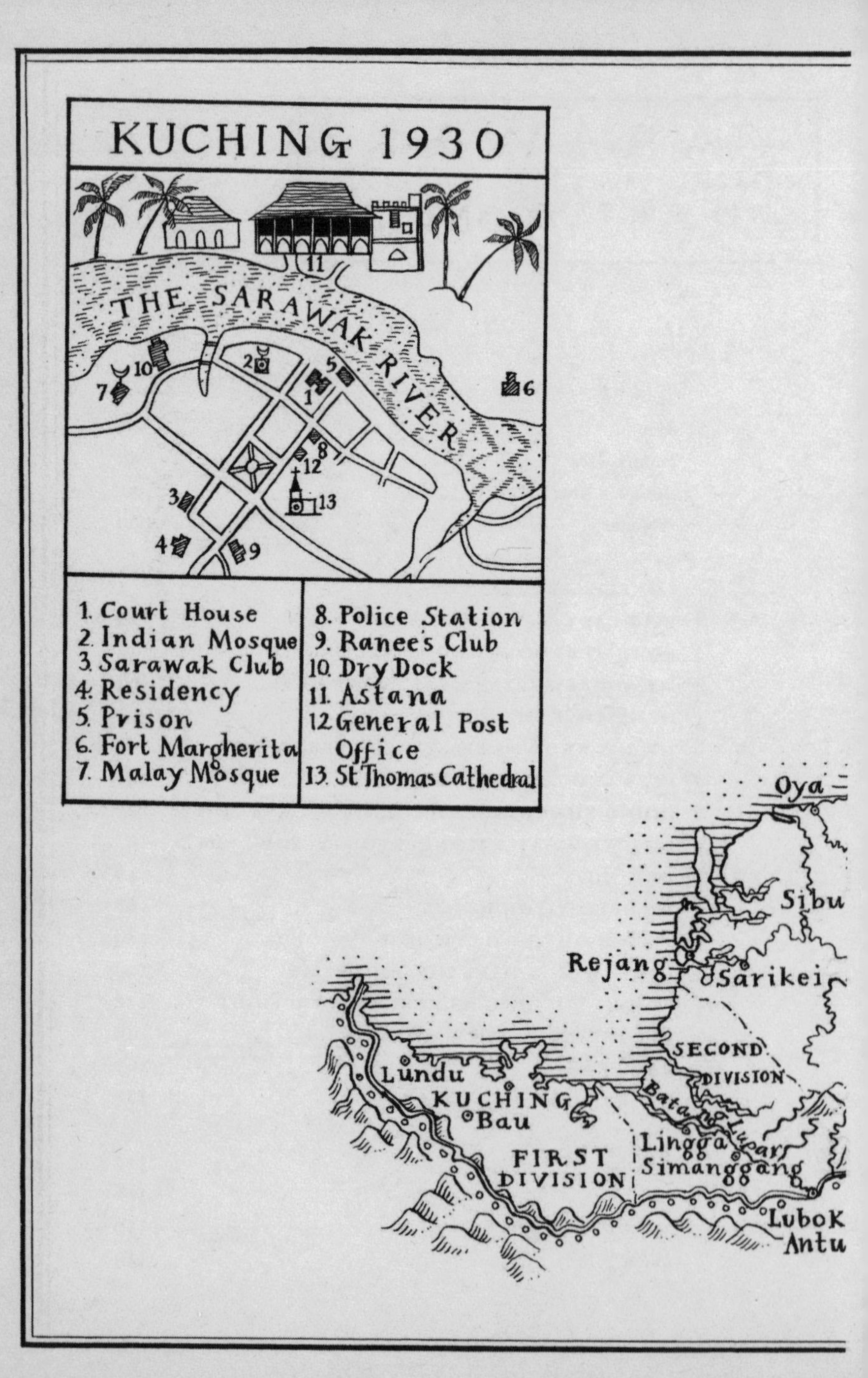
KUCHING 1930
THE SARAWAK RIVER
1. Court House
2. Indian Mosque
3. Sarawak Club
4. Residency
5. Prison
6. Fort Margherita
7. Malay Mosque
8. Police Station
9. Ranee's Club
10. Dry Dock
11. Astana
12 General Post Office
13. St Thomas Cathedral
Oya
Sibu
Rejang
Sarikei
SECOND DIVISION
Lundu
KUCHING
Bau
Batang Lupar
Lingga
Simanggang
FIRST DIVISION
Lubok Antu

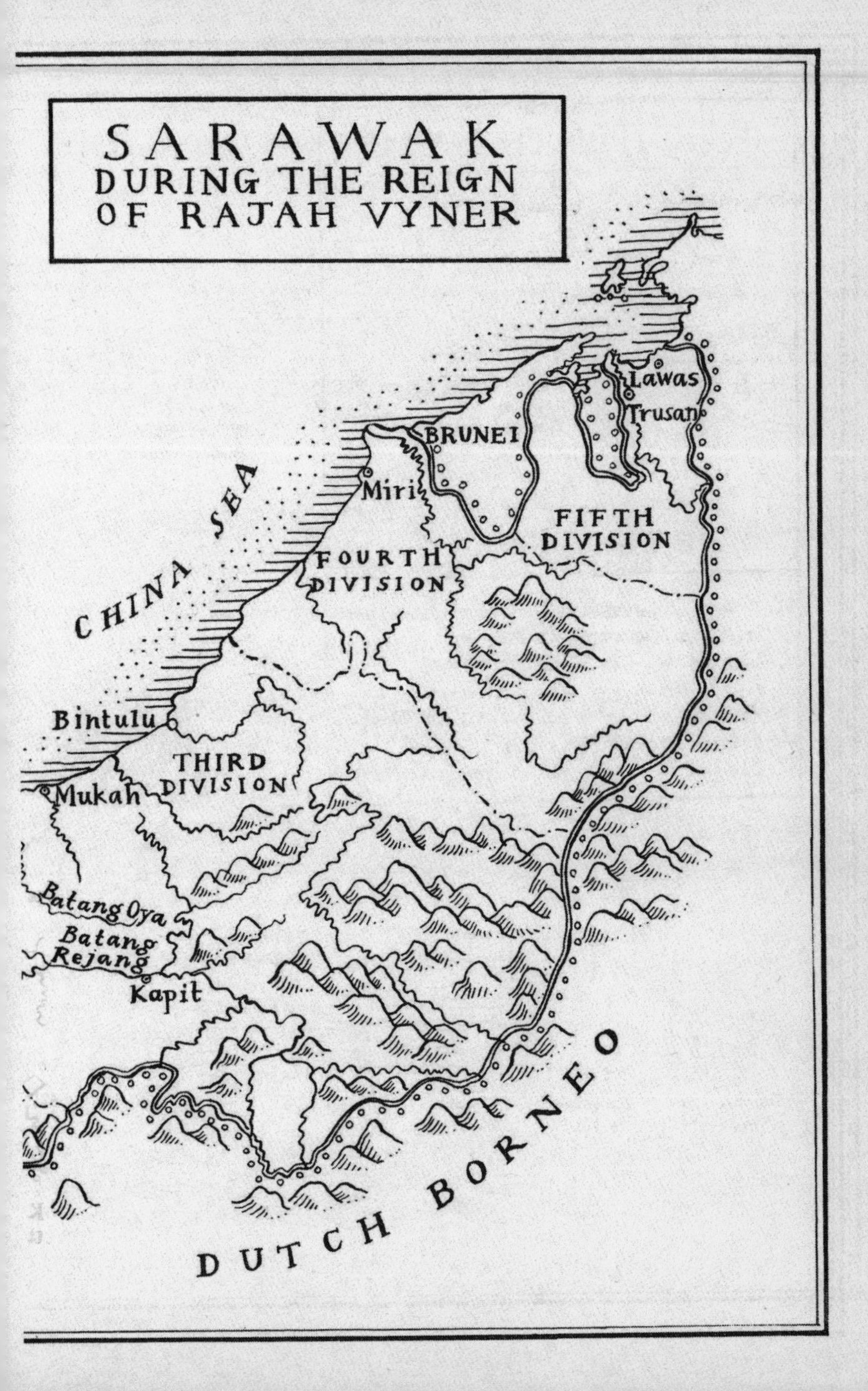
SARAWAK
DURING THE REIGN
OF RAJAH VYNER
CHINA SEA
BRUNEI
Lawas
Trusan
Miri
FIFTH
DIVISION
FOURTH
DIVISION
Bintulu
THIRD
DIVISION
Mukah
Batang Oya
Batang
Rejang
Kapit
DUTCH BORNEO

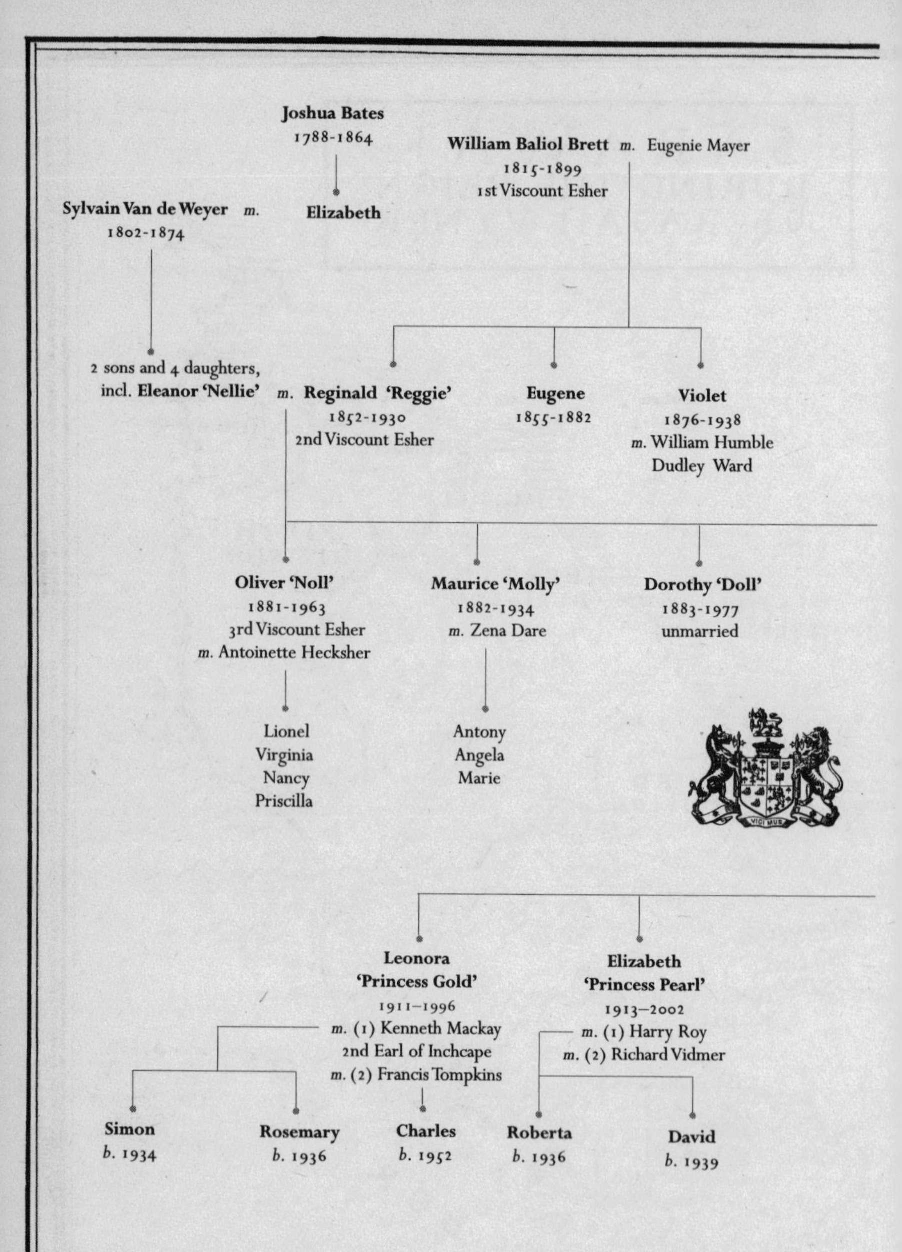
Joshua Bates
1788-1864
Elizabeth
William Baliol Brett m. Eugenie Mayer
1815-1899
1st Viscount Esher
Sylvain Van de Weyer m.
1802-1874
2 sons and 4 daughters,
incl. Eleanor 'Nellie' m. Reginald 'Reggie'
1852-1930
2nd Viscount Esher
Eugene
1855-1882
Violet
1876-1938
m. William Humble
Dudley Ward
Oliver 'Noll'
1881-1963
3rd Viscount Esher
m. Antoinette Hecksher
Maurice 'Molly'
1882-1934
m. Zena Dare
Dorothy 'Doll'
1883-1977
unmarried
Lionel
Virginia
Nancy
Priscilla
Antony
Angela
Marie
Leonora
'Princess Gold'
1911–1996
m. (1) Kenneth Mackay
2nd Earl of Inchcape
m. (2) Francis Tompkins
Elizabeth
'Princess Pearl'
1913–2002
m. (1) Harry Roy
m. (2) Richard Vidmer
Simon
b. 1934
Rosemary
b. 1936
Charles
b. 1952
Roberta
b. 1936
David
b. 1939

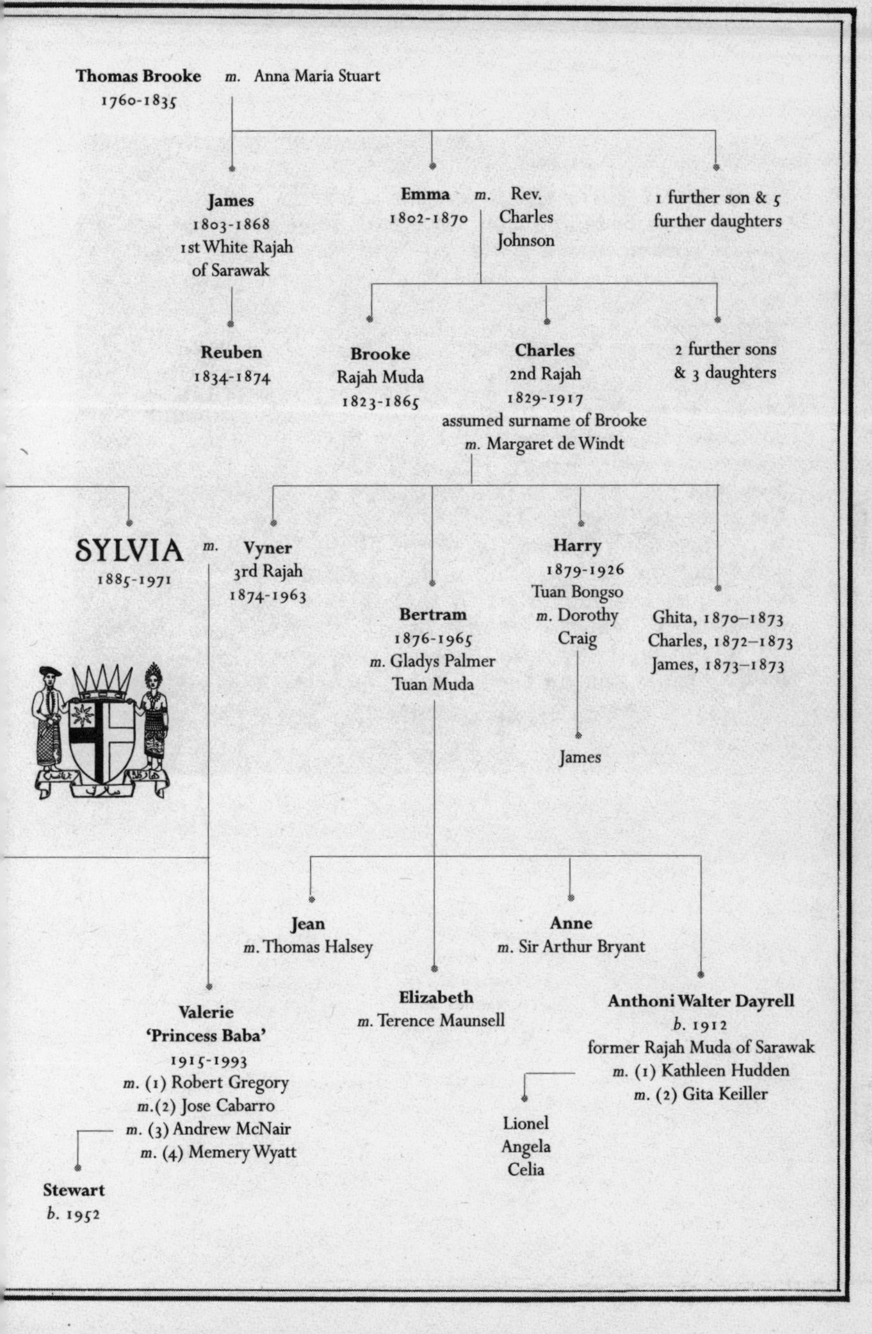

Thomas Brooke
1760-1835
m. Anna Maria Stuart
James
1803-1868
1st White Rajah
of Sarawak
Emma
1802-1870
m. Rev. Charles Johnson
1 further son & 5 further daughters
Reuben
1834-1874
Brooke
Rajah Muda
1823-1865
Charles
2nd Rajah
1829-1917
assumed surname of Brooke
m. Margaret de Windt
2 further sons & 3 daughters
SYLVIA
1885-1971
m.
Vyner
3rd Rajah
1874-1963
Harry
1879-1926
Tuan Bongso
m. Dorothy Craig
Bertram
1876-1965
m. Gladys Palmer
Tuan Muda
Ghita, 1870–1873
Charles, 1872–1873
James, 1873–1873
James
Jean
m. Thomas Halsey
Anne
m. Sir Arthur Bryant
Valerie
'Princess Baba'
1915-1993
m. (1) Robert Gregory
m.(2) Jose Cabarro
m. (3) Andrew McNair
m. (4) Memery Wyatt
Elizabeth
m. Terence Maunsell
Anthoni Walter Dayrell
b. 1912
former Rajah Muda of Sarawak
m. (1) Kathleen Hudden
m. (2) Gita Keiller
Lionel
Angela
Celia
Stewart
b. 1952

Thanks to the efficiency of Sarawak rule and the vigilance of our Sarawak Government officers, Sarawak is a far more law-abiding country than England. The blood lust is spoken of but little felt, and these tribes, although still uncivilized, have lost to a very large extent their practice of taking heads. Sarawak is, I should say, one of the few countries where you can walk abroad in safety—no beggars, no trippers, no troubles on the track. The Dyaks and Kayans really understand the meaning of the old-fashioned word "Host," and they have brought the courtesy of entertaining to the very finest art. If I wanted to spend a really happy evening I know what I should do. I should get into a boat and paddle to the far reaches of the river, to these remote places where the people live who were once upon a time the terror of the land. And there, squatting on the ground, with a plateful of rotten eggs before me, I would listen to their native songs and watch them dance, whilst over my head, in acknowledgment of my presence there, three smooth and shiny skulls would hang, with a grin on their gaping mouths.

HER HIGHNESS THE RANEE OF SARAWAK

AUTHOR'S NOTE

I am grateful to everyone who has helped me in various ways with the researching and writing of this book – even the esteemed historian who kindly wished me good luck but said he could think of nothing to contribute on 'the wretched Sylvia Brooke' or her husband and admitted to being baffled as to why I should want to write about 'that seedy pair'. Luckily I was by then too far in to turn back, and almost convinced myself to be encouraged.

The idea sprang from a telephone call in 2002 to the obituaries desk of the *Daily Telegraph*, where I then worked, from Stewart McNair, the son of Valerie, the wildest of Ranee Sylvia's three daughters, known by the popular press as 'Princess Baba'. Mr McNair – himself a headhunter, appropriately enough, albeit of the corporate kind – suggested that we might like to run an obituary of his aunt Elizabeth, 'Princess Pearl', and it was while cobbling together a piece for our page that I was drawn further in to the curious story of the Brooke family. I would like to thank him for taking the trouble to call us and for all his subsequent help.

I would also like to thank my literary agent Caroline Dawnay, for all her brilliant advice and reassuring certainty that a book centred on the racy Ranee would work, and my charming and incisive publisher Alan Samson, at Weidenfeld & Nicolson.

I owe an especially heavy debt to Professor R. H. W. Reece. During the 1970s he was responsible for assembling many of the papers in the vast Brooke archive at Rhodes House in Oxford, and for interviewing many of Rajah Vyner's officers before they died, incorporating their recollections in such carefully researched books as *The Name of Brooke* and *Masa Jepun*, which have been invaluable references for me. In 2004, while on a research trip to Sarawak, I visited Bob Reece at his home town of Perth, in Western Australia, and he has been more than generous in sharing information, insights and contacts, and most recently reading and commenting on my manuscript. I also went to see another renowned Brooke expert, Professor Nicholas Tarling, at Auckland University, who has been equally helpful.

I am extremely grateful to Rajah Vyner's nephew and thwarted heir, Anthony Brooke, now in his ninety-fourth year, and his wife Gita, who had me to stay for three days at their delightful clapboard villa on the north island of New Zealand, treated me with the utmost hospitality, cheerfully tolerated my nosy questions about his troublesome aunt and gave me free rein to rootle through his Sarawak papers.

In Sarawak, Philip Yong was most generous in arranging my stay, laying on a rich variety of entertainment – from orang-utan and crocodile safaris to karaoke at the Club in Kuching – and suggesting people to talk to, among whom I should like to thank Datuk Lucas Chin, Mrs Choo, Datuk Amar Linggi Jugah, Temenggong Datuk Kenneth Kanyan, Heidi Munan, Datuk Robert Ridu, James Ritchie, Datuk Ang Lai Soon, and Datuk Amar James Wong.

Back in Britain, the task of writing this biography would have been infinitely less rewarding without the wonderfully co-operative help of Sylvia's great-nephew Christopher Esher, the present Viscount, and his wife Valerie, who entrusted me with numerous volumes of Brett family letters which Sylvia's father had carefully bound in red leather. I was also allowed to look at the remarkable love letters between Reggie Esher and his son Maurice which are kept at Churchill College, Cambridge, and given access to the family's magnificent photograph albums.

I am equally grateful to Sylvia's eldest grandson, Lord Tanlaw, who as Simon Mackay had been Sylvia's preferred heir to the Raj. He allowed me to quote from the Brooke archive at Rhodes House and offered countless other useful insights. His sister Lady Rosemary French has also been exceedingly kind, lending me photographs, newspaper cuttings and a rare surviving copy of their mother Leonora's memoir, *My Lovely Days*. Among other books, I am particularly indebted to James Lees-Milne's biography of Reggie Esher, *The Enigmatic Edwardian*, and to Sean Hignett's biography of Sylvia's sister Dorothy, *Brett*.

I would like to say a big thank you to the extraordinarily helpful staff of the London Library, where the majority of this book was written, and to those, equally helpful, at Rhodes House, where much of it was researched, and where Lucy McCann was endlessly obliging. Among the other libraries and archives to whom I am grateful are The British Library; Churchill College Archive, Cambridge; The Colindale Newspaper Library; Guildhall Library in the City of London; Harry Ransom Humanities Research Center at the University of Texas, Austin; the Center for Southwest Research, University of New Mexico; The Bancroft Library, University of California, Berkeley; The Telegraph newspaper library, The New York Public Library, and the Kuching Museum in Sarawak.

I am especially grateful to Robert Gray and Kate Hubbard, who read the manuscript in its crudest form and suggested countless crucial refinements, to Emily Faccini for her beautiful maps, and to Christopher Phipps, for the excellent index. Many thanks also to Charles Allen, Nigel Barley, David Belton, Serena Brabazon, Rory Knight Bruce, Louise Carpenter, Lucy Cavendish, John Chancellor, the late Marie Cheyne, Sophie Coudray, the late Madeleine Daubeny, Richard Davenport-Hines, Jean Edelstein, the late Viscount (Lionel) Esher, Tom Faulkner, James and Melissa Fergusson, Natasha Galloway, David Gelber, Adrian Goodman, Tom Graves, Bea Hemming, James Heneage, Sir Michael Holroyd, the late Right Reverend Peter Howes, Christopher Howse, Jay Iliff, George Ireland, Caroline Knox, Victoria Lane, Janie Lewis, John Lloyd, Joanna Lumley, Euan and Fiona McAlpine, Belinda and Patrick Macaskie, Andrew McKie, John McNally, Lucinda McNeile, Roddy Martine, Sir Oliver Millar, Fiona Neill, Michael Olizar, Helen Oon, David Phillips, Dato Sri, John Pike, Cassandra Pybus, Dan Renton, David Roy, Rodolph de Salis, Sita Schutt, Miranda Seymour, Catherine Shoard, the Reverend Dr Ann Shukman, Roberta Simpson, Edward Simpson-Orlebar, Richard Stafford, Otto Steinmayer, Louisa Symington, Louise Tucker, Hugo Vickers, Martha Wailes, Michael Williams, Jo and Richard Wimbush, and numerous other friends who have helped me along the way. Lastly, I would like to thank my mother and father, to whom this book is dedicated.

PROLOGUE

I'M RAJAH HERE. I'LL BROOKE
NO INTERFERENCE.
Tommy Handley, *ITMA* (1940s)

On the morning of 24 September 1941 a royal salute from twenty-one cannon boomed out over Kuching, the toytown capital of Sarawak. Shortly before nine o'clock, as their last echoes died away, Rajah Vyner and Ranee Sylvia emerged from the Astana, the royal palace across the river from the government offices and main bazaar, and solemnly made their way down to the landing stage. The Rajah, a diffident Englishman who had reigned over this jungly kingdom on the island of Borneo for twenty-four years, wore an ill-fitting white duck uniform and solar topee, and walked beneath a slightly tatty yellow umbrella, the emblem of royalty in Sarawak, held aloft by a Malay bearer. The Ranee, wearing her royal yellow sarong, followed a few paces behind: besides being her husband's consort, she was also, according to custom, his slave.

Rajah Vyner's family, the Brookes, who claimed descent from the ancient English West Country family of Broke, had ruled Sarawak for three generations, during which time their realm had grown to cover an area the size of England. Popularly known as the White Rajahs, theirs was the only English family ever to have occupied an Oriental throne. They had their own flag, currency, postage stamps and armed forces, and each rajah had the power of life and death over his subjects, variously Malays, Chinese and Dyak tribesmen notorious for their custom of headhunting. The third Rajah, educated at Winchester and at Magdalene, Cambridge, was one of the few monarchs left in the world who could still say '*L'État c'est moi.*' Yet he ruled his kingdom, it was noted, rather as if it were an English country estate, with tribal chiefs always welcome at the big house. His family appeared in *Burke's Landed Gentry* as 'Brooke of Sarawak', and his career was encapsulated in one of the more arresting entries in *Who's Who*: 'Has led several expeditions into the far interior of the country to punish headhunters; understands the management of natives; rules over a population of 500,000 souls and a country 40,000 sq. miles in extent.'

It was now a hundred years to the day since an uncle of the Sultan of Brunei had ceded the government of Sarawak to Vyner's swashbuckling great-uncle, James Brooke. Everywhere in Kuching there were flags and bunting to celebrate the centenary of the Brooke Raj. All the leading chiefs and representatives from the various communities of the country had gathered together at the capital, bearing gifts for the Rajah and Ranee. The festivities would go on for a week, centred on the Grand Fancy Bazaar, with entertainments ranging from Dyak war dancing to a stall which invited participants to kick a dummy of Hitler. Boy Scouts patrolled the grounds to deter gatecrashers.

After crossing the river in the ornate state barge, a gift from the King of Siam, the Rajah and Ranee landed in front of the courthouse, built by Vyner's father Rajah Charles in 1874, where Rajah Vyner had continued to dispense justice as judge, jury and sentencer, sitting like a second Moses on the chair of state. Accompanied by his chief secretary, the Rajah inspected the guard of honour, which had been furnished by the Sarawak Constabulary, and received the royal salute. The Ranee walked to one side, escorted by the leader of Sarawak's Malay community. They proceeded to the government offices, where once a week the Rajah would receive any of his subjects who wished to talk to him, attended only by two police constables to keep the queue orderly. Detachments of the Royal Navy – four of whose vessels lay at anchor in the river – Indian Army, Sarawak Rangers, Sarawak Volunteer Force and Sarawak Coastguard stood to attention on either side of the route.

Seats for Their Highnesses had been placed at the entrance to the cool, white offices under a canopy in royal yellow. To either side there were covered stands for members of the government and leaders of the various communities. When the Rajah and Ranee were seated on the throne, a band struck up the national anthem, which had been composed by Vyner's mother, Ranee Margaret. This was followed by the reading of addresses and pledges of loyalty to the Rajah, beginning with a message from King George VI, who wished 'to convey to Your Highness My congratulations on the centenary of the State of Sarawak, and to express to you and to the peoples of Sarawak My best wishes for your future prosperity'.

Among the many other messages came one from Air Chief Marshal Sir Robert Brooke-Popham, a distant kinsman of the Rajah who had recently taken up his post as Commander-in-Chief, Far East, at the misnamed 'Fortress Singapore'. Part of Brooke-Popham's job was to organise the defence of Sarawak, guaranteed under the Treaty of Protection (1888) with Britain, which also controlled its foreign relations as a protected state. He thanked the Rajah for his co-operation in carrying out the various defence measures which he had advised. Only time would tell just how inadequate these measures were.

Rajah Vyner had always dreaded these state occasions when he was the centre of attention, but on this morning he had required more than the usual coaxing from the effervescent Ranee to persuade him to go through with the rigmarole. His ability to charm his subjects had helped make him an extremely popular ruler, but on this occasion he looked uneasy and distracted as he rose to reply to their loyal addresses. Two days later, at an all-male dinner party at the Astana to celebrate the Rajah's sixty-seventh birthday, one of the guests, a visiting naval officer, observed that his host was 'a very nice man to meet, but unfortunately he seems to have lost interest in governing his country . . .' As part of the centenary Vyner had introduced a new constitution, which would curtail his absolute powers and, in the opinion of the naval officer, it was 'just as well that he has handed over. He displayed a lack of interest and ungraciousness throughout the ceremonies, which we thought was a jolly bad show as the enthusiasm of his people was very obviously sincere.' 'The Ranee', added the naval officer, 'I think is slightly dotty, although she can be quite amusing, and what with the daughters marrying dance-band leaders and all-in wrestlers they are a pretty rummy lot.'

The events that followed on the heels of the centenary, starting with the Japanese invasion, were the culmination of a steady decline in the power and prestige of the Brooke Raj that had begun two decades previously. The whimsical Rajah Vyner, his Rasputinesque private secretary and the ham-fisted British government all bore their share of responsibility for the clumsy and seemingly underhand way in which the dynasty was brought to an end. But in many people's eyes a bigger villain was Ranee Sylvia, the extravagantly dressed author of eleven books, who was submissive consort one moment, outrageous self-dramatist the next, described by the press as 'that most charming of despots' and by her own brother as 'a female Iago'. The Colonial Office branded her 'a dangerous woman', full of Machiavellian schemes to alter the succession and often spectacularly vulgar in her behaviour. After observing the Ranee dancing with two prostitutes in a nightclub, then taking them back to the palace to paint their portraits, a visiting MP from Westminster concluded: 'A more undignified woman it would be hard to find.'

When Steven Runciman wrote his history *The White Rajahs* (1960), he conceded in his Preface that, as far as the last reign was concerned, he had been reluctant to offend those 'actors' who were still living, clearly having in mind Rajah Vyner and, uppermost perhaps, Ranee Sylvia. 'An historian dealing with characters long dead', he wrote, 'may legitimately assign motives, speculate on rumours and even indulge in a little scandal-mongering. It is neither courteous nor helpful nor wise for him to do so when he is dealing with the fringes of the present.'

Privately Runciman admitted to rather stronger views on the last Rajah and Ranee than he was prepared to publish. Writing to Vyner's niece shortly before his book came out, he said that his terms of reference (the book had been suggested and sponsored by the colonial government of Sarawak), tact and fear of legal proceedings 'kept me from saying too openly what I think about the later stages, but I hope that what I think shows through well enough . . .' 'Of the Ranee', he wrote in a subsequent letter, 'I've said very little, as I didn't want to risk libel.' This book, of which Ranee Sylvia is the central character, is subject to no such constraints, since she died in 1971, eight years after Rajah Vyner.

1

LONELY GIRL

Sylvia's elder sister Dorothy – later better known as the Bloomsbury painter 'Brett' and the third in D. H. Lawrence's *ménage à trois* in New Mexico – recalled being wheeled in a double pram with Syv by their nurse in Hyde Park one day and being told to wave to their father, Reginald Brett, who was out walking with a friend. Reggie wondered to his friend why those children were waving at him. 'Perhaps they are yours,' the friend ventured.

Reggie Brett, who succeeded his father as the second Viscount Esher in 1899 when Sylvia was fourteen, was a fabulously well-connected man, the confidant of Queen Victoria, King Edward VII and King George V, and of every prime minister from Rosebery to Baldwin. Yet he was a remote and often cruelly insensitive father to his children when they were young, apart from his younger son Maurice, whom he worshipped. Girls, in particular, were 'tiresome things until they are grown up', as far as Reggie was concerned. For her part, as the youngest child, Sylvia felt that 'nobody loved me and that I was the cuckoo in this illustrious family nest. It even seemed to me that my father's voice altered when he spoke to me, as if he were forcing his words through cubes of ice.'

For as long as Sylvia could remember, a steady stream of luminaries trooped through her family home, Orchard Lea, in Windsor Forest. This dark, rambling house was completed a few months after Sylvia was born, in 1885, to Reggie's hideous if fashionable 'Tudorbethan' design, with lead casements and low oaken ceilings. Lord Rosebery learned to ride a bicycle in the garden there during his time as Prime Minister; Kaiser Wilhelm II admired the house so much that he ordered similar ones to be built in Germany; and Queen Victoria came so often that she had her own special entrance built – it was also much used by Edward VII and Queen Alexandra. 'It was a curious life for children,' Sylvia recalled. 'The house was almost continually filled with famous people . . . At meal times we would sit dumbly listening to conversation of such a brilliant order that we became imbued with a kind of dull despair, and inferiority complex . . . I would sit there like an anaemic suet pudding, suffering the tortures of stupidity.' She also remembered spending 'a great deal of my childhood crying my eyes out in a ten-foot by twelve ivy-papered lavatory at the top of the house'.

Starved of parental love (her mother, by Sylvia's account, was usually too occupied with her 'wifely adoration' to give the children her full attention), young Syv sought it instead from her genial grandfather, the first Viscount Esher. (William) Baliol Brett, as he was before his elevation to the peerage in 1885, was a curate's son, descended, according to family legend, from William Brett, who built Brett's Hall in the County of Warwick during the reign of Henry III. He was a useful amateur boxer and captained the 'lightning' Cambridge crew that beat Oxford by a dozen lengths or more in 1839. Irresponsible and fun-loving as a young man, he subsequently knuckled down and excelled at the Bar, thanks to a remarkable memory and determination, driven to a great extent by his adoration of his French wife, Eugénie, who was forever urging him to forge ahead in his career. Elected Conservative MP for Helston in Cornwall in 1866, he was Solicitor-General in Disraeli's brief administration of 1868, and in 1876 made a Lord Justice of Appeal. Seven years later he was appointed Master of the Rolls, the second most senior post in the judiciary of England and Wales, and on his retirement in 1897 he was created a viscount, a dignity not given to any judge, Lord Chancellors excepted, for mere legal conduct, since the time of Sir Edward Coke, the great seventeenth-century judge. Baliol's last letter to his wife, written from the Lake District while on circuit, is a moving testament to his steadfast devotion:

> The lake and its hills were lovely as ever. This morning when I was going for my before-breakfast walk, the ground and the hills were covered with snow – still with the woods and hedges marking dark patches and lines, and the hills of every shape, and the lake dark in the midst of it all: it was only a new beauty in these dear lakes. I thought of nothing but you my loved and lovely one, and how happy and most happy I was there with you in the pride of your youth and beauty: and I felt again all the deep gratitude I ever feel and felt for you for having given them both to me with a loving kindness that seems to have no bounds. How gloriously happy were those days, when all was love and hope! Now, with me, all is the same love, but instead of hope is the feeling of the present. There is now in life, to me, a sense of sadness! It is I suppose, that I can no longer hope anything in myself; I know myself for what I am. For you, my love and my enchantress, you are my only hope, and my only real happiness. If I see you bright and happy, it is as Heaven; if I see you otherwise, the light is out of the sky.

As a young girl Sylvia would sit on her grandfather's knee 'stroking the snow-white hair that grew like a soft halo around his head' and implore him to marry her. 'What about your grandmother?' he would ask. 'Don't you think we had better ask her first?' But Sylvia was afraid of her grandmother, and told him that this had better be a secret between the two of them. Though by then a severe old lady in a partial brown wig, invariably slightly askew, Eugénie Brett had once featured in the popular annual *Book of Beauty* (1848), her then handsome features rendered by Count d'Orsay, the lover of the book's editor Lady Blessington. Eugénie's mother Fanny (née Kreilssamner) claimed to have been the widow of Louis Mayer, a fellow Alsatian whom she had followed to Waterloo in 1815 with her one-year-old daughter. Widowed during the battle, she subsequently married Colonel John Gurwood, a veteran of the Peninsular War, who had made a name for himself by capturing the governor of Ciudad Rodrigo. Wellington awarded him the French governor's sword for this feat, but Gurwood spent his later life paranoid that others were questioning the true extent of his heroism. Severely wounded at Waterloo, he became the Duke's private secretary and was largely occupied editing his despatches until he cut his own throat on Christmas Day 1845.

Family legend had it that Fanny was a *vivandière* and that Eugénie had been born on the field of Waterloo. Doubtful about Fanny's past, the scrupulous Gurwood had refused to let her near the Duke or other important English friends and made her stay behind in their hotel while he went into society. Instead she and Eugénie drifted into the more bohemian set centred on Gore House, where Lady Blessington and Count d'Orsay held court to an exotic assortment of émigré writers and artists. In the early years of their marriage, Gurwood had also required that Fanny leave the young Eugénie behind in Paris, thereby inviting gossip about the girl's legitimacy (some whispered that her father was Napoleon). One consequence of this was that Eugénie's admirers tended to want her as their mistress but not their wife. By the time Baliol Brett declared himself, she was nearing thirty; yet even then, busy as she was with attending the London and Paris seasons, she made him wait until he was earning enough from his briefs to support her. They married after an engagement lasting eight years and in 1852, while living in Kensington, she gave birth to their first child, Reginald Baliol, Sylvia's father.

Young Reggie spent his early life between London and Paris, and, in his memoir *Cloud-capp'd Towers*, he later recalled: 'As a child, in a poplin frock, I had been seated on the lap of a wizened old man who had once played the violin before Marie Antoinette. Later in my great-aunt's [Fanny Kreilssamner's sister Isabelle] house, I had been presented to a stout, dark-skinned man with masses of grizzled hair, an enormous hat held curiously between his knees. It was Alexander Dumas [whose mistress his great-aunt had been] . . .' Later still he had been kindly treated by the venerable Comte de Flahault, 'who, as Napoleon's aide-de-camp, had accompanied the Emperor home from Moscow, and ridden that tragic ride alongside his master away from the field of Waterloo'. Inevitably, perhaps, the boy became keen on history. He slept with one of the brown volumes of Southey's *Nelson* under his pillow, and before the age of twelve had read all of Hume's *History of England*, and all bar one of the Waverley novels.

From Cheam, Reggie was sent to Eton, where he soon came

under the spell of William Johnson, a famously short-sighted and absent-minded master who was said to wear three pairs of spectacles, one on top of the other, and was once observed, so the story goes, hurrying down Windsor Hill, grabbing at a hen in the belief that it was his hat. 'Tute', as the boys called Johnson, was nonetheless a brilliant scholar – he was a Fellow of King's College, Cambridge – and an accomplished poet, best known as the author of 'They told me, Heraclitus, they told me you were dead', translated from Callimachus, and much anthologised. He also wrote the Eton Boating Song, and was among the finest teachers in the history of the school, albeit with a notorious propensity towards favouritism. He steeped his disciples in the Greek and Latin classics and modern literature he approved of, and taught them the complementary ideals of romantic bisexual love and high-minded service to Empire. He based his ethical teachings on the classical Greek philosophers, but how far Johnson himself stuck to the Socratic ideal of restraint from passionate physical acts is unclear; he eventually resigned from Eton under a cloud in 1872, two years after Reggie had left the school, and changed his name by deed poll to Cory (that of his grandmother), saying it would save time in writing.

Johnson held Reggie Brett in the highest regard: 'I have loved other Eton boys,' he wrote to him in 1869, 'but none so *great* as he, so devoted to the public good, so exalted above me.' At the age of sixteen, when he first came to Johnson's notice, Reggie had received a letter from his tutor counselling him to 'be unworldly; don't worship celebrities, like simple people, honest people'. Some time later there was frank jealousy over 'my sweet Elliot', as Johnson referred to the future Sir Francis Elliot, GCVO, and Minister to Athens: 'I envy you being kissed by him,' Johnson wrote to Reggie, 'If I were dying like Nelson I would ask him to kiss me. I kissed his dear foot last Tuesday on the grass of Ankerwyke.'

For Reggie, though, Elliot was a dalliance. He would have deeper and longer lasting love affairs at school, most profoundly with Charles 'Chat' Williamson, a lifelong friend, a frequent and often long-term guest at Orchard Lea, and an adored confidant of Sylvia. Johnson predicted to Reggie in 1869: 'Some day, not long hence, *you* will be steeped in love for a woman as not to comprehend the old affection for boys.' Yet while he did go on to marry, and very happily, Reggie never ceased to indulge in intimate liaisons with (usually younger) members of his own sex.

His busy love life did not prevent him from passing the entrance examination for Trinity College, Cambridge, but leaving Eton was a terrible wrench, as his grandson, Lionel Brett, later explained: 'Floating in a dodger on the silent Thames then at the height of its elmy beauty, friendships were formed which were to last a political lifetime . . . To have to leave this hedonist's paradise, even for Cambridge, was heart-rending for my grandfather. Years later, the recollection reduced him to tears. It seemed a threat to his private life and created a distaste for the public arena that was to be his best-known characteristic.'

Another characteristic of Reggie Brett's was the powerful appeal he held for older women. While at Cambridge, he was taken up by Lady Ripon, the mother of his friend Olly de Grey, and he often stayed with her and her husband, the former Viceroy of India. A rich semi-invalid, Lady Ripon shared her husband's radical Whig views and their combined influence persuaded Reggie to reject his father's Toryism and eventually throw in his lot with the Liberals. Through the Ripons, Reggie also came to know Sir William Harcourt (who also happened to be a friend of his father's), who was then Whewell Professor of International Law at Cambridge and later served as Home Secretary and Chancellor of the Exchequer under Gladstone. Constantly at Harcourt's side was his son Lewis, 'Loulou', an ultimately creepy figure whose mother had died when he was born. Eleven years Reggie's junior and only nine when they first met, Loulou became one of his dearest friends; as Secretary of State for the Colonies, he would also be a potentially useful ally for Sylvia and her husband in relation to Sarawak. However, he became more widely known as a lustful pest to adolescent boys and girls, including on several occasions Sylvia's sister Doll.

William Harcourt lent Reggie rooms at Nevile Court during his time at Trinity, and later conspired with Lady Ripon to usher him into politics in 1878 as private secretary to Lord Hartington (later the eighth Duke of Devonshire), then leader of the Liberal opposition, thus launching him on his remarkable career. Though he consistently turned down jobs that brought responsibility, Reggie was an extraordinarily influential manipulator behind the scenes in the late Victorian and Edwardian eras. His love of scheming, in his case usually for the good, certainly seemed to rub off on his daughter Sylvia, if not his diplomatic finesse.

'Who is Lord Esher?' his friend W. T. Stead asked in 1910. 'Something bizarre, inexplicable, abnormal, something that does not fit in with our notions. He is a man of original genius who has carved out a unique place for himself in the world of affairs, and who in doing so has discarded almost all the usual steps and stairs by which in this country men ascend to the highest positions. He runs after nothing, but all things seem to run after him.' Esher's guiding theme, according to his grandson, was 'that as against decadent France and isolationist America only the British Empire could save the liberal values of the West from "Prussianism" '. As early as 1906 he saw the 'certainty' that Britain would have to fight Germany, and while in the popular mind he is most associated with having invented the modern jubilee and coronation, his more important achievement was the Defence reorganisation of 1904, which abolished the Commander-in-Chief, set up the Committee of Imperial Defence (of which he became a permanent member) created the Army Council and thus 'solved the vexed problem of dual civilian and professional control'. In 1909, following the success of his Territorial Army recruiting drive, Edward VII wrote to him: 'You are a wonderful man; everything you touch succeeds.' When, during the First World War, the new machinery was put to the test, Esher was in Paris acting not only as the political adviser to Kitchener and Haig but also as the confidant of the French General Staff, the only effective liaison between the two Allied governments.

Before reaching these heights, however, the young Reggie Brett had been, in his father's eyes at least, a wastrel. For four years after coming down from Cambridge he had drifted about the grand houses of England and Scotland (his parents' choice of school had paid off in this respect at least) without any apparent inclination to take up a profession. During this time he shared lodgings with his friend, the novelist Julian Sturgis, at Brayfield on the Thames. The house belonged to Sturgis's American cousin Elizabeth Van de Weyer, the only surviving daughter of Joshua Bates, the American partner of Baring's Bank, and the widow of Sylvain Van de Weyer, who had been the principal founder of the Belgian monarchy and later the

Belgian Minister at the Court of St James. From time to time Reggie would go with Sturgis to play tennis and dine with their landlady, who lived nearby in a vast Tudor-Gothic mansion called New Lodge, which had been built by her father as a wedding present on land granted to them by Queen Victoria. It was there that Reggie first set eyes on the youngest of the Van de Weyer daughters, Nellie, then aged thirteen. By the summer of 1878 he was telling friends that he and Nellie had an arrangement to marry and, although she was still only seventeen at the time, it was an arrangement that neither of them would ever repent.

According to Lionel Brett, this mousey girl was 'intelligent enough never to bore him, to defer to his own intelligence, and to know that all her life she would play Second Fiddle'. And Reggie's biographer James Lees-Milne noted that, despite her youth, Nellie was sufficiently intuitive to know what she was letting herself in for: 'Mr Brett sends word that I shake hands in a most unbecoming fashion,' she wrote in her diary in 1875 soon after their first meeting.

> This is very likely. I have never studied the becoming, which he apparently does to a very great extent, both in himself and others . . . He wishes to improve himself and everybody: he is quite right . . . Some men have such capacities for loving too. But I think I should like the same privileges allowed to me – and this is just what men are not strong enough to give. All women should take this view of married life and not be so exacting. The greatest praise a husband of mine could give me would be to say that he did not feel in the least tied down; or any more encumbered than when he was a bachelor. This is not speaking with the ignorance of a girl for I shall act up to it when married, if I do marry.

True to her word, throughout their marriage she doted on Reggie to the extent of alienating most of her children. 'She would not settle down in a room until she discovered which chair he wished to sit in,' wrote Sylvia.

> She never went anywhere, or accepted an invitation without consulting him . . . All her letters were shown to him, both the

ones she wrote and the ones she received. They were so profoundly one, it seemed a sacrilege to break in upon their devotion. Is it surprising, then, that we were afraid to approach too near; is it surprising that we felt sometimes a little unwanted and alone? My mother was sweet to us always, and attentive, but all the time we could see she was listening for him, and waiting for him. Her affection for us was a detached affection, it was an effort to tear her thoughts from his. Only Maurice could venture near, and if we ever wanted anything, we would always send Maurice to ask for it, because we knew we should get it without comment.

Reggie for his part made no attempt to conceal his foibles from his future bride. 'Why you have thrown yourself away upon one who is the converse of you in all things still remains a mystery,' he wrote to Nellie shortly before their marriage.

Very sincerely I feel quite unworthy of you, and I think you must be a kind of St Theresa, a reforming soul. Some day, like [George Eliot's] Romola, you will find me out and you will hate me. Are you prepared for this?

It astonishes me that I can write to you so easily and in this strain. You are the only girl with whom on writing I have felt on equal terms. I mean that I am sure of your not misunderstanding me and there is no necessity for elaborate detail. Does this please you or not? It is, I am sure, very unusual between a man and a woman who have anything to hide. True confidence is a heavy burden and very few men and women can bear that of those they love. But you have led me to think you stronger than most women and I have very little fear for the future. Do nothing and say nothing lightly to weaken my faith in you . . . Do not, I ask you, start thinking too well of me, for I dread disenchantment.

A further letter providing her with the opportunity to pull out met with a straightforward reiteration of her love for him. 'And do not think to frighten me with with your two-sided character – show me which side you please. I should like you as much when your whole life was laid bare as I do now, when, as you say, you have humbugged me.'

Reggie and Nellie married on 24 September 1879. A decade later he wrote to her: 'I expected ten years ago, happiness in subsequent times; but not such *uninterrupted* happiness.' And some thirty years after that: 'You have been everything to me, the love and joy of my life.'

In February 1880 Reggie Brett was elected as Liberal MP for Penryn and Falmouth. He stayed on as private secretary to Hartington, who after the Liberals' election victory declined Queen Victoria's invitation to form a government, content to serve under Gladstone, whose Irish policy in particular he felt deserved his support. Hartington was now appointed Secretary of State at the India Office, a move that gave Reggie valuable experience of Eastern affairs and his first go at pulling the strings behind the scenes (it was, for instance, through him that his old mentor Lord Ripon was appointed Viceroy of India). Hartington's subsequent acceptance of the War Office helped develop Reggie's expertise in the field in which he would make his most important mark.

Meanwhile his marriage to Nellie, whose parents had been close friends of Queen Victoria, had brought him for the first time into the Queen's private circle. On his own initiative he began sending her (via her private secretary, Sir Henry Ponsonby) confidential memoranda on India; Victoria's replies to these notes began a relationship that was to become ever closer as the years went by. According to Lees-Milne, who read all their correspondence: 'The better she got to know him, the more she was charmed by his engaging manner.'

Their familiarity was undoubtedly made easier by the proximity of the Bretts' new country house, Orchard Lea, at Winkfield, three miles from Windsor Castle at the western limit of the Great Park. This was built on land bought from Nellie's brother Victor, and it was completed shortly after the birth of the youngest of Reggie and Nellie's children, Sylvia Leonora.

Sylvia was born at the Bretts' town house, 1 Tilney Street, in Mayfair, at 5.10 a.m. on 25 February 1885. 'There was nothing momentous about my arrival into the world,' she wrote later, 'beyond the fact that I weighed only five pounds, which must have been an intense relief to my mother who had already at the age of nineteen produced a boy of over ten pounds.' The heavy boy was Sylvia's middle brother Maurice, born in 1882, a year after her elder brother Oliver and a year before her sister Dorothy.

By her account, Sylvia, too, soon became 'fat and phlegmatic and, from the time I began to think . . . obsessed by the idea that I was never really wanted'. She became a 'morbid child because I was so ugly. And they kept telling me so.' Photographs from her early childhood, however, show a far from ugly face – round, with bright, inquisitive eyes, albeit not always shown to their best advantage by pudding-bowl haircuts. Into adolescence and early adulthood her features grew more angular and, although she would never be described as a great beauty, and despite her tendency to do down her appearance in exaggerated terms, she was attractive in a pixieish way, with slim, boyish looks that were much coveted at the time and an alluring gaze that alternated between dreaminess and determination.

Dorothy, a comparatively haughty child, remembered her little sister as small and timid, 'not exactly ugly, but homely . . . every time she tried to walk, we would knock her down'. Required to fetch and carry for her elder siblings, Sylvia was often in tears. 'She did not know how to defend herself,' wrote Dorothy. 'I don't know how to describe it, just feeble.'

The first person Sylvia could remember clearly was a nurse called Mrs Jukes 'and the deep hatred I felt in my soul for her . . . She was short and ample-figured, and unrelentingly severe. She used to beat us with little sticks with dogs' heads on the handles of them, and the degree of naughtiness was made known to us by the breed of dog she made use of. For slight offences we were beaten with a pug . . . but when we had been outstandingly wicked and disobedient she belaboured our backs with the pointed nose of a greyhound.' Mrs Jukes once used a stick to beat to death Oliver's pet bullfinch, whereupon Oliver chased her around the nursery table with a carving knife. By Sylvia and Dorothy's accounts she variously drank too much, chased their mother out of the nursery whenever she ventured into it, and locked the children up in a black cupboard among her clothes, which smelled of rotten apples. She eventually resigned in a huff after the children were sent on a seaside holiday and she was not sent with them.

The children saw little of their father, who, according to Sylvia, was 'too preoccupied with affairs of State', although during the first decade of her life he withdrew, ostensibly at least, from public affairs. The slaughter of his great friend General 'Chinese' Gordon at Khartoum shortly before Sylvia was born had affected Reggie deeply and, offended by the government's hostility to his hero, he resigned as Hartington's private secretary; later that year he lost his seat in the general election and in 1886 he turned down the editorship of the *Daily News*. Instead he settled down at Orchard Lea to write *Footprints of Statesmen during the Eighteenth Century in Britain* (1892), followed by *Sketches of the Queen's Prime Ministers* (1896), while at the same time decorating the house, entertaining lavishly and indulging his passion for the turf, as breeder, owner, trainer and, disastrously, punter.

Left to their own devices for most of the day, the Brett children were brought down from the nursery to the drawing room an hour after tea to see their father 'sitting at a writing-table surrounded by books and papers, wearing a black velvet coat and smoking an eternal cigarette'. Later in the evening they would sit on the floor in their mother's room and watch her dress for dinner. Sometimes Nellie read aloud to them, and she taught Doll and Syv to crochet because she hated seeing them idle. Sylvia feigned industry, hooking and hooking at a piece of wool until she was found out. 'My whole life at that time seemed made up of petty deceptions to conceal from my parents how dull and unenlightened I was.' She dreaded her father asking her questions such as 'Who is Prime Minister?' and 'What relation is the Prince of Wales to Queen Victoria?'

Apart from her grandfather, the man Sylvia adored most of all as a young girl was Reggie's friend and political ally, the newspaper editor and spiritualist W. T. Stead. Stead appears in the first photograph of her autobiography *Sylvia of Sarawak*, dressed in a satin-collared frock coat, with a long white beard and intense, disapproving gaze, above the caption, 'My First Friend'. Sylvia remembered Mr Stead striding along the corridors of Orchard Lea deep in conversation with her father, yet always knowing when it was the children's bedtime. At the stroke of six he would 'go down on all fours, and start growling like a bear. With a shriek of delight I would clamber on his back and away he would go, still on all fours, up the stairs and along the passage to bed, with me digging my heels into his sides and pinching his shoulders and shouting at the top of my voice: "Get along, you naughty, naughty bear." I loved Mr Stead,' she recalled, 'he seemed somehow to belong specially to me.'

As a girl of six or seven Sylvia may not have been told – at least she does not mention – that in the year she was born, Stead had been sent to Holloway Prison. In a series of articles in the *Pall Mall Gazette* entitled 'The Maiden Tribute of Modern Babylon', this crusading son of a Congregationalist minister from Yorkshire had scandalised Victorian society with his exposé of child prostitution in London; with sub-headlines such as 'Confessions of a brothel-keeper' and 'Strapping girls down', the story also provided titillation. The resulting outcry helped bring in the Criminal Law Amendment Act, raising the age of consent to sixteen and increasing the legal protection for impoverished young girls. But Stead, a leading exponent of what Matthew Arnold called 'the New Journalism', and one of the most influential newspaper editors of any era, became one of the Act's first casualties. In order to make his exposé stand up, he had paid £5 to the parents of Eliza Armstrong, aged thirteen, had her medically examined to establish that she was a virgin, then sent her to a London brothel, where the proprietor dazed her with chloroform (a common practice at the time) and prepared her for use by his customers. The first 'customer' was Stead, who took her to a Salvation Army hostel in Paris for five weeks while he told her story in the *Pall Mall*, deploring the ease with which such girls could be procured. For his pains he was convicted of abduction under the new Act, and sentenced to three months' imprisonment. Former colleagues such as Bernard Shaw excoriated Stead over this put-up job and his career never really recovered, though he continued to air his rabidly puritanical views whenever the opportunity presented itself.

He also intensified his interest in 'spirit walking', as Sylvia called it, conversing with Wellington, Disraeli and Palmerston and seeing himself incongruously as Charles II. He and Sylvia would often talk about death and the 'great hereafter' and he promised to come back from wherever he went in order to see her. 'You will be certain to know me,' he assured her, 'on account of my carpet slippers.' Long after he came to his end, in 1912, on the *Titanic*, where he was 'last seen' calmly reading a book in the First Class Smoking Room – or alternatively, helping women and children into lifeboats – as the ship went down, Sylvia would look out of the window 'towards the long green slopes of the garden where he had so often walked' to see if she could see him. Although Sylvia failed to catch sight of him, in the year after his death W. T. Stead appeared to mediums as far afield as Melbourne and Toledo, and was photographed peering over the shoulder of one Archdeacon Colley.

In her second autobiography, Sylvia recalled that she and Dorothy were made aware at an early age 'that women were only brought into the world to become the slaves of men', omitting to observe that she could have had worse preparation for her later marriage to a sexually incontinent absolute monarch. Each morning, as young girls, it was her and Doll's duty to lace up their brothers' boots, so that for years to come Sylvia could not look on a boy wearing such footwear 'without having an intense desire to smack his pugnacious bottom'. The girls' sense of inferiority magnified when the boys were sent away to school ('I used to pray to God that they would never come back'), while they stayed behind to be educated at home. For the holidays Sylvia and Dorothy would often be packed off to the Isle of Wight to stay with Reggie's sister, Aunt Violet, her husband William Dudley Ward and their five children. Reggie later came to regard Dudley Ward as a fiendish drunk, though as far as young Sylvia was concerned he was 'a great, big, rollicking, laughing kind of man' who took her sailing and gave her money for decorating the dining-room table with flowers.

Back at Orchard Lea the torment for Sylvia resumed, exacerbated by what she saw when she measured herself against Doll, who as a young girl was prettier (only later did she develop rabbit teeth), more confident and more rebellious. When they built wigwams in the garden, Sylvia was always Maurice's squaw and was often kept in the wigwam all afternoon on the basis that she was too ugly to come out; Dorothy, on the other hand, was allowed to roam wherever she wanted, but mainly because Oliver could find no means of keeping her in. 'It was a constant torturing thought to me that she had all the graces I so lacked,' wrote Sylvia.

Dorothy did not take well to governesses, refused to learn anything, and smacked their faces if they dared to remonstrate. Hence there came a succession of varying nationalities (one was dismissed, according to Dorothy, because her nose twitched at dinner) until their parents gave up on the idea of having anyone at all. For a while Nellie endeavoured to teach the girls herself, giving them long lists of spellings and the capitals of countries to learn by heart, and testing them while she was dressing or having her hair done. Such exercises struck terror into Sylvia, who resorted to copying all the answers out and hiding them in her handkerchief, while the maid, Miss Vaughan, who brushed her mother's hair in front of the mirror, conspired to obscure the reflection of what she was up to.

As unalike in nature as they were in appearance, the Brett children would mostly play by themselves, Sylvia recalled, 'secret games we concealed from one another'. Occasionally, though, as well as building wigwams, they would all pretend to be cows, stripping birch branches bare apart from a bunch of foliage at the end and tying them around their waists as tails. One of them – usually one of the boys – would be cowman, but the game would nearly always end in dispute because no one would volunteer to be milked. During Ascot races, when traffic queued past Orchard Lea, they turned somersaults and cartwheels on the grass verge outside their gate, then held out their hands for pennies; as they grew older and less adept at acrobatics, they threw roses into the carriages as they went by.

According to Sylvia, their parents frowned on their ever meeting other children 'for fear of mental contamination' – Doll put it down to the fact that 'Pupsie and Mumsie could not stand the boredom of children around' – as a consequence of which she found she had no idea how to behave with young people. Apart from their Ward cousins, virtually the only other children the young Bretts came into contact with were those of Princess Beatrice, Queen Victoria's youngest daughter, and her husband Prince Henry of Battenberg (who died of malaria in 1896). They would often go across to Windsor Castle to play with the wild young Battenbergs, running noisy three-legged races down the corridors of the castle, and when Sylvia was seven she and Doll joined the dance classes that Queen Victoria had arranged for her grandchildren. 'It was only a very small attendance, but I presume select,' wrote Sylvia.

The Brett sisters keenly looked forward to these dance classes, which were effectively their only social events; they attended once a week, dressed in their best party frocks and sashes, brown silk stockings and bronze shoes. The teacher was a bad-tempered old lady called Mrs Wordsworth, who, so the children whispered, had a wooden leg and a glass eye. The children sat around and chattered until the arrival of Queen Victoria, who would enter the Red Drawing Room with a flourish, her black crinoline giving her the appearance of gliding across the parquet floor, and sit in 'a big throne chair' on the side, tapping her cane to the music and nodding encouragingly at the children. Sylvia claimed that the Queen made her stand out in front of the class because of her shapely legs. The lessons ended with a march-past in time to music, and curtseys and bows for the Queen.

Later, when Sylvia was a teenager, the young and unruly Prince Edward (the future King Edward VIII and Duke of Windsor), Prince Albert (George VI) and Princess Mary would come over with their tutor to play at Orchard Lea. On one such visit eight-year-old Prince Edward, always known to his family as David, was discovered to have killed a neighbour's ducklings and laid them out beside the lake, whereupon a furious Reggie made him go and apologise. On another, he harnessed Prince Albert and Princess Mary to the Bretts' wagonette, while he stood on the driver's seat cracking a long whip. When Reggie yelled at him to get down, Prince Edward just laughed and shook his head defiantly, at which point his tutor pulled him down and smacked him on the backside.

By the time Sylvia was seven or eight her father was growing restless and short of money. The sumptuous decoration of Orchard Lea was more or less complete and he had also spent a great deal on entertaining and racing, running up debts of £3,000. His father reminded him that he ought to be able to rub along on a private income of more than £4,000[1] but agreed to bail him out provided he gave up betting and owning racehorses. Deprived of these pleasures,

[1] This was only half the stated income of Lady Bracknell's prospective son-in-law Jack Worthing in *The Importance of Being Earnest*, which was first performed in 1895; nevertheless, at that time, for £2,350 one could have bought a house in Chelsea with '8 bed and dressing rooms, bathroom, large drawing room, boudoir, dining room, morning room opening out onto gardens and usual offices'. See advertisement in *The Times*, 11 April 1893, p.14f.

Reggie began to channel some of his energy into new close friendships, forming a passionate though platonic attachment to the Marchioness of Stafford (later Duchess of Sutherland), and becoming infatuated with a fifteen-year-old schoolboy at Eton, Teddie Seymour, who stayed for months at a time at Orchard Lea. There Reggie, apparently unconcerned by what his children might make of it all, would send him to sleep by combing his hair with his hand – 'a thing he adores'. Their relationship, which lasted three years, became common knowledge at Eton, where boys were warned against taking walks with Mr Brett. Sylvia, who had already been chided by Doll for ogling the guards at Windsor Castle, also fell for Teddie, 'so good-looking', she later recalled, 'with his golden hair and blue eyes, and lovely laughing voice . . . Of course he was spoilt by my father and he could do exactly as he liked. I used to fetch and carry for him like a spaniel. There was not a thing I would not have done for him . . . Doll and the boys would laugh at me for my devotion.'

With time on his hands Reggie also found himself more drawn to the company of his political friends, including Lord Rosebery, a fellow Etonian protégé of Johnson, who famously said of him, 'He is one of those who likes the palm without the dust.' During his time as Prime Minister (1894–5), Rosebery leaned heavily on Reggie for advice, constantly urging him to come over to Downing Street for late-night discussions or long walks in Hyde Park. When, in 1895, he made Reggie Secretary of the Office of Works, the Chief Whip (Tom Ellis) described it as 'simply execrable . . . a man with about £6,000 a year with five houses in town and country who has always left his party in the lurch'. Yet it proved an inspired appointment.

Reggie now yearned for more responsibility, and the job of overseeing all public buildings, palaces and royal parks appealed to his love of art and history while also providing him with the very welcome opportunity to further his contact with the royal household. As well as managing sweeping changes to the palaces and the layout of the Mall, he put his stamp on a remarkable series of state occasions over the next seven years. When he organised the celebrations for Queen Victoria's Diamond Jubilee, in the hot summer of 1897, the children watched proceedings from a friend's balcony, and particularly enjoyed seeing the soldiers who were lining the street fainting in the heat. On another occasion a tent that Reggie's office had put up in the garden of Buckingham Palace proved too stuffy and guests began to feel groggy. Reggie was in court dress at the time, with a rapier at his side, and this he promptly drew and thrust through the canvas so as to provide ventilation; there came a terrible shriek when he very nearly pierced a housemaid who was peering through a crack on the other side.

Overall, though, the Diamond Jubilee went off notably well, and it was followed in the next few years by the funeral of Gladstone, the opening of the Victoria and Albert Museum, the funeral of Victoria and the Coronation of King Edward VII. The impressive elegance of each occasion was thought to owe more to Reggie than to any other individual, so that he came to be seen as the inventor of modern ceremonial.

Throughout this period, Sylvia, Oliver and Dorothy received scant attention from their father, who was by this time beginning to show pronounced favouritism towards his younger son Maurice – or Molly, as he came to be called. On the face of it, it is hard to understand why this pug-faced boy should have been, as Lionel Brett put it, so 'grossly spoiled as a child and absurdly flattered as a young man'. 'There is no position, however lofty, which you will not some day be qualified to fill,' Reggie told him. 'Your beloved breast has been broadened by Providence for the stars which some day will cover it.' Lionel Brett could only assume that the extraordinary intensity of Reggie's feelings resulted from the fact that the affectionate and impressionable Maurice, who was not exceptionally clever, readily accepted the acolyte status Reggie imposed on those whom he loved. Oliver, on the other hand, who was as clever and independent as his father, always refused to do so, and accordingly Reggie never really warmed towards him. The girls, meanwhile, were simply 'written off from an early age as plain and tongue-tied, and therefore made so'.

Looking back in 1936, two years after Maurice died, Sylvia regretted various instances in her dealings with her brother, 'enacted out of passion or rage or revenge . . . and an intense desire to have everything in life I could get, and have it in my own way – I was jealous of everyone and everything, and most of all I was jealous of my father's evident preference for his youngest son. I simply could not see what he had in him that I myself lacked, and I longed to see him as the underdog and myself climbing in his place.' She remembered once leaving a glass door ajar on a gusty day, knowing that Maurice, who was playing nearby, would get the blame when it slammed shut and shattered, as it duly did. Maurice was summoned to the library by his father and severely caned, while Sylvia 'listened at the door to his tears and rejoiced'. She also recalled how Maurice's 'black devil-moods' as a young boy distressed their father so much that he would 'retire into his room: the more deaf Maurice was to reason, the longer my father remained incommunicado, with my mother pleading with him outside the door to come out and pacify his son'.

When Maurice went to Eton, in 1895, Reggie began a stream of letters to him that would later be bound in red leather and run to thirty-five volumes. On Office of Works notepaper, he addressed his thirteen-year-old son: 'My Sweet Fatty, What a duck you are . . .' and asked questions such as 'Anybody captured your heart, my Fatty? George perhaps?' Maurice was in fact heterosexual (he had a thing about actresses and later married Zena Dare), though for a time he professed to be interested in other boys, possibly as a means of pleasing his father, who in turn came to depend emotionally on his younger son. In the spring of 1897 Reggie wrote to tell Maurice that Teddie Seymour 'may be on his way to India for 4 years!! This will make a change in my life – and I shall have to turn more than ever to you, Maurice, will you go on filling up chinks?' Two weeks later, he wrote: 'I wonder whether we shall stick together, Molly. It all depends on you!'

Reggie snatched any opportunity to spend time with his son, 'a walk up High St with your dear arm in mine', a tantalising glimpse at the station, 'a very sweet half hour under the trees by Fellow's pond . . . You don't know what you are to me with your dear eyes and your murmured confidences.' He told Maurice that he dreamt of him at night 'and not infrequently by day', and that 'Sometimes you have a frigid fit! Then I am miserable!' When he felt his love insufficiently reciprocated, he turned stalker:

> I couldn't resist, inspite of a sore head and heart, coming down to you last night, and standing concealed by the shadows of the

> elms, while I called you by that old whistle. I saw your dear figure pass down the passage after a long wait. You were not in your room before supper, when I first got there. Then I got a good glimpse of your face. When you opened the window, I thought I would show myself for a moment but decided I wouldn't . . . then you went to prayers and I went gloomily home. Still I had seen you, Molly. Will you remember, years hence, how passionately you were beloved; with a real romantic passion which someday you may feel for someone else.

Occasional letters tell of a physical dimension to Reggie's love for his younger son, as when he reminisced to Maurice in 1901: 'It is many days now – how many since you used to drive home with me sitting always by choice, on my knee – and ever since those days – now years ago – no unfaithful thought has ever crossed my mind . . . I was almost certainly the first human being who kissed you at all, and quite certainly the first who kissed you passionately. I love to linger on these facts.' But Maurice, for his part, seems to have preferred not to do so, and although he told his father, 'I don't think you can imagine how dear you are to me,' two years later he informed him that he had had an erotic dream about the actress Ellaline Terriss – 'the sweetest night I have ever known in dreams'.

For the girls, meanwhile, the overriding feeling was one of being excluded. In a vain attempt to win the affection of her father, Doll began to evince a preference for boys' clothes and for playing boys' parts in plays. But at least she was close to her mother, whereas Sylvia felt she had nobody, especially after her beloved grandfather Lord Esher died in 1899, aged eighty-three. To make matters worse, she was told that on his deathbed he had sent his blessing to her brothers but not a word to herself or her sister; only the brothers were allowed to attend the funeral at Esher parish church, where he was buried in the graveyard. Feeling more isolated than ever, Sylvia took to talking to the portraits that hung on the walls at Orchard Lea. Other events, too, may have contributed to her sense of isolation. When the children's great-aunt, Louise Van de Weyer, had died, in 1896, it was to Dorothy, whose artistic sense was more in tune with 'Aunt Lou', that she left most of her money – £20,000 in trust via her mother, providing her with a modest income for life.

Aunt Lou had also left a Stradivarius violin to Reggie, which he promptly sold, spending the proceeds on adding a large room on to Orchard Lea, known as the Gallery.

By her account – and here we only have her word to go on – in the midst of her childhood despair Sylvia tried to commit suicide three times, though she was characteristically hazy on the dates. In her second autobiography she was 'a girl barely twelve years old' when she set out to destroy herself; interviewed on television shortly after the book came out, in 1970, she said that she 'must have been seven or eight'. Whenever it was, she confessed to having been 'too much of a coward to do anything violent, and besides, I was in that state of mental peculiarity when the desire for a bedroom scene and the weeping remorse of those around me grew and grew into a vivid picture that very soon became an obsession'. She first experimented with ptomaine poisoning, buying a tin of sardines from the village shop, opening it and leaving it on top of her wardrobe for seven days, before washing the mouldy contents down with water. When that failed – her father remarked on how well she looked the next morning – she sought to catch pneumonia by lying naked in the snow on the turret outside her room. That, too, left her feeling perfectly healthy, so finally, and equally unsuccessfully, she lay all night in bed wrapped in soaking towels and stockings, trying to bring on consumption. 'I pictured myself in diaphanous negligee wasting away before my parents' eyes, coughing blood.'

Given Sylvia's subsequent reputation for innaccuracy, particularly about herself, it is tempting to suspect that these stories were at least exaggerated, designed to add drama to her memoirs, which she was eager to sell. In any case, by her account again, she soon concluded that she was not destined to die, and subsequently made up her mind that she would 'live flamingly and electrify the world'.

2

LEFT LADY

To keep this promise she had made to herself, Sylvia now resolved to work harder at her education, listening more closely to conversations and retreating for days on end to her bedroom in the attic of Orchard Lea to read. In her first novel, *Toys* (1920), she would describe the young Susannah, whom she based on herself, creeping downstairs to read in the window seat of the library until the light went. 'She had a kind of passionate ecstasy for books; they were her most intimate relations . . . Shelf by shelf she read them. No subject at that time was too serious. Often she read through a book from cover to cover, and understood nothing of its contents. This, however, did not deter or frighten her; rather did she reverence the book for its incomprehensibility.' Dorothy later recalled that her sister knew 'all there was to know about everything when she was thirteen years old. She had read Zola, poked around, reading all kinds of forbidden books. She never told me because she was afraid I would blab to Pupsie and Mumsie and give the whole game away.'

Sylvia's abandonment of fresh air and exercise was at a cost to her complexion, rendering her pale and spotty, while her preference for Zola, Maupassant (in French, which she had learned from a succession of French and Swiss maids) and Poe lent new dimensions to her morbid thoughts. Yet at the same time she began to feel 'reborn . . . I gained confidence and this reading was like a strong tonic to me. I could feel my thoughts stirring and stretching and taking hold. . . . I wanted my father to be proud of me. I wanted him to see that I really was trying to climb the ladder of his intelligence, that seemed to me to touch the stars.'

Her immersion in literature also seemed to stir her romantic sensibility, and at about the age of fourteen she developed her first serious crush. The object of her ardour was George Binning, a former lover from Reggie's postgraduate Cambridge days and one of the more regular visitors to Orchard Lea when Sylvia was in her early teens. The eldest son of the eleventh Earl of Haddington, Lord Binning was 'an intelligent, affectionate, extrovert, madcap charmer', whose talent for games-playing and splendid physique had enraptured the young Reggie Brett, four years his senior. However, the result of Binning's libertinism with both sexes had been a bout of venereal disease (something the fastidious Reggie had a horror of), so that, as Lees-Milne related, 'throughout the 1880s he was a martyr to painful cures in a series of Austrian nursing homes'. Binning was in his mid-forties or thereabouts when, in the late 1890s, he captured young Sylvia's heart. He was commanding the Royal Horse Guards – 'the Blues' – and was married, though that was of no concern to her. 'All that I knew was that I loved him, and if he came into the house my legs were like cotton wool, and if he so much as addressed a word to me, the blood would rush to my face in scarlet confusion.' When the family was staying at Tilney Street she would go and stand outside Knightsbridge Barracks 'for hours', hoping that he would come out. Her infatuation, of which Binning seems to have been largely oblivious, lasted on and off for a decade, reaching an undignified finale in 1909, when she made a final attempt to fling herself at him while staying with him and his wife at Mellerstain in Scotland.

This unrequited love again made the teenage Sylvia dwell on her shortcomings, only this time she was saved from despair by a growing bond with her elder brother Oliver, then in his last year at Eton. Oliver was, she wrote later, 'the best, if not the only real friend I had at that time . . . [he] had developed in sympathy and charm. He had had a few youthful love affairs of his own, so he understood. He wrote rather beautiful poetry and would read it aloud to me . . .' Together they would sneak off to the wall of the back yard, to sit and talk and munch walnuts; she would 'always remember Oliver as he was then', she wrote, skating over the fact that her cattish behaviour towards his American wife Antoinette later caused a permanent rift between them.

Another source of happiness for Sylvia at this time was holidays spent bicycling and fishing in Perthshire. In 1896 Reggie bought a house at Callander, 'Gateway to the Highlands', where the Bretts had been going for several years. Situated between the town and the River Teith, which in full spate rushed past the drawing-room window, the Roman Camp was named after the nearby serpentine mound that for a long time was wrongly believed to be an ancient fortification; the Bretts nicknamed it 'Pinkie' for its pink-washed walls. The whole family quickly came to adore the place – especially Reggie, who was proud to descend from the noble Scottish families of Forbes and Baliol and adored the romance of the Highlands; he lost no time in extending the original house, which had been built in the early seventeenth century as a hunting lodge for the Dukes of Perth, and redesigning the garden, as well as letting rough shooting, deer stalking and fishing. In 1903 Maurice persuaded him to buy the adjoining Ben Ledi estate, and from 1919 onwards Reggie made the Roman Camp his permanent home. Thereafter, he hated the idea of Sylvia and her brood bringing their 'baskets of apples of discord', and encroaching on what he saw as the exclusive preserve of Maurice's family. But for more than two decades before that, the Roman Camp was a welcoming refuge for all the Bretts.

It was there that Dorothy, having originally set her sights on the stage, began to develop a serious interest in painting, as well as her addiction to fishing, which she continued to indulge after she followed D. H. Lawrence to New Mexico. Sylvia, meanwhile, made some of her earliest stabs at writing short stories there, hidden away in the summer house built for her use by Reggie atop a heathered tump on the lawn. 'It was a kind of paradise for us, this place,' she wrote. 'We could go into the village alone, walk alone, and be alone on the moors for hours. We could walk with the guns over the heather, and fish along the burn that wound its way down the slopes of Ben Ledi.' The Roman Camp seemed to Sylvia 'to encompass all the beauties that a home should have. It was a sanctuary for all my sadness, and I was always happy there . . . It was so free and open and clean. I could forget de Maupassant and Zola, and my own disturbed existence. I could breathe fresh air into my body and fresh thoughts into my mind.'

She recalled setting out from Pinkie each morning with a basket of sandwiches and walking up Ben Ledi, the southernmost of the big Highland hills, fishing the burn for brown trout, or just lying on the rocks and watching them playing in the shallow pools. She would eat her picnic with her back resting against the chapel that Reggie, despite his avowed lack of religious conviction, had built on the lower slopes of Ben Ledi, overlooking Loch Lubnaig, and where he intended all of the family's ashes to be buried, though none of them were. On other days she met up with the rest of the family for lunch at a black wooden hut down on the shore of Loch Lubnaig, where Reggie would be frying up cold grouse with bacon and scrambled eggs; Sylvia and Doll served as his maids, laying the table and washing up afterwards. Like Doll, Syv retained her love of fishing into adulthood, and as far as Reggie was concerned, the fact that she remained 'a very pertinacious and successful fisher' (as he described her to Maurice in 1927) was one of the few saving graces in her impossibly tricky nature.

The Roman Camp served as an ideal getaway from Reggie's increasingly hectic working life. In November 1899, six months after he succeeded his father in the viscountcy, he was asked to become Permanent Undersecretary of State at the Colonial Office. He turned the job down, as he did the next year the offer to become Permanent Undersecretary at the War Office – partly because the Queen and Prince of Wales had told him that they wanted him to remain at the Office of Works. The subsequent offer the same year to become governor of the Cape sorely tempted him. But even had he been prepared to tear himself away from his beloved Maurice, who had recently finished at Eton, he would still have wanted the approval of the Queen, who was now more dependent on him than ever. In December 1900, after she had appointed Reggie a Knight Commander of the Victorian Order, the last honour she would bestow on any subject, she remarked that no one had ever been more kind to her or attended more thoroughly to her wishes.

The next month, on 22 January 1901, Queen Victoria died at

Osborne. Sylvia could later only vaguely remember her funeral at St George's Chapel, although Dorothy recalled that the two Brett girls drove to the funeral in a carriage with their mother from Orchard Lea. Queen Victoria had instructed that there be no black trappings, but they were swathed in such heavy crêpe veils that in the dim light of the chapel they had to grope their way to their seats. Reggie had been closely consulted on the arrangements for the funeral, during which Teddie Seymour and his guardsmen carried the coffin. In his journal Reggie accounted the whole event a 'brilliant success . . . perfectly arranged from start to finish'.

The new King, Edward VII, soon made Reggie Deputy Constable and Lieutenant Governor of Windsor Castle, an appointment that accorded him, among other things, a special uniform, the official use of a room at the castle overlooking the Long Walk, control of the royal archives, responsibility for arranging the late Queen's papers and formal entry into His Majesty's court. Reggie and King Edward would regularly discuss the affairs of the day over breakfast at Buckingham Palace, and Reggie was also given the job of arranging the King's coronation, which was scheduled for 26 June 1902 but had to be postponed at the last minute because the King fell ill with appendicitis.

Appendicitis was then little understood, and, awkwardly for Reggie, it was whispered that he might have passed on an infection to the King from his daughter Dorothy, who had had her appendix removed earlier in the year, in March. Dorothy's illness had in fact been a good deal more acute, and might easily have proved fatal had the King not recommended his personal sergeant-surgeon Sir Frederick Treves – at that time one of the few men who had undertaken an appendectomy. Intercepted on his doorstep in London by a footman when he was about to leave for the weekend, Treves came immediately to Orchard Lea. He 'never hesitated', Reggie wrote to Maurice, 'and after seeing Doll, came down and explained that left alone she must die, and that the operation alone could save her. Even that was a 10 per cent risk.' Treves carried out the operation on a dining table at Orchard Lea, with several local doctors watching to see how it was done. He was by no means sure of a successful outcome, having performed the operation himself only a handful of times and seen his own daughter die following the same procedure.

But, wrote Reggie, 'It was all well managed and I think he was fairly satisfied. It was a difficult operation as there was a complication [an abscess, which burst just as Treves began to operate]. There is danger for 48 hours of course; great danger. One can only hope for the best.'

In the period leading up to Doll's appendicitis, she and Syv had not been getting on well, not least because Doll's front teeth were now beginning to protrude and she felt increasingly resentful of her more comely younger sister. Reggie had already formed the view that Doll was 'too conceited and wants snubbing' and so had little sympathy with the plight of his elder daughter, telling her after one of her many quarrels with Syv that she was like a cook complaining of the housemaid. After watching them squabbling one day, he wrote to Maurice: 'They are like a couple of spit cats and want a real good smacking. I wish you would administer it.'

The shock of Doll's illness, though, brought about a truce. Sylvia later wrote that it 'drew a kind of veil from my eyes and made me see how really fond I was of her . . . I remembered everything I had done and said to hurt her. Little unimportant quarrels, so harmless when she was well, rose now like threatening clouds before me, engulfing me with their persistent reproach. I would sit by her bedside waiting to help in any way I could.' Her remorse did not stop her from competing for the attentions of Dr Barron, who came to dress Dorothy's wound and whose youthful Germanic good looks prompted the girls to christen him 'the *Jüngling*'. Dorothy believed she was in love and could hardly wait for his visits. One morning she tied a blue ribbon round her bandages and into a bow on her stomach. 'How dreadful at eighteen to be no older than perhaps ten,' she wrote later. 'Could it be that I had been making a doll of myself, hoping that someone would love me, cuddle me?' The sisters had been aware of the dishy doctor for some time, and would often bicycle to his surgery in the hope of glimpsing him. 'There was something mysteriously fascinating about him,' wrote Sylvia, 'with his full white face and prematurely greying hair. He had a soft slow way of speaking, and his rather prominent blue eyes were heavy-lidded, hooded, almost as if to shut out the coldness of his stare.' Above all he had 'really beautiful hands. Even in those days hands were of the utmost importance to me.' But, in this instance, Doll was in the box seat. As Sylvia observed the growing bond between doctor and patient, she found herself 'torn between devotion to her [Doll] and a consuming jealousy that it was she who was ill and not me'.

Doll's recovery was painfully slow. For weeks she lay with a tube in her side draining the pus, and in June, still confined to a bath chair, it was decided that she should take the air at Folkestone, accompanied by Sylvia, who by now accounted herself 'the very best of friends' with her sister, and a nurse. While Syv and the nurse flirted competitively with the bandleader on the pier, Doll amused herself by sketching the seafront and wrote to her father describing the activities in the hotel opposite of 'the vulgarest couple I've ever had the misfortune to watch through my field glasses'.

The King's recovery from his operation, also performed by Treves, was far speedier, and the coronation took place on 9 August. Despite an ancient Archbishop of Canterbury, who at one point had to be lifted from his knees by two bishops, the event was again adjudged a triumph of organisation, enhancing yet further Reggie's reputation in matters ceremonial.

The next year, both girls came out, being presented at court by their mother on 13 March, and afterwards attending the various state balls and other events that made up the season. Sylvia enjoyed the whole experience rather more than Doll, whose 'masculine independence of spirit' meant that she scorned the ritual of matchmaking and snubbed her escorts. Doll's proudest moment, by her own account, was when her father danced with her. 'I could hardly contain myself because I knew I was the envy of all the women in the room. I never knew why he asked me unless he wanted to spite some woman who had been spiteful to him.' In her various autobiographical writings Doll attributed her hostility to men to her brothers' treatment of her and a traumatic first sexual encounter at the hands of an old Etonian friend of Reggie's – 'a contemporary of his' whom she called 'H', who had been part of the household for weeks at a time. One day Reggie had asked Doll to fetch some books from a farmhouse across the fields from Orchard Lea, and H suggested coming to help.

We walked along the path through the little wood that led to the farm and when we got inside H started looking at the pictures of racehorses that hung round the room while I collected the books. It was a dampish day so he had on a Burberry – the kind with false pockets. He took hold of my hand and pulled it through the false pocket. I suddenly felt something burning hot and soft. I can remember to this moment my stunned horror – I knew, how I knew I don't know, but I knew and I was horribly afraid. I stood stock still in an agony of surprise and fear – then I tore my hand away and turned to run. I was not quick enough. He was on me, he caught hold of me from behind and held me in a grip of iron, and began kissing the back of my neck. Wild terror broke out in me and I kicked and kicked and kicked myself free and rushed out of the house. That was my first realisation of sex and my body was stunned by it. I would let no man come near me and all I dared say was that I would never be left alone with H. But the harm was done. For years I would never let a man come near me.[1]

Some years later, after Sylvia's marriage to Vyner Brooke, Dorothy went to their Christmas party, where Vyner innocently encouraged a friend of his to kiss her under the mistletoe. 'He came up behind me and tried to kiss me,' wrote Doll. 'The old fear seized me and like a maniac I kicked that unfortunate man black and blue until, bewildered, he let me go, looking very apologetic, while I felt shaken and ashamed.'

Dorothy's biographer, Sean Hignett, is surely right to identify H as Loulou Harcourt, even if Doll is not strictly accurate in describing him as her father's contemporary. Hignett thinks it likely that it occurred when she was 'perhaps fourteen or fifteen', although given her avowed lack of worldliness at the age of eighteen, it may have been later. It was also not the last time that Harcourt tried to have his evil way with Doll. In September 1908 Reggie wrote to Maurice from the Roman Camp:

[1] Doll's cousin and patron Edward James related another version of the same incident in his memoir *Swans Reflecting Elephants*: 'He had asked her if she would like to see the grotto, taken her there and said, "I'll show you my stalactite." The poor girl got such a shock she became deaf.'

> Here is something I am not supposed to know . . . Doll, a year ago, at Olea, was kissed by Loulou, unexpectedly, and kicked him on the shins! A picture for you! He tried again and failed. At Nuneham [Park, Harcourt's house in Oxfordshire] he took her into a dark grotto, and asked her to sit on his knee. This handsome offer she rejected. These were his old games, played with both sexes for years. Curious in a Cabinet Minister, because so risky! . . . Note all the aspects. Loulou *still* not to be trusted with his *friends*. For, of course, he did not mean to stop at kissing.

According to Lees-Milne, Reggie did not approve of this kind of behaviour, and of 'what he called "harpies" who pounced on the young simply for physical gratification; for in every love affair there must, he maintained, be sentiment and romance'. Lees-Milne argued that it was unfair to bracket the 'naturally monogamous' Reggie with Loulou, and that Reggie would have been 'horrified had he known that mothers of Eton boys warned their sons against taking solitary walks with him as well as with Loulou'.

Nonetheless, Reggie's letter is extraordinarily blithe given that it was his daughter he was talking about. Sylvia, too, whom Doll had confided in, seems to have been remarkably easy on Loulou. Some two and a half years after the second incident, she stayed at Nuneham for the first night of her honeymoon, then rented a house on the estate when she and Vyner returned from Italy. In her first autobiography, published in 1936, she wrote that she had never 'met anyone since who had more charm [than Loulou]'. Her attitude is the more curious given that, by her own account at least, she too had been mauled as a young girl: once by a curious eight-year-old boy who undressed her to see what a girl was like, only to remark, 'I don't think much of that!'; on a subsequent occasion, her father's secretary 'kissed me in the dark, pressing his pale inadequate moustache into my mouth and exploring my twelve-year-old body with his secret searching hands. Thereby was laid the foundation of a wall of horror against the male sex which took me many years to overcome.'

In 1903, though, the year that she was presented at court, Sylvia put these traumas to the back of her mind for the sake of her mother, who was in despair at Doll's miserable failure as a debutante.

Determined to try harder, to 'give this coming out business a fair chance', Sylvia launched herself into the social fray full of 'heroic resolutions', as she recalled. However, she was too shy and self-conscious to dance well and the few men that came over to the chaperone sofa to ask her only did so because they had been coerced by overzealous hostesses. She was later scathing about the limited conversation of her escorts, but that was far from being their gravest sin. In Sylvia's novel *Toys* the debutante Susannah rails against the apparent stupidity of men at dances, 'but it was not because they were silly that Susannah hated them. It was because they did not ask her to dance; because they left her standing until two in the morning, the blood slowly running from her cheeks . . .'

Despite such hardships, in her autobiography Sylvia preferred to look back nostalgically 'on that wonderful first season of mine, with the doors of Londonderry House, Devonshire House, Apsley House and Stafford House flung wide open, and I know that I lived through the most glamorous and glittering finale of England's fame . . . to have witnessed the Royal Quadrille and seen King Edward VII lead his Queen on to the dance floor, Gottlieb's famous orchestra filling the dazzling ballroom of Buckingham Palace . . . to have heard Melba and Caruso in *La Bohème*. Kirby Lunn and Adelina Patti; Richter conducting the huge orchestra as it thundered through Wagner . . .' Yet, as she admitted, despite having put her all into that first season, and rather enjoying it, she too had failed dismally in the principal objective, which was to find herself a husband.

She would endure several further seasons as a ballroom wallflower before her parents accepted that there was nothing to be gained from dragging her to more dances. She spent much of the next decade convinced that she would remain a spinster, a subject on which she dwelt in early short stories such as 'The Left Ladies'. That she avoided the fate she dreaded was largely due to the initiative of their neighbour, the Ranee of Sarawak, who lived with her parrots four miles from Orchard Lea.

None of the Brett family had yet met Margaret Brooke; they merely knew that she was the estranged wife of Sir Charles Brooke, the second White Rajah, and had recently come to live nearby at a house called Grey Friars, amid the pine trees of south Ascot. Now, among her other endeavours, this determined and rather formidable

French-born lady had set herself the task of finding wives for her three shy sons. Harry Brooke, the youngest, a talented amateur actor, had for some time been organising charitable theatrical performances and in 1902 or thereabouts the resourceful Ranee came up with the idea of forming the Grey Friars Orchestra to accompany them, and inviting eligible local girls to join. She sent a letter to Lady Esher suggesting that her daughters become part of the ensemble and enclosing a list of those girls who had already accepted. Reggie, who in time would develop a pathological hatred of the Ranee, did not like the idea. 'It seemed unconventional,' explained Sylvia, 'and the picturesque title of the inaugurator annoyed my father.' But her mother Nellie thought that it might do the girls some good, and 'for the first time' her voice prevailed. So it was that Sylvia and Dorothy prepared for their first visit to Grey Friars, scouring the reference books in the library at Orchard Lea for mention of the White Rajahs of Sarawak.

The celebrated founder of the Raj was the Ranee's uncle-in-law, James Brooke, who was born in 1803 in the European quarter of Benares (old Varanasi) in India, where his father had served the East India Company as a High Court judge. Wounded during the First Burmese War, James had been invalided home to Bath, where his parents had by then retired. During his convalescence he had read all he could about the Far East, and eventually, with financial help from his father, he had gone on a trading voyage to China, which had turned into something of a fiasco. Nevertheless, when his father had died in 1835 shortly after his return, leaving him an unencumbered inheritance of £30,000, James had promptly spent it on a 142-ton schooner, armed with six 6-pounders and swivels, and after a practice voyage in the Mediterranean, sailed for Borneo with dreams of extending British influence into the far-off region of the Malay archipelago. Landing the next year at Kuching, capital of Sarawak, which was then a province under the suzerainty of the Sultan of Brunei (whose ancestors had once ruled over all of Borneo), he had found the place in a chaotic state, with Dyak tribesmen in revolt inland and piracy on the coast. The Sultan's uncle, Rajah Muda

Hassim, had been charged with quelling the rebellion but was too feeble to do so, and he had begged James Brooke to help him, eventually promising him that if he restored order the government of 'Sarawak Proper' – the size of a large English county – would be his. This, with the help of his 6-pounders, the Englishman did, and in 1841 he became the first White Rajah.

A hundred years later, in the *Sarawak Gazette* centenary number, the curator of the Sarawak Museum, Edward Banks, looked back on James Brooke as a pioneer of 'freelance government' and the spiritual ancestor of men such as Lawrence of Arabia. Both Brooke and Lawrence were distinguished by their lack of emphasis on religious matters, noted Banks, and were

> singularly fortunate in the fact that neither seems to have taken the slightest interest in the ladies of their countries, beyond the necessary slight social requirements. In the preliminary dealings with most Muslims and most heathens, this must have been an inestimable advantage, for to be able to meet the young and the old, the fair and the ugly, the flashing eye and the swelling breast and to treat them all with equal and unvarying deference, must in the end have done more than most things to gain the confidence of Arab and Malay peoples, who still erroneously regard strangers as desirous of entering into negotiations with their womenfolk. To have met men of an alien race and religion who through the years gave daily evidence of a lack of such very natural tropical feelings was just what was wanted to cement the final feeling of trustworthiness inspired by their courage, endurance and leadership – the last thread of self-interest had been removed . . .

Britain recognised Sarawak as an independent territory in 1864, four years before the death of Rajah Brooke. A bachelor with no children, he was succeeded by his nephew, Charles (né Johnson), who assumed the additional surname of Brooke in anticipation of succeeding to the Raj – his elder brother Brooke Brooke having earlier been disinherited after falling out with their uncle. Sylvia's descriptions of the Rajah's austerity were often overblown for comic effect, though she claimed to have the support of the first Rajah, attributing to him the observation: 'My nephew is too damned serious for me, or else I am too damned frivolous for him.' She also made much of her father-in-law's thrift and disdain for 'fripperies', and even his wife Margaret admitted that Charles's parsimony blighted their marriage. Nobody, however, disputed his dedication to the well-being of his subjects.

Rajah Charles Brooke was a natural leader, and his courage and physical strength won him the respect of this warlike people. He consolidated the state of Sarawak and expanded it north-west along the coast and into the interior – so that by the end of his reign it extended over almost an area approximately 50,000 square miles – the size of England. At the same time he abolished slavery, rebuilt the capital Kuching and constructed roads, waterworks and a short railway. He took pride in the absence of red tape, declaring, 'There isn't a lawyer in the whole of my dominions' and that he had 'reduced government to a miracle of simplicity . . . I don't encourage the competition-wallah when I seek an English official; all I ask for is a gentleman who can ride straight, shoot straight, and conduct himself towards the natives with a kind heart, with patience, and with sympathy.'

Perfectly at ease with the natives himself, Charles was far less so among Europeans. His lonely years at outstations had deepened his natural reserve and he was quite happy to sit for hours in silence, puffing on a Manila cigar. He was in many respects self-sufficient, but he was determined to ensure the continuation of the Brooke Raj. Unwilling to go along with his uncle James's suggestion that he make his nephew Hope Brooke (the son of the disinherited Brooke Brooke) his heir, Charles went on leave to England the year after his succession, the main purpose of his trip being to find himself a wife.

Before his death his uncle had suggested that, with Sarawak revenues at a low ebb, his rich cousin Lily de Windt, a widow living at Blunsdon Hall, Highworth, in Wiltshire, might make a good match. She was now forty and probably past childbearing, but Charles, who fondly remembered indulging in 'childish pranks' with her as a boy, went to stay nonetheless. A stiff and awkward guest, he passed his time talking about Sarawak with Mrs de Windt's sixteen-year-old son Harry[1] and going for long rides with her

[1] Harry de Windt went on to serve as Charles's ADC and later became an explorer and author.

daughter Margaret, who was then aged nineteen. On these rides he normally said nothing, so it came as something of a surprise when, some time later, while accompanying the family on a tour of the Tyrol, he scribbled some lines on a piece of paper and placed it on the piano in front of her:

With a humble demean
If the King were to pray
That You'd be his Queen
Would not you say Nay?

Margaret's first reaction was to laugh. However, the reality was that she was bored at home, and moreover she had grown to admire her taciturn suitor after reading about his dealings with pirates and headhunters, which he had modestly related in his book *Ten Years in Sarawak*. She was not in love – nor for that matter was he – but she was intrigued by the idea of being Ranee of a wild and remote country. They married some months later, much to the bewilderment of her mother and the dismay of her wider family. As they had predicted, her married life would be far from easy. On the first night of their honeymoon, they stayed in a hotel at Exeter, where the Rajah summoned a waiter.

'Dinner, sir?' the man asked.

'Oh no,' came the Rajah's reply, 'too expensive.'

Margaret made do with bread and butter, while her husband had grilled pheasant legs and a half-bottle of sherry. Lunch the next day consisted of captain's biscuits.

'It was all very dull and very queer,' Margaret recalled.

In April 1870 Rajah Charles and Ranee Margaret arrived in Sarawak aboard the Rajah's yacht *Heartsease*, to be greeted by a 21-gun salute and a deafening explosion of Chinese crackers. Later that year Margaret gave birth to a daughter, Ghita, though not before discovering that Charles already had a son, Esca, who had been born four years previously to one of his 'housekeepers' at Simanggang, where he had been stationed before becoming Rajah. Unlike his uncle James, Rajah Charles *was* interested in the women of his country, and he likewise encouraged his officers to keep native mistresses – or 'sleeping dictionaries' – as a means of better integrating and tempering loneliness when stationed upcountry, while avoiding the distractions and expense of memsahib society. The practice would continue right up until the last years of Brooke rule. In Charles's case he had kept several women at Simanggang, and according to Margaret he could become very possessive – she told how after one of them strayed with a man at the fort, 'he was furious. He had her head shaved and tied her thick long tail of hair to the flag staff!! Then she was put in a boat, shaven and shorn, and paddled to and fro in front of the campong, with a man who summoned the people to the bank by a gong, and who informed the populace of her misdeeds. In a way he was a queer fish!!'

Inevitably, perhaps, quite a number of inhabitants of Sarawak today claim descent from Rajah Charles, although Esca was the only illegitimate child he publicly acknowledged. In *Ten Years in Sarawak* he extolled the benefits of intermarriage between the Anglo-Saxon and the indigenous people, particularly as a means of producing a population best suited to developing the country. Miscegenation, he argued, would bring about 'a good cross betwixt the black race, who are deficient in mental organisation and other qualities, and the white, whose thinness of skull and nervous system are too delicately constituted to cope with the trying warmth and melting heat of these latitudes'.

But as Sylvia later argued, the plight of mixed-race children, 'born under a cloud from which they could never escape', was often a desperate one, and it became a prevalent theme in her fiction. She was not alone in observing the difficulties these children had in fitting into either the European or the Asiatic communities, especially the girls, who tended to be educated and brought up by nuns. Another writer who had lived in Sarawak noted: 'It was considered improper for the father to refer to these children in front of white women . . . Even should the father legalise his union, as few did, he could not bring his wife to the Club, nor was she invited to any public function. Should he give a mixed party, his wife and children were hidden away, a dark secret in the back quarters.'

In 1872 Margaret gave birth to two further children, twin sons, James and Charles. Twins were thought to be unlucky by some Malays, however, and in Margaret's case the superstition was aggravated by her employment of a cross-eyed English nurse and an eclipse of the sun two months before the twins were born. Her next baby arrived prematurely and stillborn in 1873 after she fell down a hatchway aboard the royal yacht – she recounted how the Malay midwife 'sat by my bed, thumping her head on the floor and screaming out, "Mati, mati!" ["dead, dead"]'. To add to her misery, the Bishop would not allow the child to be buried in the official cemetery in Kuching, as it had not been christened.

When Margaret subsequently fell gravely ill, Charles decided to take her to England on leave. But when they boarded the P&O liner *Hydaspes* in Singapore, cholera was raging, and as they sailed up the Red Sea in intense heat, all three of her surviving children died within a week and had to be buried at sea. The only child with them to survive was Charles's eldest son Esca, whom they were taking to England to be brought up by the parson at Sheepstor, W. Y. Daykin, so that he would not then be 'a bore', as Margaret put it with chilling pragmatism, when it came to the succession. For the rest of his life, Rajah Charles avoided travelling by P&O.

Margaret remained in England for over a year, and in London, on 21 September 1874, a new son, Charles Vyner, was born at 31 Albemarle Street, just north of Piccadilly (now Brown's Hotel); he was immediately proclaimed Rajah Muda, or heir apparent. Another son, Bertram, known in Sarawak as the Tuan Muda and in the family as Adeh (younger brother), was born in Kuching in 1876, and a third, Harry, the Tuan Bongsu, in England in 1879. The succession thus assured, the Rajah wrote to his nephew Hope Brooke, who had just come of age, offering him an allowance of £200 a year but warning him to 'remember not to open anything like discussion [i.e. about the succession], which can lead to nothing and do no good'.

In 1882 Margaret's health again deteriorated, and she returned to England to set up home with her sons. Provided with a modest allowance from her husband, she divided her time between London and Berkshire, moving in a circle of artistic and literary friends which included Sir Edward Elgar, Sir Edward Burne-Jones, Henry James and W. H. Hudson. They also had a house near Genoa, where for some time she sheltered the wife and two sons of Oscar Wilde after he was sent to prison. Appearances were kept up in her marriage to the Rajah and she attended official functions with him in England, but there had long since ceased to be an emotional bond. According to Dorothy Brett, Margaret was in love for a time with Hudson and attempted to have an affair with him, but 'he withstood the Ranee's advances by ignoring them'. In 1890 she had a brief but passionate affair with William Morton Fullerton, the young American journalist who at the time was Paris correspondent of *The Times*. When he broke it off, she became domineering and demanding. Some years later, Henry James told Fullerton he longed to know 'what the Ranee did to you. Are you very sure? She doesn't do things!'

The Rajah, meanwhile, continued to spend most of his time in Sarawak, relishing his regained independence. When, in 1895, the Ranee proposed going to Sarawak with their son Bertram, her husband only agreed providing she paid for her own passage; shortly after her arrival, the Rajah left for England to go hunting. It was Margaret's last visit to the country, although she lived for a further forty years.

When Sylvia and Dorothy turned up for their first rehearsal at Grey Friars, they were immediately transfixed by the Ranee, sitting in a high-backed armchair that seemed like a throne, a green parrot perched on her wrist. 'There was nothing very feminine about her,' wrote Sylvia, 'either in her manner or in the way she decorated her ordinary and almost ugly home; but she could dominate a room with her personality and enchant everyone in it.' In another account, she described how 'Her mind was never still, and all the time her lovely blue eyes compelled us to adore her. She was like Mary Queen of Scots, in her love of being loved.'

Ushered into the 'bleak little music room, with its book-lined walls and dreary cretonnes', the Brett girls were pitched straight into a rehearsal for a charity performance of *His Excellency the Governor*, the play by Robert Marshall, with Harry Brooke in the starring role. Dorothy chose the side drums and kettledrum, at which she was already a practised hand, while Sylvia, who had no particular musical skill, opted for the big drum, cymbals and triangle. Twice each week Sylvia and Dorothy attended practice sessions of the orchestra, and afterwards at tea the Ranee would tell them stories about her life in Sarawak. By Sylvia's account, she was quite candid about her relationship with the Rajah, telling the girls that the final straw in their marriage had been when he destroyed her pet doves and served them in a pie for her supper.

All eventually went according to the Ranee's plan and one by one her sons became engaged to a girl in the Grey Friars Orchestra. The first to go was Bertram, a Cambridge rowing Blue who had recently returned from military service in Egypt with a wounded leg. In 1904 he married the mandoline and triangle player Gladys Palmer, the only daughter of Sir Walter Palmer, first and last Baronet, and heiress to a sizeable portion of the Huntley and Palmer biscuit fortune – she was reported to have inherited more than £250,000 on her father's death in 1910. After their marriage she was known as Her Highness the Dayang Muda. The union produced three daughters the youngest of whom married the historian Arthur Bryant, and ultimately a son, Anthony, the future heir apparent to the Brooke Raj. But Bertram and Gladys drifted apart shortly after the First World War, during which the restlessly energetic Dayang Muda had variously built a house and run a farm near Llangollen in North Wales, opened La Ruche, a knick-knack shop in the Burlington Arcade off Piccadilly, and set herself up as a film producer. When she complained to Ranee Margaret about Bertram's coolness towards her when he returned from Sarawak, three years after the war, a tearful Margaret sought to explain: 'You must remember my family have never made their money in trade.' According to Gladys, Bertram had inherited full measures of his father's reserve and disapproved of luxury, preferring 'a straight iron bed with a mattress the hardest that could be procured' and pillows filled with straw. (Sylvia claimed he slept on boards stretched over the bath rather than in an orthodox bed.) He hated any sort of 'function', and when in England chose not to use his title, preferring to be 'one of the mob'.

His wife Gladys used her title as a matter of course, long after they separated, and was as much of a publicity seeker as Sylvia. She subsequently lived in France and went through a number of religious conversions, first to Christian Science, then to Roman Catholicism, and finally, in 1932, to Islam, the ceremony taking place aboard an Imperial Airlines flight from Croydon to Paris, with several journalists invited along to witness the event. Thereafter, she went by the name of Khair-ul-Nissa (Fairest of Women), and when she died in 1952 in Sri Lanka, she was buried in a Muslim grave.

Six years after Bertram's marriage, his younger brother Harry married Gladys's cousin, Dorothy Craig, who had pursued the Tuan Bungsu doggedly ever since joining the orchestra, but who died of consumption a few years after their marriage, shortly after the birth of their first child, a son. This left only Vyner, the plum catch.

3

BORNEO BROOKE AND LITTLE BARRIE

Charles Vyner de Windt Brooke, known as Vyner to distinguish him from his father, had first visited Sarawak with his mother when he was two. He went out again aged twelve, accompanied by his younger brother Bertram and their tutor Gerard Fiennes, who was impressed by young Vyner's reaction when he was mobbed by the natives. 'The last thing which occurs to his mind is that he is the object of their attention, and he has to be continually prodded to make him return their salutes. He always thinks they are salaaming to me. It is very nice of him to be so entirely unconscious and free from conceit.' On his next trip to Sarawak, aged seventeen, Vyner was formally proclaimed Rajah Muda before the Council Negri, the assembly of forty or so native leaders and European officers who came to the Rajah's palace every three years to pay homage to their ruler. Otherwise he grew up in London and at Chesterton House, the hunting box near Cirencester where Vyner's father spent each winter, accompanied by some twenty hunters and a splendid team of coach horses. 'His daily outing,' wrote the Rajah's adoring daughter-in-law Gladys, 'when he drove abroad behind a team of high-steppers, was an event to the people in the countryside.' His less adoring daughter-in-law Sylvia recalled staying in 'that appallingly sporting house. Foxes' heads, brushes, whips, spurs and hunting horns were everywhere. The whole place seemed to smell of bran and oats. In the passage there was every sign of slaughter . . .'

According to Sylvia, young Vyner grew up amid his parents' 'constant quarrels and reconciliations'. He was obliged to wear his father's suits cut down for him to save money and was forbidden to eat jam because the Rajah deemed it effeminate. He was also required to break in his father's hunters, while the Rajah stood in the centre of the field with an enormous whip, putting some 'life' into the horses as they cantered round. At Winchester, he excelled at athletics, while at Magdalene, Cambridge, he earned a reputation as a dashing hellraiser with an expensive passion for the turf. After graduating in the summer of 1897, twenty-three-year-old Vyner was summoned by his father to Sarawak.

For six months he was attached to the Rajah's staff at Kuching, before being despatched to his father's old stamping ground, Simanggang, seventy miles east on the Batang Lupar river. This region was home to the Sea Dyaks, or Ibans, a warlike people particularly notorious for headhunting, a custom which the first two Rajahs had so far failed to stamp out. The Dyaks traditionally saw the taking of heads as a means of consecrating important events in their lives. If a husband failed to present skulls to his wife at the birth of their child, the child was considered ill-fated. Similarly a young man needed a skull or more adorning his hut before he could be admitted to full tribal rights or successfully woo a bride. Before the headhunting expedition there would be a period of fasting and confession, of isolation in a taboo hut, before the headhunter donned an animal mask and skins to carry out his grisly task – usually accomplished by ambush, and often perpetrated on women and children of the headhunter's own tribe.

The Rajah hoped this outstation would be the place to teach his son some discipline. But the Resident Demetrius Bailey, author of *A Sea Dyak Dictionary* and a character straight out of Somerset Maugham, was hardly the man to instil it. Besides such tasks as licking stamps, doling out castor oil to the Dyaks, vaccinating their babies and occasionally performing emergency surgery, Vyner was required each morning to make his way up to the white-painted Residency and shave Bailey, whose hand shook from too much drinking, and trim his handlebar moustache. The young cadet also often found himself having to act as judge, prosecutor and garrison commander, while conspiring to conceal the real situation at

Simanggang from his father. All the while he demonstrated considerable flair for working with the Dyaks; he quickly picked up their language, enjoyed their dances, and established an excellent rapport with them.

But relations with the Dyaks were not always friendly. In late 1898, not long after Vyner succeeded Bailey as Resident, the *Sarawak Gazette* reported that a recalcitrant chief called Banting had 'obliged His Highness to organise a punitive expedition, which speedily quieted matters' – though the principal offender escaped. In 1900 the Rajah Muda took part in another, more successful expedition against Okong, the wily chieftain of the Muruts of Trusan in the far north-east of the country, beyond Brunei.

After spending most of 1901 on leave in England, Vyner returned to Sarawak to become Resident at Muka and Oya, 150 miles to the north-east of Kuching. In June 1902 he was requested to bring a contingent of Dyaks from this coastal district to join a punitive expedition against rebellious Dyaks in the upper reaches of the Batang Lupar, and on 7 June his force joined the huge flotilla of war prahus that had assembled at Simanggang. Vyner's former boss Bailey was another of the expedition leaders, and he recorded in his monthly despatch: 'More than eight hundred boats were counted passing Lubok Antu Fort in the day time (those passing after sun-set were not enumerated) and reckoning fifteen men to a boat (which is considerably understating the average complement, I am informed), the force would exceed 12,000.' Each vessel was carved and painted, with streamers flying and figureheads representing snakes, bulls and crocodiles.

They presented a magnificent spectacle, but the magnificence was overshadowed in Vyner's mind by the mysterious deaths of two men outside his bungalow the night before they were due to move off. There were whispers of cholera, but when he raised his concerns with his father, who had come to Simanggang to see the expedition on its way, they were hastily brushed aside.

For the first three days the flotilla proceeded noiselessly and safely towards its destination. With no further sign of cholera, the old Rajah's bravado appeared justified. But then, on the third day, soon after reaching Lingga, from where they were to march to the rebel stronghold, the cholera struck. As they made their way up the Delok stream, surrounded by precipitous hills, which shut out the breeze and aggravated the sultry heat, the daily death toll increased at an alarming rate. By the time they returned to Simanggang, more than a fifth of their number had died. Vyner never quite forgave his father for having failed to listen to his warning. To Sylvia's way of thinking, the whole incident proved 'more than any other what an unscrupulous and inhuman man this second Raja of Sarawak was'.

It was a year after this disastrous expedition, in July 1903, that Vyner again came back to England on leave. Sylvia had only recently joined the Grey Friars Orchestra but she had heard all about the eldest Brooke son from his doting mother. When Vyner came to watch the rehearsals, declining to join in, Sylvia was struck by his blue eyes and handsome features, his 'smooth fair skin tanned a rich brown by the tropical sun. He had the fine Brooke nose that nature has perpetuated in the outline of the Matang mountain in Sarawak; but he was so shy you felt that if you turned and spoke to him, he would rush headlong from the room.'

However, she soon became aware of Vyner watching her, and one day he plucked up the courage to ask her if he might tune her drum. 'Nineteen hostile faces glared at me,' she recalled dramatically, 'and nineteen disappointed hearts wished I would drop dead . . . I wished then that my pin curls had not blown away,' she added. 'I wished too that there were buttons in my sleeve cuffs instead of safety pins. I was desperately aware of my dumbness and the dull fixity of my expression. It hardly occurred to me that because a man had offered to tune my drum for me, he was beginning to offer his heart.'

When the orchestra subsequently folded for a while, Vyner began a flirtatious correspondence. Sylvia sent him stories she had written; he wrote back praising her 'masterpieces'. She later wrote that Dorothy asked her grimly: 'Why did it have to be you?'

By Sylvia's account, Vyner then sent a large box of violets from Cornwall, and a letter telling her:

> I love you Sylvia and have always done so and always will, but there are two barriers against me. One is that I am not literary like you and I have not the same intellectual accomplishments; and the other is that I have to make periodical visits to the East. These two barriers always loom up whenever I think of you, Sylvia, but if you do not think them insurmountable I should love sometime to talk things over. If, on the other hand, you think they are too large, I don't see the use of our meeting. That is all I have to say, Sylvia. I am not a good letter-writer and put things very crudely, but the substance of it all is that I love you – love you too much to ever cause you pain.

This straightforward declaration from the Rajah Muda was too much for Reggie, who had little enthusiasm for despotic forms of government, referred to Vyner without affection as 'Borneo Brooke', and seems to have regarded the White Rajahs of Sarawak as a Gilbertian joke. Sylvia was whisked off to the Roman Camp and forbidden from any further communication. 'Much as my parents wanted to see me respectably married,' she wrote later, 'they considered that this stranger from the Far East, the son of the woman my father so bitterly disliked, was not a suitable husband for me . . . They imagined me, shrivelled and hideously tanned, returning to them at intervals of three to five years – or else headless and buried in the barren soil of the north-west coast of Borneo.'

Up at Callander, with her mother and Maurice doing all they could to distract her, Sylvia began to think that she had imagined her love affair – until one morning when she was in the dining room having breakfast with her mother and the post was brought in. Nellie was so busy checking to see if there was a letter from Reggie that she failed to notice the spidery scrawl of the Rajah Muda. Sylvia quickly snatched the letter, hid it in her bloomers, and as soon as breakfast was over hurried to her room to open it. The letter banished all her doubts. Vyner could not understand why she had not been to see him. He was sailing for Sarawak the next day, but whatever happened, he told her, he would wait for her, 'centuries if need be'.

For good measure, before he left for Sarawak, in January 1904, Vyner also sent Sylvia a silver model of the drum he had so often tuned for her, inscribed in his own handwriting: 'From a friend'. A postcard from Port Said on his way out east was the last Sylvia heard from him for two years, despite his efforts to get through to her. 'Dear Mr Brooke,' wrote Sylvia's mother from the Roman Camp eight months after his departure,

> I received your letter yesterday, and am answering now, as I am sure you would prefer, quite openly and straightforwardly. In the first place Lord Esher's determination not to permit Sylvia to live so far from England remains unchanged, so that I must ask you not to correspond with her in any way. Secondly, if you had proposed to Sylvia in the ordinary way, I know for a fact she would have refused. I have it from her own lips – the whole thing was a chimera and a got up romance on the part of my eldest daughter – and no one was more surprised than Sylvia herself who was away at the time. I think this really closes the subject – and I am sorry to have to write this crudely – but where there has been so much mystery and misunderstanding I feel it is necessary. Yours truly Eleanor Esher.

It is not clear how Vyner took this, but for the time being he had plenty to distract him out in Sarawak, where he was fast gaining in both responsibility and reputation. His father had previously regarded Vyner as the least worthy of his sons, but he had been impressed with his handling of a raid by headhunters on the Rejang river in 1903, during which eighty women and children had had their heads cut off at a longhouse while their men worked in the fields. As the local Resident, Vyner's response had been a swift and efficient punitive expedition along traditional lines, with an attack on the headhunters' longhouse, the destruction of their property, and the placing of poisoned spikes around it.

In May 1904, following his return from England after the fox-hunting season (three months after Vyner's arrival) the Rajah proclaimed to the Sarawak Supreme Council, made up of his Malay and European advisers, that 'my son and successor Vyner, Rajah Muda, will henceforth take a portion of my duties, and make Kuching, the Capital, his principal residence, that he will take my place in the courts of law unless any question be submitted to me for any decision, that he will be entitled to use my swallow tailed flag on shore and on board at the main, and also be entitled to have the yellow Umbrella, the emblem of Royalty in this country, whenever he goes to court or whenever he may see fit to use it . . .' From now on, whenever his father was away from Sarawak – which he was for periods of up to eight months a year as he got older – Vyner would act as Rajah in his place, absolute ruler over five hundred thousand of his father's subjects.

Back in England, meanwhile, Dorothy, who had scoffed at Sylvia's spineless failure to elope with Vyner, further complicated relations between their families by developing a crush on the Ranee, whom she later credited with having introduced her to the world of art during her Wednesday-afternoon salons. Feeling herself a prisoner at home, Doll would sneak out of the back door at Orchard Lea and appear unannounced at Grey Friars. Reggie warned her that she was degrading herself, and muttered to Maurice, 'All the servants know of these back door escapes, and probably all the village by now.' Eventually the Eshers invited the Ranee to tea at Orchard Lea. Doll, who was then aged over twenty, was locked in her room for the duration of this visit, and when it was over was told that the Ranee no longer wished to see her. Feeling betrayed, Doll bicycled over to Grey Friars, climbed in through the dining-room window, 'squeezed through the dumbwaiter into the kitchen', and proceeded to chase the Ranee round the house with a carving knife. Their friendship was soon re-established, although Reggie and Nellie continued to be distrustful of the Ranee, suspecting her of having lesbian designs on both their daughters and jealous of the affection which she had given them, and they had withheld. Sylvia described how, some time later, Reggie came into her room, tore a portrait of the Ranee from the wall and stamped on it. None of this deterred Doll from seeking out the Ranee, and they remained close until about 1910, when the Ranee, in a temper, accused Doll of trying to steal her beloved W. H. Hudson from her.

When Vyner eventually returned to Grey Friars, in the early summer of 1906, he was thirty-two and coming under some pressure from his parents to get married. The orchestra was reformed, but as far as Sylvia was concerned it was far from the same as before. 'I never had a moment alone with Vyner,' she recalled, 'but the Ranee Margaret, my sister, and he were always together.' She was not the only one to presume that Vyner had transferred his suit to Dorothy. 'I am sure that she [Doll] will be Mrs Raj Moodah, or whatever they call the man, before the year's out,' Reggie wrote to Maurice in June. 'It would be the best solution.' Although he had vehemently opposed the match with Sylvia, Reggie now seemed prepared to let Vyner have Dorothy – possibly because he despaired of his wilful, eccentric and somewhat goofy-looking elder daughter ever finding a husband. Sylvia's worst fears were soon confirmed when, by her account, one rainy day at Grey Friars, the Ranee gave Vyner an enamel necklace and urged him to go into the music room and propose to Dorothy. Vyner duly entered the room, but finding Dorothy on her feet scanning the bookshelves rather than sitting in a chair reading as he had envisaged, he panicked, thrust the necklace into her hands, muttered something unintelligible, and retreated. Quite what Doll made of all this is unclear, as she does not mention it in her memoir.

According to Sylvia, 'it was after this incident that Vyner seemed to make up his mind definitely to marry me. He took Doll into partnership, and between them they worked out a scheme whereby he could approach me.' Reggie and Nellie were still distinctly unenthusiastic, but owing to Doll's connivance, whenever they took Sylvia to the opera or to Ascot races, there would be Vyner, miraculously sitting in a nearby row. When Doll invented a reason why they should drive into Windsor, there he was again, loitering in the doorway of the White Hart Hotel. One day Sylvia was in her bedroom sticking photographs into an album when Doll burst in and solemnly asked if she was prepared to run away. She drew a letter from her pocket and read it out loud: 'Dear Doll, arrange that the Parcel is delivered at the Squirrel Inn where I will collect it in my car. I will then take it away with me as arranged. Vyner.' Frightened but at the same time infected by her sister's fervour, Sylvia hurriedly packed a trousseau and ran through Windsor Forest to the Squirrel Inn, a mile and a half from Orchard Lea. When she got there, she was met not by Vyner but by the landlord with a message to say that her lover had broken down and that she was to drive to Grey Friars. While she waited for the horse and cab to be made ready, she again pondered the wisdom of eloping with a man she scarcely knew. She wondered whether Vyner really did want her, whether he had lost his nerve, whether he had been put up to it all by his mother. Her doubts turned to panic, she grabbed her bag and ran headlong from the inn and back down the forest path to Orchard Lea, where she threw herself on her bed and sobbed, while Doll stood over her calling her a fool.

Vyner assumed at that point that the game was up. As he prepared to head east again, he sent Sylvia violets from his mother's house in Cornwall: 'I hope you will forgive me for being a nuisance in the past,' he wrote. 'The more I think of it the more convinced I am how very selfish I have been in the whole matter. Anyway I can't bother you any more as I sail tomorrow . . . Your always true friend, Vyner Brooke.'

While Sylvia pined for 'the only man who had ever told me that he loved me', her parents sought to divert her by taking her to the theatre and lunching with their glittering friends at the Savoy Grill. Giving up hope of ever marrying, she determined to concentrate on her writing as 'the solution of what to me seemed a useless life . . . I wanted through my pen to be able to strike back at the world I believed had always borne a grudge against me,' she recalled. 'I wanted to hurt somebody as I felt that I myself had been hurt by my family's lack of appreciation.' According to Dorothy, when Sylvia first tried to write a novel, 'she gave it to Pupsie and he read it out aloud. Alas, I am afraid he laughed at her a good deal. It had certain mannerisms, certain silly things . . .' But Sylvia stuck at it, and eventually won a competition in a women's magazine for the best love story of four thousand words. Hers was entitled 'Sweet William' her favourite flower – and she gave her hero a stammer as a means of making up the word count. She subsequently wrote more stories for magazines, including the *Planet*, which belonged to

Harry Brooke, and the *Westminster Gazette*, whose editor John Alfred Spender was a close friend of Reggie. She would leave copies of the magazines scattered about the house in the hope that her father would see them. 'I did so want him to admire me, to look upon me at last as a human being and not as a kind of freak amidst his flock.' The ploy seemed to work. When, in January 1908, the *Westminster* ran Sylvia's article attacking the current system of bringing up girls on its first page, Reggie pronounced the piece 'Quite excellently well done', and for some time after this relations between father and daughter underwent a marked improvement.

As far as Sylvia was concerned, the fact of appearing in print was at least as important as the quality of her work. When one of her earliest stories, 'An Illusion', was accepted by the editor of the *London Magazine*, she wrote to her father: 'I don't think it matters publishing before one is any good do you? After all Charles Lamb, and Burns, and little Barrie all wrote for papers first until they became known and as I shall *never* be known in the same way I don't see why I shouldn't have all the fun.'

'Little' J. M. Barrie, the five-foot-two-inch author of *Peter Pan* (1904), was one of those whom Sylvia had met while lunching at her father's table at the Savoy; twenty-five years her senior, and then at the height of his fame, he was to become one of the several significant older men in her life. Barrie was a great admirer of Reggie, who in 1903 had arranged for him to be given the key to Kensington Gardens. He was affectionately known as the Furry Beast by the whole Brett family, but he seemed to have a particular soft spot for Sylvia, encouraging her writing, becoming, as she put it, one of her literary godfathers. When she first lunched alone with Barrie, she remembered being 'dressed up to the eyes. Fresh colour on my face, new pin curls in my hair.' She wore a black-velvet coat, which made her feel more bohemian and ultimately overconfident, so that Barrie eventually rebuked her for ordering what she wanted before he had the chance to ask her.

This was but a blip in their developing friendship, however, and he was instrumental in persuading Hodder and Stoughton to publish Sylvia's first collection of seventeen very short stories, *Pan and the Little Green Gate*, which came out in September 1908. The book was dedicated 'To Dear J. M. Barrie', and showed his influence in the use of Scottish dialect, fairies, and dream sequences and having children as protagonists. The reviews were highly flattering, the *Manchester Guardian* declaring: 'Miss Brett understands her craft admirably and works with perfect finish', the *Dundee Advertiser*: 'The author has a deep knowledge of nature and of human hearts, and she weaves her little tales and phantasies with a literary charm which it would be difficult to excel.' Reggie told Maurice that he had 'never read such a chorus of praise – enough to turn her head'. At the time, both Reggie and Sylvia were staying up at the Roman Camp, where they were shortly expecting the arrival of little Barrie. When he did arrive the next day, 'palpitating to be off fishing', Reggie was happy to give him over to Syv to be entertained. She could scarcely have been happier, fishing and basking in her good reviews in the company of her mentor. In due course she began to fall a little in love with the Furry Beast.

The day after Barrie's arrival they caught twenty-four trout, 'all good ones', so Reggie told Maurice. 'The little man got most of them, and all in the little burns . . . Very wily of him. We had tea at the Bollin and a row on the loch. He was wild with excitement . . .' Reggie noticed that Barrie talked without ceasing when alone with him and Syv, but was 'rather silent and observant at dinner'. He later told Reggie that he had never enjoyed a holiday so much.

Sylvia's next book, *The Street with Seven Houses*, a series of interrelated stories about the imaginary inhabitants of Tilney Street, in Mayfair, where the Eshers had their town house, followed hard on the heels of her first, coming out in the spring of 1909. The second story, 'The Left Ladies', reflected the author's preoccupation with spinsterhood (the protagonists were based on Sylvia and Dorothy), and the next year her predicament was addressed by another of those she had befriended through her father at the Savoy, George Bernard Shaw. 'Honourable Sylvia,' wrote Shaw,

> Yes, this is a serious matter being a 'Left Lady', but I don't think it is the plainness. If I was an attractively tattooed South Sea islander of an age at which one can engage in some adventures without becoming ridiculous and I met you under a palm tree, I should have no more hesitation (apart from shyness) than I should about eating an exceptionally delicious plum with all the bloom

on – but all these unfortunate companions and associates of yours, the title, the Windsor castle and the Royal pals and all the rest of it, make you so frightfully expensive and terrifying that the nobs can't afford it and the snobs daren't. Something must be done. The simplest way is to select your man and ask him.

Unbeknown to Shaw, Sylvia already had, possibly more than once. The previous year she had written to Reggie while staying with George Binning at Mellerstain, the Haddingtons' Palladian pile in Berwickshire, hinting that she still held a candle for her host: 'Katie [Binning's wife] has some lace collars. I should like to choke her with them.' A year later, staying in the same house, she admitted to her 'Dearest Pupsey' that she was very much in love. 'Why will they put me in a double bed, it is so insinuating.'

More realistically, as she saw it, she had also flung herself at the feet of Little Barrie. In June 1909 he had invited her to Paris to see *Peter Pan*, which was being revived for a second season there by his American impresario friend Charles Frohman. Sylvia travelled over with Barrie's wife Mary, and after a foul Channel crossing during which both of them were 'heartily sick all the way', they met up with Barrie and Frohman for dinner at the Café de Paris, before going to see the performance. 'The Furry Beast is awfully cocky about ordering dishes,' Sylvia reported to her father. 'His Savoy education has done him the world of good.' She added that Barrie was 'paying for everything – he scratches in his poor little purse all day', and that 'on the whole he looks handsome in Paris, you see his littleness does not show'.

On his return to England, Barrie learnt from his gardener that Mary had been having an affair with Gilbert Cannan, the translator and novelist twenty-two years her junior. Confronted with this discovery, Mary told her husband that Cannan was the only person in the world to her. Rejecting Cannan's suggestion that they share Mary, Barrie sued for divorce on the grounds of adultery. His wife did not defend the case, which was heard two months later in October. Reggie was among the signatories to a letter appealing to newspaper editors to minimise their reporting of the proceedings 'as a mark of respect and gratitude to a writer of genius'. Not all of them acceded to the request, so that what many of Mary Barrie's friends had known all along – that her marriage to Barrie was unconsummated – now became public knowledge.

After his divorce, Barrie seemed 'even more isolated than I was . . . ,' Sylvia recalled, 'I actually made myself believe that it was me he needed, and I sat down and wrote him a letter asking him to marry me.' She remembered the letter, which does not appear to have survived, as 'the outpourings of a clumsy frustrated debutante to this melancholy little man'. Letters that do survive from Sylvia to her father suggest that it was Reggie who put her up to it. With her spirits 'below zero', Sylvia had written to Reggie bemoaning the fact that Barrie 'thinks he can take me out to lunch, write forty letters to me, and be thoroughly kind, without my falling in love with him [but] . . . I do not inspire love in the bosom of the male sex . . . I can see nothing but myself as a grim though undeniably plump spinster, dreaming of the things that might have been.' Reggie, like Shaw, appears to have advised Sylvia to take matters into her own hands.

She later told her father that Barrie had replied to her proposal with

> a beautiful letter . . . [saying] he was an elderly fogey and that he was done with such things, and that they were out of the question for him (We know what he means by that poor darling, but of course I can't tell him I know, it is too delicate a subject). He said that what he wanted was for me to continue to be just as great a friend to him as ever, and that nothing should be allowed to interfere with a friendship which was one of his greatest joys . . . But Oh how I love him now – I can't think of anything else – I seem to have given a little piece of myself, and I'm glad, glad, glad that you urged me.

Reggie assured Sylvia that there was nothing wrong in telling a man that she loved him before he asked for it, to which she replied: 'The broadness of your mind is always a marvel to me.' The next day she summoned up the courage to ring Barrie, but that only set her off again. 'I will if I can get away from the subject of my wee man,' she promised Reggie, 'although I long to tell you how his voice sounded, and how I was sure he was looking . . .' The next week she and Barrie had lunch, when he tried to make it as easy as he could for her: 'Of course we did not mention what had passed . . . only I think really it has given him a better opinion of himself.' Though she recognised that Barrie was 'no more in love with me than my boot', she could not shake off her feelings for him, which were turning her, so she told Reggie, into a 'fussy old woman': 'Whenever there is a thunderstorm I think he may be struck, when there is a cold wind, I want to go and tell him to wrap up. If it rains his wet feet are on my mind, and when there is a heatwave, I pray that he may be in the shade.'

But the plain truth was that, however much Sylvia flattered Barrie, if he wanted to marry anybody at that time it was another Sylvia – Sylvia Llewelyn Davies (née du Maurier), the mother of the 'lost boys' who had inspired *Peter Pan*. (Sylvia Brett maintained that Barrie had told her that 'because of my love for children', she was Wendy. But there seems to be no corroboration for her assertion.) She was now stricken with cancer, deepening Barrie's gloom, and died on 27 August, with Barrie among those present at her deathbed. He was named most frequently in her will, and made guardian to her boys.

While all this was happening, Sylvia was again staying up at the Roman Camp, still worrying about spinsterhood. In reply to Shaw's letter about the hazards faced by her potential suitors, she said that she was

> dogged by the word 'Honourable' before my name . . . [though] I am nothing but a vagabond in the small circle I live in . . . In fact [so] disgraceful [a] thing am I that the so-called 'smart set' have turned me out, and the 'Souls' don't consider I have enough soul for them, and the Bohemians don't consider me sufficiently educated to belong to them, so I belong to nobody – I am not expensive, I desire nothing better than a man who can just tolerate me, the word 'love' doesn't seem to go with me – Toleration and to be left alone is all I dare ask – Now for the second item you say in your advertisement 'wanted a *young man*' – they are always fools and nearly always knaves, whereas a middle-aged or an old man has ceased more or less to be a fool and finished with his knavery. If I asked a man to marry me I

should be refused, and what then. Alas a Left Lady I must remain, the despised of my sex.

She remained in this mood for several months to come, and in November Reggie wrote to Maurice that Syv was still 'really, in her heart of hearts, worrying about that ridiculous man [Barrie] who has no intention whatever of marrying her. If Mrs [Sylvia Llewelyn] Davies had left a daughter he might have married Syv. But he can manage boys himself.'

The next month Vyner Brooke arrived back on the scene. The Rajah Muda had spent most of the past five years in Sarawak, attending with his father the historic peace meeting in 1907 at Kapit, at which his old enemy Bantin and the rebellious Dyaks of the Ulu Ai had agreed to end their feuds with the Dyaks of the lower Batang Lupar – though it needed a further expedition the next year finally to bring Banting to heel. Back in Kuching, he threw his weight behind schemes to develop the country, including the introduction of street lamps, which first appeared in Kuching in 1906, thirty years after those in Singapore, and the search for oil, which was eventually discovered at Miri in 1909. But in January 1910, while fishing in the rain in an open boat, Vyner caught a chill, which soon developed into a series of abscesses on his liver. When he was taken off to Singapore to be operated on, it was whispered in Sarawak that they would never see their Rajah Muda again.

He did eventually pull through, though when he came back to England, in June, he was still very weak. In December, after spending six months regaining his strength, he determined to make one final appeal to Sylvia. When she received his letter she was in Edinburgh, staying at the Station Hotel on Princes Street with Maurice's fiancée Zena Dare, who was on tour there playing in *The Catch of the Season*, with Seymour Hicks.

Sylvia replied straight away that she now loved someone else, but then forwarded Vyner's letter to Reggie, confessing that she was 'a little touched at this man's seeming devotion – He has been very loyal hasn't he, and the letter seems sincere enough – Indeed I feel very odd that any man should say to me "I love you". It doesn't convey reality a bit.'

Reggie and Maurice both now urged her to see Vyner, if only to prevent her becoming 'morbid and old and ill' while pining for the Furry Beast. So she sent a telegram to Vyner saying she thought they should meet on her return from Edinburgh. There followed a 'strange, shy luncheon' at Prince's Restaurant in Piccadilly, during which, as she recalled, they discussed lavatories and plumbing. Within a week they were engaged.

On New Year's Day, staying with some friends in Shropshire, Sylvia wrote to tell her father that if he still had any objection to her marrying Vyner, 'you must speak now or forever hold your peace as the thing may happen at any moment. I know you think me a fool to hurry but that is my temperament . . . personally I think we shall be very very happy.' She wrote several times to Vyner at Grey Friars, letters which he told her drove

> all my gloomy thoughts and despondencies to the winds. I want to hear you say things again yourself. You are the most beautiful being in all the world . . . and I am your slave for all time. We are now nearly halfway through the week so it won't be much longer before I see my darling and take her in my arms and imprint on her sweet lips my pent up kisses for all the days she has been away. That is to say if my darling is still sweet & kind and has not grown cold during my absence. Goodbye darling, mind and take good care of yourself & don't disparage yourself or your appearance when you write to me – *I won't hear it!* Your devoted, Vyner

'Vyner writes delightful letters,' Sylvia told Reggie, '*very* sincere, and I, like a poor deluded spirit, believe in them.' Yet she still seems to have had doubts, aware perhaps that she was less certain now of her feelings for Vyner, that young love had given way to pragmatism. A possible symptom of this was that she continued to do herself down in her letters to him. 'The only thing I don't like', he wrote on 24 January, 'is when you belittle yourself and say that I may look down on you and think little of you for being responsive to my great love for you. Darling *I won't hear it* – the only thing I want is your love and that we should be all in all to one another. If you did not show it and be cold, I should be wretched – Mind, darling, I won't have you say such things about yourself – *Allow me to know better!*'

When their engagement was announced, by Sylvia's account, most of her friends wrote careful letters of congratulation, uncertain what to make of this peculiar-sounding man from Borneo. Some imagined he was Indian, others Ethiopian; either way they supposed that she was destined for a harem. A few managed some enthusiasm, marvelling at what an adventure it would be for her to rule over savages. Letters also arrived from her older admirers. George Bernard Shaw told her he was

> not at all pleased to hear that you are in love with somebody. You ought to be in love with me. That is the usual thing and I think the proper thing at your age. I hope the other fellow is married or in some other way put on a high shelf, because it is not wise to marry a man you love, it makes you a slave and a nuisance and the poor wretch cannot live up to it, whereas if you love somebody else you have a husband with whom you can be at your ease and you can have your dream all the same without ever waking. There should always be another. He will keep well if you take care to keep him imaginary.

He added: 'It takes six years to learn to live together, and get over the most furious fits of wishing you hadn't married him, and hating him, but after that he becomes a habit and a property and you stop bothering about it.'

The marriage did not go down well with Vyner's father either. Rajah Charles suspected that Sylvia would encourage Vyner to be pleasure-seeking, extravagant and insubordinate; he also (wrongly) suspected her father Lord Esher of having arranged the match as a part of plutocratic conspiracy to capture Sarawak's natural resources.

For his part, Reggie, if friendlier than before, was still far from ecstatic about Vyner: he confided to Maurice that he was 'a good natural thing, but *not* sufficiently interesting. I don't think there is anything behind the surface, good or evil.' However, he now raised no objection to their marrying, and appeared to be warming to the ceremonial possibilities of the occasion. 'You think Westminster

Abbey do you?' wrote Sylvia to her father. 'I am for St Pauls!!!!' Through his contacts at court, Reggie established that 'Syv's official precedence when the old man [Rajah Charles] dies is immediately after the Indian Princes, and she will be treated as [consort of] a Ruler of State under British Protection'. He was also more than satisfied by the financial arrangements. 'The old Rajah has behaved very well,' he wrote to Oliver, who was in America pursuing his future wife, Antoinette Heckscher. '£4,000 p.a. and £3,000 p.a. settled on Syv in case of Vyner's death. They will be very well off.' In fact the only thing that really irked him was having to consort with the Ranee, whom he charged with constant intrigue and described as 'a treacherous beast' who had always been 'a devil' to Nellie. 'We have the infernal dinner with Mrs Ranee tonight,' he wrote to Maurice a week before the wedding. 'She proposed that we should arrive at 25 minutes to 8 and *she* at 8! as if she was the Queen. I have ordered our motor at 5 minutes *past* 8.'

But Reggie had a more important matter on his mind than the marriage of Sylvia and Vyner, and that was the culmination of his scheme to bring together his beloved Maurice and the actress Zena Dare, a match he had been pushing and orchestrating to an extraordinary degree since 1904. As Reggie's grandson Lionel Esher later summarised the situation, Zena 'was not quite the class of girl he [Reggie] had had in mind for his adored son, who would have to resign from the Coldstream Guards if he married her. But my grandfather, habitually stage-struck, had found her honesty admirable and her charm and sense of fun irresistible, and she quickly succumbed to him.' For six years, Reggie had been supplying his nervous son with tips on how best to woo Zena, telling him where to take her, when to kiss her ('All now depends upon your taking her into your arms with ardent passion,' he wrote in January 1910) and so on. On Maurice's behalf he would send Zena telegrams suggesting arrangements. He even opened her letters, explaining on one occasion to Maurice that it was 'useful, I felt that I should see it – Dear thing, she only wants your arms round her – very tight – and your lips on hers, and you need not fear for the answer'.

In the end, however, even Reggie was taken by surprise when Maurice and Zena eloped, marrying secretly on 23 January 1911 at a register office in the Harrow Road, thus avoiding a society wedding, which Zena dreaded, and enabling her to continue acting with Seymour Hicks. 'I have been bothered all this afternoon by reporters owing to a statement in the *Evening Times* (a dirty rag) that you were married this week,' Reggie wrote to Maurice three days after the event. He seemed to take the news in good part, but three months later, on Maurice's birthday, he lamented in his journal that his son was 'so absorbed in Zena that he rarely talks to me: all interest in life, except her, seems to be dead'.

Less than a month after Maurice and Zena's wedding, meanwhile, on a dank Tuesday morning, 21 February 1911, Sylvia and Vyner had been married at St Peter's Church, Cranbourne, not far from Orchard Lea, in Windsor Forest. This was the day Sylvia had longed for, yet as she got into her white-satin robe she was haunted by the defiant spectre of the morbid child she had been. The Furry Beast came up to her room as soon as she was ready, saying he wanted to be first to kiss the bride.

At the service, which was conducted by the subdean of the Chapel Royal, Sylvia was given away by Reggie and attended by several bridesmaids, led by Dorothy. Afterwards there was a large reception at Orchard Lea, with a marquee, breakfast and waiters all provided by the Savoy. It was a great success, Reggie told Oliver, who was still in America wooing Antoinette. 'The marquee and the breakfast, all arranged by Gustave [from the Savoy], were the great features. Also the boy scouts at the church. I wish you could have been there. Syv was wonderful. Very composed and looked extraordinarily well. Zena had a complete triumph, everyone clamouring to be introduced.' He made no mention of his reported encounter with Rajah Charles, who, Sylvia later wrote, 'had been dragged unwillingly to the marriage of his son'. According to her version of events, the old Rajah was anxious to leave as soon as he could and turned to Reggie without knowing who he was: 'How the hell can I get out of this damned house?' he demanded. Reggie was so taken aback that he 'meekly showed him the door'.

The hundreds who gave presents ranged from the King and Queen (who sent an enamel brooch set with pearls and diamonds) to the townsmen of Callander, who also gave a brooch, of pearl. Reggie had forecast (to Maurice) 'a very quiet wedding, no crowd, not much fuss', but the press turned out in force, eager to report the news that Lord Esher's daughter had married the heir to the 'Great White Rajah' – 'one of the most romantic sovereignties in all Asia', 'Lord and Taker of Life', 'the greatest autocrat on earth'. Sylvia's photograph appeared beneath headlines such as 'Queen of the Wild Men of Borneo', and 'Grand-Uncle of Bridegroom Won Savage Realm as Reward for Aiding Oriental Ruler'. It was further noted, on dubious grounds, that when her husband succeeded to the throne she would have the rank and precedence of a duchess at the Court of St James.

4

MY ADDRESS IS SARAWAK, THAT'S ALL

From the reception, Sylvia and Vyner went away to Nuneham Park, just south of Oxford, which Doll's old tormentor Loulou Harcourt had lent them for the first three days of their honeymoon. Some weeks before they were married, while staying at a hotel in Oxford, Vyner had ventured into Sylvia's room, but she had told him firmly that she was 'not that kind of a girl'. Now, on her wedding night, as she lay shivering in one of Nuneham's vast four-posters, the sound of her husband's approaching footsteps was 'like the beating of the executioner's drum'. That is about as much as Sylvia divulged about the first time she and her husband slept together, though in her second autobiography she tells us that the next morning he looked at her, pulled a funny face and muttered, 'Well, that's that then.'

The honeymoon did not become a great deal more passionate after they got to Italy, with Vyner assuring Sylvia that there was no such thing as love, and friendship was the foundation stone of a perfect marriage. He guided her around Rome with an ancient Baedeker, and in the evenings took her up Monte Pinchio for a view of the city as it began to be lit up. 'It was so beautiful,' Sylvia recalled, 'I wished he would make love to me then and there.' But instead he told her jokes from a book he had brought along to keep her entertained. Soon there arrived a letter from Ranee Margaret to Vyner, 'bothering him to have a baby quick'. 'Does she expect us to bring one back from Rome?' Sylvia wondered to her father.

'Anyway her talking about it almost makes me inclined not to have one at all.'

Sylvia's letters home may have satisfied her father that she was enjoying matrimony – '[Vyner] is so kind to me, and we get on as if we had been married for years, there has been none of those first four months awkwardness' – but they failed to convince him that she and Vyner were discerning tourists. 'Neither she or he are *really* objectively observant,' Reggie wrote to his old friend Chat Williamson. 'They are not educated historically either. So that they travel under severe limitations.' A few days later, he remarked to Oliver, 'No two people were ever worse equipped to go abroad.'

Moving south to Sorrento, they stayed at the Hotel Tramontano on a cliff overlooking the Bay of Naples, where they watched porpoises as Vyner rowed Sylvia along the coast. Mercifully, as far as Sylvia was concerned, he had also mislaid his book of jokes and it was in Sorrento, according to her calculations, that their first child was conceived. By the time they reached Venice she was beginning to suffer from morning sickness and found everything Vyner did a source of irritation. It was time they went home, and they soon made for London, arriving back on 13 April after more than seven weeks away.

Among the post awaiting Sylvia when they returned was a note from J. M. Barrie, praising her demeanour on her wedding day, 'so nice to everyone, especially to servants and waiters. I think the latter such a test of a nice woman, and I watched, and no one could have come more sweetly through the ordeal. I think you will be idolised in Sarawak, and we shall hear of the most romantic devotion on the part of dusky natives . . .'

George Bernard Shaw had sent a nursery rhyme:

Ride a cock horse
To Sarawak Cross
To see a young Ranee consumed with remorse.
She'll have bells on her fingers
And rings through her nose,
And won't be permitted to wear any clo'es.

'I don't know what you call it, Sylvia,' he added impishly, 'but *I* call it simple unfaithfulness . . .'

For 'tis oh my heart is left, lady
To find myself bereft, lady
Of Sylvia, my left lady
By a heathen potentate.

Shaw asked that she come to lunch and 'bring the heathen potentate – You should introduce him to the intellectual side of London. I mean, of course, to ME.' But Vyner wriggled out of the invitation, overcome by shyness: 'The prospect of having to meet somebody famous sent him straight into his shell,' wrote Sylvia. 'The instinct was so strong that if such a person called at our home, Vyner would literally lock himself up in a clothes cupboard, and stay there until the visitor had gone.'

After a month at Orchard Lea, they moved into their new home at Stanton Harcourt, not far from Nuneham, where they had leased a Victorian converted stable block from the Harcourts. Loulou had unexpectedly succeeded Lord Crewe as Colonial Secretary in 1910, in Asquith's government, and the old Rajah, who had long dreaded the encroachment of colonial methods in Sarawak, complained that 'being in Stanton Harcourt means being in Harcourt's pocket'. Pressed by Reggie, in the late summer Loulou was able to use his influence to persuade the King to make Vyner a Highness, ranking in precedence immediately after the Indian princes. Sylvia and Vyner were 'rampant with joy' with this, she told Reggie: 'Oh, the slap in the eye for the old Begum [Ranee Margaret], the hundred and one slaps in the eye for the Singapore fools who were chuckling and laughing at Vyner in their beards. How did you do it? How can I ever thank you?' The old Rajah and his supporters in the press, meanwhile, viewed all this as 'insolent' meddling on the part of the Colonial Secretary, and an unwarranted assumption of the right to supersede the Rajah on a 'purely internal' matter.

Through the hot summer months until they headed north to the Roman Camp in mid-August Vyner toiled away in the Stanton Harcourt garden, which was soon ablaze with irises, roses and rock plants, and open to the public. Every so often Loulou would turn up with his house party to admire Vyner's handiwork and generous members of the entourage would occasionally tip him, mistaking the shabbily dressed Rajah Muda for the gardener.

Sylvia began to look matronly, and experienced giddiness and fainting fits. 'Truly I have been suffering so much that I sometimes think spinsters are to be envied,' she wrote to Shaw. 'Yet I have always longed for a lapful of children so I must not grumble.' Loath to leave Vyner's side, she even went with him on rabbiting expeditions, when she would sit by the roadside knitting, waiting for him to return. They went for long drives together, and when he turned out for the village cricket team, she dutifully served the tea. She pronounced herself thoroughly contented. 'My husband and I spend so many happy hours,' she told Shaw, 'and the hours accumulate and become days, and the days become months, and we know nothing except that the sun shines and we are happy.'

Yet this was not quite the whole truth, as she later admitted. Still yearning for 'some tremendous achievement that would electrify the world', she felt restless and that she was losing momentum in her writing career. Anxious, too, not to lose touch with her literary friends, she implored Shaw to 'come and see us'. For whatever reason, it seems that he did not, with the result that Sylvia felt slighted.

It is possible that Shaw was by now beginning to find Sylvia's neediness a little irksome. His biographer Michael Holroyd thinks that she probably appealed to the submerged romantic in him, and fulfilled his need to be around unconventional people who were physically adventurous in a way that he was not, who went off and did daring and outlandish things, adding to the entertainment of life. The company of such people made him feel more whole. At the same time, notes Holroyd, his correspondence was full of people trespassing on his time and energy, asking for advice and approval, and eventually he did get tired. A characteristic of his relationships was that he tended to promise more than he actually delivered, especially as his fame increased.

Ahead of the birth, Vyner took a house in London at 8 Cadogan Gardens, near Sloane Square, and from there, on 11 November, Sylvia wrote to Shaw telling him she thought it was high time he took an interest in her, considering I am going to have a baby next week, and I don't like to think that while you are sitting at your silly old desk, I may snuff out of the world, and you not know. Perhaps you have forgotten who I am – well I am Sylvia, who married sometime past a Heathen Potentate, thereby losing your respect by becoming Her Highness The Ranee Muda of Sarawak – you gave me up after that with a shrug of your shoulders, and it is only in the very humblest spirit that I push myself under your notice again – As the plain spinster you admired me, or pretended to, well though I can no longer claim the spinsterhood I am at heart still plain – we are in this house till January, so when I am well enough you must come and see me – for if you and Mrs Shaw don't appear to take a lively interest after this letter, I shall sit down and howl.

The emotional blackmail jolted Shaw into sending a note back the next day:

Sylvia, if you have not had twenty messages from me, there is no such thing as telepathy. But I never could write them down. I can't now. When I think of it a sort of pang goes through me from the base of my heart down to my very entrails. I lose all sense of distinction between the Heathen Potentate and myself or anyone else in the world. I see no other woman on earth but you; we are Adam and Eve, and you are going to be torn to pieces and come to life again with a terrible contempt for fragile male things that would be broken by such creative miracles, and an enormous pride in having wielded all the powers of the Universe for a moment and come out triumphant . . . This is your day of battle; and everything that I can say may seem to you the trivialest twaddle. If I could go in with you, and we could rush through cheering and charging together, and sharing the wounds and howling and writhing in company, then I should not fail you; but as it is, what can I say or do? I must watch *The Times* for the announcement of the colossal relief, the victory, the triumph, and Sylvia a mother in ~~Isreal~~ Israel (there! I could not even write it properly). Its magnificent; but oh Sylvia, Sylvia, Sylvia, how I wish it were over!!!!!!!! GBS

This letter has been cited by Holroyd in his biography as evidence that Shaw 'felt a reverence and sense of humility before the fact of childbirth', of which the playwright had no first-hand experience since his own marriage to Charlotte Payne-Townshend was childless. The Shaws' lack of offspring (both of them were over forty when they married) was seized on by the playwright's actress lover Stella Campbell – the widowed Mrs Patrick Campbell, or 'Mrs Pat'. Eliza Doolittle in his *Pygmalion* in 1914 – who sought to tempt him away by saying that she could have six more children. Sylvia, in turn, exploited the affair for her own brand of mischievous fun. When, in January 1913, the Shaws had lunch with Sylvia, he recorded that she 'very devilishly' asked him point-blank, 'How is Mrs Pat?' – and 'watched to see how much damage that shell would do when it exploded'.

Sylvia's imagined agony was over sooner than expected. On 18 November 1911, at Cadogan Gardens, her first child, a girl, was born. Three weeks premature, she weighed three pounds and was delivered for Sylvia at home after three days of labour by the Royal obstetrician Sir Henry Simson. Eleven days after the birth, Sylvia wrote to Shaw, 'perched up in bed, two skinny pigtails on either side of my face, and a rather foolish smile covering my tremendous pride'. She would never forget 'the awful agony', and admitted that she had 'yelled and howled lustily, so lustily that the tears rolled down the Heathen Potentate's cheeks'. Her baby had 'so nearly died' that they were obliged to christen her there and then; so in a hurry Vyner had named her Leonora (Sylvia's second name) Margaret (after his mother, the Ranee).

Despite the fact that she had not produced a son and heir, Sylvia later recalled that Vyner was 'in the seventh heaven of delight' and showered her with flowers. But her father-in-law, old Rajah Charles, was less bucked when he heard. He was in Sarawak at the time and had prepared all sorts of elaborate ceremonies to mark the birth of his anticipated first grandson. Bell-ringers stood by to peal forth the joyful news, but they waited, hanging to the bell ropes, for a signal that never came.

Barely a year later, Sylvia's sister-in-law Gladys Brooke did give birth to a son, Anthony, and on hearing the news the Rajah ordered a salute of twenty-one guns to be fired from the fort at Kuching.

Anthony would remain to Sylvia a symbol of what she had failed to achieve, and in years to come she did all that she could to frustrate his claims as heir apparent to the Raj.

Leonora was just two months old when, on Boxing Day, Sylvia felt an excruciating pain in her stomach. Simson was sent for and he quickly diagnosed appendicitis, which evidently ran in the family, Reggie having also had an appendectomy the previous July in addition to Doll's in 1902. Like Doll, Sylvia's recovery from the operation was slow and painful, and she was obliged to the leave the care of Leonora to a nurse; Vyner, for all his delight, dared not touch his daughter. Hence mother and daughter had very little opportunity to bond before Vyner announced that he must get back to Sarawak.

Leonora was by then still only six months old and, as Sylvia recorded, perhaps a little overdramatically, 'Her life at that time hung on the thinnest of threads.' But she nonetheless resolved to go with her husband, persuaded by her father that separations were fatal to marital happiness.

The Rajah saw it as essential for the future of the Brooke Raj that Sylvia should eventually make her home in Sarawak, but he thought that Vyner's idea of taking his wife out to Sarawak for a short 'holiday' after the birth of Leonora was 'a great expense and trouble for nothing', and he made his views on the matter perfectly plain to his son. That Vyner then compounded the trouble and expense by asking Sylvia's eldest brother Oliver to go along with them only added to the strain between the Rajah and his heir.

Oliver had recently returned from America disconsolate after his fiancée, Antoinette Heckscher, changed her mind at the last minute. The idea that he should go to Sarawak seems to have been Reggie's, who deemed his eldest son in need of distraction but also spotted the opportunity of gaining an independent and enlightened view of the Brooke Raj, which he still found hard to take entirely seriously. Years later, James Lees-Milne would describe Oliver, by then Viscount Esher and Lees-Milne's superior at the National Trust, 'counting the cakes on the tea-table and calculating how many he may eat; and then gorging. Never walks a yard, saying we should hold Sir Edgar Bonham-Carter, who was a rugger blue and is now a cripple, as a warning not on any account to take exercise. Says he would rather remain in England and be atom-bombed into a jelly than emigrate to the colonies, blaze trails through the bushvelt and be eaten by scorpions.' Oliver had not been expected to accept Vyner's invitation for, as Sylvia wrote, the Bretts were 'the kind of family that rooted ourselves into places and remained there'; her brother was 'secretly glad in his heart when it rained and he could have what he called a good frowst'. Nevertheless, he leapt at the chance to go with them.

Before setting off they went to stay at Grey Friars, where the Ranee 'went for' Sylvia, so she related, accusing Reggie of conspiring to make money out of Sarawak, adding that Vyner was 'a weak-minded fool' and that the only hope for the Raj was if Bertram had a strong hand in the direction of affairs. They also lunched on successive days with the Shaws, General Sir John French (then Chief of the Imperial General Staff), who had also formed a sentimental friendship with Sylvia before her marriage, and J. M. Barrie. Shaw told Sylvia he had much admired the short play she had sent him about an actor, and then said, 'But it doesn't matter what you write, you've got such incomparable style!' Charlotte chipped in that *The Street with Seven Houses* was 'really beautiful', so that Sylvia came away 'stepping on air', she wrote to Reggie. Her literary ambitions thus buoyed, she now planned to turn her attention to a book of short stories about Borneo, which she hoped to have completed before she returned. 'My address is Sarawak,' she added, 'via Singapore, that is all; just big Sarawak and it singles out little me.'

After a final night at the Savoy, they set sail on 4 April, leaving Leonora behind in the care of a nurse. Sylvia was still in pain from her appendectomy and wore a large belt recommended by her surgeon; Vyner was also a 'leaden grey colour' after his illness; and 'Noll [Oliver]', she told her father, 'looks thin, but is perfectly cheerful – he hasn't said anything bitter yet, or abusive . . .' For their first week at sea the weather was glorious, but just after leaving Marseilles they ran into the heaviest storm seen in the Mediterranean for six years. Their vast P&O liner was 'tossed and tumbled like a piece of cork', Sylvia reported, and a great wave burst through the doors into the saloon where she was sitting after dinner. While she was recovering from all this, news reached her about the *Titanic*, which had left Queenstown on the south coast of Ireland on 11 April to cross the Atlantic on its maiden voyage, with her friend W. T. Stead among the few non-plutocrats travelling in First Class.

Stead had had serious misgivings about making the trip, having been warned by the various spiritualists whom he had consulted that travel would be dangerous in April, and that he would be involved 'in the midst of a catastrophe on water'. He had gone so far as to predict a disaster involving a large ocean liner and a shortage of lifeboats in various pieces he had written in the *Pall Mall Gazette*, but a personal summons from President Taft for him to address a peace conference in New York had eventually proved too powerful a lure.

Three days into the voyage, on the night of 14 April, Stead had been one of the few passengers out on deck, taking a final stroll before turning in, when the fateful collision had occurred. He had subsequently retreated to the First Class smoking room, and described to another passenger having seen the forecastle of the vessel full of powdered ice it had scraped off the iceberg. During the next four hours before the ship sank, he had been seen reading his book, apparently oblivious to the gathering panic around him. Later, after the ship went down, there had been a sighting of him and Colonel J. J. Astor, both clinging to the same life raft until they had released their hold and disappeared into the sea.

Reggie at first cheerfully assumed that his old friend had survived. 'Fancy old Stead in the *Titanic*,' he wrote to Maurice. 'How he will gas about it all!' Reggie's confidence reflected the mood of the country, which found it difficult to accept that this superb liner should have foundered with such huge loss of life. Two days later, when the scale of the disaster became known, he wrote again to Maurice: 'Poor old Stead. I fear that he has joined that band of immortal spirits who so deeply interested him in life. I have no doubt that he met his end bravely and well – probably with great fervour. He was a very great man, keen about everything that is worth being keen about.' Sylvia, too, mourned the loss of 'poor dear, dear old Mr Stead. I feel that terribly, he was always so sweet to me and genuinely liked me, I think. Anyway I was devoted to him.'

Icebergs were one thing they did not have to worry about in the Indian Ocean. Further east the sea became calm enough for deck tennis and quoits. Sylvia, her nose sunburnt as it was too windy to wear a hat, was roped into give the prizes at the fancy-dress ball and appointed captain of the ladies' cricket team. She told Reggie that she was still finding her new husband 'a perfect person to travel with, so good tempered and easy'. In the evenings, while Oliver frowsted in his cabin, she and Vyner would sit out on deck well into the night, while he told her stories about his bachelor dalliances. 'To put it mildly,' wrote Sylvia years later, 'he was a man who was quite incapable of resisting women . . . I realise now, that, in his honest way, he wanted me to understand his weaknesses as well as his strength; but how artless I must have been to have imagined for one moment that this old leopard would, or could, ever change his spots.'

They called in at Port Said, then Colombo, where Oliver saved Sylvia from being swept away by the undertow while swimming at Mount Lavinia, and finally Penang, from where they motored down through the rubber gardens of the Federated Malay States. Sylvia wrote to Reggie declaring that she liked the East 'better than anything I have ever done', although she admitted that she found the whites they came across in Malaya 'simply awful – you've no idea how awful they are to, and with the natives'.

At Singapore they stayed at Government House, where Sylvia inspected some of Vyner's regiment in the garage. In her first autobiography she tactfully recalled that their hosts, Sir Arthur Young and his wife, Lady Evelyn, were 'charming to us', but privately she was scornful of the governor and his entourage: 'These people are like a skit on "The gentry", a farce that half London goes to roar at,' she wrote to her father. The governor was

> like a character out of Tom Jones – a clumsy, ill-bred, beef-eating squire . . . Noll found himself discussing how to make fowls lay eggs . . . The ignorance of this man is unbelievable. He can't even tell his chauffeur in Malay to drive slowly and I've only been a fortnight in the country and yet I can do that. Fancy a Governor being unable to speak to his own people . . . Will you tell Loulou [Harcourt] with my fondest love that if he hears about Sarawak

> from *this* Governor, in any way against us – he should put them in the fire – the man's opinion isn't worth a pin's head.

Young's opinion, for what it was worth, expressed in a letter to Loulou's undersecretary, Sir John Anderson, was that he doubted the Rajah Muda or his wife 'caring for Sarawak after the novelty passes off'.

Oliver also wrote, to Reggie, a slightly pompous but well-observed letter from Government House, excusing himself for not having written earlier:

> Up till now we have been tourists and the observations of tourists are always platitudinous. Here Vyner is on his own ground and it may interest you to hear my impressions. Vyner is excellent with natives: he knows how to deal with them, how to talk to them, how to be both dignified and cordial. In our interview with the Sultan of Perah, quite a stiff and alarming business, he was quite at his ease and steered Sylvia through very well. With the whites he is not so good, being a little awkward when trying to be dignified, and as a rule inclined to be too hail fellow well met, which, as they are none of them gentlemen, they take advantage of.

Oliver noted that Sylvia was 'much better with the whites, does not forget her position and is ready to snub when other people forget it. Yesterday she was suddenly perched in the front place in the Governor's box at the races among all the local smart set behaving as stupidly and vulgarly as smart sets always do and she did very well.' He went on to describe how both the Malays and the Chinese despised the English, 'in which I heartily sympathise with them, for the type of "mean white" here is as common, louche, pushing, drunken, bad-mannered as any Western American could be'. And he echoed Sylvia's views on the governor: 'He is of course very solemn and pompous, full of sham dignity, able to make himself popular among the whites and to lead "Society" very successfully. But he is common, his manners are bad, he is ignorant & badly educated, & I disapprove of his tendency to criticise openly both the government and the King.'

On Wednesday, 15 May they embarked on the final leg of their journey aboard the steamer *Kuching*, accompanying a pungent cargo of sago and dried fish, and horses acquired in Singapore for Sylvia and Oliver. After a calm two-day crossing of the South China Sea, they awoke on Friday to a gorgeous dawn behind the distant mountains of Borneo. At about lunch time they entered a wide bay surrounded with mountains and dotted with little islands. Vyner pointed to Santubong mountain, rising three thousand feet straight out of the northern end of the bay and shaped, so it was said, like the profile of Rajah James Brooke. At the head of the bay was the mouth of the Sarawak river, tidal all the twenty miles up to Kuching.

Their reception began as soon as they entered the river and continued all the way to the capital. 'It was one of the prettiest things I have seen in my life,' wrote Oliver to his father, 'as original in its way as the Coronation.' At the village of Sijinkat banners were held aloft by the people and the hill behind was festooned with lanterns and flags, with welcoming messages for the Rajah Muda and his new bride. When their steamer was sighted, gongs were beaten, and the river bank became crowded with almost the entire population, not cheering much (it is not Malay custom), but staring, the women and children waving handkerchiefs, the men letting off hundreds of firecrackers. Vyner and Sylvia were obliged to stand by the rails in the boiling sun and wave until they were out of sight. The *Sarawak Gazette* reported that the villagers of Sijinkat had assembled there the day before, expecting the boat on the Thursday, but that they nevertheless continued their festivities until a late hour in the evening, 'and before the crowd dispersed to their homes a short prayer was offered up giving thanks for the safe arrival of Their Highnesses'.

On they steamed upriver, Sylvia in thrall to 'the broad and winding beauty of it', she later wrote,

> the little villages clamped on to the mud banks, as if the palm leaf houses had all been tumbled from a basket and left exactly as they fell. Coffee-coloured women stood waist-deep in the water with their long bamboo jars upon their shoulders; and children dived

> and swam among them like little brown tadpoles . . . There were tangled mangrove swamps along the uncultivated banks, and behind them rose the real jungle with its majestic trees and monkeys swinging from branch to branch. There was something fearsome about the richness of this ancient foliage in a land of mysterious legends and beliefs; and yet, as I gazed at all its luxuriant beauty, I knew that a long dark chapter in my life was ending.

News of their arrival had been telephoned to Kuching from the mouth of the river, and as they rounded the bend by Fort Margherita at about 3 p.m., the battery fired a salute, precipitating a general explosion of firecrackers and frantic waving of handkerchiefs on the town side of the river, where a large crowd had gathered beneath a large banner proclaiming: 'Welcome and Long Life to Their Highnesses'.

European government officers were waiting on the palace side, and as the *Kuching* dropped anchor in midstream, three of them came aboard, 'serious as undertakers', Sylvia recalled, 'and almost depressed as they viewed with unconcealed amazement my inadequate five feet'. They were taken ashore in a broad canoe, painted white, with a hood, rather like a gondola, and paddled by six Malay boys in white.

Under the covered landing stage of the Astana there were more Europeans, Malay officials and Chinese Towkeys, bowing with regal respect. They all shook hands with Vyner before being presented to the Ranee Muda. The yellow state umbrella was opened by a Malay soldier and carried over Vyner's head as they made their way up the sloping garden towards the Astana, Sylvia following four paces behind her husband, as custom demanded. A guard of honour was drawn up on the lawn, of young men dressed in neat uniforms of white, with coloured sashes, puttees and red fezzes, each one carrying a Sarawak flag; as Vyner and Sylvia passed, they presented arms. The band of the Sarawak Rangers then struck up the Sarawak national anthem, which had been composed by Ranee Margaret.

At the top of the Astana steps a large bouquet was given to Sylvia, who was by then 'hanging like an anxious limpet' on her husband's arm. Vyner said: 'Glad to see you all again: please come indoors.' 'It was exactly like a Levee,' Oliver told Reggie. 'They were all very shy and stiff, frightened as people are of Royalty, backing away if Vyner or Sylvia approached to speak.'

The verandah was later invaded by about a hundred upper-class Malay women, all dressed in their finery. 'Some of them were very pretty even to English eyes,' wrote Oliver,

> but even the plain ones were glorified by a blaze of colour, and by the flirtatious manipulation of veil. Unlike the whites they were respectful without being awkward, shy without being absurd. Always graceful, with happy, kind, smiling faces, & the most beautiful and refined manners. They crowded round Squiv till she was drowned in a sea of colour, talking away, & obviously delighted to see her. Vyner says he has never had such a crowded reception. He does the royal business with much natural dignity, knows always what to do, & is easy without 'letting it down'.

Sylvia, Oliver added, 'did surprisingly well, handicapped as she was by not knowing the language. She was rather shy of course & sometimes at a loss to know what to do next – but I think she had an enormous success. I hardly know myself, democrat & revolutionary, hardened Radical, engulfed in pomp and circumstance, bowing to "the divinity that doth hedge a King".'

The functions and handshakes went on for days: visits to the court-house and government offices across the river, surrounded by bowing officials and all the clerks standing as they passed; an elaborate feast with a leading Malay businessman who lived downriver; and tea with a Dyak chieftain (Temenggong) – 'For weird strangeness & fantastic beauty I have never seen anything to equal it,' wrote Oliver. Sylvia invariably found herself the centre of attention, even when she was at her writing desk in the Astana, where Malay women squatted on the floor watching her work, or performed solemn rites by throwing rice over her. Yet she still felt 'inconspicuous, colourless and dull', and that she did not really belong in Sarawak. 'I cared then what people thought of me, and wanted them to like me,

Above Sylvia's parents, Reggie and Nellie (inset – in fancy dress)

The Brett children in 1890: Sylvia 'Syv' (left), Dorothy 'Doll', Maurice 'Molly', and Oliver 'Noll'.

Sylvia with her grandfather, the first Viscount Esher.

The adored Maurice at Orchard Lea, the Brett family home, where the Gallery was added in 1897.

Regular visitors included (anti-clockwise from top right) young Syv's 'first friend', W.T. Stead; George Binning, on whom she had an adolescent crush; Reggie's beloved Teddie Seymour, who stayed for months at a time; and the creepy 'Loulou' Harcourt, seen here fishing on Loch Lubnaig.

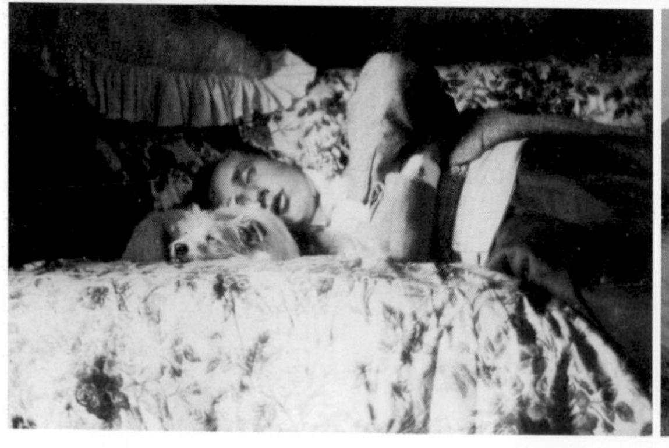

Sylvia, Reggie and Oliver at the Roman Camp, their estate in Perthshire, and the family, minus Maurice, on Loch Ard.

The budding author under the watchful eye of her mentor, J.M. Barrie, and (right) her other 'literary godfather', George Bernard Shaw.

Above The Grey Friars Orchestra, with Ranee Margaret at the piano, Dorothy seated to her left, Sylvia to her right, and Gladys Palmer clutching her mandolin, top right.

Left Rajah James Brooke, founder of the dynasty. *Below* Rajah Charles with his sons (from left) Vyner, Harry and Bertram. *Below left* Sylvia, the 'Left Lady', in 1909.

Sylvia, the new Ranee Muda of Sarawak in 1911, in Malay costume (main picture) after her marriage to Vyner, the Rajah Muda (left); and with her first baby Leonora.

Above Rajah Charles out with the Vale of White Horse; he was still hunting in his eighties.

Above right Bertram, the Tuan Muda.

From left, Maurice, his new wife Zena Dare, the actress, and Oliver, circa 1912.

Antoinette, Oliver's bride; Sylvia was endlessly cattish about her.

Left Sylvia and Vyner on her first voyage to Sarawak in 1912.

The Astana, with (below) a general view of Kuching; the building at the centre is the courthouse.

Above Race Week in Kuching, circa 1910, photographed by Charle Hose.

Left Vyner, in white, trying out Sarawak's first railway at Seventh Mile Bazaar, Kuching, 1914.

Other distractions awaited him upriver, such as Kayan dancing.

but only because my husband was so beloved by everyone and I did not want to spoil it.'

Shortly after they arrived, the Ranee Muda opened the new dry dock, amid much pomp and ceremony. 'It might have been Queen Mary doing it at Portsmouth,' remarked Oliver. 'Squiv does all the ceremonial part very well, & is I think much amused by it, enjoying the sensation of being a howling swell.' Oliver was rather enjoying it, too, against his expectations:

> This country is very different from what I anticipated, far safer, far more advanced, far happier, far more civilised . . . Vyner's whole position & life is much more dignified & 'royal' than I expected; it is exceedingly stiff and ceremonious, surrounded with pomp and circumstance, & it has all the distant & respectful atmosphere that one sees at Windsor. Sylvia cannot walk in the streets without the same staring crowd collecting that worried King Edward at Marienbad. Sentries guard us, back & front, night & day, & every time you step into the garden they present arms. The whites are respectful & frightened: & you are waited on hand & foot by silent, bare-footed, obsequious servants in quaint, gorgeous costumes who never let you do anything for yourself, & who walk always a few paces behind you to carry your parcels, your macintosh, your Chinese sunshade, your camera.

Sarawak appeared to Oliver to be 'a very happy country, guided by European brains but untouched by European vulgarity. So delicate is the control, so unobtrusive the guidance, that the native might almost imagine he was governing the country himself, & indeed he is far more master in his land, he has far more say in the direction of his own life than any other native race I have ever seen or heard of, over which a European power has control.'

With the Rajah not yet back from England, Sylvia, Vyner and Oliver all stayed at the Astana, the palace built by the Rajah as a wedding present for Ranee Margaret, who had first arrived there in April 1870 just as it was being completed. Perched on a low green hill across the river from the courthouse, it had scarcely altered since that time: three white-painted bungalows, connected by passages, raised by brick pillars some twenty feet off the ground and protected from the sun by a low-spreading wooden shingle roof and wide verandahs.

The largest bungalow at the centre housed the reception rooms and dining and drawing rooms, large, tall and cool, with a slightly incongruous castellated tower forming the entrance, where a sentry stood on guard day and night. Those on either side each contained two large bedrooms, with hard beds within rusty cages to keep the mosquitoes and bats at bay, and bathrooms attached. The Rajah and Ranee habitually slept in the western bungalow, the eastern one being reserved for visitors.

From the front of the Astana a lawn of coarse grass led down to the landing stage, bordered and shaded by bamboos, frangipani trees and betel-nut palms, clumps of red and white lilies growing underneath. Elsewhere bloomed gardenias, tuberoses, cape jessamine, filling the air with their perfume, and at the side and back of the Astana paths led off into the rainforest which stretched for miles around. In years to come the gardening-mad Vyner would lay out several acres more, with winding paths, ornamental shrubs and even a nine-hole golf course, where his officers could feel at home until their ball disappeared into a wall of jungle.

Pretty though the Astana was from the outside, inside it was spartan, the furniture having been arranged by the Rajah, so it seemed to Sylvia, to obtain the maximum of ugliness and discomfort. She later wrote that the shell of the building was 'like a lovely cloak on the shoulders of an ugly woman', and the interior a 'fantastic medley of beauty and bad taste', the result of the Rajah having filled the rooms with 'apalling imitation stuff from every period of English and French history. Cheap gilt stood side by side with poor mahogany. Early Victorian sofas rested stiffly against the walls. Crude Dresden figures held caskets in their chipped and broken hands, and mirrors were dotted on thin-legged tables. Only the ceilings were beautiful. They were heavily carved with gorgeous dragons and wide-open flowers of plain plaster, designed and executed by an ordinary Chinese workman. With Oriental furniture to match, the palace would have been a masterpiece instead of a travesty.'

Despite these aesthetic shortcomings, they quickly settled into an agreeable routine. At five in the morning, Vyner and Oliver would cross the river and ride in the cool before breakfast. Sylvia declined to get on the horse that Vyner had bought for her, preferring to spend the early morning writing, working on a short story, ''Daughter of the Crescent Moon', which appeared in the *Sarawak Gazette* in June, and a play. Breakfast was at half past seven on the verandah, after which the Rajah Muda would cross the river again to judge cases at the courthouse – twice a week he would go 'in state', under the yellow umbrella while Sylvia and her brother settled down to their books or writing.

At noon Vyner would return and they had lunch in the dining room, served by Malay servants dressed in white uniforms with broad yellow sashes coming down almost to the knee and skullcaps made of spotted cotton. On either side of the table stood two Malay boys with large yellow fans, elaborately shaped, on long bamboo sticks, with which they fanned the diners while they ate. After lunch they all slept on long chairs on the verandah. Shortly before four, by which time it was less intensely hot, they had tea, after which Sylvia would either pay her calls or join Vyner and Oliver over the river to play golf or tennis at the club – Oliver told his father that exercise was 'the best preventive of tropical liver and I go in for it strong'. Returning to the Astana for dinner, the men would change into white mess jackets; the Malay servants now wore a dark-blue uniform with gold braid on it and a red fez.

After they had been at the Astana a week, Sylvia wrote to George Bernard Shaw.

> Well, you wouldn't know us if you saw us here, and what is more you wouldn't want to know us, you with your anti-King, anti-snobbery ideas – for alas, I am no longer what I was, a humble, dutiful wife, but a howling snob with a head as swelled as the largest coconut in the land. When I tell you that every time I go to pick a flower in the garden the guard turns out, and every time I go to buy a button in the village, sixty people gather about the shop, when we go to dinner our National Anthem is played as we go up the steps, and we sit upon cloths of gold, will you believe all this and recognise the little common friend of yours who came and went without ceremony and usually in a bus?

Sylvia and Oliver were getting on tremendously, with no hint of the terrible bitterness that would shortly come between them. 'No one could be bored here,' Oliver wrote to Reggie. 'It is too lovely a place and there is too much to do. The idea that it is barbaric or primitive never occurs to one – it is a completely civilised and very, very comfortable life.' And in another letter: 'I am not Pierre Loti, & I can't describe the wonderful charm and strange beauty of the place. Vyner with the yellow umbrella over his head & followed by two soldiers, has just walked down to the river in order to go over & judge the prisoners of the day. Squiv, dressed in Malay costume, is writing stories at the next table. It really is a delightful life, & we are all enjoying it immensely.'

None of them more so than Sylvia, who loved the hawkers plying their wares in the bazaar, the sound of gongs in the mosque, the eternal chorus of bullfrogs and tree frogs at night. 'The magic of it all possessed me,' she wrote later, 'sight, sound and sense; there was in this abundant land everything for which my heart had yearned.'

5

DYNASTIC DYSFUNCTION

Sylvia's descriptions of her father-in-law often tended towards caricature, but rarely more so than in her account of his earlier-than-expected return to Kuching in June 1912, bringing to an end 'our days of freedom and fun'. 'The government officers shivered in their shoes,' she wrote in her second autobiography, 'the smiles on the faces of our Malay boys had gone. It was as if a curtain had been drawn down upon the sweetness and contentment of this idyllic land. I had only seen him for a moment at my wedding and I had forgotten how starkly supreme he was, how gaunt and unapproachable; a stern figure with a hawk-like nose, one glass eye from which a constant trickle of water dripped on to his snow white moustache, and a heart of stone.'

The Rajah had lost his eye the previous winter when out with the Vale of White Horse hunt in Gloucestershire, having ridden into a branch, which had cut across his face. Infection had set in and eventually the eye had been removed. Though by then eighty-four, he hated the thought that this would prevent him from hunting – which eventually it did – and Sylvia was not alone in thinking that the accident made him even sterner than before. She observed that 'it was the unblinking coldness of the artificial bead, which he purchased from a cheap store, that gave him the appearance of a cruel and ancient eagle, waiting to give the death-blow to his prey', alternatively that his glass eye, 'previously destined for a stuffed albatross', gave him 'the ferocious stare of some strange, solitary, marine bird'. Aided by Sylvia's colourful contributions, the stories about the Rajah's glass eye took on a life of their own. A subsequent chronicler recorded that the old man had bought several beads destined for a variety of beasts, and wore whichever one took his fancy at the time; not infrequently the eye would fall in the mud when the war prahu in which he was travelling was beached, leading to a frantic search by those who were transporting him.

Easier to verify is that during the Rajah's convalescence in hospital after the accident he had become increasingly exercised by Vyner's marriage into the Brett family, which he deemed 'unsafe surroundings'. The Rajah had an instinctive dislike and distrust of Reggie Esher, suspecting him not only of having commercial designs on Sarawak but also of exerting undue and unhealthy influence over Vyner. In the spring of 1912, as he prepared to return from Cirencester to Sarawak, the Rajah wrote to his nephew and legal adviser Charles Willes Johnson to tell him of his plan to strengthen his successor's position 'in case of his being surrounded by those who would wish to grab Sarawak when I am no more . . . [and] turn it into a money bargain'. The British government, he said, 'would be the first to encourage this movement – as they would naturally like the country added to theirs to pay for their shortcomings in Singapore and its surroundings'. The Rajah added that he intended to 'bring Adeh [Bertram] to the fore', installing him with honours as heir presumptive in case of Vyner's death or of his bearing no male issue, and electing him president of a new Sarawak Trust Committee in England, designed to safeguard the maintenance of the Sarawak Raj and prevent it from being sold or transferred. 'I know that there would be many who would try to persuade Vyner to do this.'

Vyner and Sylvia had left England before this letter was written and had no inkling of what was on the Rajah's mind, despite the Ranee's outburst at Grey Friars on the eve of their departure. But they had been in Kuching barely two weeks when a letter arrived from the Rajah announcing that he was shortly to arrive back in Sarawak, far sooner than expected, and that Bertram and Gladys were to follow.

The Rajah stressed that he was going to 'leave everything' to Vyner, and that Bertram and Gladys were simply coming out as guests for the annual race week, but Sylvia could not help suspecting that something was afoot, especially since it appeared that many officials in Kuching had known for some time before they did. Even before the Rajah arrived back in the country, there were, wrote Sylvia, 'whispered words in the Bazaar, and secret looks amongst the Government officers'. Even though Bertram sent a letter to reassure them there was nothing fishy about his visit, she and Vyner were uneasy.

The Rajah reached Kuching on the afternoon of Tuesday, 4 June, the day after an elaborate reception held for Vyner and Sylvia by the Chinese Towkeys, including sports, acrobatics, a *wayang* and a dragon procession. There was no great welcome for the Rajah, however. Mindful perhaps of the awkwardness that lay ahead, he had ordered that no salute or guard of honour should greet him, although Vyner and Sylvia did go aboard his steam yacht *Zadora* as she anchored midstream in the Sarawak river, and in the evening a small, stiff dinner party was held at the Astana. Over the next two days the Rajah said no word of his plans. He was as nice as it was in him to be to Vyner and contented himself with grilling Sylvia as to exactly how intimate her family were with Loulou Harcourt.

The Rajah had arrived 'with the documents of his plot in his pocket', so Oliver later told Reggie, but he was 'afraid to fight Vyner at such close quarters, afraid of scenes & silences', so on the Thursday he left the Astana for a small house in the town across the river. On Saturday morning he summoned Vyner to the government offices, where they spoke before no witnesses. The Rajah appeared nervous and fumbled his words while suggesting to Vyner that he thought they ought to give Bertram 'a little reception', saying that after all he was the heir presumptive, and that he had drawn up a proclamation to make that clear to everybody. Vyner, characteristically, said little in reply, but asked for a copy of the proclamation to take away with him. Back at the Astana, he went into a huddle with Sylvia and Oliver to study the document, which ran as follows:

> I, Charles Brooke, Rajah of Sarawak, do hereby decree that my second son Bertram Brooke, heir presumptive to the Raj of Sarawak in the event of my eldest son, Charles Vyner Brooke, Rajah Muda of Sarawak, failing to have male issue, shall be

received on his arrival in the State of Sarawak with a Royal Salute and honours equivalent to his rank. I further decree that he shall be recognised in future by all the inhabitants of Sarawak as being a part of the Government of the State and that such recognition shall be duly registered in the records of the Supreme Council of Sarawak.

The three at the Astana viewed this as tantamount to an attempted *coup d'état*. Vyner had nothing against Bertram personally – indeed he was very fond of him; but the fact remained that his brother hardly knew Sarawak, having not visited it for seventeen years nor undergone anything resembling the outstation apprenticeship that his father had required of him. The proclamation could mean only that his father distrusted him, while Sylvia bitterly resented the assumption that she was incapable of producing an heir. Convinced that the whole scheme had been cooked up in the venomous mind of the Ranee and pushed forward by the ambitious Gladys, they determined to resist it, and drew strength to do so from the knowledge that Vyner's income was safeguarded by his marriage settlement and that legally he could not be prevented from inheriting Sarawak.

With Oliver on hand to moderate the language, they jointly composed a letter from Vyner to his father objecting to the proclamation and asking the Rajah to clarify the vague wording regarding Bertram's participation in the government. The Rajah replied that what he had proposed was only for his eldest son's good and that of Sarawak. He accused Vyner of jealousy and of having gone back on his acceptance in the morning of Bertram's new position; he also enclosed a copy of a bill setting up an advisory committee in London, to be chaired by Bertram, which was to be passed (in the Supreme Council) after the proclamation.

This was the first Vyner had heard of the proposed committee, and he saw it as more evidence of a dark plot to tie his hands by declaring him unfit to rule and putting him under the control of his younger brother, a degradation that Sylvia and Oliver convinced him would be 'fatal in a country where natives are concerned'. 'With natives', Sylvia told her father, 'you must be a kind of God Almighty or they won't stand you.'

Sylvia and Oliver pressed Vyner to oppose all of his father's proposals, which in a series of letters over the next two days he did. He refuted his father's accusation of jealousy, saying he was merely protecting his own rights and those of his wife and children, which 'this new arrangement, secretly prepared behind my back and only announced to me at the last moment, utterly destroys'. If the Rajah chose to persist with his plan, Vyner warned, he would be reluctantly obliged to make public his protest and leave the country until matters were more satisfactorily arranged. 'The position you propose to put me in must inevitably degrade me in the eyes of the population and amounts to admitting that you do not consider me fit to govern the country without the sanction and approval of my younger brother. That is a position which I decline to hold.' After each despatch, Vyner reached for his field glasses to observe the stir around the government offices as his letter arrived.

On Sunday the Rajah gave him a last chance to withdraw his 'disobedient' letters – 'I might be a child of 5!' Vyner wrote to Reggie – then on Monday, 10 June he gave him public notice as follows: 'I shall not in future require your services in the Government offices nor in the Supreme Council . . . obedience to the Rajah has heretofore been the rule and will be so long as I am ruler. As you will have no more duties to perform in this country I recommend your leaving as soon as convenient.' At the same time the Rajah sent Vyner a private letter, far more conciliatory in tone, admitting that he had almost decided to stand down with a few conditions, and 'leave it to you to hold the Raj'. He hinted that he still might be prepared to transfer power after his return in September, and advised them not to travel too far so that they could keep in touch with events in Sarawak.

Vyner was by now in too much of a state to accept the olive branch and wrote back to say that they were 'making preparations to leave for England tomorrow morning. I regret that you should view my action in this matter as disobedience. I assure you it has been with deep regret that I felt it my duty to oppose your policy on this occasion, but I could not, and cannot give my consent to a scheme which so compromises my future. We shall remain in England until things are on a more satisfactory footing.' The next day they boarded the steamer *Rajah of Sarawak* bound for Singapore. 'All the sympathies were with us,' Vyner later told Reggie; 'everyone came to see us off, Malays, Chinese and Whites. Our departure was a tremendous triumph.'

Although Sylvia later wrote that it 'must not be thought for one moment that the Tuan Muda [Bertram] was in any way connected with this scheme', that was precisely what they all did assume at the time. Vyner blew his top in a letter to his brother, which he left to await his arrival:

> Do you suppose that I for one moment would submit to such a committee, a quorum of fools with not an ounce of brains between the lot? What do you or the others know of Sarawak or of finance? I am to do the dirty work out here while you and your gang are to say what I am to do and how I am to do it. No thank you . . . the part you have played in the whole transaction is beneath contempt, and you have done your best to oust me by plotting behind my back. If you had any moral sense (which of course you haven't) you would not dare lift up your head again from the moral degradation and treachery you have been guilty of. Anyway the Malays here, the Chinese and Europeans are well aware of what you have been attempting, you will find out their feelings on your arrival. You are doubtless proceeding to Sarawak but please understand that if you land in Sarawak, you and your wife are strangers to us for ever. I will have nothing more to do with such a man as yourself, who, while calling himself a brother and a friend plots and schemes behind my back . . . You can tell Father that I do not return to Sarawak again unless with full powers, by which I mean absolute control over the country, finance etc . . . Father talks of retiring in September and he has doubtless settled in his mind to instal you in my stead. Please understand that before he can do this he has the British Government to deal with . . .

Sylvia admitted having left an even more vitriolic note (which appears not to have survived), 'rude beyond all reason'.

Innocent on all counts, the normally mild-mannered Bertram reacted to the onslaught with equal ferocity, complaining to Oliver that Vyner's letter was 'composed of just the kind of nonsense that, were I a bit younger and as hotheaded as himself, would *bring about* the very situation that he appears to fear'. To Vyner he wrote: 'If you think the letter I wrote to you from England directly I heard from father that he had the idea of starting an office in London was a cloak for Machiavellian designs I'm sorry for you, as your temperament must make your life a burden to you, and you will have already found out how mistaken you were . . . I know you will be sorry for having written the letter, but don't anticipate your acknowledging it. So, so far as fraternal relations are concerned, good bye.'

The Rajah was inclined to blame Sylvia for Vyner's truculence. 'It is entirely his wife's doing,' he wrote to Willes Johnson on 14 June, 'as it appears she dislikes Gladys for what reason is best known to herself – a case of jealousy & spite which will in no sense alter my programme.' His wish, he added, was, 'now that Vyner has departed from me that I provide a course of safety independent of him . . . I have never by word or deed given him any equal power or any independent power in the Raj – this all his letters can prove – I will talk this over with Adeh when he arrives – of course it will lead to bitterness in the family – but that can't be helped – we are not going to submit to be advised or bullied by his wife's family.'

Bertram and Gladys duly arrived in Sarawak aboard the steamship *Kuching* on 27 June. The proclamation announcing the Tuan Muda's changed position had been issued ten days earlier, and they were greeted with the royal salute of twenty-one guns from the fort and a guard of honour, and Bertram walked self-consciously beneath the yellow umbrella. Introducing the Tuan Muda to the Supreme Council a few days later, the Rajah explained that he had directed these honours to be paid to his younger son not only because he was entitled to them personally, but also because recognition of his position in Sarawak would enable him to be a greater source of strength to the Raj. It could only be by suspicious minds, said the Rajah, that the idea could be entertained that there was any other purpose. He added that the Tuan Muda would be principally if not entirely devoted to the interests of Sarawak in England and in Europe and not in the East, 'except by express wish of his successor, namely, His Highness the Rajah Muda'. The Rajah then took Bertram and Gladys on a tour of coast stations and on a diplomatic visit to his neighbour, the Sultan of Brunei, where again Bertram was received with the honours due the heir presumptive to the throne.

Sylvia and Vyner had meanwhile arrived back in England at the beginning of July and returned to Loulou's stable block at Stanton Harcourt, where among their post was an invitation to a garden party at Buckingham Palace addressed to Mr and Mrs Vyner Brooke – 'an awful come down', Sylvia told Reggie, 'after having had the National Anthem on the way to our baths'. Three weeks later she wrote to Bernard Shaw: 'Our regality has dropped from us, and I, who was a Queen, find myself being hustled without ceremony into a 3rd Class carriage. Heigh ho, it's lucky that I have a well-balanced brain and find it easy to be a quick-change artist.'

As for Sarawak, she declared their intention 'to fight to the death till somebody's wig is on the green – I only hope it is the Ranee's', and fretted to her father about the financial dangers of the family row. Sarawak's annual revenues had quadrupled over the past twenty-five years to £150,000 in 1911, but Vyner was concerned that his 'old and crotchety' father was able to spend what he liked with no check, and did so 'on all kinds of schemes of no advantage to the country'. At present there was a reserve fund of £150,000 and no debt, but, Sylvia wrote:

> Unless we get our hold on that reserve fund we and our children will be left selling matches in the street. Why should Adeh [Bertram] control our allowance? It is disgusting to think of it even. The Ranee writes Vyner pages daily telling him to give way – Give way indeed – and let Adeh speculate all our future comfort away in rotten companies – Adeh has no idea of finance, and he is stupid, obstinate and extremely common – that's Adeh! Gladys glories in dresses, gold purses and titles – what chance has Leonora of an allowance if these foul fiends get hold of it – the Reserve fund – the thing we've dreamed of building up a safe pile for the baby – Ough it makes one mad.

Reggie told her not to make herself ridiculous, that their family quarrels were a great mistake and could only do them all a great deal of mischief. He was inclined to agree with Loulou Harcourt that the best solution would be for Vyner to get himself a private secretary 'with a good head', and that eventually Vyner would have to atone for his error in coming away from Sarawak. 'This is,' he wrote to

Loulou, 'in reality a quarrel got up and fostered by three women [the Ranee, Gladys and Sylvia] . . . silly fools all.' To Maurice, he complained that Sylvia and Vyner 'see bogies now behind every bush and mistrust everybody'.

However, Reggie did think that it would be advantageous for the Colonial Office to secure an 'immediate' treaty with the Rajah, to be followed by the appointment of a British resident in Sarawak. 'The family attempt to put Vyner under financial and political control by a Committee implies he is not fit to govern the country,' wrote Reggie to Loulou, echoing the argument put to him by Sylvia. 'If the appointment of a resident coincides with his accession to power, it may be taken by the natives to justify the action of the present Rajah and would be a reflection on Vyner's capacity to rule . . . It is', Reggie added, 'a great piece of good fortune for us that you happen to be at the Colonial Office for although your first regard will naturally be your departmental interests, you will I know do the best you can to safeguard those of Vyner and Sylvia.'

But Loulou was powerless to intervene. He met Vyner at the House of Commons and told him that the British government could not stop the advisory council, as it only had control over Sarawak's foreign relations under the treaty of 1888. He advised Vyner to be there when his father stood down. Reggie, too, suggested Vyner do nothing at present but return to Sarawak immediately he heard of his father's departure for Europe. 'He [Vyner] cannot afford not to be the man on the spot,' wrote Reggie to Oliver. 'Kings cannot, in 9 times out of 10, afford to step off their thrones, even for a short space of time. It is so jolly difficult to step back again.' He urged Vyner to write to his father explaining how much he 'felt this want of confidence on his part' but conceding that he may have in turn 'used hasty expression'.

By late July, Sylvia and Vyner had got wind of a new rumour, a 'profound State Secret', that the British government had made an offer for Sarawak and that the Rajah had accepted it. 'If Sarawak is sold,' she told Reggie, 'well, the battle is over, and we can only sit and imagine the dear Malays being turned into the jungle – for no Government would bear with their dreamy indolence.' Again she pressed Vyner to write to the Rajah to say that he would *never* give in on the committee, and to Bertram to say that if he retired from the committee, or it was not formed, he would forget the whole affair. She then went off with Vyner to tackle Loulou on what she had heard.

During their meeting on 29 July, Loulou was 'charming and endlessly painstaking', as Sylvia recalled, and emphatically denied any basis for the whispers. He later commented to Reggie that Sylvia and Vyner seemed 'quite indefinite in their plans and equally deficient in knowledge of what is happening in Sarawak. The brother is, apparently, returning home. They assume the old Rajah will do ditto almost immmediately.' Loulou added that he had found Vyner a young man to go with him if necessary, 'that is, if he can make up his mind whether he is going at all'.

Out in Sarawak the Rajah continued to carry out his plans, and at the beginning of August he informed the Council Negri of his wish to establish the committee – or Sarawak State Advisory Council, as it was to be called – as a support to the Raj in England 'so that those who might wish to intrigue should not injure and shake the independence and integrity of this country . . . Where there are riches there are always dangers,' he said. Three weeks later several English newspapers reported his speech, and on 24 August a leading article appeared in the *Pall Mall Gazette*:

> Covetous eyes are being turned on the rubber-plantations and oilfields of Sarawak, and that wonderful little State, the people of which have been redeemed from the blackest horrors of barbarism by the life work of two great Englishmen, is threatened with the loss of its independence through the influence of a cosmopolitan syndicate of financiers with a certain meddlesome Peer for a figurehead, and the Colonial office as accomplice . . . Shall this most wonderful example of what Englishmen at their best can do to promote the welfare of the savage and more backward races of mankind be sacrificed in order that a handful of speculators may fill their pockets by wringing the wealth out of the country, not for the benefit of its people, but for their own? . . . The Rajah at 83 is fighting his last fight with his back to the wall . . .

The 'meddlesome Peer' was almost certainly a reference to Reggie, with Loulou as his supposed accomplice. But the implication was almost certainly wrong: Reggie was not greatly interested in making money, and there is nothing in his journal or correspondence suggesting that he intended to do so out of Sarawak. His one venture into business, as a partner of his friend Sir Ernest Cassel's financial house, had lasted just two years (1902–4) because, according to his biographer at least, he 'hated the City'. Loulou surmised, probably correctly, that the press campaign had been whipped up by the Ranee, 'but why she should think I am anxious to annex Sarawak I can't imagine', he wrote to Reggie. As far as her suspicions concerning Reggie were concerned, the Ranee had on her side several other journalists, including Arnold White of *The Referee* newspaper, who wrote in October: 'The essence of the Sarawak problem is whether Lord Esher is to succeed the Rajah or whether, by disinheritance, the evil of an absentee, weak & extravagant despotism is to be avoided.'

It was in order to forestall such hysterical talk that Loulou again urged Vyner to make overtures to his father with the aim of effecting a reconciliation, and otherwise to lie low and for Sylvia to keep quiet. 'Of course he is right,' she wrote to Reggie, 'but I am foaming at the mouth.' She added that they were gradually getting to the bottom of the whole thing and that she had heard from Harry Brooke that Charles Willes Johnson and C. A. Bampfylde, members of the proposed advisory council in London, were going around saying, 'We're going to rule Sarawak in London.'

Out in Sarawak, the Rajah's attitude over the whole affair had hardened as time went by. Towards the end of August, after a long and reflective walk through the woods at the foot of Mount Matang, where he had built a bungalow – 'Vallombrosa' – forty-four years previously, he reiterated to Willes Johnson that the breach was 'entirely Sylvia's doing', and said it was now 'impossible to mend as I have lost confidence in Vyner . . . my policy in England will be to remain quiet and to refuse to correspond with him – unless officially . . . everything in this country is in a very flourishing state – revenue – trade – planting . . . all greatly prosperous – where is the CO [Colonial Office] going to find a casus belli to touch me or the present rule in Sarawak? The Eshers or Bretts may have other views and wish to put Vyner above me, but I am not afraid of their evil influence.'

The Rajah was right to think that Sylvia had been stoking the row, as she later conceded: 'I often wished I had never mixed myself up in the affair. But I have always unfortunately been made that way. I must interfere, I cannot keep my fingers out of the fire, no matter whose fire it is. I am nearly always to be found there disturbing it and adding on the fuel.' But he was almost certainly wrong about Reggie, who was by now growing bored of the whole saga, accusing Sylvia of being a 'damnable extremist', a 'suspicious ass' and of having picked a quarrel with the Ranee. By early September he had resolved to offer no more advice on the matter, telling Maurice that Vyner was 'old enough to manage his own affairs'.

Eventually Vyner, too, grew tired of the quarrelling, and at the beginning of October he told Bertram that he was ready not just to assent to the new advisory council, but also to do what he could to assist in its formation. In the end, a little ironically, it was a 'very persistent' (as the Rajah described it) letter from Sylvia to her father-in-law that brought about a truce: 'My Dear Sylvia,' the Rajah wrote back in reply,

> Since your letter of this morning received in bed, let all pass like a passing cloud in the tropics which is so shortly succeeded by a glow of sunshine. Not a fig of feeling of vindictiveness ever has been or will be harboured by me towards you or anyone, I may assure you, and sincerely hope that this clearing of the atmosphere may be extended towards Vyner's mother or Adeh's surroundings. Bygones will be bygones. Sarawak has not been founded on meanness or antipathies. I shall be quite well in a few days and hope you and Vyner will shortly come to Christmas. Yours very affectionately, C. A. Brooke.

So it was that the dispute was patched up and they went to stay at his 'appallingly sporting house' at Cirencester. There Sylvia discovered that even the Rajah's sister was so much in awe of him that she dared not call him by his Christian name. She learned, too, of his 'fondness of being thought a French scholar', but noted acidly that when he broke out into little French quotations they were 'usually quoted with the point of them missed out'. Presumably at that time she kept such observations to herself, thus preserving for the time being her reputation as peacemaker. She had undoubtedly helped deepen this first dynastic crisis during her marriage to Vyner, but she could at least claim to have had a hand in its eventual resolution.

6

I WANT CROWNS PLASTERED EVERYWHERE

Sylvia and Vyner stayed in England for the remainder of 1912 and shortly after New Year they visited her parents at a snowbound Roman Camp, where the Ranee Muda disported herself tobogganing down the Tump on a tea tray – 'in pink jacket and white cap turning somersaults', Reggie told Maurice. 'A truly regal sight. Vyner equally queer.' She let on to Maurice how desperate she was for another baby but disloyally whispered that trying for one made Vyner ill. Maurice passed this straight on to Reggie, who remarked: 'Syv is a goose to fuss over another baby just yet, and she talks too much.' The next day, he wrote again: 'I cannot get over her amazing statement about Vyner. The East must have a very deteriorating influence, or else Syv is dreadfully exigeante.'

Evidently, Sylvia had already got her way and, as she soon announced, her next child was due in September (1913). Her pregnancy set her thinking about the appropriate style for her daughter Leonora. 'Tell me', she asked her father, 'which you would like her to be called, Princess Leonora of Sarawak, or Dayang something? I am inclined for Princess, like the native Rajahs' daughters. Nobody will understand Dayang – Besides, Princess will annoy Antoinette [who had eventually overcome her doubts and married Oliver the previous autumn] so (there's a cattish reason if you like). Another thing – Do let me know the address of the Crest man, as I want crowns plastered everywhere – in fact owing to you

I'm a howling snob, and only think of Coronets and Crowns.' Reggie duly forwarded the address of 'Mr Burke', and Vyner went to see him. But for the time being, having in mind the troubles of the past year, they decided against re-registering the Brooke name on their own, or assuming any coat of arms or coronet without the assent of the Rajah. '*He*', Sylvia told her father, 'vigorously disapproves of what he calls all display, and although the Ranee once had the Sarawak crown on her notepaper, she hasn't dared put it on her motor. Personally *I* think it wiser to wait altogether – After all it can't be long before we can do as we please – Anyhow we will wait until you return and see what you think can be done – Vyner will do nothing *without you*, so set your mind at rest.'

The rapprochement of the previous autumn had endured to the extent that by February 1913 Sylvia and Vyner were on good enough terms with the Rajah for him to have contemplated a formal abdication at the end of the year, providing that Vyner guaranteed to spend at least two years without a break in the country. But the birth of their second child, in September, not the prayed-for son but a second daughter, Elizabeth, put paid to this plan and, as Sylvia told Reggie, Sarawak now seemed to be 'off during the Rajah's lifetime'. Broaching the subject of her 'perversely female infant', Bernard Shaw reassured Sylvia: 'My mother began with two girls and finished with me. To make a man of genius you require practice . . . When the necessary boy does come along,' he added, 'he will be so bullied by elder sisters that he will probably inaugurate his reign by cutting off every female head in Sarawak.' Sylvia affected calm, telling her father that it was 'God's doing after all', and that it was a very good thing being thwarted now and then. But the Rajah, who had returned to Sarawak in April, was less philosophical, and again the church bells in Kuching remained silent.

Shortly after Elizabeth was born, Sylvia and Vyner again went to stay up at the Roman Camp, where Reggie reported to Maurice that she fussed over her baby 'to such a degree that we cannot make out whether it is a permanent invalid or a normal child. Anyway it looks like a gnome, poor little thing, and eventually – if it survives the fuss, will be like the Ranee in a spoon . . . not a trace of Syv. They say she is over intelligent. That she certainly does not inherit from poor Vyner.' When they returned south, they moved their London base from a cramped maisonette on Davis Street, Mayfair, to Tilney House, on Wimbledon Common. Reggie agreed with Maurice that this low-gabled house in the suburbs sounded 'a bit commonplace, but perhaps there is no harm in this. Stanton Harcourt supplies enough romance, and Sarawak enough oddity, for any menage.'

Prevented for the time being from going to Sarawak, Vyner feared he would lose touch with the natives. He was not, in any case, ideally suited to a purely domestic life: Sylvia recalled that the only time he touched Leonora when she was little was to toss her in the air, which she enjoyed, only her head crashed alarmingly against the electric-light globe that hung from the centre of the ceiling. With little to occupy him beyond the turkeys he was now farming at Stanton Harcourt, Vyner set about reading all of Reggie's books. 'Every meal I am enlightened on the marvellousness of you,' Sylvia wrote to her father. 'He can't get over the fact that at an absurd age you were hob-nobbing with Dizzy and Gladstone – And laying down the law to Lord Hartington. And your ears should scorch at the praises he sings – while I listen grimly.'

Sylvia was by then back at her own writing desk, having a go variously at 'pot-boiler' short stories, she told her father, 'a long novel of the Sinister Street type only better!' and an anti-suffrage play – '*So* good, I daren't go on with [it] in case these infuriated women set fire to my babies.' In this instance, she may well have been currying favour with Reggie by disparaging the suffragettes, who had lost much of their popular support that year (1913) after part of David Lloyd George's house was blown up and Emily Wilding Davison threw herself beneath the King's horse at the Derby. In several of her other works of fiction she wrote in favour of the vote for women, upheld their right to the same extramarital liberties as men, and advocated paternal responsibility for illegitimate children, to the extent that she has even been hailed by one academic as a 'Pioneer Malaysian Feminist Writer'. That said, it was not noticeably in her nature to hold principles and stick to them.

When it came to choosing godparents for Elizabeth, Sylvia thought of asking the King and Queen or Queen Alexandra, 'just to give us a lift up in the world we so badly need', she told Reggie; but he said she should wait until she had a boy. He agreed with her other suggestions, however, including the Prime Minister H. H. Asquith, who had taken a shine to Sylvia when they'd met while staying at Nuneham shortly before her marriage and would continue to hold a candle for her until at least 1917, and Gladys Brooke, the Dayang Muda.

The choice of Gladys, with whom Sylvia had been at loggerheads for much of the previous year, hinted at an end to family conflict. But if relations with the Brookes were showing signs of slight improvement, those with the Bretts were taking a turn for the worse. The previous year Maurice had predicted to Reggie: 'Syv will ruin her life with cattishness if she is not careful.' Friends, he added, 'though amused at the moment are all rather horrified with her. Her remarks on Antoinette seem to have been terrific, and none of us seem to have been spared.'

Sylvia's childhood crush on Oliver and her rescue of him when his engagement was broken off had made her intensely jealous of his shy and occasionally awkward new wife, who would remain the object of her spite for years to come. Possibly encouraged by Reggie and Nellie – though they pretended otherwise, they never really took to Antoinette either – Sylvia delighted in trotting out her sister-in-law's social faux pas in letters to her parents.

Sylvia's hostility exacerbated the hurt Oliver felt over the fact that none of the Bretts had crossed the Atlantic to his wedding, and thereafter he worried about Antoinette's loneliness and insecurity in her new family. When the war came he got a job in uniform at the War Office so that he could look after her – 'a kind of courage not much appreciated in 1914–18', as their son Lionel drily recorded. When Oliver eventually inherited his father's papers, he was so appalled by Sylvia's poison-pen letters about Antoinette that he burnt the lot, and described his sister to Lionel as 'a female Iago'.

Throughout 1913 Sylvia also remained hostile to Ranee Margaret, unable to forgive her part in the attempted 'coup' in Sarawak the year before and perhaps now jealous of the enthusiastic reviews that greeted her mother-in-law's memoir *My Life in Sarawak*, when it was published that autumn. Though discreet about her marriage, this was an engaging account of the isolation, discomfort and dangers that the Ranee had faced on her arrival in Sarawak as a young bride forty years previously. With friends ranging from aristocratic Malays to the 'tender-hearted' public executioner Subu, whose other job was to hold the state umbrella, Ranee Margaret's affection for her husband's subjects would have been obvious to readers. Equally obvious to Sylvia was that she would be a hard act to follow.

Shortly after the Ranee's book came out, the Rajah did eventually yield to Vyner's suggestion that he should come out to Sarawak the next year, providing that this time Sylvia did not come too – if she insisted, his allowance would be stopped. Vyner departed in March 1914 and was to be away from England for more than eight months. During this, their first long parting, Sylvia wrote to her husband:

> Remember you are most of my life. Without you the world has no meaning, the sun has no warmth, and the very rains and winds are nothing to me. I wanted our love to be the most perfect, honourable and faithful thing. I wanted you to live in me and me in you for ever and ever. People tell me I should never have let you go out to Sarawak alone and that you will soon find some other woman to console you. But I am completely confident that you will never leave me and I try not to listen to anything they say. Marriage isn't a prison is it, darling? I think that each one of us should learn to live alone. I think one of the finest words in any language and within any living soul is Freedom.

Vyner never would 'leave' her, in so far as they remained married, but there were plenty of other women over the years, as Sylvia readily admitted in her memoirs, some of them apparently even procured by her (perhaps as a means of maintaining a measure of control). To a lesser extent, there would also be other men for her too, although it is not clear whether these liaisons involved much if any in the way of sex, which Sylvia later rated a 'rather ridiculous' pastime. It can certainly be argued (as some of their descendants do) that theirs developed into a peculiarly successful 'open' marriage. However, it was not always plain sailing.

Abandoned at Wimbledon in the spring of 1914 with her two young daughters, Sylvia longed to be with Vyner and resented the 'captivity of motherhood'. She began to see a lot more of her sister Dorothy, who had been all set to accompany her to Sarawak before the Rajah's intervention and who now served to combat Sylvia's loneliness when she was left at home. The sisters had developed into very different characters. Like Sylvia, Doll had inherited aspects of Reggie's wilful and reckless nature, yet she deployed them in a way that he seemed to find slightly more endearing – though he was often exasperated by her bohemian ways.

Doll had made her getaway from the family hothouse by enrolling, in 1910, at the Slade School of Art, where, like (Dora) Carrington, she was known simply as Brett. She wore masculine clothes and her hair short – in the fashionable Slade style of what Virginia Woolf called 'cropheads'. By her obvious talent as a painter Doll had not only won over the anti-aristocratic prejudice of the head of the Slade, Professor Frederick 'Nutty' Brown, but to her embarrassment also soon discovered that he was in love with her. Their relationship, which developed into what Doll termed a 'semi-engagement', caused a certain amount of consternation in the Brett family, not least because Nutty was thirty-two years Doll's senior. 'My God!' exclaimed Reggie when he first met him. 'He's as old as I am!'

Sylvia, too, had confided to Reggie, in the summer of 1912, that she found the idea of her sister with such an old man 'disgusting', but lamented:

> I think Doll is really in love with this *vieux coq*. She writes pages of rapture to me. I tried to dam the flowing tide but with terrible result. So I try being broadly skittish on the subject – I don't frankly like the idea, old men can be so awful – they are sweet as old men but awful as husbands. Yet this seems to be Doll's one chance of not being a Left Lady – she wouldn't care for a young man – the physical side of marriage appals her – she thinks poor soul that an old man would, to put it plainly, leave her alone – Well, I don't, do you?

Nutty proved her wrong. Although he and Doll did once meet in Hyde Park after dark to discuss the facts of life and what marriage involved, it appears that he did leave her alone – even though the affair rumbled on until 1916. It was not until her fortieth year that Doll experienced for the first time what he had been on about, when she went to bed with John Middleton Murry, the widower of her friend Katherine Mansfield, who had died from tuberculosis in 1923.

In the meantime Doll had consoled herself by reflecting on the advantages of celibacy; observing Sylvia 'bulging with babies', she told her friend Lady Ottoline Morrell, 'has rather helped me toward spinsterhood more than the lack of offers, so to speak – one can't paint pictures and have babies'.

Sylvia later admitted that when she was with Doll's Slade friends such as Carrington and Mark Gertler she felt 'foolish' and out of it, but she nonetheless took Doll's side in her battles against Reggie and Nellie to be allowed to use the Brett house on Tilney Street as a dossing place for them. For his part Gertler, the most frequent visitor, felt awkward at times going about with the Brett sisters, sensitive about his humble Jewish upbringing in the East End. After dining with Dorothy and Sylvia at the Savoy he wrote to Carrington: 'The richness of the place embarrassed me very much. I did not feel at ease. There was a lot of footmen in grey plush coats and stockings. They all looked at me suspiciously.'

It was on a subsequent occasion at the Savoy, on 29 June 1914, that Sylvia and Dorothy first heard about the murder of Archduke Franz Ferdinand, heir to the throne of Austria Hungary, by a Serb nationalist in Sarajevo. They were dining with their parents when Prince Louis of Battenberg came over from a neighbouring table with the news. 'R [Reggie] was full of forebodings that this was the sort of incident that might end in the conflagration of Europe,' recorded Nellie in her diary that evening. Later that summer they were all up at the Roman Camp as events led towards Britain's declaration of war on Germany. General Sir John French came north to see Reggie, having been warned that in the event of war he would be put in charge of the British Expeditionary Force to France. He was, as Sylvia recalled (perhaps with the benefit of hindsight), 'deeply pre-occupied and worried' and told her: 'I don't like it, Sylvia, I tell you, I don't like it one damn bit.'

Reggie dashed back to London on the eve of war, arriving there on 3 August. The King assured him he had in vain done all he could by personal approaches to the Emperors of Russia and Germany to maintain peace. Reggie, though, had no doubts that his country was morally obliged to go to war with Germany, a war in which his principal contribution would be to use his excellent French and understanding of the French people – gleaned from his French mother – to act as an informal liaison between French and British generals, and as adviser to Lord Kitchener. 'My father was in a turmoil of organisation,' wrote Sylvia about the war years, 'flashing like a meteor from the King to the Army, from the Navy to the Flying Corps, dispensing wisdom. Many were jealous of him, for he had no scheduled work and was not bothered by red tape. Lord Esher may not always have been welcome, but they had to admit they could not do without him.' These new roles came at a time when Reggie's influence at court was on the wane. The new King, George V, at first consulted him on such thorny constitutional issues as the Parliament Bill (1911) and Home Rule for Ireland (1914), but he was far less susceptible than his father to Reggie's ingratiating ways. Soon, as George V's biographer Kenneth Rose recorded, in place of statecraft Reggie 'had to be content with running little errands for the Queen: binding up her letters, matching the exact shade of silk for the walls of a picture gallery, seeking an elegant coal scuttle. He would flatter her shamelessly. "If you were not Queen and came into a room," he told her, "everyone would ask who you were." The Queen replied that her mother used to say the same.'

Throughout the autumn of 1914 Sylvia and Zena stayed on at Callander, where they took over an empty house – 'Inverleny' – and turned it into a twenty-one-bed military extension of the hospital at Stolehill, Glasgow. They both began as nurses, but the sight of blood made Sylvia nauseous, so she retreated to the pantry to wash dishes. In the evenings she played the piano and organised concert parties. 'The hospital is very well done,' Reggie told Maurice. 'Syv & Zena look charming in their hospital kit and work very conscientiously.'

War also altered the old Rajah's plans. Although the hunting season was upon him, he decided that his country needed him, and hurried back there, reaching Kuching on 14 December. Hearing that his father was coming out to Sarawak, Vyner took the first available boat to England, arriving back on 11 December. While Sylvia continued to go back and forth to her hospital, Vyner asked Reggie to help find him some useful war work, knowing that the Rajah would be putting it about in Sarawak that he was at the front. Reggie thought he might try to get him attached to Maurice, who was then Assistant Provost Marshal in Paris, but Maurice told his father that, much as he would like to have Vyner, having 'the arch-cat [Sylvia] over here is another matter. We are all very comfortable at present and do not need disturbing and unpleasant influences.' Instead Vyner worked very happily for a while at a factory in Shoreditch, standing at a lathe shaping bits of steel for aeroplanes, careful not to let on who he was. He also did a stint at an anti-aircraft battery on the top of Cannon Street Hotel. But when his identity leaked out he was treated with deference and it annoyed him. Eventually he unnerved himself by dropping a well-filled cartridge belt from the roof on to the street below, and promptly resigned.

Out in Sarawak the Rajah had his own troubles to contend with. In the spring of 1915 he ordered a punitive expedition against a group of Dyaks on the Gaat and Mujong tributaries of the Balleh river (itself a tributary of the Rejang), who had been carrying out a murderous spree under the leadership of a swashbuckler called Tabor. The Rajah's original force consisted of 1,200 hand-picked Dyaks and 600 Malays, but when they reached Kapit on the Rejang, they were joined by a further 10,000 Dyaks, dressed in their gaudy warcoats and hornbill feathers, who had responded to the Rajah's call, hopeful no doubt of a share in the enemy's loot.

The Rajah had come from Kuching on his yacht *Zahora*, and he made a short speech, praising their loyalty and warning them to act cautiously. As the force moved off the next morning, he stood on his quarterdeck, a short, spare figure in a blue serge coat and white duck trousers, ironed with the crease down the side, Navy style, ceremoniously doffing his dirty homburg as each boat went past with raised paddles and Dyak war cries. He waved until they had all disappeared round a bend in the river, then spent the next few days restlessly pacing the deck until they returned with the news that they had successfully routed their enemy. The Rajah later wrote in the *Sarawak Gazette* that he had lost count of the times he had commanded expeditions against the Dyaks, 'who we know are a very troublesome recalcitrant people, but like children, only more dangerous, for that reason liked more by their parents . . . I never tire of their misdeeds.'

That year also saw the opening of the first five miles of the light railway running south from Kuching. This was a project close to the Rajah's heart, and he had taken a keen interest in the laying of the track and in choosing the types of engines and carriages. It was whispered that the first engineer whom the Rajah had consulted, when he discovered the scale of the proposed project – ten miles in all – referred the Rajah to a well-known London toyshop. The railway quickly became a source of fascination for the townspeople, who would crowd alongside the track, staring as the trains went by. Each time the whistle was heard, so Sylvia recorded, the Rajah would check his watch and mutter approvingly, 'On the dot as usual.'

In this, his eighty-sixth year, there was a palpable sense that Rajah Charles's reign was drawing to a close. When he faced his chiefs, who had gathered at the Council Negri in the Astana dining room to give him fealty, one of his officers who was there recalled that, 'His gaze rested on them lingeringly, and his voice, usually so firm, was tinged with emotion when he spoke of the sixty years he had lived in the country.'

> I think [the Rajah began] after so long a period you will allow me to open my mouth and give my opinion truthfully. There may be others who may appear after my time with soft and smiling countenances to deprive you of what I solemnly and truly consider to be your right and that is The Land. It is your inheritance on which your flesh and blood exists, the source of your self-existence which, if once lost, no amount of money could ever recover. After my life the future will remain with you to be independent and free citizens, or be a humbled and inferior class without pride in yourselves or in your race. You must choose between the two, the owner or master on one side or the dependant and coolie on the other. It is for you to see that whoever rules this land the land is not granted away to strangers. This is the danger after I have passed away. I am now old and cannot live many more years, if any. I have had a long life, but my cord must have nearly reached its end. I now bid you goodbye.

Shortly after this, in August, Vyner wrote to Reggie, who had just secured him a position in the Artists' Rifles, to say that his father was coming home shortly and 'may want me out in Sarawak. Troubles in the interior I believe!' For the first time the Rajah had also suggested that Vyner should bring Sylvia with him. 'I am afraid I have been a great nuisance to you with all these choppings and changes,' wrote Vyner.

Sylvia was for once glad of her father-in-law's intervention, explaining to Reggie:

> Vyner in Sarawak is a perfectly sane, normal soul, content with everything – he is at heart half-Malay. Out of Sarawak no human being can tell what he will do next . . . He says sometimes at a dinner party that an awful sensation comes over him and he would like to rise up in his chair with a yell and tear off his trousers – now anyone who feels like that must be a bit queer. He isn't really happy in England, not for more than a few months. He misses the natives frightfully. If you had seen him as I have out there sitting amongst those naked people listening to their legends, absolutely absorbed, you'd see why he could never really be happy in England. The next thing to Sarawak he likes is me, but I can't keep him amused and interested. No woman could. I think really if he made more friends in England he would be happier. He knows so few people and won't go about. However, he is wonderful to me, and it is this devotion that makes him so sweet and easy and his humour is perfect sometimes. But the East is his home, and he's got the call badly . . .

Reggie complained to Maurice that it was impossible to make out what they really wanted. 'From what we know I cannot see that it matters much to Vyner whether Syv lives *with* him or not! He should be healthier when he is alone! She ought to have Ladies-in-Waiting, paid, and coming in in rotation. I daresay she would prefer Lords . . .'

Throughout the autumn of 1915 Sylvia dithered about whether to accompany her husband to Sarawak and risk being sunk by a German submarine in the Channel, leaving her children as orphans. She was now heavily pregnant with her third child, but even so Vyner thought she ought to go with him, especially since the Rajah had actually invited her, and moreover the people were expecting her.

Their baby was born on 2 December 1915. 'A girl, of course it was a girl,' Sylvia wrote later. 'I knew before Simmie [her obstetrician Sir Henry Simson] told me when I saw him fling up his hands in despair. I was not destined to create a future Rajah. Sometimes I feel glad, and free with the knowledge that no son of mine can wreck the dynasty and pull down what had been built with such fine hands.' The girl was called Valerie and she was no more than a month old when Sylvia steeled herself to leave her.

She told Reggie in early January that it was especially important that she went to Sarawak because she had not had a son, 'a criminal offence in the eyes of a native – There is my future with these people to be thought of. And natives are queer customers to deal with. It took the Ranee a long time to get on their right side and it will take me even longer as I am stupid at learning languages.' She added that 'though he [Vyner] writes curiously and says many things he doesn't mean, he is at heart a far-seeing, calculating and careful man, and would not expose me, who he cares for more than anything else, to unnecessary danger.' If by March her husband deemed it too dangerous crossing the Channel, she would remain behind while he faced it alone; if not she would go with him.

Reggie thought Vyner underestimated the risks, but told Sylvia that only he [Vyner] could assess the importance of the Sarawak call. 'I am really very sorry for Syv,' Reggie told Maurice, 'but this conflict of duties was inevitable, from the nature of the case.' Concerned that he might be landed with looking after her children, he asked Sylvia what provisions had been made for their inheritance, and was relieved to learn that in the marriage settlement her children had been left £500 a year each, and Sylvia £2,000 a year.

Doll once again planned to accompany Sylvia and Vyner to Borneo, telling Reggie that she hoped to return with 'heaps of paintings' and her deafness cured by the heat and sun. Ultimately, though, she was unable to tear herself away from Lady Ottoline Morrell – 'her latest mania', as Reggie called her – and the other Bloomsburies who surrounded her at Garsington. Doll's place was taken by Doris Stocker, a pretty chorus girl at the Gaiety Theatre, whom Sylvia had introduced to Vyner, guessing that he might like her. 'I had already begun to learn how much he needed the affection of a pretty girl,' she wrote in her second autobiography, 'and how the good opinion of others compensated for the poor opinion he held of himself.' On this occasion he was 'immediately attracted' and promptly asked Doris to go with them. Though almost a complete stranger to them, Doris accepted. 'It was brave of her really,' wrote Sylvia, 'and when she began to know Vyner better she realised how brave.'

Leaving the children with Ranee Margaret, they sailed, on 28 March, in the Japanese steamer *Katori Maru*, attended by their Scottish maid Cameron. Sylvia explained to her father from the Savoy before leaving that she was 'not doing this thing for Sarawak, or the people, but simply for Vyner – this year has been an unfortunate and unhappy one for him . . . I could not let him go, feeling he had failed and been foolish . . . I love my poor old Vyner, he is so good, so patient, it is almost pathetic.' Reggie thought it 'a stupid business running unnecessary risks', but they got through all right and arrived at Kuching on 21 May to a royal salute, the royal umbrella, hundreds of Chinese crackers, and the band playing the Sarawak national anthem.

At nearly eighty-seven, even the Rajah now admitted he was beginning to feel his years, although he was also in the midst of a love affair with a doctor's wife, a Mrs Waller, and therefore in comparatively good humour. Certainly he seemed better disposed towards Sylvia, and took it upon himself to show her some more of the country. Their conveyance was a small dog cart, harnessed to a spirited pony, and by Sylvia's account they nearly always ended up in the ditch. 'A little frisky,' the Rajah would say, thoughtfully dusting himself down afterwards. 'No vice, just wants to play, that's all.'

The Rajah's kindnesses did not prevent his daughter-in-law from disparaging him in her books, however. With the Rajah installed at the Astana, they stayed at the Residency on the town side of the Sarawak river – 'no hardship to us,' wrote Sylvia, 'as he [the Rajah] was hardly a genial companion at the best of times. If only he had been able to express to me the merest hint of the poetry of the country, its broad brown rivers and fertile soil, its teeming fruitfulness. But all he was interested in was economic facts, so many acres of rubber trees and sago swamps, pepper gardens and rice fields; so much per bushel – so much in the Treasury . . . There was no room in his grim world for the hibiscus or the orchid, for lolling in the sun, or a siesta in the shade.'

Once a week, the entire European population of Kuching turned out for the Rajah's Band Day, in Sylvia's estimation 'an extremely undesirable ceremony' (she was not alone in thinking that), at which

> we all dressed up in our best and gathered round the Rajah on a stretch of grass where the Police band [from Manila] would play classical music, and we would respectfully listen to discordant sounds that fortunately for him he could not hear. The Rajah's favourites would sit on either side of him, and at intervals they would scream some trivial remarks into his ear. These he would reply to at times, but more often than not he would continue beating the ground with his stick. We dared not leave until the band had laboured through their list, we just sat there devoured by mosquitoes and pouring with sweat.

On other occasions the Rajah invited senior members of the Kuching community to dine at the Astana, not, wrote Sylvia, because he was anxious to see them, 'but because it was one of his duties as Ruler of a State to be officially polite to its inhabitants'. The guests – European government officers and their wives, Malay chiefs and the principal Chinese – 'would know they were not really wanted before they arrived, and it must be admitted that he made little effort to alter this conjecture'. Sylvia and Vyner stood behind the Rajah, receiving the nervous guests as they made their way up the steps. 'There would be a little small talk on the verandah whilst drinks were being offered around. Once more the Rajah's favourites would flutter to his side like chiffon butterflies, and in shrill voices and little trills of unnatural laughter endeavour to convey to those who were not in his favour what a wonderful time they were having. Very heated and agitated, I would move from one to another, my voice also unnaturally loud and a kind of fixed grin on my crimson face.' Vyner would get as far away as he could from his father, and occasionally Sylvia would hear his ringing laugh, 'as out of place, in that palace of gloom, as a jester at a funeral'.

Sylvia also recorded the Rajah's 'remarkable habit' during these parties of relieving himself in full view of everyone. During a lull in conversation, she once proclaimed: 'Listen, it's begun to rain,' only to turn round and see the Rajah unselfconsciously 'watering the cannas over the verandah rail'. Guests would know when it was time to leave when, quite suddenly, the Rajah would move to the head of the stair and stand there with his hand held out to bid them farewell.

Sylvia found she could now speak enough Malay to go shopping in the bazaar. 'I can't talk the flowery language of the *datus* [chieftains] and their wives,' she admitted to Reggie, 'but still they love to have me with them, and sit stroking me and patting my arms and hands.' Shortly after their arrival they had attended a Malay wedding. On the wedding night the mother-in-law slept in the same bed as the married couple in order to give the bride encouragement and the benefit of her sensual experience: 'They remain in bed for a week!!' Sylvia wrote to Reggie. 'Isn't that awful.' All in all, she was delighted to be back. 'I wish you were here,' she told her father. 'A modern Arcadia, and yet perhaps not splendid enough for you. Too idle and unambitious.'

The war had barely affected Sarawak. No German raiders came and neither oil nor rubber was yet being produced in large enough quantities to be useful for the war effort. Price controls on certain essentials were imposed to guard against profiteering and many of the younger field officers who had entered the Rajah's service now returned to Europe to rejoin their old regiments – though the Rajah limited the exodus to one brother per family. After the mutiny at Singapore the Rajah ordered a wireless mast to be put up at Kuching, much to the confusion of some of the native people. Sylvia related how, while she was in Kuching, a Chinese man climbed it in the apparent belief that from the top he might see God. Once up there he lay down, then rose to his knees and appeared to be singing, before standing up and leaping over the edge to his death.

Otherwise life went on as before. At the Residency they all rose at dawn and, after a glass of pineapple juice, went to their separate verandahs to work. Sylvia began her first novel, *Toys* – a story concerning the transmigration of a soul through four women – which would take her a further two years to complete. At nine the Rajah was rowed over from the Astana in his state barge to the courthouse to hear 'requests' or petitions, with the sergeant-at-arms carrying the yellow umbrella over him and his staff that had been presented to him by the Sultan of Brunei.

There was still no mixed club in Kuching at this time. Barred from the men's club, with its billiards, bowls and tennis, Sylvia and Doris had to make do with a dingy little wooden bungalow on Rock Road that served as the Ladies' Club. Here a handful of European officers' wives would sit in the evenings waiting forlornly for male company. 'If a man passed along the road we would all rear our heads and try and mesmerise him over the hedge to join us,' wrote Sylvia. But men were banned from the premises because the Rajah disapproved of 'damned poodlefaking'. With nothing to do except gossip, the ladies would sit on the verandah and, according to Sylvia, tear their neighbours' reputations to shreds.

The Rajah's opposition to the mixing of the sexes went hand in hand with his view that if any man in his service got married, he lost the greater part of his efficiency and related less well to the local inhabitants. Sylvia later denounced the Rajah's policy as 'a vicious doctrine [which] drove white men into the welcoming brown arms of local girls, involved them in tropical entanglements, and produced a harvest that remained long after they had gone'. The half-caste offspring of these unions found happiness and fulfilment hard to come by in either the European or the Asiatic community. Even when the fathers sought to do the best for their children and send them to England to be educated, they would often find themselves stigmatised by society there, a subject that Sylvia wrote about in her novel *Lost Property* (1930).

The subordinate position of European women in Kuching society, meanwhile, meant that the young Ranee Muda's unrestrained behaviour inevitably ruffled feathers. On this particular visit, Sylvia was well aware that she had upset senior members of the Sarawak Civil Service, judging by her letter to one officer, Donald Owen, written when she was on her way back to England. 'You haven't flattered me, God knows, but you've shown me at intervals what a brute I am,' she wrote.

> You have also taught me self restraint and a certain amount of dignity, tho' dignity and I will never much walk hand in hand. I know I was rather a shock to you when I first arrived, don't think I didn't try to please you, oddly enough your dislike of me pained and hurt me frightfully. I wanted you to like me but I wasn't your style. I wasn't good enough. Your idea of what the Ranee Muda

should be wasn't me, looking like the back row of a Provincial Company. But Mr Owen, dear, you have been most tremendously kind and good, and I shall always be grateful. I promise you I will in future try to live up to that high standard you have in mind. You are quite right. The Ranee Muda should be a thing apart, but what about Syv, the mad, wild Syv, must she be choked and killed just as she has come to life? I love being the Ranee Muda, but I love being Syv as well. You don't care a damn which I am so long as I don't bother you. You are an old iceberg, ough!!! I can feel your eyes on me now. Curse me, scold me, despise me, Donald Owen, I deserve it all, but it won't prevent me from loving you, so there.

Sylvia and Doris[1] started back for England on 25 September, Vyner travelling with them as far as Singapore. For the onward leg to Ceylon they were accompanied by another Sarawak officer, Gerald 'Blue' Gifford. In her first autobiography, Sylvia described Blue Gifford as 'one of our most spectacular young officers'. He had made a name for himself in Sarawak the previous year for his part in routing the rebel Dyaks on the Gaat and Mujong tributaries, whereupon the Rajah rewarded him with promotion and the sword of honour. In Sylvia's estimation, his appeal to women was 'unquestionable'. 'He had a fine wrathful face and blue eyes that slanted at the corners, and all he really lived for was riding and his brother Barry, who was at that time fighting in France. I did not know Barry then. I had not met him. Strange, how fate unwinds a tangled skein . . .'

The Wimbledon Common Sylvia returned to had become a vast army camp, and she spent much of her time giving lunches for the forlorn officers and taking her daughters to the station to throw cigarettes for the men who were off to the front. Otherwise, with her parents and Maurice in Paris, and Doll virtually living at Garsington with Lady Ottoline, she felt profoundly lonely. She

[1] The next year Doris Stocker married Henry Segrave, the celebrated motor racing driver who later held the land speed record and died in 1930 while breaking the motor boat speed record on Lake Windermere.

even resorted to going to stay with the Ranee, but her mother-in-law spent the whole time telling her how Sarawak ought to be run. In London her only two old friends were J. M. Barrie and General Sir John French, who talked to her miserably about his replacement by Douglas Haig as Commander-in-Chief. For want of jollier company, she wrote to Blue Gifford's younger brother Barry, who was by now home on leave, asking him to dine with her.

Although she had not come across him out in Sarawak, Barry Gifford had also served the Brooke Raj for four and a half years before the war, and had been in charge of the Oya river district in January 1915 when given permission by the Rajah to return home and rejoin his old regiment, the Middlesex. Within a month of his arrival in England he had been despatched to the Ypres salient, where he was gassed and wounded on the last day of the Battle of Ypres. Reported missing, he later turned up at the Royal Free Hospital, in Gray's Inn Road, suffering from severe gas poisoning and shell-shock, talking nothing but Malay.

When he recovered, he joined the Royal Flying Corps, obtaining his wings in June 1916 as a pusher scout pilot. He was kept at home instructing until October, when he again saw action, on the Somme. On 28 October he was in the patrol that brought down the celebrated German ace Oswald Boelke, the mentor of Manfred von Richthofen, the Red Baron. Gifford later saw action in German East Africa and Egypt, and was twice mentioned in despatches for, as Sylvia put it, 'the daring courage with which he flew, and the almost reckless good-humour with which he soared above the enemy's lines'.

Before long, 'through the network of time and spaces', wrote Sylvia, this dashing pilot and his brother became her 'greatest friends'. There is also evidence that each of them became, at one time or other, rather more than that. Barry was the first one she fell for, as Ottoline Morrell observed in her journal entry in the spring of 1917 when they both came to stay at Garsington, where Doll was still more or less permanently installed:

> April 23rd, Sunday, The Ranee [*sic*] of Sarawak arrived Sat: frenzied and in a demented state about an air-man called Gifford whom she is in love with. On Sunday he flew overhead and

> dropped a message for her with a flag attached. He arrived in the afternoon – dark good-looking young man. She was quite silly about him – and I have never seen such unabashed lovers. Asquith came over in the afternoon – turmoil – as he wanted to see her too. Aldous [Huxley], Brettie [Dorothy], P [Philip Morrell] and I laughed.

Sylvia and Barry Gifford seem to have remained an item on and off until at least 1920, when Vyner appointed him as his aide-de-camp.

Reggie soon got to hear about Gifford through Lawrence 'Thrushy' Burgis, his twenty-five-year-old former private secretary to whom he had become passionately attached after Maurice's marriage to Zena. Sylvia had confided in Thrushy, and when she showed him a photograph of Barry Gifford he said he looked nice and that she was looking 'happier and more peaceful' than ever. Encouraged by this, Sylvia was soon telling her father that her airman had 'opened this new vista to me', while in letters to other friends she waxed lyrical about her passionate awakening. Reggie was hardly in a position to carp about extramarital affairs, although he did reprimand his daughter for 'kissing and telling – it spoils the romance of life'. 'You are a creature of cross currents,' he told her, 'and very attractive it is. I do not wish you otherwise. But I despise people who wear their conduct on their sleeves!'

Throughout this time Vyner had remained in Sarawak. Five days after Sylvia's departure, the old Rajah had issued a proclamation handing over 'control of the Dyaks of the Ulu Ai or interior of Rejang and Simanggang districts . . . to my son and successor the Rajah Muda'. All past disagreements, it seems, were forgotten. It was one of the old Rajah's final official acts. Not long afterwards he fell seriously ill, when a swelling on his ankle spread to his whole leg. He attempted to shrug it off as 'a touch of gout' but was forced to take to his bed after suffering fits of dizziness. Vyner moved back into the Astana to help nurse him. Occasionally the Rajah would rise from his bed and wander along the verandah, wrapped in a blanket, muttering deliriously to himself in broken French and Malay. Prayers were offered in the churches and in the mosques, and everyone waited for the flag to be lowered from the Astana tower. Miraculously, as it seemed to those in Kuching at the time, the Rajah rallied sufficiently to enable him to travel back to England in December with his girlfriend Mrs Waller, while letting it be known that he intended to return East once more in order to die.

Vyner did not relish the prospect. 'I cannot go through another illness like the last one,' he wrote to Bertram in January 1917, 'so shall hurry back to England when I hear he is approaching these shores . . . he is getting very wandering in the mind and doddery and it is hard to transact business with him.' Vyner felt that if the Rajah did come out, then his mother ought to come too. 'It is her place to nurture and look after his declining years, not mine. I think I shall suggest it to her.'

> If the old man pops off [Vyner went on], I should love you to come out and take over while I am on leave, turn and turn about. You will have full powers and of course a very considerable salary. I find my old liver is not the thing it was and I can't put in very long here at a time, perhaps 7 months in the year. If you could only relieve me during the 5 months it would be of the greatest benefit to all concerned. It would frustrate Ma. She is fully convinced that I wish to sell Sarawak, accumulate vast wealth for myself and endeavour to get a peerage. Far from it. Even my present title sickens me. Rajah Brooke plain is quite sufficient without all the high fallutin' nonsense of the HH part of it. I don't wish for any riches, just enough to live comfortably. £7 or £8,000 a year would do us admirably. This seems a lot but we have a lot of useless houses on our hands and this old Astana costs more than £1,000 a year to run with dinners, etc.

In March 1917, leaving the Resident A. B. Ward in charge of the government, Vyner headed back towards England, stopping on the way at a hill station in Ceylon, where he was diagnosed as suffering from dysentery and malaria but restored to full health within a few weeks. Soon after the Rajah Muda had departed Ward saw the giant durian tree outside the Residency burst into flames during a thunderstorm. Superstitious natives presaged a great calamity and in April, at the same time as Sylvia was going about with her airman, a cable arrived to say that the Rajah had again been taken seriously ill in London with 'a very floppy heart'. Vyner had by then reached Cape Town, but on hearing this news he hurried back to Sarawak.

The Rajah insisted that he be taken to Chesterton, travelling there by motor car, one of the 'stinking machines' he so much despised. He did briefly rally, but on 29 April Bertram reported that he was 'coughing up large bits of lung etc, so the end can't be a matter of more than a week or so at outside'. The Rajah clung on for nearly three weeks. He died at noon on 17 May 1917, some two weeks short of his eighty-eighth birthday.

7

I SEE AND I CALCULATE

Word of the Rajah's death did not reach Kuching until the next morning, when a telegram arrived at the government offices from the governor of Singapore. On being handed it, the Resident, A. B. Ward, crossed the river to the Astana, where he found Vyner on the verandah. 'I have bad news, Rajah,' he said as he approached him. Vyner turned red. 'It's all over then,' he whispered, then sank into a chair in silence.

Some time later the news was intimated to the people by the tolling of bells and the half-masting of all flags. That evening Vyner and the Resident went for a long walk. 'He did not want to meet anyone else,' Ward recorded. 'He courted solitude in his loss; he was shy in his new position.' When the Resident asked him what he would like to be called, Vyner replied that he would 'rather not be Charles II'. So he became known as Rajah Vyner, although he later combined both his names.

Rajah Charles's funeral took place at Cirencester parish church on 21 May and was followed three days later by a memorial service in the Chapel of St Michael and St George at St Paul's Cathedral, at which the congregation – among them Barry Gifford though not Sylvia, who was not at all well – stood to sing the Sarawak national anthem, the first time that it had been sung in its entirety in England.

The Rajah had recently made a new will asking to be buried in the Astana garden – 'the spot [he] selected being just outside my bedroom windows!!' Sylvia told Reggie between clenched teeth. Accordingly, he was embalmed to await transportation to Sarawak after the war. But the embalmers did not do a good job, and after he had lain for three weeks in a mausoleum at Baker Street Church it was becoming apparent that he was not going to keep much longer. 'It is so typically Brooke,' wrote Sylvia to Reggie, 'just the sort of thing that would happen to them.'

The burial arrangements soon became yet another source of friction between Sylvia and her mother-in-law. When Sylvia suggested that she had better take the Rajah's remains out to Sarawak with her in February 1918, the dowager Ranee put her foot down: 'The Ranee wants as she so charmingly puts it "Her Last Show"! before retiring,' Sylvia told her father. Eventually, it was decided that his remains would not survive the journey to Sarawak after all, and he was buried instead at Sheepstor in Devon, on 12 June 1919, under the same beech tree as his uncle James, his tomb made of rough-hewn, grey Dartmoor stone, 'firm, strong and imperishable as the memory of the man it covers', as the faithful Ward put it.

In Sarawak, for three months following the Rajah's death, government officers were obliged to swelter in mourning dress, other members of the population were invited to do likewise, and theatres remained closed for ten days. But on 24 May, the day of the memorial service at St Paul's, flags were hoisted to the mast-heads in accordance with Charles's solemn instruction that his successor should be publicly proclaimed Rajah within seven days of his death.

That morning, at a quarter to nine, Vyner left the Astana to be rowed across the river in the state barge. Awaiting him at the stone steps on the opposite bank were the leaders of the Malay, Chinese and Dyak communities, and troops lined his route to a dais which had been erected outside the government offices, strewn with yellow bunting and Sarawak flags. There his accession to the throne was announced in a hastily prepared proclamation – with no other precedent to hand, the Resident based the solemn Malay wording on that which had announced to the people of Singapore the accession of King George V. After the proclamation the new Rajah rose nervously to his feet, dripping with sweat beneath his blue serge suit, and addressed the large crowd in Malay. 'I make it known to you Datus, Pengirans, Abangs, Inchis, Chiefs and all classes of people in

Sarawak that I will on no account interfere with the Mohameddan faith or with any other religions or faiths of the people. As the white labu and the kundor fruit show white when they are split, so too is my heart unblemished towards you . . . My people, rich and poor, never be afraid if you are in trouble and have anything to complain of. I wish you all to tell me so that I can help you: therefore never be afraid to come to me.'

In this way he pledged to safeguard the traditions that had so far characterised Brooke rule, while also hinting at a slightly less austere approach to the business of being rajah. When he had stopped speaking, the guard of honour gave the royal salute, the band of the Sarawak Rangers played the national anthem, and the Resident called for three cheers for the new Rajah.

The Resident later sent a letter to Sylvia in England offering the Sarawak officers' 'hearty congratulations on becoming Ranee'. Her accession to this exotic throne was reported in newspapers throughout the world, not least in America, where the *New York Times* devoted a page to profiling the new 'Sultana of Sarawak, an Oriental Princess of Bostonese Ancestry'. This 'daughter of an English peer', it was explained, also had 'a strong strain of American blood in her veins', a reference to Sylvia's American grandmother, Madame Van de Weyer, whose Bates ancestors had been among the first settlers in New England.

Flattered though she may have been by the breadth of the coverage, at that time Sylvia was in no fit state to enjoy it. On the day that Vyner was proclaimed rajah, she was lying in a London nursing home gravely ill. Her health had been delicate ever since she'd come back from Sarawak the previous year 'very seedy with a poisoned foot', as her mother Nellie told Chat Williamson. This, Nellie added, was something Sylvia 'seemed to treat with her usual casualness but which with all we see here with blood poisoning sounded to us most dangerous. It appears that the doctor out there is not a regular accepted one – has no diploma – imagine that, when a good salary could procure the very best. It really annoys one as well as worries.'

By January 1918 Sylvia had lost more than a stone in weight and was diagnosed by a specialist as having a 'slight tendency towards tuberculosis'. By way of a cure, she proposed going to Africa for two or three months, and then on to Sarawak. But in May she took a turn for the worse and, thinking she had strained herself inside, she again consulted Sir Henry Simson, who now said she had blood poisoning. Admitted to a nursing home at York Place, she underwent an unspecified 'minor operation', as she described it, after which she believed that she could have no more children. 'The days of sons and heirs and inheritance are over,' she wrote to Reggie in June, explaining that she had 'begged Simmie not to go on fiddling with a thing that is far better left alone'. In any case, she added, Vyner no longer cared whether he had a boy or not.

During her painful recovery, she was dosed with morphia day and night; for weeks the joints on her fingers remained swollen and wrapped in cotton wool; one of her ankles was in a cage to keep it still. She grew delirious and increasingly neurotic. After visiting her, Oliver told Reggie, '[Her illness] seems to have distorted her mind and she imagines people are plotting against her, & is full of absurd fancies.' The main conspirator in her imagination was again Ranee Margaret, the latest trigger for her suspicions being the news that Bertram had been released from military service and was going out to Sarawak to assist with the government. 'Of course you are right that I make mountains out of molehills,' Sylvia wrote to Reggie from her bed, 'I always have, [but] I am afraid of Vyner's weakness . . . I personally think it looks bad in the papers . . . I should like to have seen the old Rajah have his brother within a hundred miles of the place.'

Amid her fancies and distortions, Sylvia had a point. There were distinct echoes of the 1912 'coup' in the Rajah's political will, which had been written not long afterwards, in 1913. Although he bequeathed sovereignty to Vyner, the Rajah barely concealed the fact that he would have preferred to be succeeded by his second son, directing that 'no material developments or changes in the State or in the Government thereof and no new works such as public works . . . shall be initiated by my son Vyner without first consulting my son Bertram'. The Tuan Muda was further asked 'to carry out the duties of Rajah and administer the Government of the State during such times as my son Vyner may be in England or absent from Sarawak'. At these times it was envisaged that he would occupy the Astana, and that government officers would pay him the same respect as was shown to his elder brother. When Vyner was in Sarawak, Bertram was to preside over the Sarawak advisory council in Westminster. Yet when Bertram was in Sarawak, his position on the council was to be filled not by Vyner, but by the council member with the longest record of service in Sarawak. The Rajah concluded that he hoped Bertram would be 'an additional safeguard against adventurers and speculators who would desire to make profits out of the country without regard to its real welfare'.

The longer Sylvia lay in the nursing home, the more she was assailed by perceived injustices. In a subsequent letter, she told her father that 'the plotting of Sarawak gains over me, Adeh [Bertram] goes out immediately to join Vyner, and after the War the Ranee goes out with the Rajah's body. No mention of me. As far as I can see these three intend to govern Sarawak and I shall get the good old push. Vyner is so weak, poor darling, once that old woman gets out there, he won't be able to call his soul his own.' The villain, as far as Sylvia was concerned, remained the Ranee. Bertram, by contrast, had been 'charming'. 'He tells me everything and consults me before anything is done. He is courteous and very thoughtful. You know I have never minded Adeh, I don't think he'd ever do me any harm.'

Reggie told her not to be so foolishly neurotic, and again criticised the way she had been carrying on with Barry Gifford. 'I am not quite such a damned ass as you think me,' she retorted.

> My sin is that I talk too much . . . But don't you think darling that I don't know what I am doing – I know and I see and I calculate. I am just as good as your old Katherine Bush, only not quite so much. I think she was very cruel – she calculated too much. She got what she wanted, but then so shall I. You wait until I have a house in London, a nice house, then you'll be surprised I think. What I could never do as Ranee Muda, I mean to do as Ranee. I can do it, I know I have the power. It is an extraordinary thing darling, but within the last year something new has been born in me. I don't know what it is, I can't see it when I look in the mirror, but I feel it always. A kind of power over people. People I have known for years who haven't paid much attention to me before, are now, well, more attentive. I meet new people, the same thing happens. I have hardly met a

man or a woman this year that they haven't clamoured to meet me again. Now, like Katherine Bush[1] I am watching this new power of mine and considering the effect it will have on my life. It will have a great effect now I am Ranee and can spread myself a little . . .

A month later she wrote to Reggie:

You only remember the old me, the new me is a very different person. I don't lie now, there is no reason to. I am not afraid of anyone or anything – not even of you, darling, so there. I admit I used to be terrified of you, but I am not a bit now. All that I said to Lawrence [Burgis] was true. All that I say to you is true. Oddly enough, I believe if I told you I was living with somebody you would believe me, but because I tell you I am very very good you doubt me. Never mind, one day when I am dead and gone you will be left saying 'this daughter of mine was rather wonderful, and I never knew it'. . .

When she was well enough, the new Sylvia moved to Tilney Street with a nurse, where Dorothy lent her a pianola to exercise her foot. Doll was herself at that time enduring a painful series of injections in her backside, hoping that afterwards she would 'hear marvelously'. She spent a good deal of her time looking after the convalescent Syv and her children in London, but she told Reggie that she found the wartime capital 'vile . . . the shops full of luxurious handbags and no butter, sugar or tea'. She deemed it far more sane to remain at Garsington, out of the way of the air raids, and mocked the 'sham heroics or dense stupidity' of those who were still prepared to go to London for a theatre spree on a moonlit night. Sylvia rather despised her attitude.

Doll told Reggie: 'Charlie [Willes] Johnson is simply sprawling over Syv now the old Rajah's dead – licking her boots.' The old Rajah's legal adviser and secretary to the advisory council had come

[1] *The Career of Katherine Bush* was the latest popular novel by Elinor Glyn, whose ambitious and cunning heroine overcame her unpromising Brixton background to acquire an education, establish herself in a career and marry a duke.

to visit Sylvia, kissed her hand and assured her of his loyalty, whereupon Sylvia had found herself 'giggling inwardly so much I could hardly speak to him, oily old devil'.

But although Barry Gifford spent his leave with her and oily Charlie Johnson came regularly with fruit and flowers, Sylvia's convalescence was for the most part rather lonely. On 5 July she wrote to Reggie: '. . . absolutely despondent, burning with suppressed indignation, hurt feelings and helpless, impotent rage – somehow all this week and all last week too I have been buoyed up by the fancy that Vyner was on his way home, because he never answered either of my cables – Well, he isn't on his way home, he cables to anybody, everybody except me . . . I daresay that Vyner is aching with longing for me, but why the devil can't he say so?'

When Reggie again hinted that her airman might have had something to do with her husband's coolness, she protested: 'I have done no wrong!! Nor shall I ever. I admit I am a flirt, but I put a lot of it on. It is useful in my particular position. If Queen Mary flirted a bit like old Alexandra she mightn't be so wobbly on her throne . . . I have done nothing I wouldn't tell him [Vyner] of. And he in his turn would never be influenced by gossip about me. He isn't that sort and we are not on those terms.'

As she grew fitter, she began to see more of Doll's friends, including Mark Gertler, who was himself miserable with unrequited love for Carrington and told Sylvia that not always being happy was 'an excellent sign'.

> So we both passionately desire [he wrote to her from Garsington], you Love and I to paint. However, I admit that reciprocated love must indeed be a fine thing, perhaps the most satisfactory of all emotions, but as I have never experienced it, have only in fact derived utter misery from loving, I turn away at last, in disgust, to devote myself wholly to work, which I find much more paying – I mean emotionally – as for physical passion ordinaire, well, it is sometimes quite a nice sensation, but on the whole not worth the trouble, the time or the energy. Also I find it nearly always really, rather, slightly, disgusting.

Sylvia professed to share Gertler's ambivalence about sex, and she also seemed to be in a muddle as to who it was she wanted to be doing the reciprocating. She cabled Vyner to say that, as she would not be well enough to go out to Sarawak until the next year, he ought to come home in September. However, he now hinted that he might go to China for the winter and not come home at all, even in 1918. 'He asks me to bring out his winter clothes when I come,' Sylvia wrote to Reggie on 11 August 1917. 'Supposing after my cable he still doesn't come home, what would you do? Would you go to him, or have him up for restitution of conjugal rights? The only thing is I don't want any conjugal rights just now . . . but seriously Vyner and I have been divided a year now. It is a long time and it smacks too much of the late lamented Rajah. I don't like it. Vyner writes that I am all the world to him. But it is deeds not words that count.'

As time went by, she seemed to grow more understanding and more philosophical. 'There is too much for him [Vyner] to do,' Sylvia sought to explain to her father in September. 'Too many things to be altered and gone into.' The fact of Vyner being 'all powerful' was already having an effect on him, she said: 'He seems more steady, more knit together, but on the other hand more detached than ever.' Vyner wanted her to go out in February, and 'war or no war' she intended to do so. Apart from 'the intense desire to see him', she wanted, she said, 'to regain a footing in that aloof life of his, otherwise he will drift back to his hermit days and I shall consider my marriage an informal failure. Vyner has all the eccentricity of his father, coupled with the sweetest temper and sweetest disposition in the world. I think it is very wonderful that a man like that could ever have brought himself to marry . . .' She also wanted 'to know exactly what I am and what he wishes me to be in England. I must have a definite life, and enough money to live it on, then it doesn't matter so much his living away. He will never live long in England now, so I must organise myself.' She worried that his hatred of wasting money might 'become a mania . . . and I may find myself in lodgings in the Fulham Road. And also I fear his love of being alone will make it difficult for me to resume that cosy life we led for a few years at any rate. I am not afraid of other women taking him from me. I am not afraid of him ceasing to love me. When he thinks of anyone it is of me, that I know.'

In the meantime, apart from her handful of sentimental old men friends in London and the occasional leaves of Captain Gifford, Sylvia relied on Doll and Garsington for her social life. However, as she told her father, 'I find a little of Lady Ottoline goes miles with me – Also, the house is measly I am sure.' After another visit in August 1917, she wrote:

> Lady Ottoline's entourage appals me. The COs [conscientious objectors] are so awful – Flabby cowards – over-sexed – under-sexed – never normal. The conversation consists of depraved and curious conditions in life, so that you long for an ordinary couple to come in and say well we live an ordinary life, do things in the ordinary way and have ordinary children. At breakfast with your eggs and bacon you get a minute and detailed description of life à la Oscar Wilde. By dinner time the tales become more lurid. Elinor Glyn's *Three Weeks*[1] would pale before one day in the life of Mark Gertler, or Clive Bell. Doll sits smiling, hearing nothing, but with an expression on her face as much to say 'These are real talkers and brains. Away with your great wars and your great politicians and your great soldiers, these at Garsington are men of Kultur' – Oh it made me feel very sick inside. Clive Bell, whom Doll is always quoting as if he was Jesus Christ, is a fat greasy looking creature, with long Henna-coloured hair. He has a trick, most embarrassing, of fiddling with himself – all day and all the time. Doll wanted me to tell him not to. Oh, I tell you, I had to have a mental bath when I got home, as well as a bodily one . . .

During the damp autumn Sylvia was still troubled by her foot, and very thin, weighing just over seven stone. Yet money remained her chief preoccupation. Vyner had told her that it would look bad if he increased his own allowance, having just made several 'drastic reductions' in expenditure in Sarawak in order to pay for a new water supply and for the wireless. He also planned to borrow £100,000 at six per cent to pay for lighting Kuching with electric

[1] The novel that scandalised Edwardian society in 1907 with its account of an erotic affair between a callow Englishman and a mysterious older woman, the Queen of an unnamed Balkan state; the seduction scene on a tiger skin inspired the lines: Would you like to sin / With Elinor Glyn / On a tiger skin? / Or would you prefer / To err / With her / On some other fur?

street lamps, supplying all the outstations with launches, a new trading steamer and a new yacht for himself to replace the *Zahora*. In the meantime, Sylvia resented being in the hands of agents, who, if she had people to dinner, might query 'why so much food was bought on such and such a day. Vyner didn't mean to put me in a silly position. He did it to save me trouble, but it's the wrong sort of arrangement to have.'

> Vyner is a generous man still [she went on], but before all comes Sarawak. The money he considers is the people's money. He has got to save and save for the new water supply. He would live like Scrooge, or rather like a hermit in a cave, sooner than deprive the people of their rights. That is what he would do if he was unmarried. He gives me what he believes is enough and believe me it is no ungenerous sum; but anything over and above that, any luxury or extravagance, he does not like. You know darling, Vyner's a really noble character, a wonderful character, but like Gordon [of Khartoum] he should have walked the earth alone, hand in hand with God. You can't be a dreamer of dreams, a builder of ideals, a philanthropist, when there is anything so solid or so obvious as a wife and a lusty family tagging along after you.

Sylvia was also fretting again about the status of her daughters. 'They cannot and must not be Miss,' she wrote to Reggie. 'It is absurd, if we are going to try and keep the thing up over here. All this I mean to arrange when I go out. It is no good writing these things to Vyner, he doesn't attend, one must pin him down.'

By the beginning of 1918 Sylvia was again showing symptoms of tuberculosis, though, as Doll cheerfully reported, 'she has only just begun spitting'. Learning that Vyner was also ill in Sarawak, she sent a cable suggesting they both go to Africa to recover their health. Without, it seems, having received confirmation from Vyner that he would go along with her plan, she set off on 16 January with her six trunks of luggage from Birkenhead. Again Doll had planned to go with her, telling Reggie that it would be 'something to cast the war away from one', but yet again she changed her mind. Instead she agreed to oversee the care of Syv's children, helping the Swiss nanny Juliette Baillot, Lady Ottoline's former governess, who was teaching the girls French. Doll's constant demands for money while her sister was away raised a few eyebrows at the Sarawak government office at Millbank.

Sylvia was the only woman aboard the Japanese transport ship *Kitano Maru*, which to her delight was 'crammed full of Army and Navy officers', she wrote to her father. 'I have been as good as gold amongst these boys I hardly know myself. They are all very much in love and I spend most of my time trying to keep the peace. If I ask for anything six men rush headlong in pursuit of what I want.'

When she reached Cape Town, Vyner was not there. At first she assumed that her cloud-living husband had gone to the wrong port. If only. In fact he and Bertram (who had recently been made Inspector General of the Military and Police Forces in Sarawak) had travelled to Hong Kong, 'for a change', as the *Sarawak Gazette* put it, intending to return to Sarawak in March. Sylvia did not hear from Vyner for several weeks. In the meantime, with virtually no money, she was obliged to seek the help of the governor of South Africa, Lord Buxton, who guaranteed her good name at the Mount Nelson Hotel. There, in her hysterical state and with her peculiar title, Sylvia had at first been put in a room on the disreputable second floor. During the weeks that followed, waiting for Vyner, with little to do but bathe in the surf and window-shop, she lapsed into a strange state of mind. It was, she recalled in her second autobiography,

> as if some deeply-suppressed devil within me was fighting for release; a dangerous mood of relaxation and abandonment. I had never been interested in or attracted by young men before, or felt at ease with them; but there was something about being alone in a strange city in wartime that triggered off a recklessness in me. I flirted outrageously; and, of course, it ended up with a young man letting himself into my room and announcing that he was going to spend the night with me. Slowly he removed his coat; and then carefully took out his glass eye, which he placed on the mantelpiece, while I watched the performance, quite speechless. Even if I had been the most passionate woman in the world, I could not have sinned before that glittering and baleful orb. While the young man lay sprawled and snoring on my bed, I spent the night on an upright chair. In the morning he put on his

coat, put in his glass eye and swept out of the room. Needless to say he never spoke to me again. Then there was a rather good-looking Air Force officer who turned on me in an explosion of hatred and called me a frigid flirt. He threw me into a cactus bush and it took a whole day to get the thorns out of my behind. There was really nothing to be ashamed of in these limited indiscretions, these casual encounters with desire; though they were very shocking to me at the time.

Eventually she was invited to stay at Government House, and soon after that she received a cable from Vyner sending her money and saying that he would meet her in Singapore. Reunited after twenty months apart, they returned to Sarawak together in the steamship *Kuching*, arriving at Goebilt on 31 May 1918, to be met by Bertram who had travelled downriver the previous evening. In the capital, native boats, tongkangs and launches were decorated with flags and bunting to greet the new Ranee. A royal salute issued from the fort as the *Kuching* came past, followed by the noise of countless Chinese crackers from the opposite bank. Sylvia stood out on deck waving to her welcomers.

A guard of honour was drawn up in front of the Astana and, after the salute had been taken, Vyner and Sylvia were welcomed by all the Europeans and leading representatives of the Malay and Chinese communities. After dark, at seven, Sylvia, Vyner and Bertram went 'informally' across the river – lit up by many brilliantly illuminated boats – to be met by Mr Tiang Swee and other leaders of the Chinese community, who had organised a series of lantern processions. Chinese schoolboys marched past in their cadet uniforms with martial precision, each party halting as they came before the Ranee to greet her with a song of welcome. Later they went downriver to view the illuminations, while a motor launch alongside provided 'a very tolerable selection of music', as the *Sarawak Gazette* added. 'It was not until the early hours of next morning', the report ended, 'that the last light burnt out and the last revellers went home after proving, by the warmth of their welcome, the delight of all classes in the safe arrival of the Ranee.'

A month and a half later, on 22 July, Vyner took the oath of accession before the nineteenth Council Negri and a large gathering of the general public. As usual, he was hopelessly nervous beforehand and asked that there be no visiting heads of state, which would have entailed more ceremonious formality than he could cope with. At one point, according to Sylvia, he suggested that she should attend the ceremony alone and tell the people that he had suddenly been taken ill. A stiff whisky and constant encouragement eventually persuaded him to don his green uniform, with its golden palm-leaf braiding down the front and around the cuffs. However, it promptly tore at the shoulder where moths and silverfish had been at work, necessitating a swift repair job by his attendants.

Again the organisers of the ceremony had very little by way of precedent to go on, and the Resident, A. B. Ward, made enquiries of the aged *datus* who could remember the procedure when Rajah Charles had taken his oath fifty years previously. For the first time Ward learned that the cutlass carried by Sir James Brooke when he had rid the country of piracy was regarded as the symbol of sovereignty in Sarawak. The *datus* described how the sword should be presented to the Rajah 'to be touched and remitted by him in much the same way as the King Emperor acts when the Maharajahs in Durbar offer their swords'. After a lengthy search the sword was eventually found in the Astana. Its original scabbard had been lost, however, so a replacement wooden sheath with gold ornamentation was hastily commissioned from a local craftsman.

At nine o'clock Vyner and Sylvia, in a pale-pink frock and matching picture hat, emerged from the Astana, Bertram following behind with the cutlass, which had been laid on a silken cushion and, as Ward recalled, 'looked something like a sword of State'. Crossing the river in the state barge to the stone steps on the town side, where a band struck up the national anthem, they made their way along a sunlit avenue of masts, flags and festoons to the courthouse, where the installation ceremony was to take place. Vyner walked a little ahead, as usual, under the yellow umbrella, which had received a new silk covering for the occasion. The back of the courtroom was left open, to emphasise the right of the people to access their ruler freely. Inside, a hundred hand-picked Dyak and Kayan warriors, with their feathers, shields and spears, formed the bodyguard, while outside the Sarawak Rangers provided a guard of honour.

Vyner and Sylvia seated themselves on a dais beneath a canopy of gold brocade, some of which was later used to upholster the chairs in the Astana. The two principal Malay chiefs in their silken robes then slowly approached them. In a ringing voice the aged Datu Bandar announced that he was entrusting to the Rajah the sword of state, then raised the cushion to within his reach. Vyner gently laid his hand on the cutlass, accepting the charge with a few solemn words. The two chiefs then took a few steps back and, their hands joined before their faces, gave the Malay salutation of fealty, which was then repeated by all the other Malays in the room, and many of those outside. The Dyaks and Kayans shook their spears and uttered their war cries.

Finally, Vyner stepped down from the dais and, surrounded by his council, took the oath of accession in Malay, whereupon the national anthem was played and a royal salute issued from the fort guns. In this way Sylvia's husband was sworn in as the third White Rajah of Sarawak. She in turn, as his consort, became the first resident hostess at the Astana for nearly half a century.

8

DOING THE THINGS THAT RAJAHS HAVE TO DO

Soon after the coronation Vyner took Sylvia on her first trip into the interior, exploring jungle rivers and visiting longhouses belonging to tribal people who could be relied on for their friendliness to the Brooke Raj. A cluster of fish-traps and moored prahus announced their arrival at each settlement. At the landing place the headman, holding a flag, and other members of the household would troop down to the river and mob their new Rajah and Ranee, patting and stroking their arms, singing songs of welcome.

A traditional Dyak longhouse might consist of up to a hundred and twenty dwellings, built side by side on stilts, all under one roof. To reach each one Sylvia and Vyner invariably had to negotiate a slippery mudbank, then clamber up a near-vertical tree trunk, crudely notched with steps, to the common verandah, or *ruai*. Having made this none-too-graceful entrance, they would process along the gallery to the beating of gongs and drums, squat on the clean mats ceremoniously unrolled for them, admire a programme of dancing and incantations and politely sip *tuak* – 'a horrible rice drink', in Sylvia's estimation.

In a letter to Reggie, Sylvia pronounced herself thrilled by these new experiences, adding that the heat had completely cured her lungs. Vyner was also 'better than he has been for years', although, at the age of forty-four, his hair had turned almost white. Back in

Kuching, when not discharging her social and ceremonial duties as Ranee and occasionally acting as agony aunt to some of her female subjects, Sylvia spent her days completing her first novel, *Toys*, writing from dawn till noon, snoozing, receiving visitors and playing golf in the afternoon. Her novel was 'the best thing I have ever done', she told her father. 'It is certainly the most ambitious.'

Toys was based on an idea Sylvia had had as a child that 'the world was God's toyshop' and that souls were endlessly reincarnated and dressed up 'like dolls in a shop window'. She had been reminded of her theme when, on the bridge of one of the Japanese mailboats in which she had travelled to Sarawak during the war, the captain had told her that he had known her in a former life.

The novel begins with the story of a Malay foundling, Sudarah, who falls in love with a young fisherman, only to be murdered, along with her lover, by her jealous elderly guardian, who has been hoping to sell her into slavery. Her soul is reincarnated in another Malay girl, Serini, who marries an English colonial officer but is discarded when he returns from leave with a second, English wife, whereupon, like Madame Butterfly, Serini kills herself.

The third section of the book, 'In Which the Toy Discovers Itself', features four children with the same initials as those of the Brett children and a strong element of autobiography. Susannah (the new owner of the wandering soul) and her sister Deborah are orphans – at once perhaps a reflection of how Sylvia saw her childhood and a device for leaving out her parents, who were cut from the original version after Reggie said he found the unsympathetic depictions hurtful. When the book was published, privately at first, in 1920, Reggie then felt rather aggrieved at being left out, telling Oliver: 'It is better to be caricatured than ignored.' But Oliver said he should count himself lucky. 'I think Maurice is even worse in the book than I am,' he wrote to his father, 'and everybody was asking him whether he really did undress Sylvia in the woodshed!' It is hard to imagine Maurice relishing his portrayal as the insolent gardener's son Matthew – with 'shadows in his life and grim crookedness'.

Susannah, meanwhile, has many of the traits that Sylvia owned up to in her autobiographies, including her obsession with being ugly, her hatred of boys and her envy of her prettier (at least when they were young), more self-assured sister: 'Deborah was everything Susannah would have liked to have been. She was slender and erect, her large brown eyes were a little cold in expression perhaps, but her red lips were soft and full. Her skin was like pink fruit. Susannah loved her for her self-composed refinement.' Susannah eventually marries Raymond Drydone, a colonist clearly based on Vyner, and the soul passes on to their second daughter, Elissa, a pretty flirt who 'played on the hearts of men a tune for herself to dance to'; she leads on two devoted brothers, one of whom eventually kills her.

When Doll sent her friend Katherine Mansfield a copy of *Toys*, she wrote back telling Brett that she would rather not say what she thought in case it hurt her too deeply. Oliver was similarly unimpressed, pronouncing *Toys* 'very bad & sentimental – people don't write like that nowadays'. Reggie agreed that it was 'almost unreadable' – a fair enough assessment in stylistic terms – yet he did not dismiss Sylvia's ability. 'She is a clever little monkey,' he wrote to Chat the next year, 'and full of talent.' Several of his friends purported to agree. The former Lord Chancellor Viscount Haldane wrote to Sylvia after reading *Toys* saying he 'could not lay it down. I think it is a remarkable piece of work, which shows great artistic power . . . I congratulate you.' Algernon Blackwood, the writer of supernatural fiction, hailed it as 'a consistent study of rebirth logically carried out, and in places really wonderful . . . The way you show her soul in different settings, growing, struggling, yet always the same type *au fond*, is excellent; so are her reactions to various men.' However, he went on to suggest that the book suffered from 'a certain diffuseness' and would be better cut to a long short story.

Another problem seized on by critics was that reincarnation is far from ideal as a framework for fiction: 'The idea is not inherent, and remains an imposition,' said the *Times Literary Supplement* when the book was published by John Murray in 1923. 'The restless desires and dreaminess of youth gather no charm from being recollections of a former existence.' The *TLS* added: 'The style is in that kind of poetic falsetto that irritates at first, but it has something of the poppy in it and the common sense of the reader is quickly lulled to pleasant sleep.' Annoyingly for Sylvia, Ranee Margaret's miscellaneous collection of jottings entitled *Impromptus* was reviewed in the same edition of the *TLS* and fared rather better, hailed as 'very appealing' and fully justifying the recommendation of W. H. Hudson that they should be published.

While Sylvia wrote, Vyner got on with the business of ruling Sarawak or, as their daughter Elizabeth put it, 'doing the things that Rajahs have to do'. To begin with, at least, Vyner's routine in Kuching differed little from that of his father. Each weekday morning he would cross the river from the Astana to the government offices. On Mondays and Thursdays he would go 'in state', sheltered by the yellow umbrella borne by a sergeant of the Sarawak Rangers (in later years a policeman). When he landed at the other side, a guard of about five men presented arms. He then walked about a hundred yards beneath the umbrella to the government offices, a Malay retainer bringing up the rear carrying books and a paper umbrella in case it rained.

The Rajah would first call on the Resident and the treasurer, then sit himself down in his father's old office, open to the street, where he corresponded personally with the residents in each of Sarawak's five divisions and anyone who wished could queue up to talk to him. He was attended only by a couple of police constables to keep the queue orderly, though in practice there was never any trouble. The absence of any other officers meant that his confidants could talk at their ease. It was one of the great virtues of the Brooke Raj that the relations between the Rajah and his officers and the ordinary people of the land were far closer than anywhere elsewhere in the colonies.

In the evening the Rajah's subjects were free to go up to the Astana. Dyaks could drink the Rajah's gin, chew betel-nuts, spit out of the window and generally behave just as they behaved at home, until eight o'clock, when the second time-gun signalled that it was time for his visitors to leave, as the Rajah was about to have dinner.

Like his father, though to a lesser extent than the first Rajah, Vyner occasionally took court cases in Kuching, until the arrival of a judicial commissioner from England in 1928. According to Sylvia, it was 'a most terrible ordeal' for him to pronounce the death sentence, as he occasionally did on those who had murdered 'merely for money'. Those, on the other hand, who had killed their wives' lovers were sentenced to a long term of imprisonment. The new Rajah soon gained a reputation as a soft touch, with a tendency to commute death sentences and impose hard labour instead. At one time it was said that there were nine convicted murderers working as gardeners in the grounds of the Astana.

At other times Vyner liked to wander about the bazaars dressed in a white drill suit, open-neck shirt and topee, chatting to his subjects. 'Travelling with him could be a nightmare,' recalled one of his officers; 'he would wander off among Malays, Dyaks and Chinese until we lost him – once we found him discussing school meals with the Chinese cook. He spent hours talking to people about their lives, far more interested in them than in their leaders, whose conversation often bored him.'

The new Rajah's style of ruling was more relaxed than that of his father, and he was seen as affable and approachable, although his officers attested that he could also 'chill unsuitable familiarity by a glance from his cold blue eyes'. His dignity was equal to his charm, and he was almost always known as 'Rajah' – no one, apart from his family or close friends, dreamt of addressing him otherwise. His preferred way of giving orders was to take an officer aside for a friendly chat in the course of which he would suggest what the officer should do. Provided that the officer took the hint, the Rajah would continue to hold him in the highest esteem. If the officer thought he knew better and did something else, he was apt to end up in one of the furthest outstations. 'He never sought popularity,' wrote Edward Banks, 'and must have offended many people, but he was so charming later on when he made it up, only a churl could hold it against him . . . He disliked giving orders nearly as much as being told what to do.'

Although the war had not affected Sarawak militarily, the departure of many of the younger European officers to the front meant that the Sarawak service became very short-staffed. After his oath of accession, in order to help make up the numbers Vyner was persuaded to recruit a shell-shocked friend of Sylvia's, Nigel Long, whom he gave a job in the police. The appointment was not a success. As Sylvia told Reggie, every time the five o'clock gun went off Long had to be 'strapped to his bed to prevent him running amock amongst the natives – he thinks they are Germans. It's hopeless shell-shockers coming out here . . . too bad a place for nerves.'

The Rajah still mounted occasional operations in the interior against recalcitrant Dyaks, a few of whom persisted in headhunting for criminal purposes. In April 1919, while Vyner was in England, his brother Bertram, who discharged his responsibilities in the power-sharing arrangement conscientiously and selflessly, led a successful expedition against the rebellious Gaat Dyaks in the upper Baleh river. 'With small loss of life', the *Sarawak Gazette* reported, 'a severe lesson was given to the rebels who fled to Dutch territory from where they were subsequently handed over to the government and settled under more immediate supervision.'

The wireless, one of the old Rajah's few concessions to technological progress, had rapidly become a part of life in Sarawak, bringing news from Singapore each morning in place of the weeks-old copies of *The Times* that the Europeans had previously made do with. Early in the morning of 12 November 1918 the wireless brought news of the Armistice, which had been signed the previous day and was celebrated throughout Sarawak. Vyner sent a telegram of congratulations to the King, which elicited, by way of reply, 'hearty thanks for the ready and ungrudging co-operation of Sarawak throughout the long struggle'.

Sylvia left Sarawak three days after the Armistice, returning to Wimbledon and her children. To her dismay, their governess, Juliette Baillot, had recently become engaged to the zoologist and philosopher Julian Huxley, Aldous's elder brother, who had proposed during a wintry walk while visiting Juliette up at Callander; she and the Brooke girls had been staying there in a house called Glengarry, near to their grandparents at the Roman Camp. As Juliette recalled, Ranee Sylvia

> lost no opportunity of pointing out Julian's unsuitability in almost every aspect of marriage, his unparalleled self-will which she prophesied I would never be able to cope with. I would, she said, simply be eaten alive. She also painted in glowing terms the chances of greater happiness out of his orbit, tempting me with Sarawak and its half-tamed headhunters, its deep jungle

> mysteries. Small and neat as an exotic princess . . . she sat by the fire at Tilney House and warned me by the hour. Her affectionate concern troubled me, but not sufficiently to turn me aside.

Juliette and Julian Huxley were married in March 1919, and remained so until his death in 1975; but, as Sylvia had predicted, he proved a wilful and destructive husband at times, and Juliette certainly put on a less brave face than did Sylvia when they wrote about their husbands' shameless infidelities.

While in London, Sylvia also made use of her parents' house on Tilney Street, in Mayfair, along with Doll, who was tiring of Garsington and, with the war over, now deemed it safe to be back in London. The sisters' behaviour soon upset the housekeeper, Mrs Hooper, and in the spring of 1919 she handed in her notice to Reggie and Nellie, referring gravely to the 'goings on' at their house: Doll had been allowing Mark Gertler and co. to sleep on the floor in their clothes and make a terrible mess of the place, while Sylvia had invited her friend Captain Gifford to dinner then allowed him to stay the night.

Nellie wrote to both her daughters, telling Doll that 'entertaining your friends and using the house as a furnished hotel are not the same thing'. To the charges levelled at her Sylvia responded facetiously by vowing

> hereby not to set foot in, or approach the door of Tilney Street – during your absence or at any other time should you not desire it. Nor will I ring up or in any way interfere, or shock, or create 'goings on', whatever they may be. What it is, is, one has rather believed in the milk of human kindness which in this case seems to have turned a bit sour – I know for a fact that there have been no goings on in your house and neither Doll nor I are living with any man (except Vyner) and the only man I have ever had up in your bedroom in Tilney Street is Lawrence [Burgis], who insisted on coming up when his wife was in the house, result, I have been ruled out of the Lorna menage – No, Doll and I aren't prostitutes, though we do unconventional things – I am sorry if there has been any gossip and I apologise for any folly I may have committed – It shall not occur again.

Reggie accused Sylvia of deceit. She accused her father of listening

> to the ravings of a neurotic servant [Mrs Hooper] who is so hysterical and talks so fast that she doesn't know half the time what she is saying . . . If she said that I had Captain Gifford to stay, that is true. If she said I paid for the dinner that is also true. But if she said I paid for dinner in order to keep it out of the House Books so that you should not discover, that is a damned lie. And if she said he came up to my room, that is also a damned lie. Nothing went on in your house that couldn't have happened in a glass house with everyone looking in except that I had a bath. I paid for my dinner because I had a guest, and I thought it not only unfair but rather ugly that you should have to pay for a thing which I knew would be distasteful to you – Any idea of concealing it from you never entered my mind.

Doll, too, found it hard to believe that their mother had 'swallowed whole everything Mrs H chose to tell you – a woman of highly strung nerves'. She also warned Reggie to be careful with what he said to Sylvia.

> She is very bitter, nervous people nearly always are . . . the last doctor who examined her told Vyner that he ought to look after her well because in her present condition she ran a great danger of going mad when her change of Life came. I think it was foolish of Vyner to tell Syv this, but I tell you this *privately* because it may help you in your dealings with her – only I would not say you knew to her unless she tells you herself – it is not a good thing to have pressed into one. Nerves play the very devil with people & change them beyond recognition & with very little realisation of it themselves & it does no good telling them – because I've tried & I know.

In a subsequent letter she said that she thought her sister was being a fool over her airman: 'Vyner is worth 300 Giffords.'

The whole saga seems to have persuaded Sylvia that it was time to find another London house of her own, and soon after Vyner came back in March they were installed at number 8 Airlie Gardens, a tall sliver of a house on Campden Hill. From here Leonora and Elizabeth went to school for the first time on the other side of Holland Park Avenue, at Norland Place; they played with the daughter of a chauffeur across the street and, according to Sylvia, they all lived quietly and unobtrusively and seldom went out. By way of recreation, she and Vyner began frequenting Holland Park roller-skating rink 'to be dragged round and round by eager instructors'. Visitors to their house would occasionally be confronted by the sight of the Rajah gliding past them on his skates across the parquet floor, out of control, a cushion stuffed down his trousers in case he fell.

Much of the summer was spent at Orchard Lea, which they used as a base for racing, although they had to abandon their house party during the royal meeting at Ascot to go and bury the old Rajah in Devon – 'an awful nuisance,' Sylvia told Reggie. Among the guests whom they were deserting were Doll, Maurice and Zena, Vyner's younger brother Harry Brooke, his uncle the explorer Harry de Windt, and the ever-present Captain Gifford; Carrington had declined Doll's invitation to join this motley group.

As they prepared to return to Sarawak that autumn, and to take with them all three of their daughters, Doll, who had recently healed her old rift with Ranee Margaret by paying her a visit in September, again asked if she might go with them. Vyner stalled. 'Doll would never be happy in Sarawak,' he wrote to Reggie. 'She is far too nervous and the stingy things would be too much for her. She will never be happy wherever she may be. She is too unsettled to be happy and does not know what she wants.' He persuaded her on that occasion not to go; and although she contemplated several further trips, including in 1927, when she suggested going with D. H. Lawrence, Doll never would make it to Sarawak.

Sylvia and Vyner reached the mouth of the Sarawak river at four in the morning of 11 December 1919. In view of the ungodly hour the Rajah had asked that there be no official reception, although this did not prevent the band of the Sarawak Rangers from striking up the national anthem as the *Kuching* rounded the fort. All guards stood to attention, and there was the customary salute of twenty-one guns.

The Chinese shop-houses on the other bank of the river responded with a fusillade of fireworks. That afternoon the entire European population assembled at the Ranee's Club, as the ladies' club had now become known, and warmly welcomed her back.

Six weeks after they got there they were joined by Captain Barry Gifford, who had now been gazetted as aide-de-camp to Vyner. Even taking into account his vagueness, it is hard to believe that Vyner knew nothing of what had been going on between his wife and his new ADC. Vyner had, after all, arrived back in England the previous March, a month before the row over Tilney Street blew up, and Sylvia was not renowned for her tact. Indeed, as Reggie had complained, she was positively parading her love for her airman. The fact that Gifford had suffered from shell-shock ought also have counted against his appointment in Sarawak. It is possible, therefore, that there was some quid pro quo whereby both the Rajah and Ranee would be allowed to have their liaisons.

The new ADC was expected to perform a wide variety of duties. One of his first tasks was to help Vyner and the superintendent of police fire off a few test bursts of a new consignment of lightweight Lewis guns, intended to be useful for jungle fighting during expeditions against refractory Dyaks. Later that year he took part in a scientific expedition into the interior of the Baram district; and in April 1921, by which time both Vyner and Sylvia were back in England again, he was assigned the responsibility of escorting Somerset Maugham round the country.

Maugham had arrived in Sarawak on 2 April intent on a trip into the interior to gather material for his fiction. Then at the height of his fame as a playwright and author, he had separated from his wife and taken up with Gerald Haxton, the love of his life, with whom he travelled the world. On the crossing to Kuching from Singapore he had had his typewriter and keys stolen, and further misfortune was to follow him in Sarawak.

Gifford took Maugham and Haxton first to Simanggang, where they recruited a crew of miscreants from the jail to row them on up the Batang Lupar river, spending two days in Dyak longhouses. Maugham found his Dyak hosts polite and hospitable, although, as he observed in one of his short stories, 'no one could say that there was much comfort to be found in their houses, and there was a monotony in the entertainment they offered a guest which presently grew wearisome'.

The Batang Lupar is notorious for its bore, a large wave that surges up the river during spring tide at two to three times the speed of the tidal current. The Batang Lupar's is one of the fiercest in Borneo and a careful calculation of the tides is necessary to be sure of avoiding it, a calculation the Maugham party evidently failed to make. At Lubok Naga, downriver from Simanggang, they saw two or three waves approaching from some way off but did not immediately apprehend the danger. Then, suddenly, with a roar the bore was upon them, a ten-foot high wall of water that quickly turned the boat broadside and carried it along on its seething crest. Presently they were all flung into the water. Maugham's first impulse was to swim to shore, about fifty yards away, but Gifford yelled at him to hang on to the boat as he would never have made it.

They clung on to the gunwales, still being swept along on the wave, until the boat began to turn over and they lost their hold. They regained a grip on the keel, but again the boat turned 'so that we were like squirrels in cage', as Maugham recalled. Their ordeal – later used as the basis for Maugham's story 'The Yellow Streak' – lasted for around half an hour, during which time they frequently went under, swallowed a great deal of water and became utterly exhausted. Eventually they drifted nearer the bank and two of the prisoners passed Maugham a soaked mattress, which he used as a lifebelt to enable him and Haxton to swim to the shore, again helped by the two prisoners. It is not clear how Gifford made it out. When they got back to Kuching, their survival was deemed miraculous, the *Sarawak Gazette* remarking solemnly: 'We can only be thankful that the incident did not have a more serious termination.'

Before leaving for Singapore, on 18 April, Maugham wrote to the Resident at Simanggang asking him if he could possibly commute the sentences of the two prisoners who had saved their lives. The Resident replied that one man had been set free but that he could do nothing for the other, who, on the way back to Simanggang, had stopped off at his village and killed his mother-in-law.

Maugham used his travels in Sarawak for several of his stories, published in *The Casuarina Tree* in 1926, which offer a rare outsider's view of life there between the wars. Sarawak is thinly disguised as

'Sembulu', the Rajah as the Sultan, Kuching as Kuala Solor. The stories are among Maugham's finest, particularly 'The Outstation', featuring the meticulous Resident Mr Warburton and his uncouth new assistant Mr Cooper, thrown together because they are the only two white men there. Warburton has come to Sembulu after running through a fortune in England, but even at this remote outstation he still dresses for dinner, reads *The Times* each Monday from Monday six weeks ago, and remains inordinately proud of the fact that his name figures in *Burke's Peerage*, however insignificantly. Cooper earns Warburton's contempt by dressing carelessly and – to his ultimate cost – treating the natives badly. Maugham's other Sarawak stories feature district officers who drink too much and those whose marriages are complicated by their previous liaisons with native women. As with his stories set in Malaya, those set in Sarawak caused a great deal of resentment, not least because they were so close to the bone, and many of the officers who had confided in him felt betrayed. At the time (in his 'Postscript') Maugham emphasised that his stories were fiction and the characters no more than composites of people he had met; however, he later admitted that some stories had been verbatim descriptions of what he had seen and heard, and that he had taken little trouble to disguise the material. Sylvia and Vyner could perhaps count themselves fortunate to have missed his visit.

They were at the time back in England, where during the 1920s Sylvia, partly because of her indifferent health, would spend an average of eight months a year, Vyner about six months – though sometimes longer – usually arriving back in England in time for the flat-racing season, while Bertram took charge of the government in Kuching. When they returned to Sarawak, in the autumn of 1921, this time accompanied by Barry Gifford, who had come back to England after the Maugham visit, Vyner had been away for just over a year, Sylvia slightly longer. They were accorded the usual elaborate welcome, the *Sarawak Gazette* declaring that 'all are glad to see both His Highness and the Ranee looking so well from their change home'. They arrived on 3 October in time for 'Joy Week' – seven days of parties and firework displays culminating in the all-European Fancy Dress Dance at 'the BMK', the gloomy mansion belonging to the Borneo Company. Captain Gifford won first prize in the fancy-dress competition for his 'quite unrecognisable disguise' as Mr Wu, reported the *Gazette*, while Sylvia also caught the eye dressed as a Turkish lady.

Thereafter they settled back into their old routine, which was none too arduous judging by Sylvia's description:

> We woke at 6 am and went from our bedrooms to the coolness of the verandah where we drank tea and ate mango and pawpaw. We gloried in the sun rising slowly through a soft grey mist, and the little town emerging gay and colourful from its cloak of night. Cocks would begin to crow and Chinese water-carriers would herald the dawning of the day. At 7 am, we were served with the rest of our breakfast, still on the cool verandah. During the early morning Vyner and I went about our special occupations; I to my writing and painting [during the 1920s she exhibited at several London galleries, and also illustrated some of her books, including *The Cauldron* (1925)] and he to his law chair and books. Like his father, he wasn't one for comfort, and sat in a canvas deck-chair, which was usually torn. At eight o'clock he would cross the river to the Court House. When the Court was in session he would be accompanied by his official guard, and would walk beneath the yellow umbrella carrying a walking stick with a heavily embossed silver handle which was the emblem of his office.
>
> After he had left I would often relax in the swimming pool with a gin sling, or go shopping in the bazaar, or visit some friends. At noon the cannon boomed and Vyner would return to the Astana. We would have a few drinks before lunch and then as soon as we had finished it was siesta time; at least for me, if not for Vyner. Back he would go to his old deck-chair, his cigar and his books.
>
> At 3:30pm we kept a kind of open court when the Malays, Dayaks and Chinese were welcome visitors at the Astana. There were no formalities or presentations; they just came and went as they wished. Vyner received the men in one group, while I, in my limited Malay, endeavoured to entertain the women. The talk would mostly be about the grievances and problems of their homes, the men complaining about their shrewish, jealous wives,

> and the women about the meanness of their husbands. What they were usually after was a small loan to buy or repair a house, or to purchase a sarong, bracelet, or brooch. At four-thirty these interviews would end, and we were free to cross the river to play golf or tennis, or go for a drive along our one road. Then we would go to the Club for billiards, or Mah Jong and drinks.
>
> On Saturday evenings Vyner held a roulette game, for women only; and every Sunday we had a swimming party with gin slings and an enormous curry. There was not much outside entertainment in Sarawak and we had to do the best we could with the materials to hand. But we had fun.

Vyner and Sylvia saw to it that social life for the Europeans in Kuching became livelier than it had been in the days of Rajah Charles, with more parties, more dancing, more amateur theatricals – many of them organised by Sylvia – more trips on their yacht to Santubong and race week twice a year when all the outstation officers converged on Kuching. But it was still rather limited by the standards of home, not least owing to the fact that by 1925 there were no more than three or four European women in the capital, and a decade later still only twenty or so. A mixed club was opened in 1923, though, in Sylvia's eyes, it was 'arranged in such a way that none of the men were forced into the presence of women'; and it was still very much the preserve of Europeans. Much as Vyner genuinely cared about the natives and their interests, there does not seem to have been a great deal of socialising between the different races. Stirling Boyd, the Scottish barrister who arrived in Sarawak in 1928 to take up the newly created post of judicial commissioner – the first trained lawyer to be appointed in Sarawak – wrote to his mother shortly after he got there that it was 'hardly true to say that the Rajah treats the natives as equals in society. I believe he occasionally asks a few to a party at the Astana, but he never includes them in the regular entertainments he gives to Europeans.' Those entertainments occasionally included balls, during which the Malay and Dyak mistresses of the European bachelor officers would sometimes climb into the trees in order to see how many dances their man was having with each white woman. For the natives, meanwhile, there was a weekly open-air film show at the Astana, which would be attended by up to a thousand.

Averil Mackenzie-Grieve, the writer and artist, who first arrived in Sarawak with her then husband Cyril Le Gros Clark in the mid-1920s, recalled that in the limited European society in Kuching they gave and attended 'formal and elaborate dinner parties at which we all wore evening dress and always met the same people in various permutations. After dinner there was no talk, only bridge, mah-jongg, and for tough old hands, poker and much whisky.' The Rajah, she wrote, 'had all the Brooke charm but like Disraeli's Lord Monmouth, "he wished above all cost to be amused". To this end he devised various forms of entertainment for his officers' wives and indulged his hobbies in a large way. One year he was all for making expert marksmen of us and we were invited once a week to the Astana gardens where, provided with rifles, we had to shoot an apple (cold storage) from the head of a Dyak carved figure. Prizes ranged from a length of silk to a leg of mutton.'

Like his father (who addressed his girlfriends in French), only more so, Vyner had a roving eye. It was well known that Sylvia liked to vet new appointees to the Sarawak Civil Service to ensure that they would be social assets, but Vyner was often more interested in his officers' wives, and he made no attempt to conceal his liaisons from Sylvia. By Sylvia's account he also had a string of Sarawakian mistresses, several of whom came to live with the Brooke family at the Astana, to be looked upon by his three daughters as elder sisters. Sylvia affected to have tolerated his behaviour as 'part of his colour and charm . . . his little foolishness', adding that in any case it was not entirely his fault, for although she had 'thawed considerably in the Sarawak sun, I was still, to all intents and purposes, a frigid woman'. She 'knew them all, in Sarawak and in England', she wrote, and indeed at times, she even acted as go-between. Vyner would sometimes pass on love letters he had received, and he volunteered to get rid of any girlfriends that she did not approve of. 'They came in all shapes and sizes. There was one, I remember, who had a mania for turning somersaults, presumably in order to display her very beautiful legs. There was an opera singer he took to Ascot Races, where she fainted over the rails; and there was one who liked being made love to over the back of a chair. I thought this somewhat unusual, but there is no accounting for tastes.' During more than fifty years of married life, Sylvia recalled that she only asked her husband to discard three – 'One was a gold-digger, one a thundering bore, and the other a nymphomaniac.'

In her handwritten memoir, Elizabeth, too, remembered that her father was

> madly good-looking and females swarmed around him like flies. Mummy didn't seem to mind. I don't think it would have made any difference if she did. Daddy was a terrible flirt and nanny Valentine, who was with us until we were boarding school age, and a French governess called Marie, caught his roving eye. We never had much schooling. As we were in England for half the year most of the time we had to make do with numerous governesses . . . once we had two sisters, aged between 50 and 60, draped in black – I'm sure Mummy must have chosen them to spite Daddy.

However much she told herself that her husband would never leave her, Sylvia admitted that other women 'formed the clouds that menaced my marriage . . . I was never jealous, but I was mortally afraid.' As if to get her own back, in her second autobiography, published seven years after Vyner's death, she rated her husband less than good in bed, recalling that he 'made love as he played golf – in a nervous unimaginative flurry'. She also admitted to having been a flirt herself, a fact she ascribed to her rigid upbringing which had meant that she 'knew nothing of men'. 'I was curious; I think I actually wanted to be made love to; and it was all too easy for me to encourage our Government officers that if they addressed their attentions to me, I would influence Vyner to promote them.'

After three months in Sarawak, Sylvia travelled back to England early in 1922, arriving in London on 2 February. Three weeks after she got back she learned that her former landlord, Loulou Harcourt, who had been created a viscount in 1916, had died after taking an overdose of sleeping draught. Suicide was widely suspected, and although the coroner rejected the idea as 'grotesque', suicide it most probably was. Shortly before Loulou's death Sylvia's thirteen-year-old cousin Edward James (later a patron of her sister Doll, another of Loulou's victims) had been taken to stay at Nuneham. He later recalled that the fifty-nine-year-old Lord Harcourt had spent the whole weekend trying to grope him. Before they'd left, Edward had been reluctant to go along with his mother's suggestion that he should go and say goodbye. 'Finally she made me,' he recalled. 'I came in at one end of a long, long room and he [Harcourt] was lying in bed at the other end, a bed with steps. He said, "Come nearer, child. Come nearer!" So I came a little nearer and made my speech. "Mummy wants me to thank you for a lovely weekend etc . . ." And then suddenly he threw back the bedclothes revealing a large and hideous erection; he looked like an old goat with his large drooping beard and I ran out of the room.' Edward subsequently told his mother, and soon all of London was talking about it. Not long afterwards, on 24 February 1922, Harcourt was found dead.

Reggie was in Paris representing Britain at the disarmament conference when he heard the news. He wrote to Oliver that it was 'a dreadful affair . . . Loulou is a real loss, always reliable in a crisis. It is another link with the past snapped.' It is doubtful that Doll felt quite so devastated. She had told her father the previous year that Loulou had caused her 'an irreparable injury, which was perhaps the chief cause of my seeming waywardness. Such things happen and it is natures like mine, the most unaware and innocent, that become the most suspicious and so I have had to find my own way in everything . . .' What Sylvia made of Loulou's death is hard to tell, as it is not mentioned in either of her autobiographies and her weekly letters to Reggie after 1920 were either lost or destroyed by her brother Oliver.

Sylvia's health was still not good and in the spring of 1922, while staying with her parents at the Roman Camp, she was again taken ill and confined to bed, this time suffering from jaundice. 'It is not easy to make out what is the matter,' Reggie wrote to Maurice. 'She is just as inaccurate about herself as she is about everything else.' When she felt well enough to return south, she went to lunch with Maurice, who was shocked by her pale, skeletal appearance, though at the same time he noted that 'she seemed much *nicer*, less catty etc'. Although Reggie worried about Sylvia's health, she continued to get on his nerves. As far as he was concerned, he told Oliver, she was a hopelessly silly creature, with no sort of perspective in life, while Vyner was 'a perfect loony of a husband'. In the autumn of 1922, when Vyner and Sylvia again suggested that they might like to take on Orchard Lea, Reggie refused to correspond on the subject. 'It is now scotched,' he wrote to Maurice on 26 October, 'and I am glad. But it required some diplomacy. I had rather the house tumbled down.' A few days later he wrote: 'Never *entre nous* would I have agreed. But I had to be careful . . . There is something that attaches me to its memories. Those drives home with you in the evenings. Your constant companionship. I could not stand their effacement by the Brooke family, to which I am not at all attached.'

Shortly afterwards Reggie was greatly relieved to hear that Sylvia had found another town house. 'If it comes off, it is the best solution,' he told Maurice. Which it probably was, for Sylvia as well. For although the girls were happy at Orchard Lea, neither Vyner nor Sylvia had ever felt that the house was really theirs, and while its memories may have been precious to Reggie, it evoked rather less happy ones for Sylvia. With Oliver having rejected the opportunity to live there in favour of buying Watlington Park, near Henley, and Maurice unable to afford it, Orchard Lea was eventually sold to one of Loulou Harcourt's daughters, and is now a 'business centre'.

Sylvia and Vyner went back out to Sarawak again in the summer of 1923, this time taking eleven-year-old Leonora and her Scottish nursemaid Jessie Taylor with them, and arriving at Kuching in August after stops at Rangoon and Singapore. Again Sylvia was unwell for much of the time and by the time she began the journey back to England in November, she weighed just six stone three. Leonora and Jessie stayed on with Vyner, which 'must have been a great nuisance and a bore for my father', wrote Leonora. 'Never a man who enjoyed family life, to suddenly become saddled with what almost amounted to a nursery must have cramped his style quite a bit.' Like Sylvia with Reggie, Leonora had always craved Vyner's attention: 'I would try to climb onto my father's knees sometimes when he seemed in a mellow mood. "No sob stuff," he would say irritably.' At dinner parties, if she was silent, he would shout at her down the table, 'When's the funeral?' If on the other hand she got overexcited and talkative it was, 'Stop showing off!'

At the end of the month the Rajah took Leonora and Jessie with him on a trip up the Rejang river. Travelling in the old Rajah's yacht *Zahora*, they first had to make their way round the coast through choppy sea, which always frightened Leonora. But her father was intolerant of her 'unnecessary fears'; he placed a glass of water on the deck table and told her that only when it skidded off would she be allowed to be afraid. Whenever she fell ill on the trip (during which she menstruated for the first time, and was pounced on by a naked American oil driller in his cabin) he dosed her with Epsom salts and told her it was effeminate to consult a doctor. But such was the awe in which she held him that she 'knew no harm would come to me'.

Their first stop was the town of Sibu, where Vyner presided in court for two days before continuing to Kapit, a hundred and sixty miles upriver. At the various places they visited there would nearly always be a Dyak dance in the Rajah's honour, with Leonora and her father sitting on wooden chairs draped in the royal yellow.

> To start the ball rolling, so to speak [Leonora recalled], the Chief of the Long House would kill a white cock and sprinkle the blood over us to send away any evil spirits that might be lurking about. Then, with his own fair hands, usually covered with korup, a skin ailment all Dyaks seemed to have, he would feed us eggs that had been buried for years, coal black and horrible.
>
> My father never flinched. He always knew what to say to the Dyaks; sitting smoking his cigar, joking with the women so that even the most ancient crones giggled and hid their faces. Sometimes these dances went on for hours, shining brown bodies leaping and twisting in the orange light of the torches, the sleepy beat of the slindangs and sudden war cries that would wake me from a trance. But Daddy never seemed tired or bored, and I was both. No wonder they loved him.

They stayed at Kapit for several days while Vyner conducted interviews with Sea Dyaks from further upstream who had been engaged in a bloody feud with the Kayans and kindred tribes from over the border in Dutch Borneo. The feud had a history going back more than thirty years, and had flared up in 1921 after the gruesome murder of fifteen Sea Dyaks on the Iwan river. Now a solution was being sought by the mercurial young officer then in charge of Kapit, one Gerard MacBryan. A handsome man with a very plausible manner, MacBryan came in due course to exert a mesmeric hold over Vyner, eventually threatening the very existence of the Brooke Raj.

9

BY JOVE WHAT A WONDERFUL FELLOW; BUT HE'S NUTS

The stay at Kapit was not Vyner's first encounter with MacBryan. According to Sylvia, they had both met him shortly after his first arrival in Sarawak as a nineteen-year-old in June 1920. MacBryan had at that time been posted to Limbang, in the remote far north-east of the country, to assist the district officer F. F. Boult. Boult's wife Nellie had travelled with him in the steamer along the coast from Kuching, and while she had found him charming and exquisitely mannered, she had been concerned that he appeared to be highly strung and 'full up with superstition'. During the voyage, he had told her that he had seen an enormous ghost rising from the sea while he was taking his watch. Some time after they had arrived, she had recorded in her diary that he was still 'a mass of nerves' and that although he declared himself to be a keen naturalist he 'sleeps with windows and doors hermetically sealed, jumps at insects etc'. When they had heard that he preferred to roost with the off-duty Dyak rangers in the guardroom rather than be alone in the officers' quarters in the courthouse, Nellie Boult had tactfully suggested that he might like to spend the evenings with them and sleep the night at their house. MacBryan had leapt at the idea.

Word soon reached Kuching of 'strange goings on' at Limbang, so Sylvia later related. MacBryan was said to be hallucinating that his bungalow was being attacked, and would start shooting wildly into the darkness. The crude execution by firing squad of a Malay man for murder finally tipped him over the edge, making him 'very wild and mad', whereupon Boult wrote to Kuching requesting that MacBryan be moved. So it was, by Sylvia's account, that he was summoned to the capital to be interviewed by the Rajah, at which point the Ranee also set eyes on him for the first time. He was 'tall and unnaturally thin', she wrote, 'and he wore an enormous sombrero hat. He was extremely good-looking with a pallid skin and small grey-green eyes that were never still. His greatest charm was his laugh; it shook his whole frame . . . Vyner had a talk with him; and after he had left he leaned back in his chair and said, "By Jove, Mip, what a wonderful fellow; but he's nuts." ' MacBryan certainly was unbalanced, as later events showed; Bertram recalled that in Kuching he could be heard at night hurling his bedroom furniture out of the window at imaginary assailants, accompanied by a torrent of invective. But while the spooky jungle of Limbang may have exacerbated his instability, the root causes seem to have lain in the circumstances of his childhood. Gerard Truman Magill MacBryan was born in Wiltshire on 9 January 1902, the youngest of five sons of Eveline and Dr Henry MacBryan, who ran a private asylum, Kingsdown House, at Box, near Chippenham, reputedly the oldest licensed madhouse in England. His mother died immediately after he was born. Gerard later told Sylvia how, when he was a boy, his father had insisted on taking him on his rounds and how terrified he had been of the 'incoherent ravings of the patients'. He was sent as a border to Naish House (now St Christopher's) school at Burnham-on-Sea, where on one occasion he was arraigned for stealing before an assembly of the school and only saved from being expelled by the sporting prowess of his elder brother Jack, later a Test and county cricketer and Olympic hockey gold medallist.

During the First World War, unlike his elder brothers, who had been expressly forbidden from having anything to do with the patients or staff of the asylum, Gerard became well acquainted with the whole place. But when Jack MacBryan returned from Holland in 1918, where he had been a prisoner-of-war for four years, he found Kingsdown House in a dilapidated state, his father having succumbed to drink and failed to collect the fees from the familes of his patients. Jack soon discovered that Gerard had made his father believe that he

(Jack) had been conspiring against him; within a week of arriving home he was thrown out of the house and was subsequently disinherited.

Gerard, meanwhile, entered Dartmouth as a cadet, but ultimately failed to gain entry into the Navy after failing his Navigation, despite having previously been easily top in that subject. Jack later suggested that he had done so intentionally, possibly out of fear: he said that Gerard had told him how, when confronted with the task of mounting the mast of the sailing vessel on his 'cruise', he had paid an able seaman to do it in his place. Shortly afterwards, at the Bath and Country Club, of which his father was a member, he met H. F. Deshon, a former member of the Sarawak service, with whom Vyner had led the disastrous expedition against Banting in 1902. Deshon was now retired and living in Wiltshire, and he painted in glowing colours the freedom of a district officer's life. Gerard MacBryan was excited by the idea of joining the service, and after being interviewed in London by a panel chaired by Bertram Brooke, he headed out to Sarawak. According to Sylvia, Vyner was at this time 'quite unaware that he was anything but a perfectly normal fellow, who had had an unhappy time in the Navy'.

After his unhappy stint at Limbang, MacBryan was posted as a cadet to Sibu, in 1921, and the next year he was appointed officer in charge of Kapit. Despite his nervousness, his outstanding ability quickly to master the various Dyak and Malay languages and his close study of their customs greatly impressed Vyner, who was far from being a natural linguist himself. MacBryan affected to despise Europeans and associated little with them. Yet even Bertram conceded that he was 'extraordinarily efficient with office work', and had 'an active brain, with flashes of brilliancy – his intimate personal knowledge of the lives and history of the Asiatics amongst whom he moves is unparalleled'.

Later, in 1922, MacBryan undertook the extremely hazardous journey from Kapit to Long Nawan, 360 miles upriver over countless sets of rapids and cascades, with the aim of arranging a peacemaking ceremony to end the long-running cross-border feud. MacBryan had in mind a ritual involving the killing of pigs, similar to that which had been performed to good effect at Simanggang in 1920. Arrangements were discussed, but by the time Vyner arrived at Kapit, in 1923, they had been thwarted by disagreements between the parties. So in early 1924 MacBryan repeated the journey to Long Nawan, this time accompanied by a number of senior Sea Dyak chieftains, including the famous warrior Koh, then aged fifty-four and the recognised leader of the Dyaks of the Rejang. With his heavy tattoos, boars' tusks through his ears and 'amazing muscles', Koh was a great favourite of Ranee Sylvia, who loved listening to his legends, recited in his high sing-song voice, or watching him dance, when 'the ecstasy in his half-closed eyes contained a whole alien world'.

The party were well received, and a preliminary peacemaking ceremony was held, according to Kenyah customs, at Long Nawan. It was further agreed that the main ceremony would take place in November 1924 at Kapit, in accordance with the customs of the Sea Dyaks. Vyner again made the journey from Kuching in the Rajah's yacht *Zahora* to preside at this ceremony, arriving at Kapit on 12 November with Captain Gifford. The Rajah's arrival was heralded by cannon fire from the fort, and the many hundreds of Dyaks gathered along the banks of the river in their elaborate warcoats and hornbill headdresses, uttering their war cries as the *Zahora* passed upstream. The next evening the party from Dutch Borneo arrived, 960 men (three having perished on the way in the cascades) in ninety-seven boats, saluting Vyner with their paddles as they went by and later performing an exhibition of dancing.

The peacemaking itself took place on the morning of the sixteenth, proceedings being opened by the killing of a pig and 'the sprinkling of the blood of this animal over the assembled crowd', so MacBryan later reported. Prayers were then said by each side, and on the completion of each prayer, more pigs were slaughtered, with an accompanying lamentation: 'May whosoever reopens this feud die in greater agony than this animal.' MacBryan remarked that the words implied a great deal, 'if one takes into account the length of the swine's death agonies'. On the completion of all this, both the Rajah and MacBryan made speeches, expressing the hope that peace would now prevail and warning of the consequences if it did not. So impressed was Vyner with the organiser of the ceremony that he took MacBryan with him back to Kuching and appointed him acting district officer. So began MacBryan's rapid rise through the ranks of the Sarawak Civil Service.

Back in London, Sylvia and her daughters had by this time taken up residence just north of Oxford Circus, at 62 Portland Place, the widest street in London when it was designed by the Adam brothers in the 1770s; number 62, on the east side at the corner with Weymouth Street, had formerly been the home of her cousins the Dudley Wards and in the 1930s it was one of the four houses demolished to make way for the Royal Institute of British Architects. For the time being in the mid-1920s, however, it became known as the exotically decorated home of the Ranee of Sarawak, 'that most charming of despots', as one newspaper described her at the time.

As if conscious of what was expected of her, Sylvia decorated the hall of her new home with Oriental totem poles, spears, 'and other articles that inspire fear in the casual visitor', it was reported in the press; the *Evening News* went so far as to hazard that the assortment of Dyak weapons and carvings, Chinese embroideries and lacquer furniture she had assembled constituted 'the most marvellous collection of native work that can ever have been amassed in a private residence'. If this was almost certainly an overestimation, it was not in Sylvia's nature to discourage such impressions.

The house itself was large – the girls had a suite of nursery rooms on the third floor – and sufficiently grand to reflect Sylvia's status and the growing prosperity of the Brooke Raj. Shortly after the Armistice in 1918 Vyner had felt sufficiently well-off to give the British government £30,000 towards the war effort and asked Reggie Esher to approach the government on his behalf. Now, in the midst of the post-war depression, Sarawak revenues were steadily rising, partly owing to an oil discovery: the revenue for 1924 and 1925 exceeded the expenditure by more than a million dollars – 'a sum which presumably goes largely into the Rajah's private purse', hazarded one colonial officer. Vyner was by nature frugal, but the same could not be said of his wife, or for that matter his daughters. The Brooke girls did not go short materially, and Elizabeth later recalled the frequency with which her mother would say, 'Let's all go to Hamleys for prezzies.' 'We had the biggest dolls and dolls prams that could be got and I suppose we were spoiled in that way,' she wrote. 'But I think it was just to compensate us for being with

Nanny so much . . .' To Leonora, their parents ('Their Highnesses' to the servants) seemed 'God-like beings, bringing presents when they came, leaving presents when they left. Daddy was an almost legendary figure. "Out in Sarawak" seemed like another planet to us.'

It was from Portland Place that the newly confident Ranee Sylvia began to launch herself in earnest on London society, though from the outset she veered towards show-business rather than aristocratic circles. She later admitted that she had shamelessly traded on her name, going so far as to send notes across restaurants and in this way meeting film stars such as Ramón Novarro and Carl Brisson, as well as Noel Coward, who became a regular visitor to her house and christened her daughters 'the Chicks'. According to Leonora, their house was also frequented by D. H. Lawrence (whose story 'The Rocking Horse Winner' was supposedly inspired by observing the Brooke girls), Gerald du Maurier, Gwen Farrar and Tallulah Bankhead, and their mother never missed a first night, 'accompanied by her aide Captain Barry Gifford'. The girls were often snatched from their lessons to go to a matinee in which some friends were performing. 'We always went backstage where Mummy would sit and gossip with the stars in their dressing rooms.'

In her Malay dress and the yellow sarong that she was entitled to wear as Ranee of Sarawak – not to mention the abundant elephant rings round her forearms, the occasional snakeskin headband and the red lacquer cane with tassel that she always took with her – Sylvia was an easy spot for gossip columnists about town, and a ready source of mischievous and invariably misleading stories. The ensuing newspaper articles owed a great deal to her flair for self-publicity and exaggeration. She did nothing to dispel the impression that Sarawak was populated entirely by headhunters and lotus-eaters, while her own position as Ranee remained surrounded in myth. One credulous journalist reported:

> It is no exaggeration to speak of her as a ruler, for the temperamental Sarawakians, in spite of their fondness for war and fearful practices, are very susceptible to gracious feminine influences . . . Although they practise a kind of Mohammedanism, adorned with much ancestor worship and demonology, they do

not adopt the tyrannical attitude of many Mohammedan nations toward their women. The latter are not secluded and they enjoy free companionship with the men. In the delicate problems involved in the government of Sarawak, the influence of the Rajah's wife has been of vital importance . . .

Sylvia burnished her exotic reputation by her mode of entertaining, giving, as she recalled in her first autobiography, 'Bohemian parties, unconventional At Homes and Chinese suppers at which we all squatted on the floor and ate Chinese food with chop sticks'. Her friend Max Darewski, the composer and conductor, was often prevailed upon to play the piano for these soirées, which mostly took place while Vyner was away in Sarawak. On the rare occasions when the Rajah was there he would hide in his study. He did, however, fall in with her idea that they should take up dancing, and 'learn all the modern steps'. They went along to the Empress Rooms in Knightsbridge, where Sylvia chose for her instructor Victor Sylvester, later the famous bandleader but then a world champion dancer, while Vyner spotted a sad-looking, willowy instructress whom he rather liked the look of. Too shy to ask her himself, he got Sylvia to do it for him. In due course, Toby Johns, as she was called – or 'the Woeful Giraffe', as they christened her – became yet another of the Rajah's girlfriends.

While his mania for dancing lasted, Vyner dragged his dancing mistress to nightclubs all over London – the Grafton Galleries, Chez Victors, Ciro's, the Berkeley – insisting at the same time that Sylvia went too. 'It looks better', he told her, 'that I should be out with my wife.' Yet, as Sylvia wrote, 'the sort of relationship that those two had *could* only look one way, whether I was with them or not'. Sylvia, as ever, affected not to mind what was going on – possibly because she still had one or other of the Gifford brothers on the go (Reggie and Maurice talk of 'Gifford No 2' in their letters) – and she made no attempt to hide her husband's latest conquest from her family. 'Syv came to lunch on Sunday with all her children and Vyner's new woman,' Maurice told Reggie in October 1924, 'a dancing mistress, very plain and dull.'

Vyner grew bored of dancing as suddenly as he had taken it up. 'That was his way,' wrote Sylvia, 'with houses and things and people. He drove them hard and then lost interest. I went home one evening and found our drawing room hung with wreaths. To each wreath he had attached a card – his nightclub membership cards. On a placard stretched across the room he had written: "Farewell to Night Life in London".' Despite Maurice's withering assessment, Toby Johns outlasted Vyner's dance craze and, as Sylvia recalled, 'remained one of our greatest friends until, at a very early age, she died'.

Vyner's equally faddish approach to property, meanwhile, meant that Portland Place was far from their final base in Britain. In February 1925, wanting a place in the country too, they bought Bridgeham Farm, a breezy spot on Leith Hill, the highest point in Surrey, from Jack Dare, Zena's ne'er-do-well brother, whom Vyner then employed for a spell as an odd-job man. 'Of course [Bridgeham] would not suit you,' Reggie wrote to Maurice. 'Nor me. Vyner, so uncomfortable a person, may enjoy it. We shall see.' Evidently it was too spartan even for Vyner, and before long 'that ridiculous farm', as Reggie called it, was back on the market.

When subsequently Sylvia found a house near Ascot, Reggie feared that she would invade the space of his beloved Maurice, who lived nearby at Chilston, and increase the likelihood of family skirmishes. 'Poor little Syv's personality gets more exasperating as years cumber her,' he told Maurice in 1927. 'I am getting too case hardened by everybody and everything to care much.' Yet he cared sufficiently to warn his daughter a few days later that 'in the Provinces you have to be circumspect. No Chinese parties. In London no one cares. In Ascot all the Ranee's old friends, and everybody for miles around, would be agog.' 'She is so silly,' he told Maurice.

Reggie's opinion of his elder daughter was scarcely more favourable. While he admired the way Doll had made her own way as an artist, she was nonetheless 'a queer girl', he wrote to Maurice, whose sponging habits and the extravagant way she then distributed his money among her friends annoyed him intensely. After her years spent virtually living with Ottoline Morrell at Garsington, Doll had formed a close friendship with Katherine Mansfield, lasting from 1920 until her death from tuberculosis three years later, aged thirty-four. After losing her virginity to Katherine Mansfield's widower,

John Middleton Murry, Doll then followed D. H. Lawrence and his wife Frieda out to New Mexico in 1924, the only one of Lawrence's friends to take up his invitation to form the community of 'Rananim' at Taos. The next year she wrote to Reggie announcing her intention to stay for good. 'Her "plans" are bound to vary again soon,' Reggie wrote to Maurice. 'Of course she may marry an Indian. Her deafness would matter so much less if the language was Chock Tow.' But she was as good as her word, and a brief visit to the Roman Camp that November was the last time she saw her father. 'I suppose it is a "duty" visit,' Reggie wrote to Maurice at the time, 'or she wants something. When people have drifted away for some time, they become negligible features in ones life, whoever they are. At least that is my experience. Distance lends no enchantment at all, so far as I am concerned.'

Reggie was no more enchanted by Sylvia's daughters, who were by then in their mid-teens – in 1927 Leonora's sixteenth birthday was celebrated in Sarawak, a month after the event, with a dance at the Astana. Earlier that year, she had decided that boarding school was not for her, a state of affairs Reggie attributed to her lax and pampered upbringing. 'Syv's adventure for Leonora is a failure,' he wrote to Maurice. 'The girl cannot stand the discipline after a lifetime of indulgence. How could she? getting up at 7. Drill before school – restrictions of all kinds usual in school are looked upon as grievances. Syv of course thinks it is the fault of the school. Whereas the fault lies elsewhere.' As if to vindicate his argument, the next year Valerie – or 'Vava', as she had become known – was also expelled from her school, St Mary's Ascot. Elizabeth, 'Didi', the middle daughter, avoided this fate, though in other ways she too was a disappointment to her grandfather. After her visit to the Roman Camp in 1927 with Sylvia and Barry Gifford, Reggie told Maurice that she was 'a very dull uninteresting child. She has no education and no originality. Syv herself has very little conversation, as you know, and she has done nothing for the girl except to teach her exaggeration in her view of trifles. Everything is "lovely" and that is as far as you get.'

It was really only when Sylvia fell ill, as she did from time to time in the 1920s, that she seemed assured of gaining her father's affection and sympathy, temporarily at least. In the summer of 1925 the stomach problems she had had ever since having her appendix out suddenly flared up again. She was driven from Bridgeham Farm to Portland Place, where Sir Henry Simson, her obstetrician, was again sent for. After examining her, he said that an operation was urgent. On 1 August the Court Circular in *The Times* announced that the Ranee had had to cancel all her engagements 'due to sudden illness and is now in a nursing home'. After dashing south with Nellie from the Roman Camp to visit Sylvia, Reggie wrote to Oliver that she had 'shown marvellous vitality and courage'; two weeks after the operation, he reported with relief that she looked 'remarkably well considering'.

Sylvia returned home shortly afterwards, in time for the publication of her fourth book, *The Cauldron*, a collection of short stories set in the East which she said were 'mostly true'. The reviews this time were favourable, one newspaper pronouncing it 'a brilliant book . . . [of] short stories that convey not a little of the emotion that is experienced at the first reading of *Macbeth*'. The *Times Literary Supplement* also rated it more highly than *Toys*, describing the stories as 'ingeniously macabre', with the author showing 'a sure command of the art which fits into the short story not a line more than is required to give a decisive effect'. However, the reviewer went on to say that the book 'would gain rather than lose by the omission of its illustrations' – which were also by Sylvia.

Barry Gifford was still living with them during this time as Vyner's secretary. It was he who drove her to London from Bridgeham Farm when she was taken ill, and he continued to accompany her and her family on trips to Sarawak for the remainder of the decade. It is hard to say whether and to what extent he was still the Ranee's boyfriend. Although he featured in her first autobiography, the account is all but purged of her feelings for him, and no correspondence between them appears to have survived. He did crop up quite frequently in letters between various members of the Brett family, however, and Maurice routinely referred to him as 'Sylvia's man' – which is, of course, open to more than one interpretation.

In any case, Gifford was by then a shadow of his former dashing self. 'These shell-shocked men were never really cured,' wrote Sylvia, 'there was always something evil lurking in their minds, a horror never to be spoken of, never to be lived down. Barry . . . was a charming and extremely lovable man, but the shadow of War remained with him always, and drove him slowly but surely to an early death [he died in 1932].' Unable to free himself from the horror of the war, he drank too much, something Reggie noticed when Sylvia brought him and Elizabeth to stay at the Roman Camp for her annual fishing fix in October 1927. 'Barry soaks whisky and looks awful,' Reggie wrote to Maurice, also observing: 'Whenever Syv leaves the room, even for a stop-en-route, Barry and Elizabeth rise and follow her out. When she returns, they return. It must be a very solemn rite.'

Over the years his behaviour grew increasingly erratic. Even Sylvia, never notably prone to embarrassment, admitted feeling a little abashed when, at a charity ball, he shouted, 'Here, look after this for me . . .' and tossed his opera hat towards her. She happened to be sitting next to the Prince of Wales and his entourage at the time. When the hat landed at her feet, the Prince of Wales laughed and said, 'I suppose you will sack him in the morning.' She does not say which year this took place, though by the end of the decade Gifford was reported to have 'retired' from the Sarawak Civil Service on a pension; and by the autumn of 1930, he and the Ranee were sufficiently disentangled for Gifford to marry Ivy Duke, the silent-screen star who had recently divorced the actor/director Guy Newall.

Until that time, Gifford had accompanied Sylvia on many of her trips back and forth to Sarawak, where she spent three to four of the winter months, generally arriving there in December, while Vyner would be out there for approximately half the year. 'There were certain winter months when I dreaded the sleet and the snow,' wrote Sylvia, 'and I arranged to live out East. I suppose really it was an almost ideal state – to be able to pack one's boxes and leave the cold winds and the yellow fogs behind . . .' Their movements were monitored at each end by the Court Circular and the *Sarawak Gazette*, and on each occasion, their arrival in Sarawak was greeted by a round of entertainments and welcome ceremonies, during which Sylvia might be required to inspect a parade of Chinese schoolchildren, or be borne shoulder high in a decorated sedan chair through the various Malay kampongs, flanked by a party of military torch bearers. According to the former Resident A. B. Ward, she 'impressed everyone with her originality and unbounded vivacity', and she seemed to him to take a great interest in her adopted country. However, there were also those who took against her, regarding her as out for her own pleasure and responsible for a general relaxation of standards.

One of her sternest critics was Stirling Boyd, who arrived in 1928 to take up the newly created post of judicial commissioner. Boyd was a serious-minded bachelor from Edinburgh who directed people to address him as 'Judge' and renamed his bungalow in Kuching the 'Judge's Lodgings'. He was forty-one when he first came to Sarawak – a year younger than Sylvia. He quickly formed a dim view of the Rajah, who refused to let him wear 'proper dress' in court, and whom he considered to be 'terribly changeable and prey to the last speaker', but he took a particular dislike to the Ranee – 'one of the most superficial people I have met', with 'a firm eye on the main chance'.

Boyd's opinion was shared by the equally stern Eric Mjöberg, the Swedish director of the museum in Kuching in the mid-1920s, who deplored, among other things, the way the Ranee applied her lipstick in public, 'like a chic American'. But then neither Boyd nor Mjöberg was especially popular himself. Boyd was clearly a prickly character – with one of his letters to his mother he returned some shaving brushes that she had sent him from England, asking her to enquire whether they really were made of badger hair. Mjöberg was even more disliked, it seems, judging by the bitchy review of his book *Forest Life and Adventures in the Malay Archipelago* that appeared in the *Sarawak Gazette* in January 1931. 'He [Mjöberg] had a method of dealing with the natives which was peculiarly his own,' recalled the reviewer, 'which, on one occasion, resulted in a certain District Officer having the unpleasant duty of forbidding him to go near the *kampong* at his station under pain of arrest. No one, however, can accuse Dr Mjöberg of not making the most of his stay in this country; for one thing, it was found necessary to check his baggage before he left for Europe owing to his inability to discriminate between what constituted his private property and what belonged to the Sarawak Museum.'

It was in Sarawak that Sylvia did most of her writing. In England she dabbled in journalism for the *Daily Express* and the *Sunday Graphic* – giving her opinion on such pressing questions as 'Why Did You Marry?' and 'Why Shouldn't We Gossip?' – and wrote sketches for her friend Gwen Farrar, the lesbian variety star. But in the less frenetic atmosphere of Kuching she found time during the late 1920s to write a three-act play, *Heels of Pleasure*, and a novel, *Lost Property*, which was published by Eveleigh Nash and Grayson in 1930. Both were about children of mixed blood, Sylvia's pet subject.

Heels of Pleasure was given a trial run of a week at the Arts Club Theatre in 1929 but was taken off after bad reviews. Even Sylvia admitted that it was 'clumsily constructed, and amateur and ignorant of the set rules of theatre', yet she also recorded, accurately or not, that 'one or two [of the critics] agreed that my dialogue was as good as Noel Coward's'. After reading some of the Ranee's notices, Stirling Boyd smugly wrote to his mother: 'They are, as I expected, very bad. She won't talk about her plays so much now, perhaps.'

Lost Property, which tells of the prejudices encountered by the children of a British father and Malay mother who arrive from the East to live with their spinster aunt in a small English town, fared rather better. 'Many books have been written on the tragedy of colour,' declared the *Daily Telegraph*, 'but *Lost Property* throws the whole question on the screen in a manner that is simply unforgettable.' The *Times Literary Supplement* was less effusive, but complimented the author for being 'sparing both of sentimentality and satire'.

Alongside her determination to become a famous playwright or novelist Sylvia had also conceived an ambition to get into the movie business. Towards the end of 1928 several English newspapers announced that she was intending to take part in screen productions when she passed through America on her way back from Sarawak in the spring of 1929. Rajah Charles would almost certainly have regarded this as the last straw, and friends of the Dowager Ranee sent letters of sympathy when they read the reports: 'My Dear Ranee,' wrote the punctilious courtier Sir Frederick 'Fritz' Ponsonby, 'I can well imagine how distasteful this film business must be to you, but of course the present generation do not appear to have any idea of what is good taste and what is impossible . . . not even assuming that we are out of date, it is difficult to look on calmly when one sees things being done that will have dangerous repercussions. However one thing I have learnt is that the younger generation will not listen to us but prefer to get into a mess than take advice.'

'It is really too bad,' chipped in another friend, Lord Stanmore, '& must have such an unfortunate effect in Sarawak, but I cannot see what you can do – you can't even say that Queens don't do these things for it is very much what the Queen of Romania does do. I feel for you most sincerely at this most exasperating development.' Amid the uproar, the *Sarawak Gazette*, presumably acting on instructions from the Astana, declared that the Ranee had no intention whatsoever of working in the film business, although it is hard to see where the stories came from originally if not from Sylvia herself.

When she did reach the United States, in March 1929, Sylvia was billed by one newspaper headline-writer there as the 'Queen of the Head Hunters' (thus acquiring the sobriquet she later used for her second autobiography) and portrayed in more romanticised technicolour than ever. 'She rules over one of the wildest countries in the world,' it was reported, 'swarming with tigers, venomous snakes 15 feet long, boa constrictors many feet larger and the most dangerous wild beasts and reptiles known to the Asiatic jungle. The people of Sarawak, who number a million, are addicted to headhunting, cannibalism and other fearful avocations when not restrained by their charming ruler. They are devout believers in demons, ghosts, witchcraft and all kinds of magic, and life among them is more like a story from Arabian Nights than an ordinary everyday existence . . .'

This was Sylvia's first visit to America and she loved it, admiring what she saw as Americans' straightforward 'go-getting' approach to life, not to mention the glitz of Hollywood. In early 1930 Sylvia told Doll, 'I have my finger in several Theatre and Film ventures, so at any time I may be over in New York . . .' None of these ventures appears to have come to fruition, but for the next decade and more she remained determined to make it into the movies. By the end of the 1930s one colonial offficer was noting acidly that Hollywood had become the Ranee's 'spiritual home'.

Besides her various creative endeavours, by the late 1920s Sylvia had also become increasingly preoccupied with the question of who would succeed Vyner. There had been several male pretenders to the throne over the years, including Vyner's cousin Hope Brooke, the son of Brooke Brooke, the disinherited elder brother of Rajah Charles, who in 1910 had travelled to Sarawak in an unsuccessful bid to assert his rights. Seventeen years later Esca Brooke-Daykin, Charles's eldest son by his Malay housekeeper at Simanggang, suddenly announced to the Canadian press that he was demanding recognition of his status as the rightful heir to the throne of Sarawak, together with an annual allowance of £25,000.

The Canadian newspapers reported that Sylvia was on her way to Canada to negotiate with Esca, who was then aged sixty, but whether or not this was ever her intention, the journey was never made. Ranee Margaret, meanwhile, was confident that the claim would fail because of his illegitimacy, haughtily assuring Charles Willes Johnson: 'Your uncle was monarch of all he surveyed, and certainly would not have married himself to a low Malay.' Not everyone agreed, however. In 1928 Esca met Charles Hose, who had spent two decades living in Sarawak in the late nineteenth century, and whose book *The Pagan Tribes of Borneo* (1912) established him as the leading authority on his subject. Hose was strongly of the opinion that Rajah Charles must have married Esca's mother according to Mohammedan rites, because he would have wanted to conform to the strict moral code that prevailed rather than jeopardise his position in the eyes of his native subjects. However, Hose died soon after the meeting, before he could persuade Vyner, as he had promised he would do. For lack of any other proof of his parents' marriage, Esca was eventually persuaded to give up his claim, possibly having being paid off, though he renewed it again when the cession was announced in 1946.

As things stood, meanwhile, Sylvia's daughters were precluded from succeeding to the Raj under the wills of the first two rajahs, which limited the line of succession to male members of the Brooke family, according to the normal rules of primogeniture. Sylvia had given up all hope of having a boy after her operation in 1917 for septicaemia, which seemed to rule out further children. Whenever she visited Malay houses in Kuching, women would press their hands against her stomach and say, '*Tid' ada anak?*' ('No baby?'). Always she had to shake her head and reply, 'No, no babies any more.'

With no son, Vyner's recognised heir was his brother Bertram, the Tuan Muda, and after him his son Anthony. Both Vyner and Sylvia had reason to resent this position, especially in view of Rajah Charles and Ranee Margaret's obvious preference over the years for Bertram. But given that neither Bertram nor his son Anthony was Sylvia's blood relative, and her natural tendency to feel hard done by, it was perhaps not surprising that she should feel more acutely resentful than her husband, or that she should begin to explore the possibility of changing the line of succession in favour of her eldest daughter.

As early as 1913, shortly after the birth of Elizabeth, George Bernard Shaw had told Sylvia, 'Women make the best sovereigns. The Salic law is a mistake, it should be the other way about . . .' This may have set her thinking, but it was a chance remark by King George V to Vyner on the day that he appointed him GCMG in 1927 that raised Sylvia's ambitions 'to boiling point', so Ranee Margaret later claimed. The King, explained Margaret in a letter to her friend Fritz Ponsonby, asked the Rajah if he had any heirs. 'Only daughters, sir,' came Vyner's reply. 'Never mind,' said the King. 'I will make her Begum!' Inspired by this, Sylvia left 'no stone unturned to gain her end', wrote Margaret; she had 'pestered' Vyner into not allowing Anthony to go to Sarawak for the first twenty-two years of his life, and was 'simply goading him [Vyner] into upsetting the proper laws of succession and the heirdom of Bertram and his son'.

Sylvia's determination to change things would only have been hardened by the publication in 1929 of *Relations and Complications*, the autobiography of Bertram's estranged wife Gladys. In her book the Dayang Muda went to great lengths to emphasise the mutual devotion that had existed between her and the old Rajah – knowing full well the same could not be said for his other daughter-in-law Sylvia. With regard to the succession, Gladys quoted in full a letter that she had received from her father-in-law shortly after the birth of Sylvia's third daughter Valerie in 1915. 'I see Sylvia has a baby girl,' the Rajah had written from Kuching, 'which no doubt is a great disappointment to her and Vyner – so Antoni stands so far as the hereditary prince – and I shall be quite content if nothing arrives to hinder his holding that position.'

The evidence of a 'plot' to alter the succession is far from conclusive, but it was certainly widely suspected at the time, not just by Margaret but also by other officers in the Sarawak Civil Service, and when the allegations were put to Sylvia some years later by Bertram, she appeared to protest too much. Equally widely suspected was the involvement in Sylvia's scheme of the Rajah's Machiavellian sidekick Gerard MacBryan.

MacBryan's rise through the ranks had not been without incident. Appointed acting district officer in Kuching on his return from Kapit in 1924, he had abruptly resigned after his furlough in 1925 to sell cigarettes for British and American Tobacco in Singapore and Java, where he wrote to his brother Jack to say that he was suffering from syphilis. In May 1927 he returned to Kuching on his own account and persuaded the Rajah to let him rejoin his service. For three months he edited the *Sarawak Gazette* and in August 1927 he became acting assistant secretary to the Rajah. A year later, in October 1928, he was promoted to become Vyner's private secretary and Secretary for Native Affairs – the policy area closest to the Rajah's heart. Soon he was sticking his nose into every aspect of life in Kuching, and in November he wrote to the new judicial commissioner Stirling Boyd to say that it had come to the Rajah's knowledge that 'Police Constables have been in the habit of saluting you by presenting arms when you pass. His Highness desires me to say that this action is contrary to existing orders, and I am to enquire how the arrangement by which you were accorded such a privilege was instituted.' MacBryan's strange hold over the Rajah went alongside a disdain for Europeans – he affected to prefer the company of Malays and Dyaks – in return for which the majority of his fellow officers in the Sarawak Civil Service thoroughly disliked him.

In her second autobiography Sylvia maintained that she too had always distrusted MacBryan, and that she thought him 'both ambitious and unscrupulous'. But this is slightly misleading. There were times when both she and Vyner found him stimulating company and looked on him with affection, nicknaming him 'Baron' (von Münchhausen) for the outrageous stories he told. 'I know MacBryan is a complete crook,' Vyner once said to a friend, 'but he amuses me. I enjoy watching him and trying to work out his next move.' The same friend described how, despite his general unpopularity, MacBryan was 'always a great favourite with the Ranee and her young daughters'. It was even whispered that the Ranee and MacBryan were having an affair, and while their letters to one another do not bear this out, they do suggest a friendship of intermittent intimacy in which Sylvia blew hot and cold.

Fast as his rise had been, in the late 1920s MacBryan still had some way to go if he was to realise his ultimate ambition, which was one day to become rajah – or at least regent. Inspired by the example of Sharif Ali, a native of Taif, Arabia, and a descendant of the Prophet Muhammad, who married a daughter of the second Sultan of Brunei and later ascended the throne as the third sultan in 1425, MacBryan's ploy for achieving his goal was to marry into the Brooke family.

In order to prepare the ground, in 1928 MacBryan persuaded Vyner to nominate several new *datus* to Sarawak's Supreme Council. His aim was to reduce the power of the three hereditary Malay chieftains and secure a majority who would support a petition for the line of succession to be switched to the Rajah's eldest daughter and her descendants. MacBryan had already used his linguistic skills and understanding of their culture to establish close links with the Malay community in Kuching, and he now attempted to persuade them that his proposed change in the succession would not only delight the Rajah, but would also greatly please the King of England because of his intimate friendship with the Ranee's father, Lord Esher. Four new *datus* – among them an illiterate businessman deemed 'most unsuitable' by Bertram – were duly appointed, three of them on the Rajah's birthday in September 1928, the other in 1929. But in the end the petition was dropped before it could be presented to Vyner owing to the firm stand of the chief *datu* (Shahbandar), who said that going against the will of Rajah Charles would render him liable to the 'vengeance of departed rulers'.

In her autobiographies and correspondence Sylvia freely acknowledged MacBryan's ambitions but always made out that he had been acting on his own initiative – rather than as her accomplice, as was alleged by Bertram and others. In a letter written in 1940 she told Bertram that MacBryan had begun his campaign by 'making violent love' to her middle daughter, Elizabeth. 'I don't think Didi was more than fourteen at the time,' she wrote. 'But as you know MacBryan was determined to get into the family somehow . . .' When Elizabeth showed no interest, MacBryan transferred his suit to Bertram's youngest daughter, Anne, who, after her parents separated, often stood in as hostess at the Astana during her father's stints in Kuching. MacBryan went so far as to threaten suicide if Dayang Anne refused to marry him, causing Bertram to have him removed him from the capital. But MacBryan subsequently admitted to his wife that while he had imagined himself in love with Anne Brooke, ambition had at all times been at the root of his desire for her.

Aside from his schemes relating to the succession, MacBryan was presumed to be behind Vyner's sacking his chief secretary H. B. Crocker, which also took place in September 1928 – creating a power vacuum, which MacBryan then filled. A year later he was said to have instigated the removal of Charles Willes Johnson, the Rajah's cousin and legal adviser, allegedly for taking commission on securities dealing and on the Rajah's life assurance. The dismissals contributed to a general feeling of insecurity among the government officers in Kuching. 'One can't help wondering whose turn it is next,' wrote Stirling Boyd to his mother.

MacBryan and Willes Johnson had long been at odds, but Sylvia, no fan of the latter, helped intensify the feud by telling MacBryan (by letter) that Willes Johnson was spying on his house, situated just below the Astana, with field glasses. Boyd saw the Ranee's intervention as typical of the way she operated. 'I don't suppose for a moment that he was spying on the house,' he wrote to his mother,

> and if he were why does the Ranee want to write a letter about it? It shows the sort of atmosphere of suspicion there is. The other day there was a dinner party at which the Ranee was present and she announced before the whole company that Mrs WJ [Willes Johnson] was an impossible woman and wouldn't be allowed to land in Sarawak. I gather that this is more or less true but how frightfully indiscreet of the Ranee of all people to proclaim it in such a very small community . . . ordinarily to be disliked by the Ranee is on the whole a compliment as in general people who

have any moral stamina are not popular, and the same applies in large measure to the Rajah.

Having persuaded Vyner not to replace Crocker as chief secretary in 1928 – pointing out that the Rajah could run the country directly from the Astana, while he, MacBryan, did all the work – MacBryan appeared to gain almost complete control over Sarawak, professing to be the Rajah's mouthpiece across a wide range of state and personal matters. The extent of his influence was not only irritating to other members of the service, but also deeply baffling. Some even suspected that the Rajah was being blackmailed, perhaps on account of his sexual transgressions. But this seems unlikely, given that Vyner appeared to care insufficiently about his reputation to mind having anything exposed. It is more likely that he deemed MacBryan indispensable owing to his peculiar genius for dealing with delicate local matters and doing the dirty work; he understood the undertow of the East better than the Rajah's other officers, was a far better linguist than the Rajah and knew how to manipulate everyone, regardless of their race. The service as a whole regarded him as the Rajah's hatchet man, charged with carrying out all the unpleasant jobs. 'Hatred and resentment against him were enormous,' recalled one officer, 'but all the time he seems to have been doing the Rajah's wishes.'

MacBryan's deviousness appealed to certain traits in the Rajah's own character. One of those who knew both Vyner and Bertram well, deemed the Rajah

> a cleverer man [than his brother] and a very shrewd judge of his fellow men, but he is perverse and irresponsible. He cares about nothing but his own amusement, is easily bored, especially by a virtue in other people to which he has no wish to attain, and he uses his gifts, which are many, to minister to his own perversity. Whenever he returned to Sarawak he started at once to undo everything that the Tuan Muda had done in his absence, no matter how wise or far-sighted these measures might have been, for the pure joy of setting people at loggerheads; so that it was not long before neither European nor native officers knew where they stood and conditions became chaotic. Behind all this is the

personality of the Ranee, of whom the less said the better, and of one MacBryan who is at present the Rajah's private secretary.

It seems that MacBryan eventually proved too much even for the Rajah, however. In December 1930, shortly after arriving back in Kuching with the Rajah, Ranee and their three daughters, MacBryan was asked by Vyner to resign, which he did, citing 'personal reasons', and left the country. Vyner later maintained that he had been unaware of his private secretary's intrigues at that time, which seems a little unlikely. More probable is that he had simply grown tired of MacBryan's underhand ways, and/or bridled at the way he had tried to court his daughter. We cannot be sure about the extent to which Sylvia connived with MacBryan in his various schemes or indeed influenced her husband to demand his resignation, but in later years MacBryan blamed her 'capricious' behaviour for his troubles. In any case, this would be not be the last they heard of him.

10

TO HELL WITH DIGNITY

The year that ended for Sylvia with the departure of MacBryan from Sarawak had begun with the death of her father in London. On the morning of 22 January 1930 Reggie had returned to 2 Tilney Street after staying with Maurice and his family at Chilston. He was due to have lunch with his protégé Lawrence Burgis at Brooks's Club in St James's and was in high spirits, chatting and laughing with Nellie before going into his dressing room on the ground floor to change. There, with a thump, he fell to the floor behind the door.

Reluctant to believe that her husband could have died so suddenly, Nellie telephoned Sylvia, who was in London at the time, and asked her to come over and 'make sure'. Recalling all this in her second autobiography, Sylvia wrote: 'I had never seen anyone dead before. I touched his hands, and they were still soft and warm. He looked young, the lines gone from his face, and peaceful. I remember thinking to myself, "You will never be able to hurt me any more." I had no feeling of loss or sorrow because I had never really loved him.'

Forty years after the event she may have overstated the hardness of her heart; after all, during her father's lifetime, she had constantly craved his love and approval. On the other hand, she sounded less than devastated when she wrote to her sister shortly after he had died: 'It is really only for Mumsie it is sad. A shutter has closed on her entire life, as she only lived for him . . . Don't you fret Doll, there was nothing we could do. Pupsie liked us, but he was only half interested.' Her chief disappointment, she said, was 'that Pupsie did not live to see me a famous playwright . . . My view of the whole thing is that he was spared the pain of his grandchildren disappointing him as his children did.'

It is fair to say that none of the Brett children really lived up to Reggie's hopes for them. Even Maurice had latterly fallen in his father's estimation, not least because he was forever grumbling about money, and as Lees-Milne later wrote, Reggie had 'transferred his worship' to his grandson Tony, lavishing attention, advice and money on him, and 'addressing to him rapturous poems about youth and beauty'. After Reggie's death Maurice took on the task of editing his father's journals and letters, but then died suddenly himself, shortly before the first two volumes were published, in 1934. Reviewing *Journals and Letters* in the *Daily Telegraph*, Harold Nicolson wrote: 'No man has ever had his finger in so many pies. Nor would it be fair to suggest that he was a busy-body, an intriguer, an adventurist. He was the most perfect of all lubricants . . . half soldier, half a politician, half a diplomatist, half a man of letters, half a man of taste [it was] Esher more than any other man who created the influence of King Edward's court.'

It was partly the contrast between the behaviour that Reggie had grown used to at the Edwardian court and the way Sylvia conducted herself as Ranee that made him so disillusioned with his younger daughter. Writing about Sylvia some years previously, Reggie had remarked to his dear friend Chat Williamson: 'Dignity does not enter into her scheme of life.' One of the consequences of Reggie's death was that, free from the threat of her father's chastisement, Sylvia seemed to become even less bothered about her dignity than before. That at least was the impression of the more punctilious officers in the Sarawak Civil Service, and indeed of other observers from outside the country.

Stirling Boyd, who was promoted to Chief Justice of Sarawak in 1930, noted in letters home at the beginning of the new decade that 'the amount of smut in Her Highness's conversation is unbelievable', and regarded the annual trips to Sarawak of the Ranee and her daughters as 'a great waste of money'. 'Their chief influence here seems to be to stir up trouble,' he observed. When they left, he added, 'an almost holy calm descends'. Nor did increasing age seem to moderate the way the Ranee behaved.

Some of the 'trouble' referred to by Boyd during the early 1930s may have had to do with what Sylvia cheerfully described as her daughters 'playing havoc' with the emotions of the government officers – taking their lead from the amorous escapades of their father. 'They had all their father's mischievous desire for adoration,' wrote Sylvia, 'and a great deal of my longing for love, without my inhibitions. Vyner looked on with tolerance, because he saw himself in them, and only put his foot down when their affairs interfered with the work of his officers.' Sylvia, meanwhile, appears to have done more than merely tolerate her daughters' dalliances – her accounts suggest that she positively egged them on. She lived vicariously through them, relishing the fact that their lives were easier, that 'they never had to stand in a row of anxious virgins as I had done, waiting to be asked to dine or dance. They had beauty, and a certain notoriety, for their Sarawak background made them ready-made material for the gossip columns.'

Among the Malays of Sarawak Leonora became known as Princess Gold for her 'fair hair and golden complexion'; Elizabeth became Princess Pearl, and Valerie, the youngest, Princess Baba. The names were eagerly taken up by the popular press in Britain and America, and equally eagerly disputed by Vyner, who protested that their correct title was *dayang*, not princess. But the newspapers paid no attention to the Rajah's complaints, and as Sylvia recalled, 'everything the Three Princesses did was exaggerated and glamourised'. In time, the 'dangerously beautiful' Brooke girls married eight times between them; their various husbands included an earl, a bandleader and an all-in wrestler.

In the late 1930s their cousin Anthony, the heir apparent, pointed out that their all too frequent appearances in the newspapers had turned Sarawak into 'a music hall joke'. Even Sylvia conceded that the country had been 'cheapened and ridiculed in the eyes of a sensation-loving world', though she was hardly blameless in this respect, with her tendency to come out with wildly inaccurate statements whenever she came across a journalist.

The Colonial Office had long had its own designs on Sarawak, and the comic-opera public image of the country in the years before the

Vyner seated between Sylvia and Bertram and surrounded by his Dyak warriors, in Kuching to celebrate his installation as Rajah in 1918, and (inset) processing after the coronation beneath the Yellow Umbrella; Bertram follows with the Sword of State.

Below right The new Ranee with one of her Malay friends.

Below left The ballroom at the Astana; Sylvia saw to it that there were more dancing parties than during the reign of Rajah Charles.

THE RANEE OF SARAWAK AT GARSINGTON.

Sylvia in her Oriental garb, which was always sure to attract attention in England. Here she is opening a fete; on either side of her are Lady Ottoline Morrell and her husband Philip, the MP.

Her sister Dorothy, 'Brett', with Aldous Huxley (left) and the painter Mark Gertler, also at Garsington; and some years later, at Taos, in high boots and sombrero.

Sylvia's favourite Dyak chieftain, Temenggong Koh, with head trophies.

The communal verandah, or ruai, of a typical Dyak longhouse.

A Dyak head feast.

Sylvia sporting another Oriental creation in about 1920, and at her most appealing in a photograph by Paul Tanqueray.

An official portrait of Vyner from the 1920s.

Tea at the Astana, 1920. To Vyner's left are their daughters Elizabeth and Valerie. Sylvia is at the other end of the table, with Leonora standing on the far right.

Sylvia and a teenage Leonora, poolside behind the Astana.

Rajah Vyner with his Sarawak Rangers.

Ranee Sylvia and her 'princesses', photographed for a newspaper at home in London.

Off to Sarawak.

Sylvia, Vyner and Valerie arriving in splendour, Kuching.

The multi-talented Ranee, seen on the left sketching, and (right) her painting of Leonora.

RANEE BECOMES SCENARIO-WRITER

TO WRITE FILM PLAYS: The white Ranee of Sarawak and her daughters.—To-day's "Evening Standard" photo.

Never one to shun publicity, she was often featured in the press, advertising her skills.

White Ranee Of Sarawak

PLANET.

The Ranee of Sarawak, daughter of Lord Esher, photographed in her boudoir at her country house in Berkshire. Her husband, Sir Charles Vyner Brooke, inherited the title of Rajah from his father. Sarawak, on the island of Borneo, was a grant from a Sultan to the Brooke family.

Leonora, Sylvia and Elizabeth at the society lawn tennis match held each year by Lady Wavertree at Sussex Lodge in July 1928.

Sylvia with her sister-in-law Zena Dare and daughter Elizabeth at the Royal Academy in May 1934.

Vyner taking the salute during a visit to Kuching by the Governor of the Straits Settlements in 1930. Sylvia, his slave according to Sarawak custom, stands four paces behind.

Second World War helped harden opinion there that the Brooke Raj had had its day. Like the French monarchy before the revolution, for almost a hundred years the rule of the White Rajahs had been absolute and popular. Now the present Rajah appeared to be suffering a drastic loss of power and prestige.

Since the end of the First World War, progress in the world at large had made the Brooke Raj appear increasingly anachronistic and amateurish in its methods of administration. In his book *Durch die Insel der Kopfjäger*, published in 1931, the disapproving former Sarawak museum director Eric Mjöberg had remarked: 'Everything in this obscure little country bears the stamp of slackness and hopeless disorder.' 'Here we take it easy,' he recalled being told on his arrival in 1922; and he found that no one was in his office except between 9 and 11.30 a.m. and 2 and 3.30. p.m. The Rajah meant well, Mjöberg thought, but he was indecisive and a hedonist. When his officers talked to him he would say, 'I see, I see,' while his thoughts wandered.

Yet even critics of the regime conceded that the Rajah 'was a very important factor in native administration and that it would be extremely difficult to substitute another government for that of the Brooke family'. Thus, instead of a takeover, the Colonial Office wanted to have a British Resident in Sarawak to advise the Rajah and bring about a gradual process of change. However, as early as 1912, when Loulou Harcourt was Colonial Secretary, Sylvia had told Reggie that the idea was 'entirely impossible . . . if they put a Resident here, Vyner would be obliged to sell out and go. You would see in a minute if you came out, and Loulou too, how ridiculous it would make Vyner look – a white Rajah ruled by a white Resident – the Malays simply wouldn't understand it.'

Sylvia was echoing Vyner's view that he had to be an autocrat in order to command the loyalty of his subjects. If the Colonial Office hoped that Vyner would be more amenable than his father to relinquishing some of his power, they were disappointed. The idea of an adviser was put to him on several occasions, but he proved impossible to pin down. Nor, to begin with at least, did he evince a willingness to 'sell out', as, before his accession, it had been confidently predicted he would. Meanwhile, the peculiar position of the Brooke Raj in British society and public opinion limited the pressure that the Colonial Office could reasonably apply, in effect leaving it up to the Rajah to make the first move.

Within Sarawak itself even Sylvia shared Anthony's concern, albeit for different reasons, that her husband's authority over his subjects was diminishing. Writing in 1939, she observed that the spread of mission schools into the jungle meant that the white man was 'no longer a synonym of mystery and law. Equality of race, familiarity of contact, have taken away power and put in its place a sort of precocious liberty that has made the the Dyaks and Malays more difficult to control.' All this, she said, meant that 'Vyner's reign was not – and is not now – an easy one'.

Meanwhile, the older Vyner grew – in 1930 he was fifty-six – the more idle, impulsive and eccentric he seemed to become. No one questioned his genuine and benevolent concern for his people, yet at the same time the day-to-day business of government clearly bored him. He seemed to care far more about his various horticultural and farming projects and whatever happened to be his latest craze. In 1932 it was cooking and, as Averil Mackenzie-Grieve related, 'a marble-slabbed kitchen, fitted with a batterie de cuisine worthy of a cordon bleu, was fitted up under the Astana'. Each afternoon at five o'clock Mrs Mackenzie-Grieve and the other wives of the European officers were obliged to sit around at little tables 'eating our way doggedly through soggy fruit cakes and hard scones; sweat beading on our foreheads'.

The Rajah's new hobby annoyed Boyd, among others, since His Highness would often put off tennis matches 'because there was a cake in the oven . . . Other minor questions such as what is to be done about the deficit of 1 million dollars on the current estimates are put aside for the moment,' added Boyd. 'What a country!'

The Chief Justice was concerned that the Rajah's whims were damaging his authority, especially now that it was also being undermined by a deteriorating economy. Having fared better than most countries during the 1920s, Sarawak was now feeling the full effects of general depression in trade, with prices for all agricultural products in 1930 standing drastically lower than they had a year earlier. The downturn was felt particularly acutely by the Dyaks, who had taken to growing rubber and other jungle produce on a large scale and who now instinctively blamed their Rajah for the disastrous drop in prices

– especially now that he was imposing higher taxes on them as well. The fact that the depression hit less than a year after the Rajah had given £100,000 to the British government fuelled the controversy. 'I don't imagine it is pure altruism!' Boyd wrote cynically to his mother at the time of the donation. 'I shouldn't be surprised if HH is after an earldom.'

The resentment caused by the slump culminated in a rebellion led by a Dyak chief called Asun – the first serious unrest in the interior since MacBryan's peacemaking ceremony at Kapit in 1924 – and several expeditions were needed to quell the trouble and round up the dissidents. Asun eventually gave himself up in December 1932, whereupon he was sent into comfortable exile in Lundu.

The depression also meant that some of the ceremonial trappings of the Brooke Raj had to be dispensed with. Among the many belt-tightening measures was the disbanding of the Sarawak Rangers, whose primary function had changed over the years from combating headhunters to putting on ceremonial torchlight tattoos and displays of Dyak dancing. The band's last performance was to herald the Rajah and Ranee's arrival with their daughters in December 1931. Thereafter, the Brookes had to make do with the constabulary band to accompany their comings and goings. The 'air force' had also been disbanded two years earlier, though it had only ever consisted of two seaplanes, one of which had crashed soon after arriving.

At the same time Vyner also ordered a twenty per cent reduction in his privy purse (though he had earlier drawn a considerably greater sum than his personal allowance for the year), and just after Christmas 1932 he wrote to his niece to say: 'Masses of Europeans are under the axe now for the coming year. We are trying to cut down departments to skeleton proportions but it is as difficult as removing oysters from their bed with a toothpick to get dept heads to sack their men.' For his own part he admitted, 'I am just as lazy as I ever was, & very seldom visit the offices. Brings on the blood pressure.'

His health concerns were more genuine than they sounded. Earlier that year, when the Rajah's blood pressure had got too high, his doctor had advised him to 'knock off the stengahs and the pahits' and to limit himself to five cigarettes a day. The doctor also recommended that Vyner return to England two months earlier than he planned, and he duly departed on 19 March. Sylvia, though, was determined not to miss out on Kuching's jolliest time of year and so stayed on with her two younger daughters for a further five weeks. Boyd wearily reported to his mother that the Ranee was 'threatening to paint the place red'.

Shortly after Vyner left Sylvia was at the racetrack watching her husband's horse leading in the main event of race week when a seaplane swooped down, unannounced, on the Sarawak river. As Sylvia would soon be delighted to discover, the plane belonged to Richard Halliburton, the 'movie star handsome' American daredevil who had climbed the Matterhorn, re-enacted Lord Byron's swim across the Hellespont and swum the length of the Panama Canal, for which he had paid a 35 cents toll. Now, in a bid to recoup a fortune lost in the Wall Street crash, he had bought an open-cockpit biplane, 'The Flying Carpet', and hired a pilot, Stephens Moye, so that he could write a book about flying round the world.

When they landed opposite the Astana, Halliburton's arm was heavily bandaged after a close shave with the propeller a few hours earlier at Pontianak. No sooner had they come ashore than they received a summons from Sylvia to appear at the Astana that evening for the Grand Prix Ball. Halliburton later described how,

> half-encircled by a bank of orchids, the Ranee, in white and wearing a magnificent diamond necklace, greeted her guests, assisted by Princess [*sic*] Elizabeth, age eighteen, and the Princess Valerie, sixteen. Every woman present was jeweled and smartly gowned in the latest (minus eight weeks!) Paris mode; and every man resplendent in military or civil uniform . . . scarlet jackets, medals, ribbons. A Filipino orchestra played for the hundred couples dancing in the great banquet hall, from the walls of which gazed the portraits of Sarawak's Rajahs, past and present . . . and outside, the head-hunters, dressed in gee-strings, watched from the lawn. It was as beautiful and graceful picture of social life as I've ever seen.

Halliburton and his pilot, Stephens Moye, each with a 'princess' on his arm, later led the Grand March.

Halliburton purported to have found the Ranee 'slim, vivacious, keenly alive' and impressively unfazed by his arrival. He asked his hostess if he might dance with her. 'I always like to dance with Americans,' came her reply. 'I was fortunate,' he wrote gallantly, 'because the Ranee was decidedly the best dancer at her party.' When he suggested that she might like to go up in their plane the next day, she leapt at the idea, to the dismay of government officers, who dreaded having to tell the Rajah if something went wrong. Halliburton recorded that 'it almost caused a civil war', and that Sylvia urged them to take off quickly before a cable arrived from Vyner forbidding her from making the flight – the first by a woman in Borneo, she was proud to record. Sylvia was impressed by Halliburton's breezy willingness to take on the responsibility. 'I hadn't time to protest,' she wrote afterwards in the *Sarawak Gazette*, 'I hadn't time to be alarmed – that's America!'

Amid considerable relief, they landed her safely and were soon on their way again, though not before having flown over the Astana and dropped the helmet Sylvia had worn, inscribed with the slogan: 'Long live the Queen!' They then proceeded to Kapit, where at Sylvia's suggestion they took her old friend Koh (who had been raised to Temenggong after the peacemaking at Kapit in 1924) for a flight – the first on record taken by a Dyak.

There is no suggestion that anything improper occurred between Sylvia and Halliburton – although, at the age of forty-seven, she was probably still susceptible to the charms of a handsome and dashing young airman (Halliburton was thirty-two, at the time).[1] However, Vyner may well have been annoyed at his wife's irresponsibility in accepting a ride in a stranger's plane while he was away and thereby causing a great fuss in Kuching. The episode served to demonstrate the daredevil in Sylvia. She could be undeniably courageous, as she showed on other occasions when she accompanied a crocodile-hunter in a small open boat in a search for the creature that had eaten the hunter's wife, or when she became a regular visitor to the leper camp just outside Kuching, despite, by her own admission, feeling 'fear and revulsion' when Vyner first asked her to go.

[1] Halliburton disappeared seven years later, in 1939, while attempting to take a junk across the Pacific.

Most of all she channelled her bravery into being outrageous, whether it was staging a riotous party in Kuching when she knew full well that it would offend local sensibilities, or, as has been alleged, asking new recruits to the Sarawak Civil Service whether she had slept with them before. There seems little doubt that at times Vyner found Sylvia's flamboyant behaviour a useful foil for his shyness, but it is hard to believe that he did not also occasionally feel uncomfortable with it.

Throughout this time, Sylvia's hopes regarding the succession to the Raj had continued to be vested in her eldest daughter Leonora, who attained the age of twenty-one in 1932. At the beginning of that year, while the rest of her family were in Kuching, Leonora had remained behind in Europe, fielding prospective husbands. Having rejected various hopeful bachelors in Sarawak, the Rajah's daughter was now, so Stirling Boyd told his mother, 'being run by some rich Rumanian widower' with whom she had gone to Paris 'at his expense' and attended a 'bed party'.

In the autumn of 1932 Leonora and the Romanian, a railway and steel magnate called Max Ausnitz, became engaged. Ausnitz was 'charming and kind, and immensely rich', wrote Sylvia in her first autobiography (privately she also remarked to Doll that he was 'most prodigiously plain – a case of Cyrano de Bergerac'). Yet the dowager Ranee Margaret was alarmed by the prospect of Leonora marrying a foreigner, however well-heeled, and she asked friends to look into his background. 'With regard to the *haute société parisienne*,' one of them responded, 'Max A is not *très ré pandu*. He may know people belonging to it, but he is not in it. First of all he is a Jew . . . If you want more details I can write to Bucharest.' Before further details were called for, Leonora got cold feet and called it off.

The next January – 1933 – on her way back from Sarawak aboard the P&O liner *Carthage*, Leonora met Kenneth Inchcape. Twenty-four years her senior, Inchcape had divorced his first wife in 1931 and succeeded his father as the second earl the next year. Leonora had no idea that he owned the ship until he invited her to dinner in his quarters. After a brief courtship their engagement was announced in April and they were married in July at St George's, Hanover Square, with Vyner giving his daughter away.

Shortly before the wedding Ranee Margaret had been visited in Cornwall by a reporter from a London newspaper and asked whether there was any truth in a communication they had received 'from someone very highly placed regarding the succession to the Raj [stating] that the Rajah has seen fit to disinherit his brother in favour of his eldest daughter Leonora'. Guessing that the information had come from Sylvia, Margaret told the emissary that 'so great a lie' would be immediately contradicted by the officials at the Sarawak Agency in London and would 'do the paper no good'.

Nevertheless, the rumour that Vyner was contemplating a change in the succession soon found its way to the Colonial Office. On 1 March 1933 the Secretary of State Sir Philip Cunliffe-Lister sent a cable to the Rajah pointing out that under the agreement of 1888 between Britain and Sarawak any question as to the right of succession had to be referred to His Majesty's Government for a decision. Vyner cabled back that the rumours were 'absolutely false', yet talk of Sylvia's so-called plot persisted at the Colonial Office and in Sarawak.

Her alleged accomplice was by then back in England. After his resignation MacBryan had drifted to Australia, where he unsuccessfully prospected for gold near Alice Springs, suffered a nervous breakdown and, in 1932, married an heiress, Eva Collins, who had taken pity on him. The couple – whose marriage, by her account, was never consummated – returned to London, where MacBryan worked for his brother Jack as a stockbroker for a time before persuading his father to sign a deed of gift assigning to him possession of the Kingsdown House asylum. While in London he renewed his friendship with Sylvia and Vyner – he was among the guests at Vyner's birthday party at the Savoy on 26 September 1933 – and began to press them to be allowed to return to Sarawak. This last request they refused, but MacBryan made sure to keep in touch with events in Kuching through the few friends he still had there. In due course the Colonial Office became aware that he had been asked 'very confidentially' by Leonora's husband Lord Inchcape to investigate 'the claims of his wife to succeed the present Rajah and so upset the present heir presumptive, the Tuan Muda'.

Lord Inchcape's enquiry was almost certainly prompted by the birth of his and Leonora's son, Simon, on 30 March 1934. Sylvia and the Inchcapes now appear to have pinned their hopes for the succession on this boy, and the next year the Inchcapes travelled out to Sarawak to inspect what they hoped would one day be their son's realm.

This was Kenneth Inchcape's first visit to the country, and Vyner and Sylvia made sure that he was given a warm welcome. Arriving at the mouth of the Sarawak river in February, the Inchcapes were met by Vyner and Valerie, transhipped to the Rajah's yacht *Maimuna* and escorted upriver to Kuching by three launches, decorated and manned by Malays in colourful costumes, to the beat of drums, the sound of gongs and the reports of small cannon. Opposite the Astana scores of decorated boats were moored and from there came further strains of music, while hundreds of people waved their handkerchiefs. The state barge took the party ashore and that evening a garden party was held to introduce the Inchcapes to representatives of the various communities.

Their two-and-a-half-week stay was crammed with dinner parties and receptions. The busiest day was the Ranee's birthday, 25 February. All ships in port were dressed and at eight in the morning a salute of twenty-one guns was fired from Fort Margherita. A morning regatta, during which Sylvia and the Inchcapes ventured out in two of the largest racing boats, was followed in the afternoon by a tattoo staged at Fort Margherita by the Sarawak Constabulary, including a display of physical drill done to music, carried out, as the *Sarawak Gazette* noted, 'with the smartness and precision that can only be attained by careful instruction and much practice'. After that came a varied programme of Sikh wrestling, Malay and Dyak dancing and 'a demonstration on a machine called a Gymnoframe, by one who is obviously an expert'. Eventually, the drum and fife band struck up, and there were two short 'humorous' sketches, a fall-in, and finally three cheers for Her Highness.

When the Inchcapes departed, on 7 March, they accompanied Sylvia and her other two daughters as far as Singapore, from where, for the first time, Sylvia, Elizabeth and Lord Inchcape's daughter Pat Mackay were due to fly back to England. Their carrier was Imperial Airways, who began flying to Singapore at the end of 1933 and advertised: 'British standards of service. Comfortable saloons. No tips. Nights spent on land.' The journey took nine days, with overnight stops for Sylvia and her entourage at Bangkok, Calcutta, Jodhpur, Sharjah, Basra, Rutbah (due to a sandstorm) and Alexandria. They landed for the last time at Brindisi, and caught a train to Paris. Sylvia later recalled Elizabeth's anxiety about 'this long journey through the skies' and that it was only her daughter's 'intense desire' to return to her beau of the moment that induced her to attempt it.

At the age of twenty-two, Elizabeth (or 'Didi') was a far cry from the 'dull little girl' she had been according to her mother, 'colourless and plain [with] a plate across her teeth'. She had grown up 'different and dark' and 'was of constant interest to those about her', wrote Sylvia. 'Even if she did not speak, she subconsciously attracted. From out of her tangled hair, her eyes loomed – they were like jungle pools, half green, half brown. Her skin was like ivory, and her lips a broad thread of scarlet. Her capacity for love was immeasurable. She had to have it, it was meat and drink to her.' Sustenance came mainly and, to her mother's satisfaction, from the world of show business, and among those whom Elizabeth fell for was George Metaxa, who, by Sylvia's account, 'sang for the first time in England in my house', and the debonair song-and-dance man Jack Buchanan, who spotted Elizabeth's potential as an actress and offered 'to build her into a star'. But Buchanan soon realised that Elizabeth did not really know what she wanted. According to Sylvia, her daughter's 'moody indifference' caused her to 'go out night after night smoking and drinking, and creep back in the early hours of the morning unhappy and profoundly bored'. Eventually Sylvia persuaded Elizabeth to enter the Dramatic School of Art and, in 1932, at a cocktail party in London, she met the bandleader Harry Roy.

Roy was almost twelve years older than Elizabeth and they shared little in terms of background. He had been born in East London to Jewish parents; his father was a box manufacturer and master bootmaker. Yet by the time Elizabeth came into his orbit Harry Roy was a star: 'London's loudest-blowing hot jazz conductor', as *Time* magazine described him, he could afford a flat on Park Lane, rode each morning along Rotten Row, in Hyde Park, and even owned his own cricket pitch. As far as Sylvia was concerned, artistic celebrity was a more than adequate substitute for heraldic quarterings, especially since he seemed to have succeeded in banishing her daughter's sulks and injecting some ambition into the girl at last.

Even so, their courtship did not go entirely smoothly – by Sylvia's account it ran 'an uncertain and uneven course for many months'. But, convinced that they were right for one another, she vigorously promoted the match, and Harry Roy later told the press that it was the Ranee who had urged him to propose. Vyner, when he was asked for his permission, cabled from Sarawak to say, 'Quite OK Eliza Provided No Publicity Or Newspaper Excitement'. But his pleas fell on deaf ears, and when Princess Pearl and the King of the Hot-Cha announced their engagement, in June 1935, there was considerable excitement in newspapers across the world.

Sylvia, meanwhile, received anonymous letters accusing her of 'letting the blue blood of England loose upon the soil', but she recalled that 'the roar of disapproval and talk meant nothing'. She claimed that Vyner and her mother all 'stood in line' and 'defied all comment', and she hailed her daughter as the pioneer of a 'new belief' in social equality.

Vyner returned to England that summer but left again before the wedding with the convenient excuse that the new governor of the Straits Settlements, Sir Shenton Thomas, was due to visit Sarawak in August. In order to get back in time, for the first time the Rajah travelled to Kuching from Singapore by flying boat – 'all rather awkward', Bertram wrote to his daughter Anne from Kuching, 'as we shan't be sure of how or where he is to be met until the last moment'.

Vyner took Valerie with him, and when they arrived, on 4 August, Bertram commented that she was 'looking awfully pretty . . . sandals, no stockings, and brilliantly carmine toenails'. The Tuan Muda was a little apprehensive of what the governor would make of his niece, and was relieved to see that 'Miss Governor' was similarly got up when they arrived four days later. Bertram was also impressed by how 'improved' Vava was. 'She's a dear, and funnily enough seems totally unspoilt. I think she is doubtful as to the Roy marriage turning out a permanent success. She's very sensible about it. She doesn't run him down at all but says he is intensely jealous, and will expect Eliza to sit through every night while he is performing, so as to wait for him and go home with him.' He added that Vava also had a prospective bridegroom in tow. 'He sounds an awfully good fellow . . . a well-known amateur yachtsman, who has already been let down twice by girls he is engaged to . . .' Valerie was to let him down too.

The governor was greeted by a full twenty-one-gun salute, but during his speech afterwards Bertram was at pains to emphasise that this was not to be taken as a signal that the governor was visiting Sarawak in the course of an official tour but was rather 'His Highness the Rajah's welcome to Your Excellency as the personal representative throughout Malayan territories to the King-Emperor, and therefore as a living link between Sarawak and the protecting power'.

Elizabeth and Harry Roy's wedding took place on 6 August 1935 at the Caxton Hall in Westminster. A crowd of five thousand fans had gathered outside the register office, and several times they broke through the police cordon. Eventually mounted police had to be called in, but even they were unable to clear a way for the bride when she arrived – wearing 'a simple white Paris day frock and wide picture hat' – accompanied by Sylvia, Leonora and grandma Nellie Esher. After the ceremony, as the couple emerged, Harry's band serenaded Elizabeth with 'Sarawaki', the love song that he had composed for his bride. The crowd, who had been waiting there since early in the morning, joined in with the chorus:

Sarawaki, skies of blue
Sarawaki, I'll always dream of you
I see you waiting 'neath the golden bamboo-oo
Oh! Sarawaki, my heart is there with you.

'Seldom has a register-office wedding commanded such exciting scenes,' remarked the *Daily Mail*.

Among their presents, it was reported, was a Sunbeam sports car from Vyner and Sylvia, and a large tapestry-covered stool that Nellie Esher had embroidered with the words 'Rhythm Romance'. The reception was held at the Mayfair Hotel, where Harry's band were then performing. 'Sarawaki' quickly became a hit and it was probably what most people associated Sarawak with in the late 1930s. 'It did become a little irritating to be asked from time to time if Harry Roy was your Rajah,' remembered one of the former missionary priests there.

After honeymooning in the South of France the Roys embarked on a tour of provincial Britain, with Elizabeth doing her bit as a backing jazz singer, before beginning work at Elstree on *Everything is Rhythm*, a jaunty musical film in which Elizabeth – billed as 'Princess Pearl' – played a princess in a mythical kingdom, her husband the dance-band leader who won her heart. 'She photographs marvellously,' declared Roy about his wife during filming. 'She sings well. She acts well. Everyone in the studio agrees with me . . .' With her exotic title it was confidently predicted that it would only be a matter of time before Elizabeth was snapped up by Hollywood.

After travelling north to see them perform in Glasgow in early September, Sylvia, meanwhile, had set off for Sarawak, where she was to join Vyner and Vava and work on her autobiography, the manuscript for which she had promised to the publishers Hutchinson and Co. on her return. Again she made the journey by air – landing by seaplane on the river opposite the Astana. Her travelling companion this time was another of the guests at her daughter's wedding, Gerard MacBryan.

For more than two years MacBryan had been badgering Sylvia and Vyner to be allowed back to Sarawak, and eventually they had relented. The pretext on this occasion was that he was on his way to Australia, ostensibly to arrange for his divorce. He was told firmly that his invitation to stay with them at the Astana was on the condition that he keep out of politics, and that his re-engagement in the Sarawak service could not be contemplated. But no sooner had he arrived in the country, on 30 September, than he renewed his request to rejoin the service. On being refused, he proceeded to pick up again his intrigues with the Malays where he had left them five years previously.

In mid-October, a few days before he was due to leave, MacBryan suddenly announced that he had cancelled his visit to Australia. He had decided to become a Muslim and go on the pilgrimage to Mecca with a local woman called Sa'erah. The beautiful daughter of a Dyak father and Melanau mother, Sa'erah was a twenty-four-year-old divorcee and 'a former prostitute', according to Vyner. MacBryan, then aged thirty-five, had taken her as his mistress after she was discarded by a European friend of his in Kuching.

After holding a farewell tiffin party at the Rest House and giving Sylvia (Vyner was by then away from Kuching) a written promise never to return to Sarawak, MacBryan and Sa'erah left on 21 October for Singapore, where he converted to Islam and was given the name of Abdul Rahman by the All-Malaya Muslim Society of Singapore. He and Sa'erah were then married and set off for England then Mecca – though his wildly inaccurate descriptions of Arabia in general and Mecca in particular led some to doubt that he ever got there.

On his return he collaborated with the author Owen Rutter on a book entitled *Triumphant Pilgrimage: An English Muslim's Pilgrimage from Sarawak to Mecca*, in which he was given the pseudonym David Chale but appeared in Arab garb on the frontispiece. Besides recounting MacBryan's supposed journey to Mecca the book also set forth his ambition of becoming the British Muslim leader of the Far East, ruling from Sarawak. According to Sylvia, this all demonstrated MacBryan's 'almost megalomaniac imagination' and she vehemently denied any complicity in his scheme. He had 'attempted to enlist my sympathy', she wrote in her second autobiography, 'and when I wouldn't have anything to do with his wild schemes, he tried his blandishments on Noni [Leonora] – but she merely laughed at him.'

In Sarawak, after his departure in 1935, nothing was heard from MacBryan until he reappeared in Singapore in April the next year and began putting it about that he intended to return to Sarawak and start a company promoting pilgrimages. On hearing this, Vyner telegraphed the governor of the Straits Settlements, Sir Shenton Thomas, asking him to prevent MacBryan from sailing. The governor said he could not, whereupon Vyner had an Undesirable Person's Order drawn up preventing MacBryan from landing.

MacBryan was warned about this before leaving Singapore, but he took no notice and, wearing his Haji robes, boarded the steamship *Vyner Brooke* bound for Kuching.

On arrival at the signal station outside Kuching harbour, the ship was boarded by two English police officers and MacBryan was arrested, taken ashore, and shown a copy of the Rajah's prohibition order. He was bundled off to a private house twelve miles from the capital and kept under guard for three days – the officers detaining him were instructed to treat him with the greatest possible courtesy and consideration and he was also permitted to see Sa'erah – before being put back on the *Vyner Brooke* to Singapore. There MacBryan lodged a complaint with the British Resident and threatened to publish the story, offering various newspapers 'an exposé of Brooke rule'; he claimed that the real reason for his deportation was the Rajah's fear that he would supplant him as ruler of the state. Vyner later explained to the governor that it would be 'quite impossible in a small place like Kuching to have a European ex-government officer recently converted to Islam cohabiting openly with a Malay woman of known bad character . . . and [furthermore] since both he and the Malay woman were Hajis, to have tolerated such a state of affairs would have been to run a grave risk of outraging local Mohammedan opinion'.

While under arrest in Sarawak, by his account, MacBryan had asked to see the Rajah and was refused, but he was told that he would be pleased to see him in England. Accordingly MacBryan returned to London by Imperial Airways and awaited the Rajah's return. When Vyner came back, in May, MacBryan visited him at his flat. At that meeting Vyner reiterated that he wished him to stay away from Sarawak and cease meddling in the affairs of the country. The next day MacBryan sent Vyner a letter in which he gave his 'solemn word of honour' to abide by the Rajah's wish 'in every detail'. In return for MacBryan's undertaking, Vyner promised, 'Dear Baron', to attempt to 'clear any stigma that may be attached to your name during recent events in Sarawak and Singapore. Sa'erah, your Haji friend, can do exactly as she likes, and her movements will in no way be restricted.'

Sylvia had left Sarawak shortly after they celebrated their silver wedding anniversary, in February 1936, and so missed the drama of

MacBryan's deportation, but she would remain closely involved in the continuing saga for years to come. In June, in London, she attended with Elizabeth and Harry Roy the première of their film *Everything is Rhythm*. Later that summer saw the publication of her first autobiography *Sylvia of Sarawak*, which she dedicated 'to my Husband – the man who has been my greatest friend – the man who has never let me down – and the man who has made me laugh more than anyone I know'. It was, Sylvia declared in her Foreword, 'not an ordinary biography. Indeed I never intended that it should be. Facts to my mind are insufferable, and dates fill me with fear.' But the shortage of specifics did not seem to bother the critics. H. E. Wortham (best known in his day as Peterborough in the *Daily Telegraph*) wrote in the *Sunday Times* that her life was 'pictured in a pattern, vivid, highly coloured, sometimes garish. But whatever the tone it possesses the underlying unity of temperament and personality. It is this that places her autobiography apart from the normal examples of its kind.' He added that, 'whatever the distinction of her father, this young Edwardian had quite unusual qualities to be able to command so many loyalties of friendship'. The *Times Literary Supplement* paid tribute to the Ranee's 'adaptability, her enthusiasm for life, her unconventionality and perhaps above all her sense of humour'; the reviewer also praised the 'engaging spontaneity' of the Ranee's writing. 'It is intimate without being indiscreet, frank without being malicious: in fact the only person Her Highness is hard on is herself.'

Undeterred by the disapproval of her mother-in-law, and doubtless spurred on by the example being set by her daughter Elizabeth – whose next film, *Olympic Honeymoon*, came out in December – Sylvia had also written a film synopsis about the first White Rajah, and in October 1936 Warner Brothers paid her £500 for the motion-picture rights. A clause in the contract stipulated that they would indemnify her if the film upset either Rajah Vyner or the dowager Ranee Margaret. Sylvia wrote excitedly to Doll in New Mexico asking her to come and visit her in Los Angeles the next spring, where she would be superintending 'a big Sarawak film'. Before that, she would spend the winter as usual in Sarawak.

Before leaving London, Sylvia called on Ranee Margaret at her dreary flat in Albert Road, off Regent's Park. Although she was by now in her eighty-seventh year, the dowager Ranee was 'still beautiful', recalled Sylvia; 'her eyes, so like my husband's, were still as blue'. She wore grey chiffon, with a black-velvet ribbon round her neck, a chiffon headscarf, her gloved hands resting on her lap. She seemed confused as to who Sylvia was and asked why her maid had dressed her up: 'Why does she make me sit here when there is nothing to do and no one to see?' By the time Sylvia reached Sarawak, on 7 December, Ranee Margaret had been dead for a week.

The Times saluted 'one of the last of those who helped to make the richly coloured pattern of Victorian society'. The *Sunday Times* mourned the 'passing of a vital personality', breaking a link with the old days of colonial expansion: 'The "White Ranee" came to her Eastern throne when the world beyond Suez was still mysterious and romantic; and when she withdrew from Sarawak there remained half a century of vivid life in Europe. A creature of commanding presence and beauty she dominated her circle by the force of her personality and her deep emotional response to the best in the writing and painting of her times.' Another newspaper noted that, when Queen Victoria received her at Windsor, she kissed her on both cheeks as a queen.

As if to accentuate the break with the past, in the same issue that carried obituaries of the dowager Ranee, the *Sarawak Gazette* announced that Sylvia's onward destination in the spring was to be Hollywood, where the Ranee would 'take part in the production of a film dealing with Sarawak's early history'.

For the time being, however, Sylvia was caught up with the continuing machinations of MacBryan, who was again threatening to descend on Kuching. On 29 December she wrote to him from the Astana. 'My dear Baron,' she began, and thanked him and Sa'erah for the 'really lovely sarong' they had given her for Christmas, which had been 'enormously admired'. 'Now listen Baron,' she went on:

> Why my dear boy do you go on trying to come out here when you know it is quite hopeless? It might not have been if only you had listened to my advice. If you had played your cards right you might be here now living at Bedil [his house near the Astana]. As it is you trusted the Malays a little too much. You believed they wanted a leader other than the Rajah. You wanted a Mohammedan country with a Mohammedan leader. The Malays might have

> followed you Baron had you been fabulously rich. As it is they sit on their hams and wait and see what happens. Unfortunately for you they did not wait silently – they talked. And their talk hasn't helped you towards your ultimate desire. Besides, you yourself in all you have written and signed have made it impossible for you to come out here again during this Rajah's lifetime. Had you ventured to some other country you might by now have been an amazing personality. Or had you been loyal to us from the beginning you might have gone very far. But I am afraid there is too much, far too much against you. When I return from Hollywood I will tell you what I mean. Do nothing until you see me. Don't spoil any chance you have for the future. You are young. We are not – keep quiet and be patient and one day I think you will be very near your goal. But only over our dead bodies Baron . . . Wait for me to return and I can tell you much.

Before receiving this, MacBryan had sent a seven-page letter to the Permanent Undersecretary of State for the Colonies setting out his grievances over his treatment the previous year and claiming that Vyner had failed to abide by his undertaking to 'clear the stigma' on his name. MacBryan said that this had resulted in his 'suffering considerable damage to my business and livelihood' and he considered himself 'no longer bound by any promise I made to the Rajah of Sarawak'. He was seeking the intervention of the Secretary of State over the deprivation 'of my proper rights and freedom of movement as a British subject . . . without affording me an opportunity of hearing or trial'.

The Colonial Office replied that they were seeking a report from the Sarawak government. MacBryan soon wrote again 'in order to give such explanation as I can as to the true cause of the sudden change of attitude towards me by the Rajah of Sarawak with whom I have enjoyed a long and unbroken friendship and have received numerous expressions of liking and regard'. He claimed he and his friends in Sarawak 'cannot but feel that the underlying cause of the change is the influence of the Ranee whose treatment of me has been most capricious, alternating between affection and abuse. Among her obsessions is that I am too intimate with Malays and am in some way plotting against her interests. This idea is not only a fallacy but is quite fantastic to the knowledge of all reponsible officials in Sarawak.' To bolster his exculpation he cited the fact that he had recently received letters from the Ranee's son-in-law Lord Inchcape 'expressing his appreciation of my advice on questions of succession and inheritance in Sarawak'; and, as evidence of what he called the Ranee's 'curious mentality', he sent the Colonial Office a copy of Sylvia's letter of 29 December.

The Colonial Office found the Ranee's 'theatrically-worded effusion' highly entertaining, one official noting: 'The whole story is fantastic, and throws grave doubts on Mr MacBryan's sanity. The Ranee's reference to her visit to Hollywood is strangely appropriate; only there would she find activities so bizarre!' Yet at the same time there was confusion as to the nature of her dealings with MacBryan. To Bertram, who eventually saw a copy, the letter indicated that MacBryan and the Ranee had initially been plotting, 'and that he double-crossed her by embarking on a covert enterprise of his own to supplant the Rajah by a Moslem ruler'. Sylvia's unspecified 'advice' to MacBryan may well have been, as Professor Bob Reece has suggested, that he should bide his time while Vyner was still rajah, so that he would still be in a position to act as a guiding eminence for Leonora in her possible future role as regent for her son Simon.

In any event the letter helped convince the Colonial Office that the Rajah had been fully justified and had acted within the law in excluding MacBryan, 'an undesirable character', so that there was no ground for intervention by the Secretary of State. Soon after having been informed of this decision, MacBryan withdrew his complaint and for the time being contented himself with some stockbroking in London.

11

WATCH OUT, HOLLYWOOD

In mid-February 1937 Sylvia set off for Hollywood as planned, leaving Vyner to rattle around on his own at the Astana in Kuching. Travelling with her secretary Freddy Mann, she sailed from Singapore in the vast steamship *Empress of Japan*, the fastest, largest and finest trans-Pacific liner. En route they stopped in Japan, a visit organised by the Japanese company Nissa Shokai, which had been engaged in various farming and mining activities in Sarawak since the beginning of Vyner's reign. The previous year Nissa Shokai had arranged for a Japanese rear-admiral to visit Sarawak. Notwithstanding Japan's withdrawal from the League of Nations three years previously and its increasingly bellicose actions, the admiral and his party were given a twenty-one-gun salute from Fort Margherita. In Japan, Sylvia too was treated like royalty, even though she was not a state guest. When they put in for a night at the port of Kobe, just west of Osaka, on Japan's inland sea, no one, reported the *Sarawak Gazette* – not even the wife of the President of the Philippine Republic – was allowed on or off the ship until the Ranee had disembarked; audiences at cinema houses throughout Japan were later treated to a newsreel of this great event.

When eventually they reached Los Angeles, awaiting Sylvia at her hotel was a film script, *The White Rajah*, written by Errol Flynn. Flynn had recently made his name with his swashbuckling performance in the pirate adventure *Captain Blood* (1935) and he saw himself as perfect for the part of James Brooke. Indeed, he told Sylvia that he had always imagined that the two of them were remarkably alike. Before becoming an actor, Flynn had spent much of the time between 1928 and 1931 in New Guinea, running a coastal sloop, mining for gold, and growing tobacco and coconuts, although some attributed his more exotic 'memories' – trading slaves, abandoning a sinking ship, et cetera – to his ability to bluff, to make things look a little more exciting than they were. He had used more than a little artistic licence in the script that now lay on the Ranee's dressing table.

Though she was hardly a paragon of factual accuracy, Sylvia decided that Flynn's film script was, historically speaking, 'an absurdity', and she wrote to Warner Brothers to tell them so. The result was that Flynn asked her to dinner. Arriving at his house, she was shown into a large sitting room with leopard-skin rugs on the floor and 'furnished in the glossiest style'. She was told that Mr Flynn would be down shortly.

> I waited; and suddenly the staircase became brilliantly floodlit. On it there appeared Errol Flynn himself in a pair of white close-fitting trousers that showed every nerve and muscle of his body. Slowly and gracefully he descended, giving me plenty of time to appreciate his entrance – and him. He flashed a smile at me that would have sent a thousand fans into hysterics and then he started to make me a drink . . . The lights slowly dimmed, and I could only just see him across the room. We had no time for conversation before the lights blazed on again, to herald the arrival of Lillie [Lili] Damita [Flynn's tempestuous French wife]. She also wore white; a gorgeous creature, holding an enormous Persian cat in her arms. She greeted me briefly and proceeded to lie on the floor with her cat.

Eventually they went in to dinner, in the course of which Flynn took exception to Sylvia's strident criticisms of what she later described as his 'ridiculous story about a girl who dressed up as a boy and chased James Brooke through the jungles of Sarawak'. It had made James Brooke out to be a Casanova, which was ridiculous, she said, given that the wound he had received in Burma had 'for ever stilled his sexual passions'. Flynn protested: 'You can't have a motion picture without love.' 'And you can't have James Brooke with it,' came Sylvia's reply. They parted friends, as she recalled, but although Flynn was paid $25,000 for his pains by Warner, and correspondence and negotiations rumbled on for years afterwards, the film was never made.

Sylvia stayed on for a further month in Hollywood, where she was reported to have acted as 'technical advisor on a photoplay about Sarawak' – presumably a reference to the doomed Flynn venture – and done some radio broadcasting. She was also, it appears, visited there by her sister Dorothy, whom she had not seen since 1924, when Doll followed D. H. Lawrence and his wife Frieda to Taos, New Mexico, installing herself in a cabin that she called 'The Tower Beyond Tragedy'. Doll had spent the intervening thirteen years painting the landscape and native Indians of Taos Pueblo. She had published a memoir, *Lawrence and Brett: A Friendship*, three years after Lawrence's death from tuberculosis in 1930, quarrelled a lot with Frieda, and taken American citizenship in 1936. Away from her family, she had grown more forthright and built a reputation as a village eccentric; in later years, her biographer Sean Hignett notes, she would become a tourist attraction. But she never quite escaped from the spell of her father, naming a series of dogs after him (Reggie, Baliol, etc.) and painting the Esher arms on the door of her adobe studio. She also stayed in sporadic touch with Sylvia by letter and, in 1931, when she drew up her first will, she bequeathed to each of Syv's daughters one of her Indian blankets; in addition Leonora was to have her silver belt, Elizabeth her beadwork gloves and Valerie her Indian bead belt.

When Aldous Huxley came to stay with Doll in the summer of 1937, he found her 'still' not speaking to Frieda and 'odder than ever in a Mexican 10 gallon with a turkey's feather stuck in it, sky blue breeks, top boots and a strong American accent'. It would be 'difficult to imagine anything too exaggerated or conspicuous for Brett to wear', wrote Hignett, yet she nevertheless shuddered at Sylvia's clothes when she saw her in Hollywood: 'My sister tells me she never wears anything now except Native dress,' Doll wrote to her friend Una Jeffers, 'which means Malay costume . . . heavens, how embarrassing.'

From Hollywood, Sylvia returned for the summer to England, where she was joined by Vyner and in October attended the première of Elizabeth and Harry Roy's third film, *Rhythm Racketeer*. The next month, however, she was off again across the Atlantic in the luxurious Cunard liner *Aquitania* (with its Adam-style drawing room in first class) to New York, where she announced on arrival that she was to remain for two months. The Ranee's ostensible purpose this time was to promote her autobiography at the National Book Fair – where she inevitably regaled reporters with more overblown accounts of her life among the headhunters in 'the last Eden' – but the length of her stay suggests that equally compelling reasons for the trip were her well-known love of nightclubbing (a subject on which she later contributed a wonderfully incongruous essay to the *Sarawak Gazette*) and to enable her to spend time with the latest man in her life.

Jack Golden was a nightclub pianist, the accompanist, musical director and drinking buddy of Harry Richman, the phenomenally popular song-and-dance man known as 'Mr Broadway' in the 1920s and 1930s. 'Like most of my friends,' Richman wrote in his memoir *A Hell of a Life*, 'Jack was a character. He loved to drink. I could handle the booze, or thought I could. Jack thought he could handle it, too, but he didn't have the experience I had.' Wanting to be more than just Richman's accompanist, Golden was forever going off to start bands of his own; but, as Richman recalled, 'his ideas were far ahead of their time so he never got very far'. By the 1960s, he was running a haberdashery near Baltimore.

It is not clear where or when Jack Golden and the Ranee had met for the first time, but Sylvia was soon referring to him in her letters to Doll as 'my beloved boy' (he was some years her junior), 'anchorage', or simply 'my boy friend'. As with previous boyfriends, she made no attempt to keep his existence from other members of her family, and on the eve of the Second World War her mother Nellie went so far as to urge her to go to New York to be with him. Vyner, too, appears to have known all about Jack Golden, and during the war he even gave him power of attorney over his wife's affairs and, according to Golden, promised to pay him £500 a year for his pains.

Back in London, meanwhile, Valerie had taken advantage of the absence of both her parents to get married. Sylvia's youngest daughter was 'a natural flirt', according to her mother. Having turned down the handsome amateur yachtsman whom her uncle Bertram had deemed so suitable and broken off a further engagement to the actor Kenneth Duncan (who was briefly touted as 'Britain's Clark Gable'), in the autumn of 1937 Vava had fallen into the clutches of the European middleweight 'catch-as-catch-can' wrestling champion. A divorcee whispered to be Cuban and known in wrestling circles as 'The Gable of Grapple', Bob Gregory was not quite what the Rajah and Ranee had had in mind as a husband for their youngest and most beautiful daughter. Vyner, who was still out in Sarawak, threatened to disinherit her if they married, but no sooner had Sylvia left for New York than Valerie announced her engagement. On more than one occasion she failed to show up at the register office, but the ceremony eventually took place on 22 November at Marylebone. Neither of Valerie's sisters knew about it until after it had happened. On the marriage certificate Gregory gave his occupation as a 'physical culturist'. Once again, there was no shortage of newspaper excitement.

Exasperated by this latest development, Vyner stopped Valerie's allowance for a while, and remarked to a friend, 'Thank God I haven't four daughters. What a family!' Sylvia, too, expressed her disapproval – publicly at least – although in the opinion of Stirling Boyd, she was entirely to blame for bringing her daughters up 'like tarts' (he remarked to another friend: ' "Princess Baba" was out here when she was well under 16, and their moral training is an imaginary quantity!'). The wedding was attended by a blaze of publicity, which the Gregorys eagerly fanned by driving around London in a white open car with 'Baba and Bob' painted on the back of it and Valerie carrying a toy fur monkey, larger than she was, wherever she went.

The next summer – 1938 – they moved to California, where Valerie tried without success to get a screen contract with a Hollywood studio, despite an alluring perfomance as a cooch dancer in Universal's *You Can't Cheat an Honest Man* (1939), leading one newspaper to label her 'The Siren of Sarawak'. 'At home, Princess Baba would expect any hoochie-coochie dancing to be done by the servants,' the paper hazarded. 'In Hollywood the Princess is GLAD to brush the sleep out of her eyes, straighten her tousled hair and slide out of bed at 6 a.m. to be on set by 7.30.' On other occasions, 'Princess Baba' was observed sitting loyally ringside during her husband's bouts – by her account there was a clause in his wrestling contract stipulating that she should be present watching each contest. The couple were reported in *Time* magazine to be expecting a baby and to be planning to buy an island in the Netherlands East Indies, to be called 'Babaland', where, according to Valerie, 'every man would be Rajah'. 'We're going to have a democracy,' she declared, 'but with a court and things – maybe an aristocratic democracy. I think a country without lots of uniforms and braids is no fun.'

The 'fantastic publicity' surrounding both Valerie and Elizabeth eventually led Vyner to issue a statement to the press saying that it was

> of constant annoyance to the natives and to myself that my daughters should be referred to as 'Princesses'. This title is a pure fabrication of the Press, a slogan which has been used and used and misused until not only our country but every country in the world is heartily sick of the sound of Sarawak. I wish to state definitely here and now that none of my daughters are princesses. Before they were married their names were Miss Leonora Margaret Brooke, Miss Elizabeth Brooke and Miss Nancy Valerie Brooke. At least that is what they were christened. We have done our best to try to put a stop to the statements that have been pouring out from California and New York, but we are helpless in the hands of this undignified sensationalism that some people make use of as publicity. I would be extremely obliged if the gentlemen of the Press would realise once and for all that there are no such people as Princess Gold, Princess Pearl and Princess Baba, but that I have three daughters whose names are: The Countess of Inchcape, Mrs Harry Roy and Mrs Bob Gregory.

When Harry Roy and Elizabeth arrived back from a tour of South America soon afterwards, they affected nonchalance at the Rajah's statement. Reporters could not help noticing that 'Princess Pearl' was painted on her luggage.

By this time Sylvia was beginning to feel that time was running out for her to do something about the succession. For many years a combination of her hostility and Bertram's tact had kept her godson Anthony Brooke (then widely known as Peter) away from Sarawak. The youngest of Bertram and Gladys's four children, Anthony had had, by his own account, a 'strange' early life. His mother had left when he was 'four or five', and thereafter he had lived in a succession of boarding houses at St Leonards-on-Sea, on the south coast of England, looked after mostly by his nanny. He had seen his mother, who lived in Paris for many years after the separation, irregularly. His father would disappear from time to time to Sarawak, but Anthony was 'strangely uncurious about what went on out there . . . I don't remember asking him what he did while he was away . . . I was a very shy person, with a bad stammer, which was accentuated by my early days at school, when people laughed at it. There was one schoolmaster in particular who was very brutal about it.'

This nervous, stammering boy was nonetheless still the heir apparent to the Brooke Raj, and in 1934, at the age of twenty-one, after Eton, a year at Trinity, Cambridge, and a stint learning the Malay language and Muslim law at the School of Oriental Studies in London, it was time for him to learn the ropes. In June that year, with 'Auntie Syv' safely back in England, Bertram brought his son out to Sarawak, where he entered the service as a cadet. In the same way that Vyner had been, Anthony was rather abashed by all the attention he received wherever he went: 'Everybody is bewilderingly embarrassing here – they will insist on showing me through doors first and getting up when I come into the room and altogether seem to do all they can to make me feel different. And I'm not quite sure I like feeling different! However everybody is terribly nice and I daresay I'll get used to it as with any luck I may be in this country another 50 years or so! (If God and the Japanese are willing.)' He made a favourable first impression, though. Charles Macaskie, chief secretary since 1932, told Ranee Margaret that he had 'charmed all hearts. His intellect is remarkable and his poise and manner here were perfection. The Tuan Muda must indeed be proud of him and the way in which he handled himself in his future kingdom.'

After a tour of the outstations, Anthony was seconded to the Malayan Civil Service, where he served variously as an acting resident and magistrate before returning to Sarawak in 1936. He did stints at the outstations of Nanga Meluan and Marudi, and at the Kuching Secretariat, before going back to England in 1938 to take a course in colonial administration at Rhodes House, Oxford, taught by the celebrated imperial authority Margery Perham. After Bertram suffered a nervous breakdown that year, rendering him no longer capable of discharging his responsibilities in the power-sharing arrangement with Vyner, it was widely assumed that Anthony would succeed his uncle as rajah.

This growing assumption now steered Sylvia towards an alternative strategy. Increasingly taken as she was with America, the romance of Sarawak was beginning to wear thin for her, and besides, as she and Vyner grew older, the constant to-ing and fro-ing was becoming tiring. As an alternative to handing the Raj over to Anthony, for whom neither of them felt much affection, the possibility of ceding Sarawak to Britain in exchange for a financial settlement seemed at least worth investigating. In 1913 George Bernard Shaw had told her: 'The sooner Vyner hands that unhappy island [*sic*] over to the British Government for thirty millions or so, the better.' More than twenty years later, with Anthony now carrying all before him and money worries beginning to weigh on the minds of the Rajah and Ranee, that idea began to seem increasingly attractive.

In the summer of 1938 Sylvia asked Reggie's old friend and private secretary Lawrence 'Thrushy' Burgis, who was by then at the Cabinet Office, to sound out the likely attitude of the British government if Vyner offered to transfer to the British Crown his sovereignty over Sarawak. After obtaining Vyner's authorisation, Burgis duly made contact with the Colonial Office. He explained that the Rajah was extremely shy and could not bring himself to make a formal and official approach to the government, but that he had made it clear to him (Burgis) that he was 'desirous of divesting himself of the burden', providing that he was suitably compensated – a figure of £5 million was said to have been mentioned.

After a further 'long talk' with Vyner, however, Burgis admitted that he thought that 'the Rajah did not have so clearly in his mind as the Ranee had in hers' a complete transfer of sovereignty. 'The Rajah appears to be obsessed with two chief anxieties,' noted the assistant secretary Edward Gent after his interview with Burgis,

> viz, his own and the Ranee's financial interests, and a desire not to appear to the natives of Sarawak to be throwing them over. He wants to preserve his position in these two respects, but at the same time to be relieved of any active duties or practical responsibility in the State. He expresses no concern for his three married daughters, and hopes that in any event his nephew Peter [Anthony] Brooke could be retained in the Colonial Administrative Service, while the Ranee according to Mr Burgis does not conceal her desire that the 'White Rajah' system should be terminated once and for all on a satisfactory financial settlement for herself and her husband. But the Rajah for his part is unable to make up his mind between such a complete cut and the less revolutionary step of handing over the administration to a British Adviser appointed by the Crown on much the same lines as the procedure in one of the Malay states . . . Burgis is inclined to doubt whether the Rajah is capable of achieving any distinct preference without guidance.

A lunch meeting was proposed between the Rajah, Ranee, Burgis and Gent, and at Sylvia's suggestion, a restaurant was chosen at Leicester Square – 'Very typical!' noted Gent. But even the prospect of such an informal beginning as this was too much for the Rajah and on Monday morning (the day of lunch), Burgis telephoned Gent to say sorry but the Rajah was unable keep the appointment. There were no further discussions before he and Sylvia returned to Sarawak, arriving in Kuching on 24 October.

On that visit Sylvia remained for her customary three months, during which time the *Sarawak Gazette* ran an article based on her Ranee's experiences the previous year at various Manhattan nightspots. When she departed again, on the 16 January 1939, it was on the first flight from the newly completed Kuching aerodrome, which would in due course become a stopping-off point between Singapore and Hong Kong, and allowed for three air mails a week. The *Sarawak Gazette* reported that the Ranee was seen off by 'the Rajah, native chiefs, friends, well-wishers and a band of Dyaks in their native dress, who brandished their knives and spears as they danced and sang their farewell'.

On the day that Sylvia arrived back in London, 10 February, a short notice of her next book, *The Three White Rajas*, published by Cassell, appeared in *The Times*. The reviewer suggested that 'the appeal of the book lies in the Ranee's personal approach to her subject rather than in its historical importance' – a delicate hint perhaps that, while her book contained engaging passages on Malay and Dyak legends and a collection of colourful anecdotes about the rajahs, the Ranee was not to be entirely relied on for facts. The foreword was written by Vyner without having read a word of the book. The next day the *Times Literary Supplement* also carried a review, which observed that the aim of the Ranee's biographical sketches was to 'appeal to the popular imagination and with that end in view she relies on the presentation of character rather than on the marshalling of facts or the discussion of politics'. It also drew attention to the inconsistencies in her appraisal of her father-in-law, Rajah Charles. 'On page 124 she speaks of his justice, his wisdom, his immense foresight. On page 127 he is described as "unscrupulous and inhuman"; and on page 148 she refers to him as "this fine old man".'

In the spring Sylvia received a call from her daughter Valerie, who was still in Los Angeles, to say that she was ill (it is possible, given the earlier reports of an expected baby, that she had had a miscarriage), and could she come? So in April Sylvia again travelled to California for what *Time* magazine called a 'public reconciliation' with Valerie – who was still Princess Baba to the American press however much the Rajah protested.

When she opened the door to their small apartment in Los Angeles, she found her son-in-law 'doing physical jerks with an enormous crowbar in his hands, completely oblivious to everything else', and the kitchen 'stacked with unwashed dishes'. It was soon evident that 'Bob and Baba' were far from being a happy couple. The previous autumn they had separated for some months while Valerie tried in vain to get into motion pictures in London. She had subsequently returned, but she told her mother that she was still miserable and increasingly irritated by the crude way that her husband used her exotic identity as 'Princess Baba' to promote his own interests. 'She had something of Vyner's hatred of public exposure,' wrote Sylvia, 'his repugnance to trading on his name.' Valerie soon fled back to England again, on the pretext that it was easier to find work there. She never saw her husband again.

For Sylvia the visit to California in the spring of 1939 was the first of several trips to America that would keep her away from Sarawak for the next two and a half years. Having for the time being given up hope of either selling the country or changing the succession, she seemed resigned to the fact that Anthony would succeed to the Raj. This was the last thing that Sylvia wanted, but it was hard to see what could stop him.

While the Ranee had been in Los Angeles, Anthony had returned to Sarawak to take up the post of district officer at Mukah. He had not been there long before one of his junior officers complained to him of having been harshly dismissed from the Sarawak service (for understating his debts while applying for a government loan). Anthony felt that the man had been 'savagely' done by, but he also saw this as an opportunity to have a go at members of the committee of administration in Kuching, who he thought knew nothing of Sarawak outside the capital and were becoming too fond of the increased power recently bestowed upon them by the Rajah. The chief secretary, Edward Parnell, and the financial secretary, H. M. Calvert, were '*openly* referred to as Mussolini and Hitler by the *Chinese* in the bazaar!!' Anthony told his sister Jean. He persuaded his uncle Vyner to allow him to launch an enquiry into the affair. The enquiry ('not exactly a model of judicial procedure', as one Colonial Office official noted) had dramatic results, leading to the resignation of five senior members of the Sarawak government, including Parnell, Calvert and Sylvia's bête noire Stirling Boyd, the Chief Justice. All of this suited Vyner, who held that 'a native state cannot be governed from an office table' and that the government so formed was 'drifting away from native interests' – which had always been his primary concern as Rajah; and, of course, it was convenient to have his dirty work done for him. As far as many of the natives were concerned, meanwhile, it restored their confidence in the government, as it spelt the restoration of the Rajah as the supreme head of government.

In April, shortly after the enquiry, Vyner appointed Anthony as Rajah Muda – albeit cryptically, letting it be known that this had no bearing on the succession – and when the Rajah departed for his annual furlough in England soon afterwards, he left his twenty-six-year-old nephew with absolute autocratic powers in charge of the country.

While the popular press in England paid more attention to the birth of a daughter, Roberta, to Princess Pearl and Harry Roy, the Colonial Office watched with interest the political developments in Sarawak. The five senior administrators were deemed to be 'of no great loss' – Sir Shenton Thomas in Singapore added, with regard to Edward Parnell, a personal friend of Vyner: 'He has a Japanese wife who knows everything that is going on in Kuching. She is better off out of the country.' The Colonial Office also saw in Anthony a straightforward young man with whom they could do business (they probably knew nothing at that time of his passion for astrology and other transcendental pursuits), in contrast to the idle and increasingly whimsical Rajah and his 'dangerous' wife.

The Colonial Office was still keen to secure the appointment of a general adviser in Sarawak, concerned that to sanction a British citizen having absolute dominion over such a territory was becoming increasingly untenable. In 1937 it had received its first hard information about conditions there from M. J. Breen, a senior administrator from Hong Kong, who had spent three months in Sarawak producing a report in response to an original request by the Sarawak government. Breen's report did not make happy reading, observing that until recently Sarawak had 'maintained an uneventful and on the whole contented existence. The Rajahs ruled the country on the lines of an hereditary country estate, and their officers appointed by favour regarded themselves as personal agents not as officials of an Administration . . . But the system is now breaking down as modern progress and patriarchal conditions cannot be reconciled.' His damning conclusion was that 'the natural resultant of a lethargic ruler vested with absolute authority and an amateurish council of advisers is spasmodic administration, makeshift policies and an absence of discipline'.

Sir Shenton Thomas, for one, considered Breen's report overdrawn, but even he did not dispute the large proportion of the total revenue that seemed to be appropriated by the ruling family (in 1936 it amounted to £34,000 – one-sixteenth of the total revenue for the year) and the fact that less than one-twentieth of the Brookes' emoluments were spent in the country. In his note to the Colonial Office concerning Breen's report Thomas added that, while the Rajah could safely be seen as 'the father of his people', the Ranee 'intervenes in official matters . . . and so is a menace as well as being a nuisance'.

'Sarawak is a territory of very great economic possibilities & of defence importance,' noted Gent in May 1939, '& it is essential to keep this iron hot & not lose the opportunity, which appears to present itself, to ensure an orderly introduction of modern ideas of progress.' Gent was far from alone in apprehending Sylvia's attitude to the new Rajah Muda as heir presumptive to be hostile, and predicted: 'We may yet have a dispute on that account to settle.' He advised the Undersecretary of State for the Colonies, the Marquess of Dufferin and Ava, that it would be unwise to press the Rajah on whether Anthony was to succeed, as it might 'stir up great opposition from the Ranee' and might wreck the great opportunity now offered to the Colonial Office of getting a foothold in Sarawak.

Lord Dufferin, who knew Sylvia and Vyner socially (their daughters had been bridesmaids at his marriage to Maureen Guinness, one of the three 'Golden Guinness Girls', in 1930 and they often met each other racing), agreed: 'The Ranee is a dangerous woman and I think if we let matters take their course Peter Brooke will almost automatically step into his uncle's shoes.' 'The important point now', he added, 'is to get the Rajah to agree to the appointment of an adviser. He is so shy and suspicious that it is a delicate matter approaching him. If either of us get an opportunity of meeting him in the natural course, we might raise it if a suitable opportunity presents itself.' The Colonial Office eventually got its wish in July, with Vyner agreeing to the appointment of W. E. Pepys, formerly general adviser to the State of Johore, as general adviser to Sarawak – though he firmly refuted the suggestion that this indicated any change in the relations between the British government and Sarawak.

Anthony, meanwhile, while acting head of the Sarawak government, had enacted various education reforms that would assist the Malay population and stand him in good stead with the anti-cessionists after the war. Sensitive to the prevailing climate of colonial reform, he had also amended the penal code and orders on whipping, the protection of women and girls and the punishment of mutiny, and widened the criteria for those deemed to be natural-born Sarawak subjects. One of his last acts during his six months in charge was to issue a proclamation supporting Britain's declaration of war against Germany and Italy.

On the outbreak of war, in September 1939, Vyner hurried back to Sarawak, arriving there on 9 October. Sylvia was by that time zig-zagging her way across the Atlantic in the *Queen Mary*, in order to honour her commitment to do a lecture tour of America, raising money for Sarawak's lepers, but also longing to be back with Jack Golden and keen to sell some of her Dyak designs of textiles and jewellery. 'I think all the Jewish blood in our family must have poured itself into me,' she wrote to Doll, 'I love business. Everything I do is commercial, that's the sort of mind I have I am afraid.' There was a certain amount of necessity about her trading activities. With the Sarawak government office in London unable to send over her allowance during wartime, she was reliant in New York on the money that Vyner had sent to Golden, who, besides serving as an emotional prop to the Ranee, now had power of attorney over her affairs. However, her allowance never seemed to cover her expenditure and for the next few years she was permanently strapped for cash. By 1942 she had run up debts of $7,000 in America alone.

In the autumn of 1939 Sylvia made two trips to Hollywood, on the second occasion breaking her journey to visit Doll in New Mexico. She told her sister afterwards that 'it would break my heart to live in Taos', though she admitted that the scenery was beautiful and the people were 'charming'. 'It made me so happy to see you amongst a crowd like that and to know how much they all think of you. You certainly have gone to the right spot for you and I can't see you anywhere else.'

Sylvia had been hoping that Vava was going to come over to California, but soon learned from her cook (her most reliable source of news from home at that time) that her daughters were enjoying

London too much, 'out every night at the Café Anglais, and then on to the Embassy Club . . .' Vava had also fallen in love with an 'awful' man, reported the cook. This development Sylvia kept to herself when she called on her son-in-law, who was in a sorry state anyway, having just been thrown headlong out of the ring. 'I am afraid he is too light a weight to wrestle much longer,' she told Doll. 'He wants to start a fish and chip shop, so I am going through the details with him to see if I can't perhaps help him a little.'

When she returned to New York, in December, Sylvia heard that Gregory had sent Vava divorce papers and told Doll: 'I hope to God it is true.' It was – they were eventually divorced the following November (1940). Sylvia was planning to spend Christmas in Manhattan, holed up with Jack 'together like Scrooges . . . He hates going out, and I don't like it without the kids.' Instead she set to work on her latest novel, *A Star Fell*, about an epileptic Tamil, Rama Chandra, brought up by missionaries whose teachings have a lasting effect on his unhealthy imagination, creating in him a particular obsession with the story of the Immaculate Conception. The American publisher Harrison-Hilton had bought the book after seeing the first two chapters, and now wanted 60,000 words more from her by the end of February, 'which would be easy', she told Doll, 'if I wasn't going around on this bloody tour talking my head off from Jan 9th until the second week in March'.

On 29 December Jack abandoned her to go to Florida. Faced with the prospect of seeing in the New Year on her own, she was rescued by Doll's friend and patron at Taos, Mabel Dodge Luhan[1] who held a party at her fabulous apartment at number 1 Fifth Avenue. She urged the Ranee to come in her 'full Malay dress', thinking that it would entertain her artistic friends, and Sylvia, who rarely required much encouragement to don her Oriental garb, was only too happy to oblige.

At the beginning of January Sylvia set off on her lecture tour. Billed as 'Queen of the Headhunters' and once again sporting her royal yellow sarong, she criss-crossed America by train, speaking

[1] A wealthy heiress from Buffalo, Mabel had married a Taos Pueblo Indian and built the 'Big House' on the outer edge of pueblo land, where she invited D. H. Lawrence *et al* and so effectively founded the artistic community there.

each evening at a different venue and afterwards taking questions from the floor – the commonest one, so she remembered, was: 'Why the heck d'ya marry a nigger?' By 24 January she had reached Pittsburgh, where she was encircled by journalists seeking her reaction to the news that Vyner had deprived his nephew Anthony of his title – the culmination of a sequence of events in Sarawak of which she seems to have been completely oblivious.

The previous October Vyner and his nephew had overlapped in Sarawak for about two weeks. During this time, observers noticed one or two signs of tension between the Rajah and Rajah Muda, notably one evening at the club in Kuching, when Anthony had lured all the ladies away from the Rajah's roulette table by performing card tricks, with the result that the Rajah left in a huff. Two days later Anthony had departed on two months' leave for Rangoon, where he was to be married to Kathleen Hudden, the sister of a district officer in the Sarawak service. When he passed through Singapore, the governor, Sir Shenton Thomas, noted that the Rajah Muda had 'developed considerably' and seemed enthusiastic to make Sarawak a model state. The governor thought he would make a first-rate rajah. However, the reigning Rajah was beginning to have other ideas.

As soon as he arrived back in Sarawak, Vyner had begun to hear disturbing reports about Anthony's behaviour while he had been away. Among the criticisms were that the Rajah Muda had been supercilious, reluctant to take advice, extravagant with government money and had tended to judge officers according to their horoscopes. In a letter to the Scottish MP Sir John Kerr, Stirling Boyd later quoted 'another man in the Service' who said that the Rajah Muda had made himself 'incredibly unpopular during the time that he held the reins of Government and there is not a soul, young or old, who has a good word for him. He was inverted to a pathological extent and I think most of his queer ideas on dignity and things of that sort arose out of his crushing sense of inferiority.' When asked about these allegations, Anthony pointed out that, having caused the resignation of the entire government 'on a matter of principle', he would hardly have been 'the flavour of the day among men in the

Service'. Comments about his 'queer ideas on dignity and things of that sort' would have been natural and predictable reactions.

In her second autobiography Sylvia went further, charging Anthony with having been an exhibitionist and displaying 'symptoms of folie de grandeur'. She wrote that he had had a golden cardboard crown clamped on to his car, and issued instructions that all ox-carts, motor cars, and rickshaws were to draw to one side at his approach. Anthony is adamant that his aunt made all this up. 'Having cardboard crowns made and pinned on my car? Stopping the traffic? No! What else can be – or need be – said?' He is probably the last person alive who would be able to remember.

One can certainly conceive of Sylvia inventing these kinds of details, but, to give her her due, in this case the stories seem to have emanated from those 'men in the Service' who bore a grudge against Anthony on account of his youth and unclubbable behaviour. In his letter to Kerr, Boyd too reported hearing that 'Master Peter' had 'insisted on having the traffic stopped for him' on his way to his office. Whether or not the stories were true, 'if [this] came to the ears of the Rajah, he would undoubtedly have seen red', remarked Boyd. He concluded that the demotion was most probably due to an accumulation of incidents that caused the Rajah to deduce 'not only that Peter was trying to run the country but that he was trying to run him. That would be the last straw.'

On 17 January 1940 Vyner issued a proclamation: 'It appears to the Rajah that Mr Anthony Brooke is not yet fitted to exercise the responsibilities of the high position and all authority and powers vested in Mr Anthony Brooke by proclamation in March last year are hereby derogated and brought to an end.'

Shortly afterwards Vyner wrote a letter to Bertram, saying: 'No one could have started off under fairer auspices than Peter did, but I come back to find everything changed.' Vyner said he blamed himself for having put his nephew in sole charge of Sarawak with so little experience. Nevertheless, he thought Anthony had 'got very much up against the people of Sarawak, probably through tactlessness or over zealousness or something, and the best thing for himself is to be away for a bit and let things settle down'.

Anthony, meanwhile, had had intimations that his uncle was unhappy with him, having received a cable in Singapore accusing him of being 'extraordinarily generous' with government money in furnishing the house of the new general adviser. But he did not learn of his demotion until he reached Athens, where he stayed with his mother on his way back from his honeymoon and where he saw a copy of the proclamation in a newspaper.

12

I JUST WON'T HAVE NO SAID TO ME

Confronted in America by headlines such as 'White Rajah Degrades Nephew: Not Fit to Rule', Sylvia told reporters that she was 'amazed' by the news. 'I knew the nephew was considered a little young and had made a rather unfortunate marriage,' she said, 'but I didn't expect anything so drastic. It is so unlike my husband to do anything so determined as this.' At the same time she made no attempt to hide her delight, declaring that she felt 'pretty sure' that her daughter Leonora, Lady Inchcape (who had been recently widowed and was by then driving an ambulance in England), would now become Crown Princess of Sarawak and succeed to the Raj.

Referring to Anthony's 'rather unfortunate' marriage to the 'commoner' sister of a Sarawak government official, Sylvia explained: 'I don't like to be snobbish, but the natives are very particular about these things.' The Ranee's comments exacerbated the sense of outrage at the Colonial Office about Anthony's demotion. 'Good Gad!' minuted Edward Gent when he saw the press cuttings.

In Athens Anthony also read what Sylvia had to say. His sister Jean urged a dignified silence, but instead he fired off a volley of letters, aimed, he told Jean, at stopping

> this rotten cheap publicity about Sarawak which looks like continuing in the Press so long as the Ranee remains capable of wagging her tongue – ie so long as she is alive. Sarawak must not

> continue to be regarded with the contempt for which the Ranee has herself been solely responsible, and the next couple of months will show whether I was right to take this line or pathetically wrong. At some future date it may be useful for the Press to have known that I do not intend to associate myself with the whole Sarawak 'ballyhoo' . . . The whole world must know that Sarawak is a reputable country . . .

In another letter on the same day he added:

> The Ranee's statement, even though it appeared in the sort of papers read by nobodys, provided me with a perfectly irresistible opportunity of showing her that she is not 'top dog', and that I did not intend to lie down and be kicked while in that position . . . since I have reason to believe that history will impute to her some connection with the recent proclamation (which the Rajah is by this time bitterly regretting) I'm none too certain that life, for her, will continue to be a bed of roses . . .

Convinced of Sylvia's 'malicious intent' to damage his reputation, Anthony also wrote to his solicitor:

> If you would be good enough to let the Ranee know on my behalf that I will on this occasion be satisfied with a private written apology if it is couched in terms, alternatively the Ranee must publicly deny these remarks were made . . . Since the Ranee does not always appear to find it easy to control either her speech or her imagination, it would, I think, be a kindness to add in language that will leave her in no doubt that I mean precisely what I say, that I shall not tolerate the publication of such mischievous libel, neither shall I hesitate to take action against any such unfounded attacks on my private life.

He further asked his solicitor to inform 'the various controlling authorities of the world press' of his course of action and to say that he would be 'grateful if they could refrain from associating the activities of the Ranee and her family from those of myself and my wife'.

Quite aside from the feud over the succession, Anthony had for some time been bridling at the detrimental effect that the antics of the Ranee and her daughters were having on the image of Sarawak. When Bertram sought to calm his son down, saying that he should read the press notices as an ordinary member of the public, Anthony insisted that

> in the interests of Sarawak the Ranee should be silenced . . . The Rajah has now, as always, my genuine sympathy for her [Sylvia's] irresponsible and uncharitable conduct towards her kith and kin and for the most irretrievable damage she has caused to the prestige of Sarawak and to the name of Brooke by her deplorable public behaviour in recent years. I am very sorry for her too, if only because during her lifetime she has succeeded in bringing unhappiness both to herself and to others, and one would have to be made of marble to feel no pity with so sad and unenviable an earthly history.

It was certainly true that, besides the news about Anthony, Sylvia had few reasons to feel happy at that time. She was permanently estranged from her only surviving brother, Oliver – who told Doll in January: 'My views on Sylvia can never be altered' – increasingly apart from Vyner, separated for the time being from her boyfriend Jack Golden, and worn out by her lecture tour. In early February, she learned of the death of her mother Nellie, the Dowager Viscountess Esher – 'one of the last to have known Queen Victoria with real intimacy', as her obituarist in *The Times* noted. Sylvia was unable to return home for the funeral because of her lecturing contract. 'What could I do?' she wrote in her second autobiography. 'The show had to go on!' 'I must say I would like to have been with her,' she wrote to Doll at the time. 'But there it is, she has gone on a great adventure back to the man she loved.' As when her father died, Sylvia may have been more affected than she let on. The next month she was admitted to hospital in New York suffering from nervous exhaustion.

She recovered quickly enough, however, helped by a spell with Jack Golden and Harry Richman in sunny Florida. But her lecturing payment was halved because she had broken her contract by failing to appear at her final two venues. By now her daughters were 'yelling for me to come home', she told Doll; 'their love affairs are all mixed up, and they know I will get them out somehow'.

When Sylvia returned to London, shortly afterwards, she may not have been overjoyed to learn that Bertram had brokered a truce between Vyner and Anthony. Bertram's role as go-between was made easier by the fact that he had had some sympathy with Vyner's actions in demoting Anthony in the first place. Two weeks after the proclamation he had written to his wife Gladys saying that their son had not been 'branded for life' and that it was a case of 'least said, soonest mended . . . He [the Rajah] hasn't done it just for fun,' wrote Bertram. 'He is fearfully perturbed by the idea that Peter, with what amounts to Dictator's powers, even temporarily, might suddenly see fit to use them as a Dictator in some way (with the best intentions) which might be injurious to the State, or antagonise those with whom he is working . . . He is probably quite wrong in thinking this (if he does think it); but if he does think so one can't blame him for acting on it.'

In any event, Vyner felt slightly sheepish about the whole business. In March he wrote to his nephew apologising for the 'claptrap' publicity coming from America about the proclamation, and in due course he agreed that Anthony could return to Sarawak in January 1941 as a district officer and work his way up in the service once more. However, he warned Bertram that his son would have to watch his step from now on: 'There's an Indian proverb that says "when one lives in a tank it's just as well to keep on good terms with the crocodile". There's a good deal in this . . .'

Notwithstanding this rapprochement, Sylvia again sought to tackle the issue of the succession while she was in London. At the beginning of July she wrote to Bertram to say that he must know how popular her daughter Leonora Inchcape was with the Sarawak people and that there was a large body of opinion among Malays that the succession should be altered in her favour. The fact that Anthony had fallen out with the Rajah and was 'far too impulsive' to be trusted to rule the country had greatly increased the feeling, she said, especially since Lady Inchcape now had a son who could be educated for the Raj.

Bertram answered, as he recalled, 'quite politely that of course like everyone in Sarawak I knew that she and MacBryan had for years been trying to get the line of succession shifted, but his [MacBryan's] attempt to coerce the Malay members of the Supreme Council wasn't very successful'. He added that, while Sylvia herself seemed to think that it would be a splendid idea to make Leonora's son Simon the heir, there was no reason to believe that the Sarawak people had ever entertained such a notion, and that Sylvia was obviously unaware that the line of succession had been laid down in the wills of the first two rajahs.

The accusation that Sylvia was in cahoots with MacBryan brought a vehement rebuttal. 'I am so glad you wrote as you did although I consider your letter is first cousin to a STINKER,' she wrote to Bertram on 8 July.

> But no wonder, if you had all those thoughts harboured in your mind, it is enough to make anyone mad. How could you have me to dinner the other evening, and how could you always have been so sweet to me if you felt in your heart that I was plotting against you and Peter. I never imagined in my wildest dreams that you could believe such a thing of me . . . You know Vyner doesn't care a twopenny damn who inherits really because he says he will be well underground. . . . The whole thing has really grown from the evil seeds in MacBryan's brain,

she added, and the only reason she had written was that Vyner had been 'foolish enough' to allow MacBryan back into the country, 'and as Peter is supposedly on his way out there, I thought trouble might spring into the arena again'.

MacBryan was already on his way out to Sarawak when Sylvia's letter was written. For much of the past four years he and his wife Sa'erah had been living in London, renting a flat on Marylebone High Street until 1939, when his father died, whereupon they moved down to Kingsdown House to supervise the asylum, which would remain in operation until after the war. In the spring of 1940, however, MacBryan was called up for National Service. Faced with the prospect of being away for an indefinite period of time and leaving his Sarawakian wife alone in the depths of the Wiltshire countryside, he wired the Rajah asking for permission to take her back to Kuching so that she could live with her family there. Vyner, who did not return to Europe at all that year owing to the war, agreed to this, providing that MacBryan abstained from any form of political activity or any contact with the government. MacBryan then applied for an exit permit from the British passport authorities, stating that the sole purpose of his visit to Sarawak was to escort his wife, since her English was not sufficient for her to travel alone or to remain in England when her husband had volunteered for service, as he promised to do on his return. They left England in June and arrived in Kuching in August. Bertram, for one, immediately assumed that with Anthony out of the way MacBryan planned to wheedle his way back into favour with the Rajah and advance his own schemes for the succession. He also strongly suspected Sylvia's involvement, despite her denials.

Before he left Britain, MacBryan's passport was endorsed with a signed undertaking by him to return by 25 October 1940 to fulfil his obligations under the Defence Act. Shortly after arriving in Sarawak, however, he contrived 'accidentally' to drop it in the middle of the Sarawak river. The Sarawak Constabulary had made a note of the endorsement when MacBryan arrived, but when MacBryan applied for a new Sarawak passport, Vyner ordered the endorsement to be omitted, having by then apparently decided to make use of him after all.

The Rajah arranged for MacBryan to be taken on as art curator at the museum in Kuching and shortly afterwards readmitted him to the Sarawak Civil Service in the specially created post of political adviser. In the autumn he took his new adviser with him on a tour of Sarawak's far north-east, which included a visit to Brunei. In January 1941, having persuaded the Rajah to let him act as his envoy in settling a territorial dispute with the Sultan, MacBryan made a second visit to Brunei, this time travelling with Sa'erah in the royal yacht *Maimuna*. They anchored opposite the Astana, where MacBryan, in Arab garb and going under his Muslim name of Haji Abdul Rahman, went ashore to treat with the Sultan. Before long they had reached an agreement whereby, in return for a cash payment, the

Sultan would acknowledge the Rajah's sovereign rights over Limbang, the neighbouring territory formerly belonging to Brunei that Rajah Charles had controversially annexed in 1890. MacBryan then proceeded up the Limbang river to the disputed territory, where he reached a settlement of the longstanding claims for compensation of the descendants of Rajah Muda Hassim, who had ceded Sarawak to James Brooke. Anthony later claimed that the Limbang agreement was merely 'a cloak to conceal a secret arrangement' whereby MacBryan would lend support to the Sultan's claim that under Brunei law the succession could pass to his daughter, his only legitimate child, and the Sultan would in turn support the succession of the Rajah's daughter Leonora in Sarawak. If this was the case, it is possible that Vyner knew about the pact, especially since he later told Bertram that the Limbang settlement had been his idea not MacBryan's.

When MacBryan returned to Kuching, the Rajah congratulated him on his diplomatic coup and appointed him political secretary with a place on the Supreme Council. Within a month, however, during a visit to Sir Shenton Thomas in Singapore, the Rajah was forced to cancel the agreement, the British Resident in Brunei having pointed out that it was contrary to the treaty of 1888, under which Sarawak's relations with all foreign states, including Brunei, were to be conducted by the British government, or in accordance with its directions. Government officers in Kuching feared that the controversy over the Limbang agreement would now be used by the British as a pretext for increasing their control over Sarawak's affairs.

The British authorities, meanwhile, were becoming increasingly suspicious of the Rajah's 'adviser' and commissioned a full intelligence report on him. In addition to his trickery over his passport, MacBryan was held to have violated certain wireless restrictions that existed in Brunei, while within Sarawak he was rumoured to have cultivated acquaintances with the Japanese community in Kuching and to have advised the Japanese on the purchase of land near military installations. When he and Sa'erah accompanied the Rajah to Singapore in February (en route to Vyner's holiday home in the Cameron Highlands of Malaya for a three-week break), the British military authorities there urged the governor to arrest him and have him deported back to England. However, Sir Shenton was reluctant to be seen to be interfering in Sarawak, and Vyner was able to persuade him that he could not do without his adviser until after the centenary celebrations in September.

On the other side of the world Sylvia had returned to America from England in late July 1940, crossing the Atlantic in the company of 600 evacuated children. Before leaving England, she told Doll, she had 'mixed [herself] up' with the evacuation committee in a bid to sort out the 'hopeless way that England has dealt with the thing'. One of the gravest problems, as Sylvia saw it, was that no one in America knew where the children had come from and what sort of lives they had been used to. She cited the example of 'a bunch of kids' who had been landed in Canada:

> Ten very well brought up ones, and about five of London's lowest. What happened? The Canadians weren't told, and the Cockneys found themselves in a big house with a swimming pool and telephones under every bush. Their meals were given to them on the terrace, and they were given food they had never seen before. What do you think is going to happen when those very same kids go back to England and to the home that they once had? . . . I am not a snob, but I don't see why the hell Duff Cooper's butler's boy should have HIS meals brought out to him on the terrace.

In September Sylvia told Doll that Vyner had written asking her to go over to him. 'I really think Sarawak is in great danger, and if there is going to be trouble, I am certainly going to share it with him. So I am leaving for Vancouver tomorrow, and taking a boat shortly for Shanghai . . .' But, like so many of Sylvia's plans, this one soon altered and, for whatever reason, she stayed put in New York, working on various writing projects. 'The only reason I try', she told Doll, 'is that if the Japanese take Sarawak we shall all be so damned poor, it is worth trying to save and make a bit before the crash comes.' She had learned to live on 'practically nothing as far as food is concerned, but I must have my GIN as you know.'

By November she was back in California, trying 'to beat my way into Hollywood', she told Doll. 'I just won't have no said to me.' She was also making more speeches, 'sometimes twice a day', endeavouring to 'create a better feeling between Britain and America' and 'combat Fifth Column activities' among the large German population there. On 11 December she wrote to Anthony Eden at the War Office offering to do 'a definite job' for propaganda on behalf of the British government. 'Because although I say it as shouldn't, I have made a big hit over here . . . Is there anything you could suggest that I could go on tub-thumping over . . . They will listen to me. What does England want?' But while the American people were hailing her as 'the best Ambassador that England has ever sent over' (so she told Doll), members of the press there were increasingly inclined to poke fun at her – as when she reportedly referred to some of the evacuated children as 'the young riffraff of England' (a misquote according to Sylvia), or made a rather public show of donating a pint of 'her blue blood', as *Time* magazine sarcastically reported it, to help Britain's war effort.

For Christmas, Sylvia wanted to go to Florida, but wrote to tell Doll: 'My old prim and proper Jack wouldn't let me in case I got talked about.' So she stayed on in Hollywood, translating a book of Sarawak legends, which she turned into a children's book, and hatching various money-making schemes. One was to do a lecture tour of South America, where 'English people are badly needed to counteract the Nazi influence', she told Doll. She was hoping that Pan American Airlines would sponsor it, but evidently they declined the opportunity. In February she returned to New York, putting up at the Winthrop Hotel on Lexington Avenue and 47th Street, and writing from six in the morning till lunch time each day. She recorded an advertisement for the Château Martin Winery (for $50) wrote articles (one entitled 'I want a job', for which she was paid $150 by *Pic Magazine*) and did some radio work. But by August she was again broke and told reporters she had 'walked the streets of New York for days without enough to eat, looking for work'. In her second autobiography Sylvia described this as 'one of the most bizarre and miserable periods in my life. Vyner had vanished; the British Ambassador [Lord Lothian] – whom I had known as an extremely tiresome small boy and to whom I applied for help –

professed himself unable to do anything; I tried for numerous jobs, and failed to get any of them; and was finally reduced to telling fortunes at Leon and Eddy's Bar, where I was known as "Toots". Meanwhile I lived on hot dogs in my room, and crept in and out under the increasingly hostile eyes of the manager.'

Her salvation was a commission to write a 3,000-word article for the magazine *American Weekly*, headlined 'The Inside Story of the Three White Rajahs', for which she was paid 'a wonderfully, ridiculously large sum of money'. The piece was crammed with colourful and improbable tales. Sylvia recalled, for instance, how, not long after becoming Ranee, she had been 'sitting in the Palace grounds one day, shaded by a golden bamboo tree' when she was approached by a young Dyak girl by the name of Mala. 'She was troubled I could see. She held something in her hand . . . Now as Mala came nearer and I saw what her burden was I was horrified . . . It was a young girl's head that Mala carried so carelessly by the hair, and she must have travelled several days with the hideous thing, for the Dyaks do not live near the capital.'

The head belonged to the former lover of Mala's husband, and he had cut it off in order to prove to his wife that the affair was over. Mala now wanted her husband to take the head back to the girl's relatives – as the Rajah had decreed should happen in such cases – but the husband had refused for fear of incurring bad luck. 'That she [Mala] objected to the head and wanted it sent back', wrote Sylvia, 'showed the strides the first two Rajahs had made in putting down this terrible head-hunting habit. But it also showed me the strides my husband and I still had to make before the custom would vanish from Sarawak.' Her lucrative article rambled across several subjects besides, including her assertion that there was 'no feeling of race discrimination in Sarawak' and that 'when a white man in Sarawak falls in love with a native girl the Rajah and I encourage him to marry her'. She also wrote that Sarawak boasted 'an excellent beauty parlour and the women no longer have to depend on betel nut for red colouring many of them have learned to make themselves up in a modern and sophisticated way that would make them the envy of many a white society girl. All who can afford it have bobbed hair with soft, glistening permanent waves. Fingernails are well-manicured and brightly enameled, eyebrows are gracefully arched and the coffee-coloured skins of these girls are beautiful.'

The increasingly chaotic finances of Sylvia and her daughters were widely assumed to have prompted the next big event in Sarawak, the announcement on 31 March 1941 that the Rajah intended to mark the centenary of Brooke rule by divesting himself of absolute power and giving Sarawak a written constitution.

The background to this was that, in January of that year, MacBryan had gone to the Treasury in Kuching with a letter from the Rajah authorising the transfer of £200,000 from state reserves to the Rajah so that he could set up a trust fund for his family in London. The acting treasurer Cecil Pitt-Hardacre refused to transfer the money, and threatened to take the keys to the Treasury with him to Singapore if the Rajah chose to dismiss him.

Early in March, after returning from three weeks at the Rajah's holiday home in the Cameron Highlands, MacBryan again raised the question of financial provision for the Rajah and his family with Pitt-Hardacre, who now conceded that some provision should be made but demanded a constitutional guarantee that there would be no more demands in the future. Shortly afterwards, the treasurer received a note from the Rajah saying something like: 'Dear Pitt, you can have your Constitution.' Pitt-Hardacre later observed that, given the sequence of events, it was impossible to conclude that the offer of a constitution, far from being a forward move by an enlightened ruler, was motivated by anything other than the Rajah's desire to raise a large sum in cash. He assumed furthermore that the prime mover in all this was MacBryan, 'who no doubt received a substantial commission for his work'. The Rajah had recently given MacBryan the title of *datu*, made him a life member of the Supreme Council and Council Negri, and granted him a pension for life of $2,000 a month in the event of the Rajah's death or abdication.

On 17 March MacBryan sent a memorandum containing 'a preliminary advice of His Highness's intentions' for the future of the Raj to the chief secretary, J. B. Archer. The Rajah was proposing to appoint Anthony as his heir, on probation for no more than five years. There would be a new constitution designed to eliminate the autocratic power of the Rajah, who would now have to conform to the majority opinion of an advisory council. MacBryan also asked that a cheque for the dollar equivalent of £200,000 payable to His Highness should be made ready by the time the Supreme Council next met in mid-April, when the Rajah planned formally to announce the new form of government.

On the same day MacBryan also wrote to Anthony, who had returned to Sarawak with his wife and baby son in January to work as a district officer at Sarikei. Anthony received a copy of the memo along with an invitation from the Rajah for him and his family to come and stay at the Astana for the meeting of the Supreme Council and remain until the end of Race Week. He replied that, while he was 'exceedingly gratified' that his uncle was thinking of appointing him as his heir, he could not accept this honour, since it depended on his father Bertram renouncing his rights as heir presumptive, which he had shown no indication of doing. Anthony suggested 'with the greatest respect' that the whole matter be left in abeyance.

The tone of that letter may have been perfectly tactful and conciliatory, but on the same day he wrote a more inflammatory note to his uncle suggesting that one of the first acts of the planned advisory council might be 'to recommend that Mr MacBryan be removed from Sarawak as soon as arrangements can be made with the immigration authorities at Singapore to receive him'. Anthony also wrote to Archer pointing out that 'any advice rendered by MacBryan seems fated to be dishonourable and tainted with intrigue', and urging him to do all he could to convince the Rajah of this. 'There are many forms of subtle bribery and corruption,' wrote Anthony, 'and MacBryan is the Master of them all.' Archer replied that he entirely agreed but that the Rajah was 'apparently completely in his hands and all our efforts to curb this have so far failed'.

Keen to limit MacBryan's influence once and for all and insure against any future raids on state funds, the committee of administration now sought to bring matters to a head by drafting an agreement, the details of which were kept private. Under the agreement, which was signed by Vyner on 31 March, the Rajah undertook to transfer legislative powers from himself to the committee, which would in turn be responsible for drawing up a constitution; the Rajah also promised that neither he nor any member of his family would make any further claim on state funds other than those set out in the agreement. In return for all this and for assuming full financial responsibility for the Ranee and their three daughters, the Rajah was to receive £200,000 in cash within two weeks; the loan on his house in the Cameron Highlands of 32,000 Sarawak dollars would be written off, and he would be allowed 60,000 dollars each year for the upkeep of the Astana and 21,000 dollars for charitable purposes. His salary would be lowered from 10,000 to 7,000 dollars a month, to reflect the reduction in his responsibilities, but he would continue to receive interest from the pre-existing trust fund in London (at that time 50,000 dollars a year). He would also continue to be entitled to the sole use of the Astana and the royal yacht *Maimuna*, and had the right to dispose of his personal property in Sarawak, to confer and refuse titles and decorations on his own family and others, to visit any part of Sarawak, 'to exercise his customary prerogatives in accordance with the advice of responsible advisers', and to maintain existing annual payments from Sarawak funds to members of his family and the *datus* then in office.

A hastily prepared ceremony announcing the new constitution took place on the same morning as the signing of the private agreement. About a hundred officers and men of the Sarawak Constabulary lined up on the Astana lawn, along with the brass band. After the royal salute and national anthem, the troops formed a hollow square, while the Rajah took his place before the assembly, the Supreme Council sitting on his right, the committee of administration to his left, and proceeded to read the address. 'I have always been positive,' began Vyner, 'as was my father, that it was never the intention of Sir James Brooke to establish a line of absolute rulers. What he set out to do was to protect the natives of Sarawak, the real but backward owners of this land, from exploitation and oppression, until such time as they could govern themselves. I hope that it may be fairly said that this worthy aim has in large measure been achieved.' He concluded his speech by naming Bertram as his heir, then dismissed those who were present before going inside the Astana, where he invested the officers responsible for drafting the proclamation with the Order of Sarawak.

Privately the Rajah had also bowed to the committee's demand that MacBryan leave the Sarawak service. But when the announcement of his resignation appeared in the *Sarawak Gazette*, on 1 April the Rajah immediately re-engaged him as his private secretary, paying his salary himself. That morning MacBryan was sent across from the Astana to the Treasury to insist upon immediate settlement of the £200,000 in cash, notwithstanding the treasurer's pleas that this would imperil the financial integrity of the state. It was whispered that the Rajah was anxious to get his hands on the money in case the governor of the Straits Settlements decided to intervene.

Shortly afterwards the Rajah set about disposing of property he owned in Kuching, including the hugely popular Sylvia Cinema, which he had built in 1934 and which he was observed to sell with 'undue haste' to a Chinese syndicate despite the fact that the Borneo Company had a valid option to buy at an agreed price and was only awaiting approval from their London board of directors. MacBryan, meanwhile, was rumoured to have been paid £10,000 by the Rajah as commission for negotiating the deal, and he bought large quantities of land and housing in the Kuching and Sibu districts.

News of the constitution had been wired to the governor of the Straits Settlements on the afternoon of 31 March. On the whole Sir Shenton approved of the idea, writing the next day to Lord Moyne, the newly appointed Secretary of State for the Colonies, that it would mean much more effective administration 'as the Government will no longer be at the whim of an irresponsible ruler under the influence of a crook'. Moyne was now keen to have a British adviser in Sarawak, but Thomas suggested that, before insisting on this as a condition of approval, it might be wiser to await the draft of the constitution.

In June 1941 Britain's former general adviser to Sarawak, W. E. Pepys, travelled to Kuching to take soundings on the idea of a British representative, and reported a consensus among European officers that Sarawak could no longer continue to be regarded as a museum piece, having been 'pitchforked into the Imperial limelight' owing to its strategic importance in the looming conflict with Japan. Pepys noted: 'Practically every lady is engaged in some sort of war work,' and that the former hard drinking had noticeably decreased: at the Island Club, Sibu, notorious formerly for its alcoholism, members had introduced 'No treating' – 'a change indeed', commented Pepys. In general the morale was good among the European community, who were 'war-minded and like to think they are doing their bit'.

However, at the same time Pepys observed that talk of the private agreement concerning the £200,000 had 'rather shattered' the reputation of the Rajah. There was some doubt among his subjects about whether he would stay around to discharge his responsibilities as a constitutional monarch, or even attend the centenary celebrations. Many officers also objected to the 'high falluting' wording of the proclamation, arguing that it would have been far better for the Rajah to have said, 'I'm getting old and tired and wish to pass the burden of government on to younger shoulders.' 'Everyone would have understood and sympathised,' wrote Pepys, whereas the proclamation caused only confusion among the Rajah's subjects, especially since the Rajah was proposing to hand over his powers to a committee of bureaucrats whose predecessors he had effectively dismissed two years earlier.

To diehard officers who had been drawn by the peculiar romance of Sarawak, meanwhile, the whole idea of a constitution seemed a great shame. 'It has just about degenerated in one fatal step to the level of a colony instead of being independent,' wrote one customs officer in his diary. 'I don't say that it may not lead to the State being governed in a better way, but it is nevertheless the end of a piece of history – it has just sunk to the common standard of the rest of the world.'

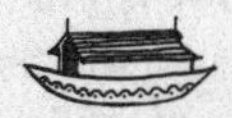

The fiercest opposition to the Rajah's constitutional proposals came from his own family. Sylvia, who had remained in New York throughout this time, wrote later that she considered the proclamation ill-timed, that she 'could not help seeing MacBryan's work in it', and that 'Vyner was agreeing to become what he had always sworn he never would – a puppet king'. Bertram, who was in England, took issue with the reasons Vyner gave, in particular his claim that his predecessors had foreseen a time when the natives would be able to govern themselves. 'Rajah James cannot have had any such idea,' wrote Bertram at the beginning of May, 'for he died (long before anyone regarded such a scheme as coming within the scope of practical politics) providing for a chain of succession to the Raj, with remainder to the British Crown, for ever, in his will.' Bertram added that 'Rajah Charles would certainly have mentioned the matter in his political will had the possibility ever entered his head', and quoted his father's statement urging 'that the policy and methods of Government of Sarawak as hitherto carried out by the first British-born Rajah and myself may not be departed from after my death'. Bertram suspected MacBryan of writing the speech and Vyner delivering it 'without really considering what importance must be attached to the sincerity of any public utterance of one in your position'.

Bertram branded the constitution a 'dangerous experiment' that threatened the racial harmony that the Brooke Raj had fostered in Sarawak as well as the way in which the people viewed their Rajah. 'Because the present system has been built up through the course of 100 years to suit a paternal autocratic regime, it would be inviting disaster to try and tinker with it and make it suit something radically different.' In his view there could be no system of self-government that would make the people of Sarawak happier and more prosperous.

His son Anthony agreed, observing in a letter to his father that the constitution would mean the Rajah vesting the trust of his people 'in a small oligarchy comprising a majority of European officials'; the people themselves had expressed no desire for this change and might lose confidence in their Rajah when they discovered that it had been effected. While he conceded that the time was right to impose some limit on the Rajah's power, he thought it would be sufficient for the Rajah to be required to give the British agent written reasons on any occasion when he did not accept the advice of the councils. Above all, he felt that it was vital that the Rajah's authority should not be weakened in the eyes of his subjects.

Anthony's reaction to the constitution did not endear him to Vyner, still less did his attempts to dislodge MacBryan by way of complaints directed at both the Rajah and the governor of the Straits Settlements. On 4 April, shortly after the proclamation, Anthony turned up unexpectedly in Kuching from Sarikei. After addressing the committee of administration and gaining its support, he went to the Rajah to tell him that MacBryan posed a threat to the internal security of Sarawak and should be deported. MacBryan threatened to sue Anthony for libel and a furious Vyner demanded that his nephew be disciplined for leaving his post without leave. He subsequently let it be known that he would have nothing more to do with him, and that henceforth he would regard him as 'merely a junior Government officer'.

Yet neither this, nor the approbation of the governor, who saw the constitution as a means of extending British influence in Sarawak, dissuaded Anthony from continuing his campaign of opposition. In July he wrote to the new chief secretary Cyril Le Gros Clark deploring 'this impersonal and revolutionary monstrosity', which Anthony said he intended to oppose 'with all the legitimate means in my power'.

As the months passed and Anthony's opposition intensified, so did Vyner's antipathy towards his nephew. One result of this was that the Rajah seemed to grow increasingly determined to divest himself of virtually all responsibility and had to be persuaded to shoulder any legislative burden. He even admitted that his motive was to ensure that Anthony should have none of the sovereign powers of his predecessors. Kenelm Digby, the legal adviser who did most of the drafting of the constitution, explained to a friend that the Rajah, 'seeing death gradually approaching, decided to tie his nephew in such a way that he could not avenge himself for the various slights he had suffered from the Rajah's friends and relatives'.

In the final draft of the constitution, the Rajah's existing powers and prerogatives were to be exercised with the advice and consent of the Supreme Council, the majority of whose members would be European officers of the Sarawak Civil Service. The one power left to the Rajah was to nominate members of the council. Below the Supreme Council was the Council Negri, which would be responsible for passing all legislation enacted by the Rajah-in-Council. The Council Negri would consist of twenty-five members, fourteen of whom were to be drawn from the Sarawak Civil Service.

Anthony's protests culminated in a furious cable he sent to Sir Shenton Thomas on 11 September 1941. The constitution, he wrote, had 'a background of intrigue, treachery, humbug and bad faith, sufficient to condemn the people of this stricken land to hang their heads in shame and misery for years to come'. He then left his post and travelled to Kuching, where he was handed a letter from the Rajah dismissing him for insubordination, at which point he departed for Singapore.

In the days and weeks that followed, the Rajah began for the first time openly to express his desire to make his grandson Simon Brooke Mackay the next in line to the throne after Bertram. In this it is safe to assume that he was actively encouraged by Sylvia, who was by now back in Sarawak after an absence of two and a half years. Sylvia had sailed from Los Angeles in the passenger liner *Mariposa* on 3 August, clad, so it was reported 'in a green-gold sarong and wearing gold earrings shaped like British lions'. She arrived in Kuching on 24 August 'looking very fit', Vyner told Bertram. 'She is full of her American lecture tour and is giving a weekly lecture at the Club and also will address the Rotarians. Syv tells me she has been all over America, sometimes giving two lectures a day. She is not staying long but leaves for England in October after the Centenary Show.'

Three days after the Ranee's arrival the Rajah gave what he called a 'hoi polloi' dance for Chinese girls and boys at the Astana in honour of her arrival. 'Very popular turns,' he told his brother, 'already had three of them. About 200 turn up and Chinese girls are wonderful dancers & keen as mustard. Also I have installed a billiard table here [in the old library] and occasionally have pool parties. My other entertainments are poker parties. So we don't do so badly even in wartime. I *occasionally* give a pompous dinner to highbrows, bigwigs and honourables but only about once a month as it means a stiff shirt & collar which are not needed on my more plebeian occasions.'

The centenary was now almost upon them, with the preparations inevitably being masterminded by MacBryan, including the issue of a commemorative set of stamps, which did not, however, reach Sarawak until after the war. The centenary would also see the new constitution come into force, and on 19 September Vyner telegraphed Bertram asking him to state whether or not he wished to remain as his heir. Bertram cabled back to say that he did not consider a reply necessary as the line of succession had been laid down in the wills of the first two rajahs and confirmed in the treaty of 1888. On 23 September Vyner told the chief secretary Cyril Le Gros Clark that if Bertram wished to remain his heir, he must publicly accept the constitution and that an Act of Succession must be passed establishing Leonora's son Simon Brooke Mackay as the next in line to the throne. In the event of the Rajah and Tuan Muda both dying during Simon's minority, Leonora should be proclaimed regent until her son came of age and could become rajah. Vyner said he considered these measures necessary because 'my nephew Peter Brooke, given two great opportunities by my good-will, has proved himself irresponsible and unfitted to become Rajah of Sarawak. And I feel it to be my foremost duty to Sarawak and its People to prevent the possibility of there ever being a Rajah who is unprepared and unwilling to defer to the opinion of a majority of his Advisers and to accept discipline.' This did not, however, prevent Vyner later from dismissing rumours as to his favouring any change in the succession as 'ridiculous'.

The festivities had meanwhile begun, on Saturday, 20 September, with a regatta on the Kuching river, followed by a garden party the next day at the Astana, hosted by the Rajah and Ranee. On the Tuesday there was a football match, 'European v Chinese', and on Wednesday, Centenary Day, the official ceremony at the court-house. Two days later, Vyner's birthday, at a ceremony in the Astana garden, the Rajah appointed the Ranee and MacBryan Grand Masters of the Most Excellent Order of the Star of Sarawak.

Vyner's all-too-apparent lack of interest in the week-long programme of events culminated in his declining to attend either the Centenary Memorial Service at St Thomas's Cathedral on the Sunday, or even the two race meetings, where he was due to present cups to the winners. In the film footage that was taken of the centenary celebrations, Sylvia looks to be enjoying herself rather more than her husband. On the last day, Monday, 29 September, she wrote to Doll of the 'wonderful simplicity, and yet perfect orderliness of the affair . . . In what other country could two Rulers sit exposed to thousands of people without the slightest protection anywhere near them?'

Five days later she was off, flying from Kuching to Singapore on 4 October, then on to San Franscisco via Australia, New Zealand and

Hawaii. She later maintained that her quick departure was due to the fact that the 'clouds of war' had caused Vyner to fear for her safety. However, at the time she wrote to Doll saying that it was 'most important' for her to see Leonora, and that she return to England before Anthony did, in order to be on hand in case he 'attacked' the Sarawak government or sought to contest the assertion that Leonora's son Simon was now the rightful heir to the Raj. Anthony had been insubordinate and disloyal to Vyner, she wrote, and 'proved himself absolutely unfitted for the trust that has been placed on him, and utterly unsuited to inherit this lovely land'.

Vyner left Sarawak with MacBryan on 29 October, bound for Singapore, his house in the Cameron Highlands and eventually Australia, where he intended having an additional holiday, leaving Cyril Le Gros Clark in charge of the government of Sarawak. His departure was against the advice tendered to him in Kuching, according to the judicial commissioner H. Thackwell Lewis, who wrote later that, 'in view of the tense situation with regard to Japan [it] might be regarded as the action of a man no longer having that interest in his country or that sense of duty towards it that would have been expected from a ruler really interested in the welfare of his people'. Because of the way in which he felt, Thackwell Lewis declined to attend the farewell function at the Astana to say goodbye to the Rajah. In his memo, which he sent to Anthony at the end of the war, he pointed out how, prior to leaving, the Rajah had been at pains to liquidate his personal interests in the country, 'selling the Cinema, rubber gardens and other holdings for ready cash'. Thackwell Lewis was told by the treasurer that the proceeds had been transferred to Singapore, where the Rajah endeavoured to buy American gold dollars with it, but did not succeed. 'If this is true it would indicate a strange attitude at that particular stage of the war.'

On his way through Singapore, Sir Shenton Thomas also asked the Rajah to reconsider his decision to go to Australia in the light of the constitutional position of Sarawak. But as Vyner would later explain, he felt that at the age of sixty-eight he 'badly needed' a break, and that 'an exaggerated degree of importance was being attached to the new constitution in some quarters and by reason of my long experience of Sarawak affairs I felt best qualified to judge what was good for my own country'. He did agree to curtail the length of his absence, although he was adamant that he had no idea that the outbreak of war with Japan was imminent.

13

YOU IN KUCHING MUST STAND AND FIGHT

Vyner may have apprehended no immediate danger to Sarawak from Japan at that time, but by many people's reckoning the threat of an invasion had significantly increased in August 1941, shortly before the centenary, when the Americans, British and Dutch blocked the export of oil to Japan in response to its invasion of southern Indochina. It was logical to assume that Japan would now turn its attention towards the oil-rich Dutch East Indies, and the ill-protected British protectorates of Brunei and Sarawak, whose oilfield at Miri had been a major supplier of oil to the powerful Japanese Imperial Navy before the embargo. Shortly before the centenary the Sarawak government froze the assets of the 136-strong Japanese community in Kuching as a pre-cautionary measure – although that did not deter them from contributing one of the decorative arches for the celebrations.

From time to time during his reign Vyner had made voluntary contributions to Britain towards the cost of his country's defence, measures that had included the building of airfields at Kuching and Miri during the 1930s. Between late 1939 and early 1941 the Rajah's contributions totalled two and a half million Sarawak dollars, and in March 1941, as war in the East approached, he had taken the opportunity to remind Sir Shenton Thomas that he expected Britain to fulfil its side of the bargain under the treaty of 1888. The governor responded by sending an officer to Sarawak to report on its defence, and in April the 2/15 Punjab Regiment was despatched to Kuching. Six months later, however, Sarawak's secretary of defence, J. L. Noakes, was still of the view that Britain's measures for the protection of Sarawak were 'totally inadequate' and that this tiny garrison of 600 men who had no experience of jungle fighting would be quite incapable of resisting an invading force.

Noakes's report was sent to Lieutenant General A. E. Percival, who had arrived in Singapore in May to take on the daunting task of defending Malaya. Percival's resources were already hopelessly stretched as Churchill gave priority to the Near East and Russia, but he promised two anti-aircraft guns within the next six months, and said he would like to see more men and some RAF aircraft stationed in Kuching. He admitted that with Britain's desperate obligations all over the world, its deployment of armed forces in the region was far from sufficient, but pointed out that Sarawak was no worse off than any of the other protected territories. At Noakes's invitation, Percival subsequently visited Sarawak, arriving in the destroyer *Vampire* on 27 November 1941, the very day that the Colonial Office issued a warning that war with Japan was imminent. Percival recommended that the few Punjabis should concentrate on defending the airfields, and sternly told members of the Supreme Council as he departed: 'There have been too many retreats. You in Kuching must stand and fight.'

On 8 December, less than two weeks after Percival's visit, news reached Kuching that Japanese torpedo and dive bombers had destroyed much of the American fleet at Pearl Harbor the previous day, and that the Japanese were now advancing against British and Dutch possessions in South East Asia. That day all Japanese civilians were rounded up and interned in a camp at the government rest house, the Sarawak Volunteer Force donned their uniforms in readiness for active service, and all oil installations at Miri were destroyed to deny them to the enemy. Japanese seaplanes soon appeared in the sky on reconnaissance flights and, after some preliminary bombing, on 16 December an invasion force of ten thousand troops landed at Miri. Three days later Kuching was bombed from the air, killing or

wounding eighty-three of its inhabitants, and by Boxing Day the city was in enemy hands, the Japanese having come up the Sarawak river in a flotilla of small motor boats dressed in Sarawak uniforms.

Sylvia was by this time in New York, where she was able to catch up with Jack Golden, and wrote to Doll promising that she would be 'returning to Sarawak about May, war or no war, and I hope to bring Noni [Leonora] too'. When she learned of the Japanese landings at Miri, she reassured the press that 'everything the Japs want has been destroyed' and that, should they attempt to penetrate inland, Sarawak's headhunters could handle them. She added that she was on the point of leaving for England to break the news that Leonora's son Simon Mackay had been nominated by the Rajah as his successor, which prompted the headline 'Nine-Year-Old Boy Heir to Sarawak' in the *Daily Mirror*.

'My daughter [Leonora] is unaware of the purpose of my trip,' the Ranee was quoted as saying, 'and I am afraid it will be a great shock to her. It means that her son will soon have to prepare himself for the day when he will rule Sarawak.' Leonora and Bertram both subsequently dismissed this notion as 'ridiculous', on the Rajah's authority, only to discover later that Vyner had charged his ministers with the obligation of passing an Act of Succession before he left Sarawak.

The Rajah and MacBryan had just reached Sydney when they heard that war had been declared and Miri demolished. They made immediate arrangements with the Australian authorities to fly back to Sarawak, and on the day that the Japanese landed at Miri, Vyner sent a cable to his stand-in head of government Cyril Le Gros Clark: 'I deeply regret not being with you in Sarawak to share this time of anxiety and trial through which you are now passing. I send you this message of good wishes and encouragement coupled with an expression of my full confidence that notwithstanding these days the tide will soon turn. I am hastening to return to Kuching to join you with the utmost speed possible and you may expect me to arrive in the near future.' Vyner planned to return to his country via Dutch Borneo, and he requested that the district officer of Lundu and Bau, to the west of Kuching, be informed so that he could make appropriate arrangements to receive him at the border.

The Rajah and MacBryan reached Surabaya on the north coast of Java on Christmas Day, to be greeted by the news that Kuching was already out of radio contact. They pressed on to Bandung, the military headquarters of the Dutch East Indies, where, on 29 December, they met up with the Dutch commander-in-chief, who grimly informed them that Kuching had fallen three days previously. The Punjab Regiment had fought magnificently, they were told, but the population of Kuching had adopted an anti-British attitude. Unable to bring himself to believe this latter piece of information, the Rajah determined to send his private secretary over the border to find out for himself.

It was agreed that MacBryan should leave that afternoon with a Dutch expert in guerrilla warfare, Colonel Gortman ('a spitfire of a man', as the Rajah described him, 'full of blood and thunder'), for the frontier with Sarawak, where he was to make contact with those Europeans who had escaped from Sarawak, persuade them to accept Gortman's command and make an assessment of the support that could be gained from the Dyaks for a guerrilla campaign. As he later told the British High Commissioner in Canberra, Sir Ronald Cross, the Rajah hoped that the presence in the interior of Borneo of 'the most skilled jungle men in the world' might well prove to be 'invaluable as a strong pro-British asset'. He predicted that the Japanese would content themselves with control of the coastal areas and doubted that they would attempt to move into the interior. His main concern was for the safety of his European officers and the Chinese. 'I think natives will get off all right,' he wrote to Bertram, 'as propaganda given out by the Japs is all pro natives.'

A number of the Rajah's officers, accompanied by their wives and children, had by now made it through the jungle to Pontianak, on the west coast of Dutch Borneo, two hundred miles from the frontier with Sarawak. There, on 31 December, they were taken aback to see MacBryan, wearing the striking uniform of a Dutch officer, with jackboots and revolver strapped round his waist, arrive on an aeroplane with Gortman, bearing a letter of credence signed by the Rajah. One of the officers, John Gilbert, later recorded that when MacBryan suggested the idea of their returning to stir up discontent among the Dyaks against the Japanese and waging a guerrilla war, they told him 'in no uncertain language that we knew more of the attitudes of the natives in Sarawak than he did'. They thought it highly unlikely that the Dyaks would want to sacrifice themselves against the well-armed Japanese, and besides, wrote Gilbert, 'none of us had any time for this gentleman, and were certainly not going back under his command'. Further tension arose when MacBryan attempted to withdraw the Sarawak state funds that had been deposited in the bank at Pontianak by the Sarawak treasurer, B. A. Trechman, brandishing a letter of authorisation signed by the Rajah. Trechman refused to co-operate, saying the Rajah had no constitutional right to authorise anybody to draw on state funds.

Following these rebuffs, MacBryan and Gortman then drove on by car to the Dutch airfield at Lidau, fifty miles from the border with Sarawak, where they met up with the remnants of his 2/15 Punjabi Regiment, commanded by Colonel C. M. Lane. Lane had commissioned the intelligence report on MacBryan before the invasion, written by B. J. C. 'Shot' Spurway, and he needed no persuasion from the other European fugitives that it would 'extremely inadvisable' to let the Rajah's private secretary cross the border. Lane now asked Spurway to write another security report, which accused MacBryan of having cultivated relations with and sold land to the Japanese in Sarawak before the war, and of spreading anti-British and anti-Brooke propaganda while on a visit to Sibu in November 1941. The report concluded by alerting the authorities in Singapore to the possibility that MacBryan was a 'Quisling on his way back to form a puppet state in Sarawak with himself as head, a position he is well fitted to hold due to his influence over natives and landed interests'.

When Spurway's latest report reached Sir Shenton Thomas, the governor demanded that MacBryan be arrested, which he was, on 3 January 1942, by the Dutch, who also confiscated all the Rajah's personal papers that he had with him. The local Dutch commander was said to have wanted him shot on the spot, but instead he was taken under armed guard and put in the gaol at Pontianak, then shipped to Palembang on Sumatra, and thence to Batavia (Jakarta), where he was prevented from communicating with the Rajah, who had remained there to await news from his emissary. On 11 January MacBryan was flown to Singapore, where he was served with a warrant for his arrest and taken off to Changi gaol.

By a stroke of good fortune, a few days later the Rajah's solicitor Roland Braddell happened to come to Changi to visit a client and was 'astounded' to see MacBryan, whom he knew well from his many meetings with the Rajah. After listening to his story, Braddell challenged Sir Shenton to produce evidence against him or let him go. As Braddell had surmised, the governor was hard pushed to prove that MacBryan was a Japanese spy, Spurway's allegations having relied mainly on hearsay from European officers who were decidedly ill-disposed towards 'the Baron' – Spurway effectively conceded as much when MacBryan threatened him with legal action after the war. It is possible that, as a fluent Japanese speaker, MacBryan had wanted to try to negotiate with the invaders, either regarding the possibility of making Sarawak neutral – an idea the Rajah had toyed with before the war – or to enlist Japanese co-operation in his scheme for an Islamic confederation of South East Asian states. But the governor had no reliable evidence of this either; so he reluctantly released his prisoner and put him on the next evacuee ship bound for Western Australia.

On 30 January MacBryan flew from Perth to Melbourne to be reunited with the Rajah, who had by then also made the journey from Java. The next day, having been told the whole story, Vyner wrote a long letter of protest to the British High Commissioner in Canberra, Sir Ronald Cross, complaining that the governor had never even told him about the arrest of his private secretary and claiming that he had been actuated by feelings of personal antagonism towards him – a suggestion that was later strongly refuted by Lord Moyne. As a result of the arrest, wrote the Rajah, 'My special messages to the leaders of the tribes and my subjects urging them to stand firm, to assist the British and Dutch authorities in every way possible, and to await patiently the day of their deliverance were not conveyed to them.' He added that the treatment of his personal representative had 'reflected seriously upon my personal prestige in those places', and that it crowned 'the generally antagonistic attitude which Sir Shenton Thomas has persistently maintained towards

Sarawak and myself during the past few years and which has caused me such profound distress'.

Sylvia had by then made it back to England, having been granted 'priority' in her passage by the new British Ambassador to the United States, Lord Halifax, 'owing to serious conditions in Sarawak'. Halifax's intervention, which may have had something to do with the fact that he and the Ranee had known each other since childhood, bemused the Colonial Office, not least because shortly beforehand the Ranee had sounded off to the press about the 'titled fools' who represented Britain's interests in America. And it did not prevent the Ranee from venting her feelings about Britain's miserable failure to defend her husband's realm as soon as she got home. 'We all knew there was not a hope for Sarawak from the first,' she said in typically hyperbolic style at a luncheon of the Overseas League in London in February. 'Fifty years of my husband's life and about thirty-five years of my work with him have been wiped out in only five days of fighting. All our people have been taken prisoner and my husband is missing. I have not the slightest idea whether he is in Australia or whether he actually made his way to Sarawak which seemed to be his intention.'

She told her audience that, before leaving Sarawak, she had gone 'round all our defences – and what a pitiful array they were! Our front door was invulnerable, but there were a hundred and one back doors where the Japanese entered unmolested.' The 'excellent little airfield' they had constructed stood 'lonely and depressed without a single plane on it', and was used by the Punjab Regiment for their afternoon football ground. When 'our people' were being drilled in home defence, they 'looked on it as some sort of a game. They shouted, laughed and turned somersaults, just like a bunch of schoolboys at play. The Punjabis ran about like mad things, pulling down trees for no apparent reason, and putting up barbed wire just behind the Palace, so that every time the Rajah went for a walk he was caught up in it.'

Her brother Oliver, though, was succinctly scathing about the part that Sylvia and Vyner had played, or rather failed to play, in the whole episode, writing to Doll in January: 'Neither of them were where they ought to have been in a crisis in their country's fate. They had a chance of being like the Kings of Norway and Greece, & now the heroic moment has gone. And so has their country, their money and their future. For I cannot believe the Rajahs will be reinstated after the war.' Two and a half years later he wrote to Doll: 'I hope to goodness the British Government will not be so foolish as to put Sylvia back on the throne of Sarawak – that is *not* one of the things we have been fighting for!'

In 1942 Sylvia was herself far from optimistic about their chances of being reinstated, telling Doll in June that there was 'no chance of Mop [Vyner] and I ever being more than a couple of nomads for the rest of our lives'. With this in mind, she decided to sell her house at Lancaster Gate and rent a large flat at 45 Albion Gate, overlooking the northern edge of Hyde Park, which she shared for a short time with Leonora.

Leonora had been widowed three years previously, in June 1939, when her husband Kenneth Inchcape had suffered a coronary thrombosis that was misdiagnosed by his doctor as indigestion. Left alone at the age of twenty-seven with their five-year-old son Simon – the Crown Prince of Sarawak in Sylvia's eyes – and eighteen-month-old daughter Rosemary, Leonora had had little time to grieve before the outbreak of war three months later.

Before the war her husband had suggested that she ought to learn to become an ambulance driver – 'driving was something at which he considered me competent,' she recalled – and in wartime she put her skills to use driving a mobile canteen in East London, then an ambulance during the Blitz. Before coming to live with her mother, she had also suffered two further family tragedies: first the suicide of the butler, Willey, who 'hanged himself in the gun room with Nanny's ironing flex', and then, in August 1941, the death of her eighteen-year-old stepson Jimmy (Kenneth's third son from his first marriage), who fell over a cliff while shooting rock pigeons.

By the time she moved in with Sylvia, Leonora was feeling 'free and lonely', and going out most nights, sometimes escorted by her eldest stepson – also Kenneth – who was only five years younger than she. In due course she became the merriest of widows, embarking on a succession of transient love affairs, and each weekend at the house near Salisbury where her children were looked after by their nanny she would appear with a different man in tow. Her daughter Lady Rosemary French remembers that 'they all brought us presents so we didn't mind; those that we didn't like we laid traps for'.

Back in London during the week, Leonora was now working for the Bundles for Britain campaign, 'standing in a confusion of other people's clothes from early morning until late at night, sorting and wrapping and tying up parcels'. Sylvia, too, wanted to do her bit but 'nobody seemed to think there was anything I could do; it seemed I was too late'. Soon after she arrived back in England, in January, she had written a letter to the Prime Minister, imaginatively claiming she had just 'escaped' from Sarawak and volunteering to set out on a lecture tour of Britain to tell people all about the Far East. She maintained that there was no one better suited to this 'extremely necessary' task. The Ranee's offer was referred to the Colonial Office, who were determined not to turn her loose. The Assistant Undersecretary of State Edward Gent minuted that 'the Ranee of Sarawak's public utterances are not such as to suggest that she would be fitted to be entrusted with any official mission (or encouragement) to explain the Far East to the people of the UK'. Her 'vituperative opinions for the Press' and 'remarkable statements about the succession in Sarawak' were characterised by 'extravagant misuse of language'. 'In short,' Gent concluded, 'her tongue style is thoughtless and sensational, and her inclination is towards an inverted and malicious form of snobbishness. She should not be trusted with any publicity task by the Govt.' Another of his colleagues agreed that he 'could think of nothing calculated to do less good and more mischief than a lecture by this lady at the present moment'.

Shortly afterwards the Colonial Office also had to decide whether the Ranee should be granted dollar exchange to cover the debts of $7,000 that she had run up in America. Most of these had for the time being been paid by Jack Golden, who was also claiming the $1,000 which he said the Rajah had promised him in return for looking after his wife's affairs. Assistant secretary Leslie Monson observed: 'It seems to be a case of balancing the value of the dollar exchange concerned against the possible loss of prestige to our cause by the leaving the debts of this "British princess" as she is no doubt known in the USA, unpaid.' He proposed that the Ranee should be granted sufficient exchange to meet those debts that were 'reputable' and those which the British consul considered could not be left unpaid without damage to the British cause. But the Colonial Office declined to transfer funds to pay the divorce expenses of the Ranee's daughter Valerie, who had by this time divorced Bob Gregory in America and wished also to obtain her freedom in Britain. For this she needed to have evidence of adultery in America, and a firm of lawyers in New York was ready to undertake this task on receipt of an advance of $1,000 for expenses and a $1,000 retainer.

By late spring 1942 letters were beginning to reach Sylvia from Vyner, including one from Batavia relating his thwarted ambition to become a guerrilla leader. In May she received another from Melbourne, where the Rajah was by then living in a tiny flat and limiting himself to one drink a day. 'I have it with two pals who are also dead broke owing to the Japs,' he wrote. 'We have all our meals in a hamburger shop also around the comer. We get a hamburger, bread and butter and cup of tea – all for one and six.' Vyner told Sylvia that he loved living alone and doing his own cooking. She mournfully concluded that the invasion of Sarawak had put him in a mood whereby he wanted to be alone and 'cut away entirely from his home and family'.

In another slightly dotty letter to his niece Jean Halsey, Vyner described how he was 'doing my own chores – cook[ing] all my foods which I have to personally carry from the village. Its no joke carrying eggs in one of one's coat pockets, & a collyflower [*sic*] in the other & also a loaf of bread and perhaps one or two books in ones hands . . . I am adept at cooking joints, chickens, brains and tripe . . . whatever happens when I get back to England I have no use for cooks – oversexed harpies.'

'Ordinary Australians', the Rajah told his niece, 'are awfully nice and very matey.' He appears to have preferred their company to those of his Sarawak officers, among them the hostile former Chief Justice H. Thackwell Lewis and deputy treasurer Cecil

Pitt-Hardacre, who had also made it to Australia. The Rajah chose to remain in Melbourne rather than join them in Sydney, where for a few months they operated as a government in exile – there being more than the quorum of three members needed to convene a meeting of the Supreme Council. The Rajah showed almost no interest in the council's business, and some time in late February or early March, he wrote to the council to the effect that, as far as he was concerned, the British or Dutch could have Sarawak after the war. According to Thackwell Lewis, he was proposing 'the winding up of the Government commitments, the pensioning off of the services and presumably the handing over to himself of the remaining assets of the state [amounting to 13 million dollars]'. When his council refused to have anything to do with this idea, the Rajah asked that his letter be destroyed. Thackwell Lewis, never one of Vyner's biggest fans, deplored the 'shameful defeatism' of Vyner's communication, which he considered amounted to 'the most cynical repudiation of his own obligations to his country'.

It did not take much to persuade Vyner to fall in with the opinion being expressed by both Bertram and the Colonial Office that Sarawak's affairs would be better off being run from London. He also seemed to have caved in on the constitution, writing to Bertram, in March, that if after the war his people did 'wish me back (wishful thinking!) I should only do so on my own terms & with complete powers. All red tape, Councils, bureaucracy, etc. etc. to be completely eliminated. I am sure you will agree in this.'

In April the Rajah disbanded the Supreme Council in Australia and appointed a Sarawak Commission in London with Bertram as its president. This was to operate from the Sarawak government offices at Millbank, and would have as its foremost duty the custody of Sarawak's reserve funds. The Rajah planned to stay on in Australia until the situation in the Pacific improved, retaining £200,000 of Sarawak's funds under the supervision of Pitt-Hardacre for payment of salaries etc., while £100,000 was to be transferred to London. He also told Bertram that he was dispensing with MacBryan's services as private secretary, saying that he was 'thoroughly fed up with him'. However, this seems to have been little more than a device for making his brother more amenable to whatever he decided to do next – he assured Pitt-Hardacre that Bertram 'would fall in with any proposals that were suggested providing Mac had no fingers in the pie' – and Bertram suspected that the Rajah, Pitt-Hardacre and MacBryan 'were engaged on some deal – with MacB as secret agent'. Anthony, who had arrived back in London in mid-January via a visit to his mother in Athens, was equally suspicious of his uncle's motives, writing to Edward Gent at the Colonial Office that, while it was possible that MacBryan's power was broken at last, it was just as likely that he had 'prevailed upon the Rajah to make this gesture to put those concerned in good humour and to prepare the ground for a final appeal to my father for a sum of money which would enable the Rajah (and MacBryan) to retire gracefully from the Sarawak scene together'.

Sylvia, as one might have expected, was busy with her own scheming during this time, and in mid-June 1942 she wrote to Jack Golden hinting at a plan she had for the liberation of Sarawak: 'I wish I could tell you about it, but I and eleven others I have mustered are sworn to secrecy. If one little whisper of this leaked out, it would spoil all our show. The only thing that may be an obstacle and difficult to overcome is the Tuan Muda (heir apparent), and he is FAR too apparent for the likes of me. He hates my soul, and would on principle oppose anything in which I venture. But we are hopeful, this little band and I, and we mean to do what we have in mind to do in spite of the Tuan Muda.'

Early the next month she again wrote to Jack, saying:

> It may so happen that I shall disappear for a while, not yet, but sometime in the near future. I don't want you to be anxious if you don't hear from me, but trust me and know that what I am doing is what I want to do with all my heart and soul. I can't tell you a thing about it, but if all goes well I'll turn up again at the end. All should go well, but the utmost secrecy and care has to be maintained. I must confess it is MY idea, but I couldn't make any headway until I found my company of friends who think and feel as I do. Please don't worry about me, the only way you will know that I am fulfilling my dream is that you won't get any letters for a

> spell. I can't let you know any other way. Nobody knows what I am contemplating doing . . . The only ones that know are those that are in it with me.

Two weeks later she wrote to explain 'why I feel that this thing must be done. I am, and have been ever since Sarawak was taken, deadly ashamed of the show we Englishmen and women put up . . . it is no use beating about the bush . . . we DID let our natives down, and I could never look them or GOD in the face if I didn't do something about it.' Her 'little band of men', she said, consisted mostly of Sarawak officers, along with 'one or two' Americans. 'We are now waiting for the arrival of one Sarawak man from Australia who has all the dope, and will give us a good idea of what is going on over there . . . after this we can get cracking . . . There is nothing foolhardy or crazy about the plan. We have laid it well, and I have one Sarawak survey man with me who knows every inch of the Sarawak coast. The thing is feasible. Vyner may be a stumbling block to me, but I am not telling him anything about the part I plan to play in this.'

The letters were intercepted by the censors. To Leslie Monson at the Colonial Office they indicated that the Ranee had 'some cracked-brain exploit in hand. There may be nothing in it but she is capable of anything and it might be as well to consult MI5, who have been sent copies of the extracts, in case they have further information on her plans.' A colleague thought that it sounded 'like mystery for its own sake rather than anything likely to deserve serious attention'. Gent agreed: 'She is a neurotic person – something of an exhibitionist.' However, he thought that it might be worth watching to see whether there was any connection between her plans and those of MacBryan. In May the Rajah's former private secretary had tried in vain to join the Allied Intelligence Bureau in Brisbane, run by Captain Roy Kendall, who wanted to land two Brooke officers by submarine to gather information about occupied Sarawak. The Sarawak man from Australia 'with all the dope' for whose arrival the Ranee was waiting was presumed to be Pitt-Hardacre, who was in fact already secretly working for Kendall, and who had been sent to London by the Rajah with orders to try to clear MacBryan's name with the War Office. According to what Sylvia later told Anthony, the War Office had earlier asked her what she thought of MacBryan, and she had answered that he was 'a kind of evil genius', that he had a brilliant mind, but that the Rajah was not deceived by him. Even bad people have their uses and MacBryan could be used, she said, but on the other hand he was the 'perfect Quisling type'.

The extent to which Sylvia's liberation scheme existed outside her imagination is unclear, as is the connection, if any, with Kendall's plan; but we do know for sure that she never did 'disappear' from London, and in September she wrote to the Colonial Secretary Lord Cranborne with another offer of her services. She was now volunteering to help break down the 'cruel and unjust colour prejudice' encountered by colonial servicemen and war workers, who, she ventured, 'must be mighty lonesome over here'. She suggested that she might take them sightseeing and 'entertain some of the coloured people here in my house, which is full of interesting relics from my own beloved Sarawak and might interest them. I think after thirty-eight years amongst Malays and Head-hunters I understand coloured people more than I do my own race.' Once again the Colonial Office did not deem it expedient to take advantage of the Ranee's offer.

Instead Sylvia made do with working in the canteen of the Washington Club for American servicemen, and later at the American Red Cross Club, experiences which only confirmed to the Ranee that she and Americans had a special rapport. In 1940, in the midst of her US lecture tour, Sylvia had told Anthony Eden that 'Americans DO like the way I address them'. Now, during her war work with the GIs, she wrote to Doll in much the same vein: 'I get on with Americans, I love them. They have such a gorgeous sense of humour . . .' Leonora later described how when four American officers moved into the flat below her mother's, the Ranee went into 'a dither of excitement'; she and her maid Lotty 'were like girls, running up and down with flowers and things, and even food' for the new arrivals.

Not that Leonora proved immune to their charms. She had never met any Americans before, recalling, 'To me they were either gangsters, movie stars or over-sexed private eyes.' But these men 'came like a rush of fresh air into our lives', she wrote in her autobiography. She was dazzled by the abundance of food and alcohol on offer at their officers' club and enjoyed being 'treated as though one were special instead of a sort of useful encumbrance . . . Was it any wonder we women got swept off our tired and run down feet?' George VI bade his subjects to 'take an American into your home for Christmas', and Leonora was only too happy to do the King's bidding. She fell in love with several, including the *Time & Life* correspondent Noel Busch, before eventually plumping for Colonel Francis Parker 'Tommy' Tompkins, the most senior of the officers billeted in the flat below her mother.

By the spring of 1943 Leonora and Tommy were living together. Sylvia seemed quite happy with the arrangement, telling Doll that he was 'very sweet . . . quite a big man in the American Army [he was head of the intelligence branch at the United States Headquarters] and likely to go far'. 'He is married,' Sylvia added, 'but then, American marriages aren't that binding, and maybe she'll settle with this one. He isn't young [in 1943 he was forty-seven] or good looking. But he has been wonderful to her and she adores him.'

Elizabeth, meanwhile, had been swept off her feet by another of the flat's occupants, Colonel Richards Vidmer, a forty-four-year-old former sports columnist for the New York *Herald Tribune*, who 'knew his way into women's hearts as surely as into their beds', wrote Sylvia. Elizabeth and Harry Roy had been drifting apart for some time now. During the early part of the war she had spent most of her time living in Wales with their two children while he continued to perform with his band in London, and although she came to stay with her husband every now and then, Sylvia observed to Doll in June 1942 that 'he doesn't seem to count in the picture at all'. Not that Sylvia minded. She, too, had by now taken against her bandleader son-in-law, owing to what seems to have been a mixture of snobbery, anti-Semitism (despite or perhaps because of her own Jewish ancestry) and disapproval of what she saw as his louche and uncouth ways. 'He isn't a bad little man,' she remarked to Doll, 'but crude, and it just gets me down to see him with the kids. Maybe it is that I so dislike the Jews . . . I can't help it Doll. If you could see how they are behaving through this war, even YOU would dislike them.'

When Sylvia told Doll the next April that Elizabeth had left Harry for the American colonel, she wrote: 'I thank God on my knees every night,' and added that 'their marriage had been rooted in incompatibility from the start'.

> I can't tell you all the circumstances [she went on], but I think when I do tell that he [Harry] has slept with both Noni and Vava, amongst many others, you won't think it wrong of her to leave him. With her kids growing up, and the filth of his language and conduct, she has every right to free herself. She has stood eight years of an almost concentration camp marriage. Even I haven't been able to dine out with her for eight years without taking the blooming Roy family . . . Didi hasn't been an entirely moral wife I know, but she has been, and is, a wonderful mother. She has brought up her two kids quite beautifully. He hasn't done a thing, he doesn't even support them financially in spite of all his money.

When Doll passed all this on to Oliver, he cautioned her: 'If I were you I would not believe what Sylvia says about her children; she no more tells the truth about them than she does about everyone else.'

Valerie, or Vava, was living with 'that awful Spaniard', as Sylvia described him to Doll – Jose Pepi Cabarro, an orange-importer with a hefty frame and 'the face of a meditative goat'. Sylvia told Doll that Cabarro had been living off her youngest daughter for the past three years but refused to marry her lest she became a Spanish subject and her assets were frozen. Valerie was living 'like a tramp' in a small cottage by the Thames at Maidenhead, with 'no bath, no hot water, no electric light . . . She cooks and slaves whilst he sits on his fat hams and reads the papers all day. I hate his guts. Bob Gregory was worth a million of him . . . he was a crook of course, but a nice crook.' The next month, May 1943, Valerie and Pepi were married. 'I could see nothing alluring in him myself,' Sylvia wrote later, 'but perhaps, for her, his very size was symbolic of security and peace.'

Throughout this time MacBryan had remained with the Rajah out in Australia, seemingly as much in favour as before despite ceasing to be private secretary. The Rajah had supported his application to work for Roy Kendall's intelligence operation in Brisbane, and when the War Office refused to give MacBryan security clearance, the Rajah complained to General Douglas MacArthur, Commander of the American forces in the South-west Pacific, that he had been 'prevented from using his special knowledge in the service where it could be most useful' owing to 'mud-slinging' arising from jealousy over his friendship with the Rajah. MacArthur declined to intervene, however, and in October the Rajah re-employed MacBryan as a 'confidential agent' to liaise between himself, the Sarawak government office in Sydney and the office of Captain Kendall in Brisbane.

In January 1943 Bertram got wind of MacBryan's plan to return to Sarawak at the earliest possible moment as the Rajah's viceroy. He wrote to Vyner saying that he held 'no feelings of personal animosity towards MacBryan, who can't help indulging in scheming and meddling and political jugglery any more than people can help having clubfoot or arthritis, or some other disability. But the fact is that . . . the enormous power he has wielded latterly in Sarawak, with the most deplorable results, is solely derived from his having acted as your mouthpiece . . .' The Tuan Muda warned his brother that he would not really know to what end his powers would be exercised, and that it might suit MacBryan for the Raj to come to an end, 'and for Sarawak to revert to its former state of vassalage to the original ruling power [Brunei]'. 'A plenipotentiary commission for use in Sarawak given to MacBryan', Bertram remarked, 'is rather like giving a man with a partiality for arson a box of matches or a torch and giving him the free run of your granaries.'

With war still raging, the commission remained on hold for the time being, and in February the Rajah wrote to MacBryan reappointing him as private secretary on his old salary of 835 Sarawak dollars, and suggesting that he accompany him to London, where the Rajah would attempt to clear his name once and for all with the War Office. He added: 'I will take you to Sarawak if I return.' They arrived in England on 9 June after having spent several weeks in America en route.

By the time Vyner got back to London, Sylvia had retired her maid, Lotty, and Lotty's husband Tom, to a house she had bought for them near Leeds, and was now living alone, doing her own cooking and housework – though Lotty still came up to London on occasional long visits and slept in a room below the Ranee's flat. 'I must say I love doing everything myself and I can cook fairly well now,' Sylvia wrote to Doll. She had moved several times within the same street on account of the air raids, which she admitted rather thrilled her, the big guns in Hyde Park setting the skies ablaze, 'the German devils streaking across the sky and turning and twisting like moths caught in the candle light . . . I think it must be my sadistic side, but it really excites me when I hear those sirens go.' She was working on a book (which appears never to have been published) of short stories about the effects of the war on women, 'rather horrible and morbid. They start all right, and then become gruesome and bestial. Maybe as I get old I get cruel, or maybe it is my answer to all this unhappiness and separation.'

In Sylvia's case it was not just the separation from her husband Vyner – which she said made her life 'sadness itself' – and boyfriend Jack, but also from her only friendly sibling Doll, who had now put down permanent roots in New Mexico, where she was growing more eccentric by the year. Feeling decidedly more patriotic and warlike now than she had during the 1914–18 war, Doll had taken to displaying the Union Jack and Stars and Stripes on her car, and told Oliver excitedly in 1943 that she was 'painting BOMBERS, beautiful B 24's, I just love the Flying Fortresses and B 24's and P 38's . . . I buy all the mags full of flying planes . . .' To another friend she wrote: 'I paint in the mornings and in the afternoon I fold bandages: my day is divided into war and peace.' Some time later she wrote to Oliver asking him to 'wangle' a job for her in a Flying Fortress: 'I am scared blue of bombs but I would lump even bombs to get over the Pacific in a bomber . . . I could then paint for Britain.' She added that Lord Halifax 'must remember Pupsy' and so could speak up for her.

Sylvia's relations with Oliver remained as acrimonious as ever. He told Doll in September 1942 that he took 'jolly good care not to go within a thousand miles of [Sylvia] or to have any communication with her'. Sylvia, for her part, complained of having been cheated out of the money settled on her by Reggie when she married. Under the settlement she was to receive £20,000 on the death of their mother,

Nellie, subject to prior settlements on Oliver and Maurice (whose share now went to his widow Zena) of £50,000 and £20,000 respectively – with recourse being had to the properties at 1 and 2 Tilney Street and Orchard Lea if the funds were insufficient. Oliver told Doll he was 'much amused' to hear that Sylvia was proposing to bring an action against himself and Teddy Seymour as trustees, and said he was 'astonished' that Doll should 'still treat what she [Sylvia] tells you as "facts" when you know what a liar and mischief-maker she is'.

'It is not our fault that she comes last on the list for distribution of assets & that there are no assets left to distribute,' he went on. 'It is the sort of thing that happens to people who love money too much. You say she is generous. To whom? When? I have never seen any signs of it. She certainly showed no generosity of behaviour to Antoinette when she arrived a stranger in England. And all that about being "thwarted" will not wash. Life thwarts everybody, & she was no more thwarted than the rest of us. But there, you cannot help liking her, while I find it quite easy to avoid doing so.' Sylvia more than reciprocated the dislike, describing her brother to Doll as 'poor silly pompous Viscount Esher'. In another letter she wrote: 'Nothing will ever make me believe that HIS blood is ANY thicker than water.'

The various estrangements inevitably made her feel lonely, and so, in the spring of 1943, she was 'thrilled to death' by the prospect of Vyner's imminent arrival. She had arranged the flat so that he had his own suite and could do 'exactly as he likes irrespective of me'. She could not wait to see him and to hear what he felt about their future prospects in Sarawak. At the same time she worried that Vyner would be shocked by how much she had aged. Getting old, she told Doll, was 'a damnable affair . . . I don't feel a day older than when I married, but my poor old hulk doesn't seem to get around so easily. Besides, THINGS come out on one. A mole here, or a hair there. I don't mind lines, they give character, but scraggy necks and flabby chins get me down.'

For whatever reason, Vyner did not stay long under the same roof as his wife. By the time of Sylvia's next letter to Doll, a year later, in May 1944, he had moved out to Jewell's House at Stanford Dingley, Berkshire, where he resumed his interest in gardening, took up small-scale farming and developed 'a new pash' on the woman who lived next door. 'I like her very much,' Sylvia told Doll; 'she is amusing, intelligent, and excellent with him.' Nor, apparently, had this new love interest diminished Sylvia's regard for her husband, who was, she added, 'the most amazing man living at this moment . . . and I still get a tremendous kick out of being with him. So much humour, so much originality. One could never get bored with such a man.'

The previous year Doll had suggested to Sylvia that she must occasionally feel jealous, but she had denied it, explaining that she and Vyner had 'too good an understanding for that'. Two years later she told Doll that they had 'made a glorious success of our marriage just because we don't behave like any other husband and wife have ever behaved. We have our own separate flats. We go out together, dine together, have lots of fun, and then at night we call it a day, and go back to our virgin beds. No-one who has ever married has so hated the sleeping together more than either he or I did . . . It's alright when you are young, and it's alright if you want kids. But as an act it is both ridiculous and awkward, and I take a very poor view of it indeed.'

But if her days of sleeping with her husband were long since over, Sylvia continued to exert an influence over him in matters relating to Sarawak. In the spring of 1943 her love–hate relationship with MacBryan was going through one of its hate phases, which may explain why the Rajah's loyalty to his private secretary faltered so soon after they reached London. On 26 June the Rajah, with characteristic caprice, terminated MacBryan's service once again. When he protested that the Rajah's dismissal of him would prejudice his chances of finding war work, Sylvia was deputed to dine with him on 1 July and, according to what Vyner later told Bertram, 'gave it to him hot and strong'. Vyner added that he was 'jolly glad to get rid of him, you don't know what days and weeks of boredom I have had in his company . . . My pity for him was entirely misplaced.' MacBryan slunk off to his asylum at Kingsdown House, from where he wrote to Bertram in a bid to ingratiate himself with that side of the family, now that his relationship with the Rajah had broken down. His aim, he told Bertram, was to 'convince you of the sincerity of my motives' and correct 'those bad impressions which I am regrettably led to believe you have formed'. Bertram refused to have anything to do with him.

Sylvia's status and identity as Ranee, meanwhile, remained as important to her as ever, and she continued to be governed by what she admitted to be her slightly guilty conscience about the invasion. In November 1943 she seized the opportunity presented by the arrival of the new Colonial Secretary Oliver Stanley to volunteer to return to Sarawak with the reoccupying army in order to help in 'the re-establishment of normal life'. 'I think I can say without too much conceit but with pride that all the natives in Kuching were genuinely fond of me,' she wrote to the Colonial Office. 'If I went out there I feel that I could help regain a little of the white man's prestige with care and tact.' After consulting Frederick Pollard, a member of the Sarawak service and a near relative of the Rajah, Leslie Monson minuted that he [Pollard] 'had no hesitation in stating (though not for publication) that the Ranee was completely devoid of any qualifications that would be of service in the rehabilitation of a liberated Sarawak'. Gent tersely concurred: 'She ought to be the last civilian in the queue. Her spiritual home is Hollywood.' Sylvia received a polite and non-committal reply.

The next spring – 1944 – Sylvia wrote to Doll to say: 'The war is going well, especially out OUR way, and I am beginning to air my sarongs, and polish up my Malay for the re-entry into Sarawak. That is my one incentive. The thought that keeps me going. I want to go back there and make good, and wash out the unfortunate fact that I wasn't taken prisoner with the rest. Always I will have a guilty conscience that THEY are there, and WE are here.'

14

RELUCTANT RAJAH

The terms on which the Rajah and Ranee would return to their realm, if they ever did, were still far from clear, not least because Vyner was so ambivalent about the whole prospect. 'If I elected to return to Sarawak I feel I should be putting my head into a veritable hornet's nest,' he wrote to Bertram in November 1943. 'The only thing that bothers me is finance. Supposing I renounce my rights, what will the BG [British government] do about my salary? I don't much mind about myself but I have an expensive family to keep going, also a lot of dependants. If this point is settled I should be much relieved!'

Bertram pointed out that the British government would be likely to examine state disbursements for at least a year before the fall of Sarawak, and his brother might then be required to repay the £200,000 he had controversially acquired before the introduction of the constitution. Vyner retorted that that money 'certainly wasn't a loan' and he would rather go to gaol than repay it. He had decided that it would 'simplify matters a great deal' if he offered to return to his country and this was the line now being pushed by Sylvia, who was 'very keen about this'. He doubted that 'even the hard-hearted British Government would keep me out there for more than a two or three years stretch, which I am quite prepared to do if my health stands it'. However, he did not want to be obliged to 'sit in committees, meetings etc etc & absolutely refuse to be buggered up with a lot of red tape in the interim before leaving for Sarawak'. 'I suppose,' he added, 'if I were received on my return by curses and hisses from the natives, the BG would allow me to clear out.'

By mid-1944 the tide of war in the Pacific and South East Asia had turned, and Japan's positions in the region were looking defenceless. Guadalcanal had fallen to the Americans in 1942, Tarawa in 1943 and in early 1944 Kwajalein and then Saipan, where, as part of the Japanese strategy that its people should never be captured, women and children were made to jump off the cliffs when the Americans landed. In June 1944, shortly after the landings on Saipan, the Colonial Secretary Oliver Stanley wrote to Vyner saying that, given the progress of the war, it was 'not too soon' for them to discuss the future government of the Rajah's state. He said that Parliament and public opinion at home and among Britain's allies would inevitably hold the British government responsible for the future development of Sarawak, and existing agreements between the two countries were insufficient to enable it fully to discharge its responsibilities. He invited the Rajah to come and discuss the matter.

Vyner had by then settled into a bucolic existence on his smallholding at Stanford Dingley, where his correspondence tended to get buried beneath packets of vegetable seed. Only occasionally, when the weather suspended his farming operations, did he venture to London to see Sylvia, and he was unwilling at this stage to get involved personally in such talks, so instead he sent along his government agent H. D. Aplin. Aplin reported back that the Colonial Office now wanted a British representative to advise the Sarawak government on political, social and economic matters, and for the King to have jurisdiction in Sarawak's internal affairs under the Foreign Jurisdiction Acts of 1890 and 1913.

On hearing this the Rajah wrote to Stanley saying that while he thought that 'nothing but good' could come from closer liaison, he could scarcely be expected to accede to the arrangement being suggested at the present time when, 'owing to the unavoidable inability of the Protecting Power to preserve them from invasion', the people of Sarawak were under alien rule. 'I should be willing', he concluded, 'to return to Sarawak for a short period on its reoccupation, if thought desirable, but I feel that the future must lie with those who have the physical vigour not only to make a fresh start, but to continue firmly along such lines as will ensure internal peace within the state.'

In early October, at Vyner's suggestion, Bertram went to the Colonial Office for a 'frank talk' with Edward Gent, who was an old friend of his, during which he re-emphasised the Rajah's reluctance to enter into what might be seen as a secret treaty, but nevertheless agreed that the Colonial Office should now bring to the table 'detailed suggestions for future relations between the British and Sarawak governments'.

Before these suggestions were received, at the end of December 1944 Anthony Brooke arrived back in England from Ceylon, where he had been serving on the staff of Admiral Lord Louis Mountbatten, the Supreme Allied Commander in South East Asia. Anthony's hopes of one day becoming Rajah had lately been revived by a letter he had received from his father, saying that the government of Sarawak was 'no septuagenarian's job, and no septuagenarian who suggested that he was the chap to carry it out would be entitled to much confidence'. With MacBryan for the time being out of the picture, the Rajah had been making more conciliatory noises about his nephew, and Bertram felt able to reassure Anthony that he was now likely to succeed to the Raj. Nonetheless, Anthony still thought, 'The old boy will hang on as long as possible,' as he wrote to his wife Kathleen, and he doubted that the Ranee had entirely given up her machinations.

In November Anthony received a cable from his father informing him that he was on the point of being reinstated as Rajah Muda, and on 2 December the War Office authorised Mountbatten to release him from his post. On his way back to England, Anthony spoke to American journalists in Delhi with the object of 're-educating the American people away from the dance band and all-in-wrestling associations with Sarawak', so he told his wife. Soon after he arrived back in England, Vyner appointed him head of a 'Provisional Government', the successor to Bertram's Sarawak government commission, which meant that Anthony now took charge of negotiations with the Colonial Office.

Grateful for this responsibility, the Rajah Muda was also keen to play an active part in the reoccupation of Sarawak, especially in view of the fact that no member of the Brooke family had been present in the state 'in the hour of the people's greatest need'. It was, he considered, 'imperative, if the Raj is to continue, that a member of the family should land and be with the people at the hour of their liberation from the Japanese'. The War Office and Colonial Office were less keen on this idea, fearing that it would create 'almost insurmountable difficulties' if Anthony became involved in the military operation.

In the meantime, Anthony began setting down on paper how he saw the future of Sarawak, but when he sent his proposals to the Secretary of State, Stanley observed mildly that they did not appear to be 'altogether in accordance with the basis of discussion expressed in my letter to the Rajah of 19 June 1944'. Letters went back and forth, with Anthony objecting to the Colonial Office's demands for the right to legislate for Sarawak under the Foreign Jurisdiction Act, and that the British representative be given an effective voice in domestic policy. Stanley, meanwhile, refused to be restricted from 'raising in the discussion any proposals which commend themselves to His Majesty's Government'.

Subsequent meetings at the Colonial Office failed to resolve the impasse, with Stanley and his colleagues arguing that the world had changed since 1888 in such a way as to make the existing relationship no longer tenable: the Secretary of State would have to answer to Parliament in regard to Sarawak affairs, while American people were likely to hold the opinion 'even more strongly' that a native country governed by a white rajah was an anachronism; there might well be a popular outcry at American lives being spent in order to hand back Sarawak to a system of government which was in a constitutional sense 'irresponsible'. They warned Anthony that it would be a serious responsibility to oppose their policy with 'nothing more solid than sentiment'.

As far as Anthony was concerned, though, he was representing the interests of an independent sovereign state, and he refused to submit to a 'unilateral decision' of the British government. When the Colonial Office put forward its legal advisers' 'considered view' that Sarawak possessed 'no personality whatever' in international law, and was 'simply a territory within the British Empire', discussions were suspended while the Sarawak team sought advice from their own counsel.

In mid-July 1945, by which time Allied troops had already entered Sarawak, Stanley was growing impatient and wrote to the Rajah to say that, regarding the discussions, 'unfortunately . . . little progress has been made and all these meetings have been suspended for over two months while your representatives seek legal advice . . . You will, I am sure, share my concern at this long delay, in view of the fact that the Sarawak representatives have so far shown themselves personally unresponsive to the proposals of His Majesty's Government.' Vyner forwarded the letter to Anthony with a terse note: 'Please deal with this.'

Although relations between Vyner and Anthony had never been notably harmonious, lately they had been making an effort to get along better. Sylvia, who had eagerly fostered the enmity in the past, entered into the new spirit by lunching with Anthony at Ciro's Club, her favourite haunt in the West End of London, in early August. The atmosphere was 'exceedingly friendly', as Anthony recorded in his note of their meeting, and they agreed to put their differences behind them. 'She'd said a lot of queer things, but that was all over and we now had the future to deal with.' Sylvia said that the Rajah had felt much more cheerful and confident since the Rajah Muda had visited him at Stanford Dingley. He was delighted that they had 'come together' again and would both go out to Sarawak after the liberation. She added that her husband had 'always had something of an inferiority feeling' and had become profoundly depressed about Sarawak and afraid that the people would never want to see him again in view of the circumstances of the Japanese invasion. But with the turn of the tide he was now 'perking up' and 'definitely wanted to return . . . if only to say goodbye'.

Sylvia candidly admitted that MacBryan had been exceedingly useful to the Rajah in the past, especially with regard to money, but assured Anthony that he was no longer part of the equation, that the Rajah was no fool, that MacBryan had no hold over him whatever, and that the Rajah certainly had 'no intention of taking him back'. She saw MacBryan from time to time and promised to keep Anthony informed of what he was up to. She guaranteed that the Rajah would have no more to do with him.

Shortly after their lunch, Sylvia wrote to Anthony:

> I am genuinely glad we are all friends again Peter . . . I think you will find that you and Vyner will have a wonderful reception in Sarawak . . . Vyner needs your youth and assurance and you will be able to do all the things he hates so much such as ceremonies etc. I had a few harsh words with MacBryan last time I saw him . . . and told him plainly that from now on Vyner was working with you and therefore he should take no more part in political controversies. He was *extremely* annoyed! I am coming back to London Sept 3rd then I positively *must* meet your 'Commoner' wife as I am supposed to have called her according to the damned American Press.

Sylvia's hold over her husband was not so strong as she suggested, however. By the end of August the changeable Rajah was once again proposing to take MacBryan out to Sarawak as his private secretary when he returned in March. With the progress of events, the Rajah evidently felt he now needed his 'evil genius' at his side to help deal with the pressure that was being put on him by the new Labour government, which had swept to power in the general election in July and was demonstrating rather more determination than its predecessor to bring an end to the Brooke Raj, subject to the payment of compensation. In early August, the atomic bombs on Hiroshima and Nagasaki and Japan's consequent capitulation brought forward the need to decide what would happen to Sarawak after the war. With the formal Japanese surrender in Kuching now scheduled for 11 September, at the beginning of that month the Cabinet decided that, unless a satisfactory agreement with the Rajah was reached within two months, the British government should take matters into its own hands. In November, the new Colonial Secretary George Hall reported back to his Cabinet colleagues that there was nothing 'in our formal Agreements with the Rajah which would enable his rule to be brought to an end by unilateral action on the part of HMG', but added that this was no longer necessary since the Rajah had himself now proposed to cede Sarawak to the British Crown.

Precisely when or why Vyner decided to abdicate is not clear from the available Colonial Office files. According to Sylvia, in the months leading up to her husband's proposal, the office had 'questioned him closely as to what he would do when the war with Japan was over and Sarawak recaptured, and how he would ever raise sufficient funds to set the country on its feet again'. The cost of reconstruction, estimated at £8 million, considerably in excess of Sarawak's remaining reserve funds, helped persuade Vyner that cession was an attractive option. 'We could of course have borrowed the money,' Sylvia later wrote to Doll, 'but in order to pay back, we would have had to have taxed the people heavily. Vyner is 72-years-old and he didn't feel he would outlive that debt and see his people free again.'

However, his eventual decision was clearly also actuated by what he (and Sylvia) saw as the unsuitability of his likely heir, Anthony, his intransigence during negotiations with the Colonial Office, and his presumptuous attitude to the succession. As so often, it was the Ranee who made the Rajah's feelings known. 'It isn't an easy or a particularly envious position to be an heir apparent,' she wrote to Anthony on 8 September 1945, 'and only with the utmost tact and understanding and complete knowledge of the Raja's character can it be successful . . . The Raja hates being bossed as you know Peter, and so did his father before him. After all there is nothing he doesn't know about Sarawak and the way to rule it.'

Sylvia said that the Rajah wanted Anthony clearly to understand that he 'insists on keeping in with the Colonial Office'. She went on to say how annoyed the Rajah had been when Anthony referred to 'my people' when he wrote to the newspapers thanking the Admiralty for naming a ship after Sarawak. 'It was only a slip of the pen Peter, but it was a bad slip and the Raja was extremely annoyed. You are the Raja Muda, the Heir Apparent, that is your standing, it is a position on its own, and you don't have to represent the views of the Raja, only yourself. What the Raja wants you to understand is that as long he is alive and capable, he wants to rule Sarawak in his own way, there will be plenty of time for you to rule it AFTER he's passed out.'

In view of the Rajah's decision to re-employ MacBryan, Sylvia reiterated that he had 'NO HOLD over the Raja more than that the Raja finds that Mac's particular form of genius is extremely useful to him, and there are certain things that MacBryan can do for the Raja no one else could possibly accomplish. The Raja is perfectly aware of Mac's failings and faults and has him well in hand.'

Two days after Sylvia's letter to Anthony, Vyner announced that he was resuming his powers following the liberation of his country and the end of the war in the Far East, and that Anthony's position as officer administering government would therefore be terminated. The provisional government felt the Rajah was exceeding his powers under the 1941 constitution and requested an interview, but an hour before it was due to take place, on 19 September, Sylvia telephoned to say that the Rajah was unable to keep the appointment. When Vyner invited Anthony and the other members of the provisional government to submit their resignations at once, they replied: 'Such plans as Your Highness has in mind can only be considered after Your Highness has properly resumed the powers of Rajah-in-Council and Head of the Provisional Government of Sarawak.' On 4 October the Rajah wrote to Anthony saying that he regarded the letter as 'a direct affront to myself, and I can only regard your action as an act of insubordination without parallel in my experience of State Affairs'.

Later that evening the Rajah called on the Colonial Secretary to tell him that he had dismissed his nephew as head of the provisional government. A week later the Rajah again wrote to Anthony to say that he was 'deeply shocked' by his intransigent attitude towards the Colonial Office, and by his extravagant purchase of a £20,000 residence in Regent's Park. 'You may neither use in future the style and title of Rajah Muda,' he concluded, 'nor consider you have any right of succession to the Raj of Sarawak.' Shortly afterwards, on 23 October, Sylvia wrote to Anthony to say she did not see why they could not continue having 'our lunches, only I think it is a little too soon to resume them yet . . . I am sorry it all ended this way but I guess you and Vyner just don't agree on any one point in connection with Sarawak. I think had I known you better many things might have been avoided, on the other hand it is so easy to be wise after the event.'

In the aftermath of this latest falling-out between the Rajah and his nephew, Anthony was offered the deeds of the Regent's Park house and £2,800 a year on the condition that he did not in future 'interfere in the affairs of Sarawak nor discuss publicly or privately in any way, malicious or otherwise, Sarawak affairs or Raja Brooke or his Highness's family'. But Anthony was in no mood to be silenced, especially since he had by now received his counsel's opinion, which upheld Sarawak's status as an independent sovereign state. He stepped up his press campaign challenging the right of the Colonial Office to enter into direct secret negotiations with the Rajah to settle the fate of the Raj, attracting the sympathy of politicians on both sides of the House. When his allowance was temporarily cut, in January, Bertram urged his son not to do anything intemperate, but at the same time wrote to Vyner accusing him of being 'petty and stupid . . . merely spiteful' for quashing the title of Rajah Muda. 'I know Peter is damned difficult,' wrote Bertram, 'but so far as your relations in Sarawak are concerned, it is greatly your fault.' He warned Vyner that Anthony might drag up the Rajah's 'dismal financial record' and that he had some 'very influential friends' – among them Anthony's former tutor at Oxford, Margery Perham, the former colonial secretary Oliver Stanley, and the popular historian Arthur Bryant, who was married to Anthony's sister Anne.

The Colonial Office, meanwhile, was still striving to reach an agreement with the Rajah that would be acceptable to the people of Sarawak. After almost four years of occupation the Rajah's prestige among his subjects remained undiminished, so the Colonial Office was informed by Charles Macaskie, the former chief secretary of Sarawak who was now a brigadier in charge of post-war political planning for the three British territories on Borneo. The Rajah was still regarded with 'almost religious reverence' and the local population were 'perfectly amenable to instructions so long as they are persuaded that these instructions either emanate from the Rajah or at least represent his wishes'. However, Macaskie warned that the Dyaks in particular might be troublesome if they felt that the status of the country was being changed otherwise than in accordance with the wish of the Rajah.

Among the Rajah's wishes was that the Colonial Office should now carry out its negotiations with him via MacBryan, a man the office had long regarded as a scoundrel. During the two years since he had last been dismissed by the Rajah, MacBryan had divided his time between the Berkeley Hotel in London and his asylum in Wiltshire, where he was said to be making '£7,000 a year net' and drinking a bottle of whisky a day. From September he began dealing with the Colonial Office on the Rajah's behalf – he later claimed to have been offered a knighthood by Hall for his role – and officials at the CO had to grin and bear it. After one meeting in January, one of the CO's legal advisers minuted that he 'found [MacBryan's] suave obtuseness (real or feigned) coupled with a tendency to dogmatism very trying to the patience and I should prefer that on any future occasion (if such cannot be avoided) he should be accompanied by a solicitor'.

Besides his helping to reach a financial settlement, the Rajah also wanted MacBryan to go out to Sarawak as his envoy to drum up local support and obtain the approval of the Supreme Council for the cession. The Colonial Office had grave reservations about this, but eventually bowed to the Rajah's insistence that he was the only man who could gain the support of the non-European leaders for the transfer of his country to the British Crown. It was also no secret that MacBryan would be taking £55,000 out to Sarawak, some of which was earmarked for what the Rajah called 'final distributions' to the *datus*. One colonial officer observed: '[This] sheds more light on the form which the consultation with the native authorities is apparently to take.' Hall scribbled alongside the minute that while it did not look very 'pleasant, we are in no position to interfere'.

MacBryan was to be accompanied on his mission by an officer of the Malayan Civil Service, W. C. S. Corry, who was instructed not to let him out of his sight. They arrived in Kuching by flying boat on New Year's Day, and were put up at the Astana, which by that time was being used as the Australian Military Headquarters' Mess. MacBryan immediately set about visiting each of the *datus* privately in order to obtain their signatures to a letter authorising the Rajah to proceed with the cession, and to distribute the Rajah's payments – $12,000 to the senior Malay chief, Datu Patinggi, and $10,000 to each of the others. Many of the *datus*, Patinggi included, had collaborated to some degree with the Japanese and it was strongly suspected that MacBryan also promised them immunity from prosecution if they supported the cession. In addition, MacBryan appears to have deliberately misled them and other people in Sarawak by suggesting that Anthony and Bertram had consented to the Rajah's proposal.

In any event, all five *datus* eventually allowed MacBryan to convene a meeting of the Council Negri, on 5 January, with the aim of legitimising all unconstitutional actions that the Rajah had taken since the invasion of Sarawak, and authorising the setting aside of $1 million from state reserves for the Sarawak State Trust Fund. The Rajah was to have absolute power over the formulation of the trust deed and the selection of trustees, and the stated purpose of the fund was that the Rajah and his ministers should be 'independently maintained' after the cession. The next day the Council Negri repealed the 1941 constitution, after which MacBryan then distributed money from a suitcase, before leaving for Singapore, where he cabled the Rajah to say that the agreements reached were unanimous and 'fulfil in every sense Your Highness's expectations' and expressing the hope that the Rajah and Ranee 'may be moved soon to come to Sarawak where a great welcome will await you'. Corry, who was still supposedly keeping an eye on MacBryan, reported that, as far as he could see, it would now be 'perfectly fair to go ahead with the change of status'. He subsequently remarked that the distribution of sums of money was 'in accordance with the Rajah's normal practice from time to time' and said that no particular political significance should be attached to them.

By the time they returned to London, Anthony's anti-cession campaign was gathering momentum and Sarawak had become a topic of some controversy among the British public. On 6 January the *Observer* newspaper's leading article suggested that there appeared to be 'no logic in the Government's attempt to coerce the people of Sarawak to give up their independence and come under the Colonial Office while it presses on with self-government in Malaya and

Burma'. When it emerged that the meetings of the Supreme Council and Council Negri convened by MacBryan had not been properly constituted, the Colonial Secretary decided that in order to make cession appear legitimate, the Rajah would have to go out to Sarawak himself and put the proposed cession before properly constituted meetings of the two councils.

As a prelude to his visit, on 6 February the Rajah sent a message to his people to say that the King had agreed to his proposal. The initiative, he said, had been his; the transferral of Sarawak to the Crown would fulfil the hopes of the first Rajah Brooke, and his intention was that his people should enjoy 'more direct protection of His Majesty, and those inestimable rights of freedom which His Majesty's citizens enjoy . . . We believe that there lies, in the future, hope for my people in the prospect of an era of awakening, enlightenment, stability and social progress such as they have never had before.' He further declared that in Sarawak

> all authority derives from the Rajah. The people trust the Rajah and what the Rajah advises for the people is the will of the people . . . No other than myself has [the] right to speak on your behalf. No one of you will question whatso'er I do in his high interest. No power nor personal interest shall subvert my people's happiness and future. The happiness of your future lies within another realm. There shall be no Rajah of Sarawak after me. My people will become the subjects of The King. Now draws near the time when I will come to you. Expect me soon. This is for your good my royal command.

When he read the final passage, Bertram observed: 'Its egotistical and flamboyant vulgarity is entirely inconsistent with his [Vyner's] character, which has many aspects – but vulgarity is not one of them.' He assumed that the message had been drafted by the Ranee and MacBryan, though Sylvia acquitted herself in her second autobiography, declaring it to be the work of the Baron 'indulging his lust for power in the only way open to him'.

On the same day the Colonial Secretary made a statement to the House of Commons. Hall's Conservative predecessor, Oliver Stanley, responded by asking whether the Colonial Secretary could be satisfied that there was 'a real desire in Sarawak for this complete cession' given that the Rajah had been absent from his country for some time, and for several years had abandoned any connection 'even with the Provisional Government in this country', and that the Rajah's emissary was one in whom the Colonial Office had 'no confidence whatever'.

Hall assured the House that cession would only be effected after the Rajah had himself visited the country and convened a properly constituted meeting of the Supreme Council. He also said that the Rajah intended handing over Sarawak's accumulated reserve funds amounting to £2,750,000, on the understanding that £1,000,000 would be set aside for a trust fund to provide for the Rajah and his dependants and certain local functionaries during their lifetimes, before eventually reverting to Sarawak. When Anthony Eden asked for assurance that Parliament could 'fully discuss and approve this step after adequate discussion', the Leader of the House, Herbert Morrison, remarked: 'I am bound to say there is something curious about this indignation of the Conservative Party over a little bit being added to the British Empire.'

A headline in the London *Evening Standard* that afternoon interpreted the cession as: 'Britain buys Sarawak'. The next day the *Daily Express* reported that the Ranee had been out celebrating their '£1,000,000 compensation' with a dinner party – with guests including her daughters and MacBryan – at Ciro's Club, while the reclusive Rajah stayed at home. 'I think the Rajah deserves it after all his years in that country,' the Ranee told reporters. 'He has been striving for incorporation in the Empire all his life, just as the first and the second rajahs fought for it all their lives. We believe it is the best thing for the people. We thought that we could give them no better protection than the name of the King.'

Notwithstanding this unequivocal public endorsement of her husband at the time, in her second autobiography, published twenty-four years later, Sylvia wrote that cession was one of the few points of conflict between them; Vyner had 'put too much trust in MacBryan', and the cession amounted to an 'unnecessarily hurried finale to a legend that had been such a splendid thing'. It was 'tragic and heartbreaking to those who had to stand by helplessly and watch it happen', she wrote. For the first time, 'I felt a door had been slammed in my face for which I held no key. I simply could not understand his reasoning; all I could do was bewail to myself the fact that my beloved and admired Rajah had allowed himself to be stampeded by a half-crazed young man, when he should have relied on his own instincts and judgment.' In another passage in her book, she reflected that this was a moment when 'Vyner's isolated and secluded character needed a wife with more authority and confidence than I had. Through all our married life I had given way to him, complied with his wishes, and been at his beck and call. I have always believed that a woman should be subservient to her man, and remember, according to Sarawak custom, I always had to walk four paces behind my Rajah . . .' An element of regretful hindsight almost certainly coloured her memories. For one thing, if she really was so distrustful of MacBryan, what was he doing among her guests at Ciro's?

There was little doubt how Anthony felt, however. In a letter to the *Manchester Guardian* he branded the deal 'crude Imperialism' that would 'defile the pages of British and Sarawak history'. 'Whatever the Rajah and British Government may say, sovereignty resides in the people of Sarawak and the rights of the people are not for sale.' He promised to 'personally oppose the measure by every means in my power'. Bertram, who first heard about the cession from the BBC, opposed it on similar grounds in a letter to *The Times* on 9 February, in which he pointed out that, as heir presumptive, he had never been consulted on the 'proposed sale of Sarawak's independence'. Among those who sympathised with Anthony and Bertram's position was Sylvia's brother Oliver, by then a much-admired chairman of the National Trust's historic buildings committee, and of several other 'heritage' committees besides. 'You ask me what I think of Sarawak,' he wrote to Dorothy. 'Hanky-panky I suspect. Intrigue with the Secretary against the heir. But you know what I think of Sylvia & her ways. It seems however that she has netted a million to spend at night-clubs.'

Of the British newpapers, the *Observer* and the *Sunday Times* came down most vociferously on Anthony and Bertram's side. Others regretted the end of such a romantic kingdom but seemed to feel that weak states had no place in the post-war reconstruction of South East Asia. The *Manchester Guardian* took the pragmatic line that while the cession was 'a queer business', to reverse it would only create more instability.

In Sarawak, the *Sarawak Tribune* had casually mentioned MacBryan's visit in January but gave no hint of the Rajah's proposal for cession until 8 February, when it printed his message to his subjects. However, the recently formed Malay National Union had already put up posters telling their people to 'Wake up! Be conscious! . . . Be it known that our native land has been sold secretly . . . now we must stand up as the people of Sarawak.' Following the Rajah's message, they convened an anti-cession meeting, in response to which the Rajah published further messages in the *Sarawak Tribune*, telling his people that he would pay annual visits to Sarawak to help them through the period of transition, reassuring them that he would consult the two councils and had 'only the interests of the people at heart'. The Malay National Union shot back that if the Rajah considered himself too old or ailing he should hand over the government to the Tuan Muda or his son.

There was a more favourable response from the Chinese. The majority of whom seemed to think that cession would mean faster economic and commercial development and more opportunities for the working classes and natives. It was assumed, furthermore, that Sarawak would form part of the Malayan Union, and that the Chinese would enjoy equal rights of citizenship and be able to take part in politics.

Many of the up-country Dyaks, meanwhile, remained oblivious of the proposed change. The police inspector Edward Brandah, himself a Sea Dyak, or Iban, predicted that it would take some of them years to realise that there was no longer a Rajah. 'The Ibans will lose a great and kind protector,' he wrote. 'Our fears are like that of a small boy who is sent to boarding school.' But he added: 'We may forget the Rajah only in words but not in heart and mind, for what he has done, it was done for our future happiness and prosperity which lies in another realm under the protection of His Majesty the King.' At a subsequent meeting of the newly formed Sarawak Dyak Association, it was decided the Rajah should be allowed to explain the situation before they made up their minds.

Back in Britain, Hall was given an awkward time by Opposition MPs in the Commons on 13 February when he revealed that the meetings of the two councils that MacBryan had arranged were regarded only as exploratory discussions. The next day, in a letter to *The Times*, Margery Perham questioned whether the dynasty 'under some improved method of British surveillance' and 'increasingly constitutional in function', might for the time being 'prove the best focus for the unity of a racially mixed people and the best expression of its sense of historical identity'. But Margaret Noble, who was also lobbying on behalf of the anti-cessionists, found that the image of the Brooke family, particularly the Ranee and her daughters, did not exactly help their cause, and that there seemed to be little interest in the remote kingdom beyond such subjects as headhunting and 'those peculiar girls and their extraordinary marriages'.

The Colonial Office, meanwhile, continued to take its own soundings, and in February it received a letter from the former governor of Singapore, Sir Shenton Thomas, who had spent the war as a prisoner of the Japanese before being liberated in Manchuria by American forces in August 1945. Thomas said that while the Rajah's policy of keeping his people 'out of the world' had had its attractions, it had become very clear later that this deprived people of advantages which were, or ought to have been, available under the British flag. Expenditure on social services undoubtedly lagged far behind that of other countries. If Bertram were fit to take over, Thomas would have expected 'very considerable improvements', but he was not, and Anthony Brooke, the likely successor, had 'failed miserably' when left in charge of the state in 1939 and done

> all kinds of tactless and unnecessary things, which aggravated the Service and annoyed the Rajah who censured him severely. Since then he has become more and more obstinate and arrogant. When the Rajah authorised the new constitution in 1941, Anthony Brooke left his post in direct contravention of orders and came to Singapore to protest to me. I told him he had no sense of discipline and that by acting in such a way he was presuming on his Brooke connection. I told him also that I was entirely in favour of the Rajah's action. I can see no hope for Sarawak under the Brookes and I am certain that HMG has done the right thing in accepting the Rajah's offer.

There was also an interview with Noel Hudson, who as bishop in Kuching during the 1930s had formed a dim view of Sarawak's 'incompetent and corrupt' government. Immorality and drunkenness were rife among the civil service, he said, and encouraged rather than discouraged by the Rajah. The Rajah himself, for whom, in spite of his faults, Hudson still had a sneaking liking, was subject to sudden caprice and held the fate of his civil service in his hands. At any moment, on idle gossip, individuals might be dismissed, administrative decisions set aside and even judicial decisions reversed. The Ranee was far worse than the Rajah, Hudson thought. Bertram Brooke was the best of the family, whereas his son, Anthony, was a man with ideals but without the capacity or the balance to succeed as rajah under the present constitution. Hudson had long ago reached the conclusion that the Rajah's personal administration must end, but at the same time he was not happy that Sarawak should become an ordinary Crown Colony. Whatever might be said about the Rajah, he was still regarded as the father of his people. They liked his paternalism. They knew that he was quite prepared on appeal to reverse the decisions of the administration. He therefore favoured a British representative whose advice the Rajah would be bound to take. If the proposal for cession were pursued, however, Hudson was emphatic that the idea of obtaining the views of the two councils was 'ridiculous' as the members of the councils were the Rajah's yes-men and could be relied on to endorse whatever the Rajah proposed. In no sense could they be considered representative of the people of Sarawak.

In order to defuse the critics and garner international respectability, Hall decided he needed to show by another means that the Rajah's proposal was broadly acceptable to the native communities, and on 27 March he announced that he was despatching a parliamentary mission to Sarawak to gauge local opinion. Two MPs were allotted the task, D. R. Rees-Williams, the Labour MP for South Croydon, who had been a lawyer in Penang before the war, and David Gammans, the Conservative MP for Hornsey, who had worked in co-operatives in Malaya and had since become the Opposition spokesman for Far Eastern affairs. Their trip to Sarawak was timed to coincide with that of the Rajah and Ranee, and to enable them to cable their findings to the Secretary of State ahead of the decisive meetings of the Supreme Council and Council Negri in May.

The wedding of Leonora, 'Princess Gold', and Kenneth Inchcape in July 1933, reported here in the unlikely setting of the *Ironwood Daily Globe*, Michigan

GLOBE, IRONWOOD, MICH. NINE

Read the Classified Advertisements

English Earl Marries Daughter Of Rajah, Who Lived in Jungles

The happiness of all June weddings . . . reflected in the marriage of Leonora Brooke, left, daughter of the white rajah of Sarawak, and the war-veteran Earl of Inchcape . . . while her father ruled his Dyaks in primitive Borneo.

Ceremony Unites Two Families With Movie-like Careers.

This is the last of six stories on the most romantic June marriages of 1933.

BY MILTON BRONNER

London, June 24—When "Princess Gold Pretties" knelt beside the Earl of Inchcape at the altar of historic St. George's church in Hanover Square, Dyak head-hunters on the other side of the world threaded their way through the jungle paths of Borneo all unknowing.

But it was the daughter of their sovereign (they knew her as "Princess Gold Pretties") who was being married in London, the daughter of Sir Charles Vyner Brooke, the white Rajah of Sarawak.

And though the daughter of the third Rajah of Sarawak, "Lord and Taker of Life," was marrying the second Earl of Inchcape, World War soldier and shipping magnate, the wedding ceremony was one of the quietest and simplest of 1933's June ceremonies. There weren't even any bridesmaids. Yet for all the simplicity of the ceremony, here was the uniting of two families each with so bizarre a career that if you saw it in the movies you would sneer that it was impossible.

Real Adventure

Back in 1840, the grandfather of the bride was a young man, just discharged from the Indian army, and unwilling to settle down to a quiet life in England. The East had gotten into James Brooke's blood. So he took all the money he could scrape together and chartered a ship. He filled it with equally adventurous friends and plenty of arms. Then he sailed for Borneo, seeking adventure. He found it.

The Sultan of Brunei, to whom Sarawak belonged, was in the midst of an unsuccessful struggle with pirates who were terrorizing his entire domain. Brooke and his friends offered their services as soldiers of fortune. They cleared out the pirates, and as a reward the grateful sultan made Brooke a rajah, with Sarawak as the domain over which he was to have absolute rule.

James Brooke became the white rajah, and third in line from him, the father of the present bride, now rules Sarawak.

Cannibalism Still Found

Once Sarawak's capital Kuching, was seized by Chinese pirates and only recaptured after a bloody battle. But the constant battle of the white rajahs has been against the ignorance and barbarism of their own 500,000 subjects spread through a jungled area the size of Kentucky. Tigers are as common as alley-cats, and the head-hunting Dyaks and other Malay subjects like nothing better after a victorious war than a little filet of speared enemy, rare.

Brooke, was knighted, his nephew succeeded him, and then his son, the present rajah, returning from Cambridge, led expeditions against the head-hunters. He married the Hon. Sylvia Brett, daughter of Lord Esther, who became thus Ranee of

Lake Streeters Win Two Games

The Ironwood Sokols baseball team met defeat yesterday when it played host to the strong Lake street team. A doubleheader was played and at the end of each game the score of 10 to 9 in favor of Lake street.

Both teams played good ball, but the Sokols had a few costly errors and they showed themselves in need of batting practice. The games were nip and tuck affairs and a point or two would have swung victory the other way.

Fans who attended were well satisfied and declared the return games between the teams should be

News Oddities

By the Associated Press

Port of Spain, Trinidad, June 24 Threatened with death by the Hindu Goddess Kali, Seepersad Nailpaul, native writer, yesterday offered a goat as sacrifice to appease the hunger of the goddess.

Naipaul wrote newspaper articles revealing that native farmers of Hindu origin had defied government regulations for combatting cattle diseases and were substituting ancient rites of the Goddess Kali to drive away illness attacking their livestock.

CASHIER HELD FOR SHORTAGE IN BANK

Young Banker Charged With Misappropriating $37,000 in Funds.

Manitowoc, June 24—(AP)—A warrant for the arrest of Charles O. Drumm, 35, charging that as cashier of the State bank of Manitowoc he misappropriated $37,000, was issued yesterday.

Last night the young banker, a leader in Manitowoc's commercial life, was in custody of his father in law, Sheriff Herman Schuette. Officials did not indicate whether the warrant had been served. It had been issued earlier in the day by Municipal Judge O. T. Bredesen.

Disclosure of the shortage caused a sensation throughout the city.

The State bank of Manitowoc issued the following statement:

"Charles O. Drumm, a former employe, has been found short in his records to the amount of $37,000 and has been dismissed from the organization. The amount of the shortage is covered by bond and will be recovered from the bonding company."

and with her first baby, Simon Brooke Mackay, Sylvia's choice as Crown Prince.

Elizabeth, 'Princess Pearl', with her bandleader husband, 'King of the Hot-Cha' Harry Roy, in a scene from the musical film *Rhythm Racketeer* (1937).

Gladys Brooke, the Dayang Muda, at Croydon Airport in 1932, boarding the Imperial Airlines flight to Paris during which she was to convert to Islam; journalists were invited along to witness the event.

Sylvia looking pleased with herself after becoming the first woman in Sarawak to fly, in 1933.

With her friends 'Blue' Gifford, in Monte Carlo (left), and the Nawab of Pataudi, whom she also clearly admired.

Vyner with his nephew Anthony Brooke, who took a dim view of the colourful antics of the Ranee and her daughters.

Gerard MacBryan, the Rajah's private secretary, after his supposed pilgrimage to Mecca in 1936. His wife Sa'erah was Sylvia's lady-in-waiting and later chief procuress of 'comfort women' for the occupying Japanese.

The Sylvia Cinema in Kuching, opened in 1934: perhaps the ultimate tribute.

Valerie, 'Princess Baba', with her all-in wrestler husband Bob Gregory in 1940; and modelling 'Baba's Beachwear' in California, 1939.

The tribulations of Rajah Vyner, as interpreted by the *Port Arthur News* in Texas.

Headline "Headaches" of a Headman—in Borneo

The Rajah of Sarawak Can't Keep His Royal Daughters from Marrying Band Leaders and Wrestlers, and Even His Wife Has 'Gone Hollywood'

THE WHITE RAJAH OF SARAWAK
Sir Charles Vyner Brooke Has a Large Part of the Island of Borneo (Indicated Above) in His Palm, So to Speak, But He Can't Keep His Own Daughters in Hand.

PRINCESS PEARL
Otherwise, Elizabeth Brooke, (Right) Upset Her Father, the White Rajah, by Marrying Harry Roy, London "Swing" Band Leader.

THE RANEE OF SARAWAK
She Spends Little Time in Kuching, the Capital Where She Is Queen, for She Is Busy in the Occident Most of the Time, Keeping an Eye on Her Daughters.

PRETTY BABA
(Left) Valerie Brooke Lost All Her Liking for the Title of Princess After She Saw Bob Gregory (Below) Wrestle.

By Cedric Stuart

THE "wildmen of Borneo," famed in song and story and the bogeyman of childhood for ages past, are addicted to cannibalism, head hunting and kindred uncivilized and indelicate pursuits.

But their marriage code is the strictest in all the world, with sharply-divided caste lines and innumerable tabus to make thorny the path of dark belles and warriors who fall in love.

No such inhibitions, however, restrain the family of the suave, cultured Englishman who rules over half a million of them living in the northwestern third of the East Indian island shared by the separate states of Sarawak, Dutch Borneo and British North Borneo. He has three charming daughters, this white rajah of the savage tribes, and here is how their marital affairs stand:

One is married to a jazz band leader.

One braved parental wrath for the love of a divorced wrestler.

The third married a belted earl, but the fact he had been divorced two years previously puts even this union in a class apart from the rigorous restrictions on wedlock as obeyed by the "wild men of Borneo."

In Oriental countries the father is the undisputed head of the house, and his slightest wish is supposed to be law to his women folk. The sensational romances of his daughters have naturally been embarrassing to the ruler of a people to whom "loss of face" is a dreadful occurrence.

The most picturesque ruling family in all the world is that of Sir Charles Anthony Johnson Vyner Brooke, the white rajah of Sarawak, which is about the size of Kentucky, whose youngest daughter, Valerie Brooke, 21, otherwise known as "Princess Baba," recently announced her intention to marry Robert Gregory, 25-year-old and handsome middleweight catch-as-catch-can wrestling champion of Europe.

From his up-to-date, air-conditioned palace in wild and woolly and faraway Sarawak, Rajah Brooke voiced loud and violent opposition. He threatened to disown "Princess Baba" if she became plain Mrs. Gregory, but Valerie, knowing her father's anger comes and goes with the suddenness of the tropical storms among which he lives, thought nothing of it.

She and the rest of the world recalled that Papa Brooke stormed in equally violent fashion when her sister, Elizabeth, picturesquely called "Princess Pearl," married Harry Roy, the leader of a London's "swing" band a few years ago.

The daughter who married an Earl and thus met with almost all of the Borneo stipulations as to the fitness of bride and groom was the eldest of the three, Leonora.

She, too, had a royal title and was "Princess Gold" to her family and intimates before she became the wife of the Earl of Inchcape.

When the cables from Sarawak brought to London's West End the full force of Rajah Brooke's opposition to the latest marriage, "Princess Baba," like the little Audrey of other renown, just laughed and laughed and laughed.

"Papa just doesn't like publicity," she said. "I know that's the whole trouble."

"Papa" had his full share of distasteful publicity when Elizabeth married Harry Roy. For Roy marched his whole band, saxophones, clarinets, trumpets, bass drum and all, to the Claxton Registry Office to greet him and his bride with a rollicking dance tune when the marriage bond had been sealed.

The Rajah apparently is the only member of his family, incidentally, who does abhor publicity. His wife, the attractive Ranee of Sarawak, went to Hollywood not long ago to work as technical adviser on a photoplay about Sarawak and do some radio broadcasting. Before the Gregory episode, Valerie got a lot of publicity with reports she planned to marry Kenneth Duncan, an English film actor whose fans like to regard him as Britain's "Clark Gable."

When this report was published, the Ranee lost no time in denying it, and inferentially indicated a daughter of a multi-millionaire Rajah would never marry an actor. Wrestlers were not in the picture at that moment.

The Rajah of Sarawak has to live alone in his castle in his modern capital at Kuching, except for his servants and retainers, for neither the Ranee nor any of his daughters cares much for Borneo's wild men or its tropical climate.

Sir Charles takes his job very, very seriously and regrets he has no son to succeed him, though he is ready to hand the sceptre over to his younger brother and heir apparent, Bertram W. Brooke, His Highness the Tuan Muda, whose present wife is Gladys Palmer, biscuit fortune heiress. She has been a Quaker, Protestant, Catholic and Mohammedan in faith all within a few years.

The Tuan Muda has a family of his own, and his eldest son, A. W. D. Brooke, will inherit the title, which descends only to males. Lady Inchcape has a son, who is next in line, so there is little real possibility that the offspring of a band leader or a wrestler may ever become the Rajah of Sarawak. However, anything can happen, as is shown by the story of how 63-year-old Sir Charles Vyner Brooke came to be the ruler of 500,000 wild men of Borneo.

Back in the 1860's an English adventurer named James Brooke fitted out a schooner and sailed 'down' into the East Indies as a trader in Borneo. He found the Sultan of Sarawak unable to cope with a revolution of some tribes. He helped the Sultan subdue them, and as a reward was made the Sultan's successor—the first white man in all history to become an Oriental potentate. When James died, he willed the Rajahship to his nephew, Charles Brooke, who ruled until 1917 under British government's protection. Then came Sir Charles Vyner Brooke, the present title-holder.

Sarawak is a lush tropical country some 40,000 square miles in extent, which exports much rubber, oil, coal, sago, pepper, rattans. Its daily round of life passes almost unnoticed by the world at large, with Sir Charles now safe and secure in his leadership, although a few years ago it was threatened by a pretender.

This happened when E. Brooke Daykin, a businessman of Toronto, advanced claims on behalf of his daughter, Grace, said to have been a descendant of Tia, the first wife of the present Rajah's father.

Tia was the daughter of a chief and member of a former ruling house. Daykin produced records to show she married the second Rajah under the laws of her country, making her his consort. As a result, Daykin claimed, Grace is entitled to the throne and he went further to say that many natives of Sarawak had seen her pictures in the newspapers, liked her, and wanted her for their queen.

The white rajah consulted lawyers and then announced briefly and to the point that the claim was out of order and unjustified. There the matter had to rest, for the rajah had the British government back of him.

It is no concern of the British government that the rajah's daughters have a predilection for orchestra leaders or wrestlers.

"I have been madly in love with Valerie since the night I met her months ago," Bob Gregory, the wrestler, said.

"At that time I was friendly with her mother, the Ranee.

"But since Valerie and I became sweethearts I am afraid that friendship has cooled off. Many barriers have been put in our way."

Their most enthusiastic supporter, naturally, was the Princess Pearl, for she never quite got over the criticism that followed her own marriage to a band leader.

There is a precedent among the older members of the Brooke family for theatrical marriages. The present Ranee, the former Sylvia Brett, is a daughter of the late Viscount Esher and a sister-in-law of the present Viscountess. The latter before her marriage was Zena Dare, an English actress worshipped by a generation of London theatergoers. She was one of the most popular musical comedy stars of the pre-war decade.

Lady Inchcape, Nee Leonora Brooke, Was the First to Present the White Rajah with a Grandson.

"WILD WOMEN OF BORNEO"
These Subjects of the White Rajah, Who Are Shown Holding Heads Collected by Their Husbands, Are Not Typical Now. The Rajah Is Rapidly Civilizing His Domain.

White Rajah Denies Unrest in Jungle Kingdom

STORIES of unrest, culminating in the retirement of four high officials, in Sarawak, romantic jungle land ruled by the "White Rajah," were officially denied last night.

It was reported by the B.U.P. from Singapore earlier in the day that the Chief Justice, the Chief Secretary, the Financial Secretary and the Chief of the Survey Department had resigned as a protest against the introduction of reforms by the Rajah's nephew while Sir Charles Vyner Brooke was home on leave.

The news agency stated that an official of the Federated Malay States Civil Service was leaving to investigate, while Sir Charles would return to Sarawak immediately.

THE RANEE.

• • The Rajah, an Englishman, rules over a country of 30,000 square miles with a population of about half a million Dyaks and Malays

Rajah's Statement

In a statement to the *Birmingham Gazette* last night the Sarawak Government Agency in London stated:

"The Rajah wishes it to be known that so far from there being any unrest in the service at the present time the service is now more peaceful than it has been for years past.

"The officials resigned because the[y] disagreed with a policy which th[e] Rajah wished to pursue, and [he] allowed them to retire on pensio[n] Their positions have been filled [by] promotions from the Service, and [a] barrister who has had previo[us] experience in the East is short[ly] leaving England to become Judici[al] Commissioner.

"There is no truth whatever in the report that any inquiry by the Colonial Office has been suggested This rumour may have arisen from the fact that the Rajah has for some time past been contemplating the appointment of a retired Colonial administrative officer to his staff."

The Ranee of Sarawak told th[e] *Birmingham Gazette*: "It is n[ot] frightfully important. The officia[ls] have received handsome pensions."

No unrest said the headlines, but shortly afterwards Vyner surrendered his absolute powers on the eve of the Centenary celebrations in 1941 (right); the Centenary was marked by the issue of a new set of stamps, which did not arrive till 1946 due to the war.

The Japanese forces Sarawak surrendere on 11 September 1945 and in April 1946 Rajah Vyner received the Sword State from the Datu Pattinggi, with Rane Sylvia looking on.

The last picture of the Rajah and Ranee with their most senior aides.

Vyner signing the document ceding Sarawak to Britain, at the Astana in May 1946. Next to him is the British representative, C.W. Dawson. Standing behind them in uniform is the acting chief secretary, J. B. Archer, for whom the controversy surrounding the cession proved too much; he shot himself shortly afterwards.

bove Anthony with his mother Gladys in 1947 at 'Sarawak Lodge', Singapore, from where hey orchestrated the anti-cession campaign; and (below left) with his second wife Gita in weden, in a later incarnation as a self-styled 'travelling salesman' for world peace.

ylvia also spent much of the rest of her life living out of suitcases, flitting between London, merica and Barbados, where she remained an inveterate party-giver to the end.

Rajah Vyner, aged 80, in his London lair, surrounded by his pin-ups.

The Ranee with her walker Frank de Buono.

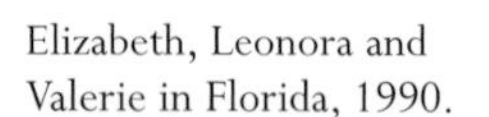

Elizabeth, Leonora and Valerie in Florida, 1990.

15

RACY RANEE

Before the Rajah and Ranee were due to leave England for Sarawak, in April 1946, Sylvia recalled having made 'one last desperate effort to delay the cession . . . to break Salic Law, and place Leonora on the throne; but Vyner would have none of it; and indeed, by then, he was already too deeply committed to draw back'. Her version of events may well be distorted by her muddled memory in old age and innately cavalier approach to facts, but there is some corroboration for what she suggests. However committed Vyner was to abdicating, he was perfectly capable of changing his mind at the last minute, and it was presumably at his instigation – quite possibly having been persuaded by his wife – that before cession was finalised the Sarawak government agent J. A. Smith went to visit Leonora's son Simon Mackay at his prep school in Oxford. Simon, later Lord Tanlaw, an independent peer on the cross benches, had long been the Ranee's preferred choice of heir to the Raj. He recalls that the purpose of Smith's visit was to explore the option of putting in a regent until he attained majority; but it was eventually decided that he was too young. That a regency was still being contemplated in the Rajah's circle at this final hour may explain why around this time MacBryan revived his ambition to marry into the Brooke family, setting his cap now at Leonora. Since having returned to England three years previously, MacBryan had been openly cohabiting with his private secretary, who was tersely portrayed in a note by Bertram at the time as a 'buxom blonde'. However, some time during the period leading up to the cession, according to Leonora, at one of her father's Sarawak get-togethers, MacBryan 'got me into another room and after kissing me with such vehemence he almost dislocated my neck, he told me he had always loved me to distraction'. By Bertram's account again, one evening in MacBryan's room at the Berkeley, his mistress was heard to scream at him after discovering that he wanted to get rid of her and marry Leonora. There was also a 'stormy scene' at the Rajah's flat in Albion Gate on 25 February, during which the Rajah 'abused' the Ranee and said that he was going to refuse to go out to Sarawak and was 'fed up with the whole thing'. The row, noted Bertram, 'seemed to have something to do with Leonora and marriage', and the apparent upshot was a notice in the newspapers two days later announcing that Leonora's forthcoming marriage to 'Tommy' Tompkins, who had recently obtained a divorce in America, had been postponed. Thereafter MacBryan continued his campaign by sending Leonora 'the most wonderful love letters I have ever had'. 'Annoyingly,' wrote Leonora, 'my father was all for a marriage with him. "Dear Old Baron" sort of thing. But he was not for me.' So it was that she soon married Tompkins after all, presumably to the disappointment of not only MacBryan but also Vyner and Sylvia, whose initial enthusiasm about Tommy had quickly worn off; she told Doll, in 1944, that he was a 'dull little American colonel'.

While all this was going on, Vyner was growing anxious about reports of unrest in Sarawak over the proposed cession, and he wanted reassurance that if he and Sylvia did go out there they would not be 'spat at'. Two European Sarawak officers were duly despatched to carry out a quick countrywide survey of opinion. They reported back that two-thirds of Sarawakians were in favour of obeying the Rajah's wishes, although there were fears in the Fifth Division that it would mean a return to rule by Brunei, and one of the officers carrying out the survey privately admitted that cession was 'understood by no one', himself included.

The Colonial Office, though, was adamant not only that cession should be understood but that the procedure for effecting it should leave 'no room for doubts and possible criticisms'. One consequence of this was the decision to drop the proposed £1 million trust fund, which would not only have depleted Sarawak's reserves but also, under MacBryan's control, risked becoming an embarrassment to the British government. Instead, there was an agreement that £30,000 would be paid annually from Sarawak state revenues to trustees, who would then pay the pensions to the Rajah and his dependants that were to have been paid from the trust fund. This compromise seems to have been reached after discussions between the Colonial Office, MacBryan and the Sarawak government agent J. A. Smith, and without the knowledge of the financially naive Rajah, who continued to believe that the original trust arrangement still stood.

Meanwhile, the fact that Bertram and Anthony had not been consulted about the cession was swept under the carpet. Vyner initially also refused his brother permission to go out to Sarawak, but eventually relented provided that he agreed to accept the decision of the two councils on cession. When, shortly afterwards, Bertram learned about MacBryan's 'distributions', he sent a cable to Sarawak asking the *datus* what they were for. The *datus* replied that they were compensation for 'the tribulations we suffered under the Japanese occupation', and that far from being compelled to sign anything, they had consented to the Rajah's proposal in pursuit of 'greater prosperity, freedom and happiness for the country and the people'. By another cable on 12 April a sceptical Bertram warned the *datus* that they had an 'immense moral responsibility' to vote in accordance with the real wishes of their people, and not to commit themselves until they had met him face to face.

By that time Vyner and Sylvia were already on their way out to Sarawak, having left Poole aerodrome on 7 April. MacBryan was to have accompanied them, but instead, as Sylvia recorded, he had 'simply vanished, leaving Vyner to face the music alone'. Possibly, the Baron anticipated a difficult time in Sarawak, or it may have had something to do with Leonora. According to Vyner, his absence was due to 'a difference of political opinion regarding the visit of my brother, the Tuan Muda', but Bertram himself suspected that there was 'some camouflage' about his non-appearance, and that he was bound to join them later on. Those who did travel with the royal party included the new British representative, Christopher Dawson, who was charged with carrying out last-minute negotiations with the Rajah and would later become the first chief secretary of the new colonial government; William Dale, a hastily appointed legal adviser from the Colonial Office whose job was to ensure that everything about the cession was in order legally; and a handful of Sarawak officers who the Rajah felt could be relied on to support cession – others who did not were asked not to return to their posts until after the vote.

There were ten of them in all, including the Rajah and Ranee, and between them they brought 1,400 lbs of personal baggage along with 1,600 lbs of freight, including such items as bed linen and, as Dawson noted in his diary, 'a good deal of gin & whisky . . . Evidently the Rajah does not intend to be caught short when he resumes his administration.' After overnight stops at Biscarosse, in France, Cairo, Bahrein, Karachi, Calcutta and Rangoon, Vyner and Sylvia met Mountbatten in Singapore to discuss the wording of a proclamation handing the government of Sarawak back to the Rajah. On Sunday, 14 April they completed the final leg by flying boat, landing at the mouth of the Sarawak river and transferring to the royal yacht *Maimuna*. As in the old days, Sylvia stood out on deck waving her silk scarf to the crowds on the river banks all the way upriver to Kuching.

'Never before had we received such a tremendous welcome,' she wrote later:

> hundreds of little boats lined the river banks, and behind the boats the crowds were so dense they looked like a forest of dazzling flowers with their golden sarongs and little coloured coats. No one shouted abuse at us or raised a dissenting voice; they only waved their handkerchiefs and tiny flags. When we reached the steps of the Astana we thought we would never be able to break through the multitude pressing towards us. The people went mad as they hugged and patted my husband; some of them had tears streaming down their cheeks.

As they went ashore, a twenty-one-gun salute sounded from Fort Margherita, and as they moved among the people, Sylvia walking in her customary place four paces behind her husband's royal umbrella, Malay women surged through the guard to prod Vyner with their fingers, teasing him that 'the Rajah has got fat'. 'They giggled and tittered and touched him and their little bracelets jingled in his ears,' Sylvia recorded; 'they pounded me, too, asking me why I wasn't with child. I didn't remind them that I was now sixty-two.' Later on, as they looked down from their upstairs verandah at the Astana, the crowd sang 'Salamat rumah Tuan Rajah' ('Blessings on your house, Rajah') and 'Salamat Tuan Ranee'. Sylvia said she 'would have felt further from tears if some of them had denounced us and called down curses on our heads instead of invoking this gracious and merciful benediction, this unanimous affection. I wondered if it was crossing Vyner's mind not to go through with it.'

The next morning – Monday – the Rajah went across the river to the chamber of the Supreme Council, where the proclamation for the withdrawal of the military government was read out by Brigadier Gibbons, the officer commanding the 32nd Borneo Brigade. The Rajah then read another resuming his government, after which Datu Patinggi presented him with the Sword of State. In the evening they took a drive around Kuching, with crowds lining the route and showering the royal car with yellow rice, schoolchildren singing and waving flags. The only signs of discord were some anti-cession placards in the Malay kampong, an unprecedented display of dissent that reportedly so astonished Ranee Sylvia that she stopped the car, leapt out and exclaimed to the protesters: 'What! No cession?'

The Datu Patinggi also gave the Rajah a letter from the Malay National Union suggesting that the Rajah should hand over to his brother or nephew if he felt unable to carry on; but, overall, Dawson noted that there 'was not the slightest sign of anything but gaiety' and he wondered whether the dissenting placards signified anything more than 'an effort by a vocal handful'. Both he and the Rajah were only too well aware, though, that MacBryan's visit in January smacked of 'dirty work', an impression the Rajah attempted to dispel in a statement to the press the next day. The payments to *datus*, he said, represented the annual allowances due to them since the outbreak of the Japanese war. 'We have not had any opportunity of explaining the true position to the chieftains, who are under a misapprehension if they think the money was a bribe.' The main accuser was the venerable Datu Patinggi, who had informed the British military authorities and handed the money over to them pending an investigation – but they appear to have turned a blind eye. It was whispered among European officers that Datu Patinggi had been influenced by the posters. He was old and frail, they said, and nervous of his personal safety. During the occupation, he had 'played a part in a half-hearted way' with the Japanese, and was rumoured to have asked them to make him rajah and for a monopoly on the right to collect turtle eggs, a subject long close to his heart.

On Tuesday various Dyak chiefs came to the Astana to tell the Rajah of their wartime experiences. The visitors included Sylvia's old favourite Temenggong Koh, who, at the age of seventy-six, was looking younger than he had before the war, so the Rajah told Dawson, and appeared 'refreshed' by the renewed headhunting engendered by the occupation. In Sarawak as a whole it was estimated that fifteen hundred Japanese had been liberated from their heads, which were particularly prized by the Dyaks for being 'nice round heads with good hair and gold teeth'. 'Most of it was mere murder,' recorded Dawson, 'but there were some stories of real attacks by Dayaks on Japanese troops, machine gun posts captured etc.' He added that the Sarawak officers seemed to be of the view that 'this three and a half years of glorious hunting' would not make the Dyaks out of hand, but rather the fact that they had replenished their head supply would 'tend to keep them quiet'.

Over the next few days Vyner rarely left the confines of the Astana, but Sylvia went out and about to observe some of the effects the occupation had had on Sarawak and its people. 'It was as if they had been subjected to some subtle corruption,' she recorded.

> They no longer greeted us with the graceful Malay salute, their fingers touching their foreheads and their hearts, but gave that stiff, typically Japanese bow of their heads. And this was only an outward sign of more fundamental changes. It was apparent that they had not been so much in awe of the Japanese as interested and impressed, for only those who had been maltreated and half-starved seemed to bear any resentment. Yet there had been some ghastly cases of brutality. One of our most promising young Government officers, an exceptionally brilliant boy, had

> been taken from the prison camp, day after day, for questioning, and tortured with such unimaginable cruelty that he had locked himself in the lavatory one morning, broken a glass water bottle, and cut his throat.

Sylvia discerned 'two ill-fitting sides of the Japanese character'. On the one hand they had brought toys to the convent schools at Christmas, and trees with coloured candles, yet at the other extreme

> they had destroyed Vyner's library, with most of his valuable diaries and books; and they had found some love letters from some of his girls and crudely framed them round the walls. An urge to destruction, and a kind of sentimental creativity, seemed to go together. There were shattered houses, devastated rubber plantations, and ploughed and broken padi fields; and yet there were signs of quality and culture in the roads they had made, and the delicate little gardens. Wherever they went they had left these monuments – these miniature gardens, and these softly-surfaced roads.

They visited the concentration camp where many of the European officers had been interned, a 'gloomy ramshackle building with wire fencing round it and etched deep with all the signs of misery and despair: crooked initials carved on the wooden walls, days and months and years marked off; torn pin-up girls, a grass bracelet, a broken wrist-strap . . .' Many of the European officers had been routinely tortured or had died of disease and malnutrition. A number had been murdered, including the former chief secretary Cyril Le Gros Clark, who had shown exceptional bravery while acting as the prisoners' leader and spokesman; during the Allied bombing raids in July 1945, he had been taken to a gaol in North Borneo and executed, along with four other prisoners. Nothing on the scale of the Sandakan Death March – from which just six out of more than two thousand Allied prisoners survived – happened in Sarawak, but the death toll was still appallingly high in places owing to malnutrition and disease.

During these first few days accompanying the Rajah and Ranee around Kuching, Dawson was struck by the demonstrations of loyalty, 'yet,' he noted in his diary, 'they do not seem to be interested in much beyond their own possessions and comfort. There must be something more, or perhaps *was*, in the past, to account for their great popularity.' However, he thought that Sarawak was a notably 'happy and individual country and the CO [Colonial Office] must be made to understand that this atmosphere will be spoilt if a cold, hard colonial system is substituted for the present somewhat happy go lucky but personal rule from the District Officer upwards . . . how it is to be hoped that they will not be bound in a straitwaistcoat of unnecessary legislation and red tape'.

On Monday, 22 April, when they had been there a week, Lord Mountbatten came to visit, accompanied by his twenty-two-year-old daughter Patricia. According to Sylvia, the thought of having Mountbatten beneath his roof 'put Vyner in such a panic that he was literally chewing his handkerchief with nerves. Yet no one could have been more charming or done more to put Vyner at his ease.' The Mountbattens landed first on the town side of the river, where the 'Supremo' inspected guards of honour provided by the Punjabis and Sarawak Constabulary, whose band played instruments recently recovered from their hiding places during the occupation. They were then paddled over to the Astana, where they were met by the Rajah and Ranee, and where Patricia Mounbatten admired a large, flamboyant wooden bird which stood in the main drawing room; Mountbatten recorded in his diary that the Rajah 'with true Oriental munificence, promptly gave it to her; rather to her embarrassment!' Over lunch Vyner and Sylvia told Mountbatten of the troubles they had had with their nephew. Mountbatten sympathised, having known Anthony from his stint on his intelligence staff in Ceylon. Anthony had 'appeared to all of us to be somewhat unbalanced', wrote Mountbatten in his diary, and in the circumstances cession seemed 'the only reasonable solution'. 'There is one thing there is no doubt about,' he added, 'and that is [the people of Sarawak's] genuine affection for . . . the present Raja; and if he were 41 instead of 71, or if his brother were young enough, I am sure they would never agree to cession.'

Heavy rain during lunch put paid to the afternoon's programme of sightseeing, but eventually, at tea time, they visited the museum. After dinner they were paddled in two barges to Fort Margherita to watch a tattoo; Dawson, who had joined the party, noted that it was 'pretty long' and seemed to bore Mountbatten, though Mountbatten himself professed to have enjoyed the Dyak dancing by 'genuine headhunters from the hills' and his encounter with 'one old boy' who pointed to a wristwatch that he was 'incongruously' wearing. Dawson told Mountbatten that it had been appropriated from the Japanese District Commissioner, the Dyak having first dined with him and then cut his head off.

Before leaving the next morning, Mountbatten drew Sylvia aside and told her that not until many years after the death of her husband 'and the true history of Sarawak is written, will the world know what a great gesture this truly great man has made'. When she told Vyner this, she recalled, he looked up from his book, grinned, and said: 'Intelligent fellow.'

Over the next few days, with the help of Dale, Vyner set about untangling the constitutional mess created by MacBryan in January. Members of the Supreme Council who had died or been murdered by the Japanese also needed to be replaced. When he had filled the vacancies, the Rajah called a meeting of the council on 24 April, at which he assured his people that the British government would bring greater progress and stability, that the *adat lama* (established custom) and principles of the 1941 constitution would continue to be observed, and that he, the Rajah, was not abandoning Sarawak, and would continue to make his visits to outstations. He took the opportunity once again to dismiss the notion of Anthony as a future ruler: 'I have given him three chances to prove his worth, and he has failed. My heir must be the King.'

At the end of the week Vyner and Sylvia travelled by plane to Sibu, again accompanied by Dawson, who recorded that they flew over a series of 'little steep hills, cleared of most of the jungle, planted under this wasteful method of crop and move on, the only way the Dayaks can grow anything'. When they arrived, they processed on foot through the village streets, the Ranee escorted by young Dyak girls in their dancing costumes. The indiscriminate American bombing prior to the liberation had destroyed schools, shop-houses and a church, and killed 150 local people and no Japanese, but Dawson noted that it was 'queer how they [the Sarawakians] seemed to take it, just as part of the war'.

At the courthouse, the Rajah made a statement about the cession in a way that suggested to Dawson that 'either HH has lost interest (which wld be fatal) or he is supremely confident of the outcome . . . I wonder if the old boy is really trying.' In his later report Dawson noted that the Rajah's casual manner when talking about the cession contrasted with the concerned way he listened to the natives' applications regarding fishing and customary rights and hearing about their Japanese headhunting exploits – 'giving the impression that *these* were the really important affairs about which he had come to visit them'. Later on Dawson watched as Sylvia did some 'not very good' pencil sketches of Dyak and Malay girls. 'Ranee affects to be so attached to them, but I wonder how much is genuine. I sometimes feel they regard the thing as a stunt and a bore.' Later, they went to the club to watch 'some exhilarating Dyak war dancing'. Dawson liked the Dyaks, whose manner he found preferable to the 'somewhat circuitous oriental approach of the Malay. It is man to man, & no inferiority business. I could happily live among these people . . .'

On this, their final trip to the Rejang, Vyner and Sylvia then proceeded upriver to Kapit, where Temenggong Koh had summoned an assembly of hundreds of Kayans and Dyaks in their war boats. They were dressed in their scarlet capes and hornbill-feather headdresses, and when the Rajah came ashore and made a speech, they all fell silent. He spoke in Dyak, and as Sylvia wrote,

> he was amongst the people that he loved; and as always in such circumstances, his shyness disappeared. I don't think I have ever admired Vyner more than I did then, as he stood, a tall informal figure in a khaki suit and an old white topi, addressing his warriors and their wives, explaining to them the reasons for the Cession. He did not read his speech, but told his story in their legendary language and in the only way that they could really understand; and their faces remained as fixed as bronze images, and their fierce lashless eyes never left his face.

Later they spent their final night in a longhouse and the next morning inspected a collection of Japanese heads, which had been smoked and hung in a special corner of the longhouse. According to

Sylvia, the Dyaks told them how they had sent their prettiest daughters down to a pool in the jungle to bathe, and when the Japanese had crept up to stare at them, 'they had simply lopped off their heads as they went by'.

Besides providing an account of Sylvia and Vyner's visit to Sarawak, Dawson's diary dwelt on his own frustrations as a married man of almost fifty tempted by the 'dozens of pretty appealing faces', the brown-skinned, bare-breasted girls they encountered at almost every turn. Dawson, whose wife had refused to leave him at the outset of the war and so had been interned along with her husband by the Japanese, allowed himself the odd flirtation but left it at that, if his diary is to be believed. 'In myself I propose to avoid unnecessary complications,' he wrote, 'though there is an urge to strike a blow in the fast fading cause of romance.' The legal adviser, Dale, demonstrated less self-control, however, and raised a few eyebrows by making a beeline for MacBryan's estranged wife Sa'erah, who was high on the list of wartime collaborators, having lived with a Japanese naval officer in one of Kuching's large bungalows during the occupation and acted as chief procuress of 'comfort women' for the occupying forces. Dawson conceded that Sa'erah was 'really quite pretty', but at the same time observed that she was as 'wicked & clever as her husband'. It is unclear whether or not she resumed her position as Sylvia's lady-in-waiting at this time.

After a further spell in Kuching the royal party set off on another trip, on 30 April, this time travelling by launch to Simanggang, where the Rajah again heard various petitions and cases, including a polite request by some Sea Dyaks that they be given some Japanese heads to replace those of four Chinese collaborators, which they had been forced to return to their victims' families. He also set out his case for cession, after which Dawson wrote in his diary that 'simple Dayaks will accept it', but they would also 'certainly expect HM [the King] to pay them a visit!'

They began their return journey down the tidal rips of the Batang Lupar, the scene of Somerset Maugham's near drowning in 1921. Dawson gathered, presumably from Sylvia or Vyner, that it was

'Maugham who showed the yellow streak on the occasion in question'. Having spent more time in their company, Dawson was coming round to the Brookes, writing in his diary that the 'R & R [Rajah and Ranee] are such pleasant people when they are alone and natural; he particularly, really charming & nice'.

When they got back to Kuching, they met the two MPs, the Conservative David Gammans and his Labour counterpart David Rees-Williams, who had recently arrived by flying boat and were staying aboard the naval minesweeper HMS *Pickle*. According to Gammans, the MPs were obliged to share a small cabin infested with cockroaches and rats, but Dawson noted that they nonetheless seemed reluctant to leave their ship and refused to go anywhere that would necessitate spending a night ashore – hence planned visits to such places as Marudi and Simanggang had to be cancelled.

Before setting off on their tour of the country the MPs went to tea at Datu Patinggi's house, outside which stood hundreds of Malays bearing banners with such slogans as 'No Cession' and 'We want the Brookes'. The chieftain said he feared unlimited immigration by Chinese and others, swamping the Malays, and openly accused MacBryan of bribing him. When they held a meeting the same evening, it appeared to Gammans that the only people who supported cession for its own sake were the Chinese, who believed it would lead to more trade, and although one or two Malays such as Datu Patinggi were dead against it, the vast majority regretfully acquiesced in what they felt was inevitable, or else were prepared to trust the Rajah in his statement that cession was the best thing for the people.

The next day the MPs set off on their tour, accompanied by Dawson, who, as the British representative, cannot have been an entirely impartial chairman of the various meetings they set up; he more or less admitted this when he told Hall later that he had been able to 'establish a suitable atmosphere' with his introductory remarks. They began in the far north-east of Sarawak by visiting Limbang and Lawas, where Gammans, like Dawson, was horrified by stories of the 'senseless' bombing carried out by the Allies before their landings took place. Communication problems and the fact that they had come at such short notice meant that Malays and Chinese were far better represented at their meetings than indigenous tribes from upriver. In these places, and at Miri and Bintulu, the general feeling was against cession, owing largely to the people's love of their Rajah, and Dawson feared that the report of the two MPs might not be favourable. But at Sibu, the largest town in Sarawak after Kuching, they encountered a very different atmosphere. The MPs regarded the Sibu district as the best gauge of Iban (Sea Dyak) opinion, and so could not fail to have been impressed by a letter in favour of cession presented to them by Sylvia's friend Temenggong Koh. Koh claimed to have had the assent of thirteen Iban chieftains (*pengulus*) and all the Ibans of the Third Division. This may well have been an exaggeration, but the fact that the Rajah had recently visited Sibu to explain his policy had undoubtedly made a difference. As Koh explained to Gammans, they trusted the Rajah. Other Ibans also told the MPs that cession would mean better education and general development for their people. Shortly afterwards, the MPs despatched an interim report to the Secretary of State advising: 'In our view, there is sufficient acquiescence or favourable opinion to justify the matter going before the State Council on 15th May, and we strongly urge no postponement.' Gammans was very impressed by what he had seen of the Dyaks, and the fact that during the occupation 'they lopped off 1,500 Japanese heads. One of them – which they wanted to present to us – was the head of the Japanese director of education. It was a noble cranium, as befits an educationalist and when it was alive it wore glasses. The Dyaks still kept the glasses on, and took them off every day and wiped them.'

By the time the MPs returned to Kuching, Bertram had arrived and was staying at the Residency. Vyner had written to his brother in advance suggesting that it would 'look silly' if they avoided each other entirely and that, whatever their views were on the future of Sarawak, 'I think, if you agree, an outwardly friendly attitude should be observed between us.' While in Kuching, Bertram refrained from active propaganda against the cession but stated his case to those who came to ask for it. Among his visitors was Rantai, a Sea Dyak of the Ulu Ai, who had been given the impression by the Rajah during his tour of the Second Division 'that cession would entail no alteration of anything' and that the Rajah 'would continue to visit them in future in the same way as in the past'. The Datu Patinggi, members of the Malay National Union, and many of the European and native officers also came. The revelation that the Tuan Muda had never been consulted about the cession, let alone given his consent, changed many people's minds over the issue, including for a time Temenggong Koh, who was reported to have exclaimed: 'In that case the Rajah has cheated us!' However, Koh would later fall back into line and voted in favour of cession.

Some felt that, had Bertram campaigned vigorously against cession, he might well have prevented it from going through, but he chose not to, telling Vyner on his arrival that, however great the difference of opinion between them, he did not intend allowing the matter 'to become the subject of a family dogfight'. However, a week later he did protest to Vyner about the 'secrecy and unnecessary speed' with which the question had been handled, and he was said to have shaken his fist at the acting chief secretary J. B. Archer and asked him how much he was getting out of it. Interned by the Japanese during the war, Archer had refused recuperation leave so that he could help the Rajah with the cession.

Before the meeting of the Council Negri on 15 May there was a final burst of lobbying, with the Rajah summoning all the European members to the Astana. There were stories of native members being subjected to varying degrees of pressure, including an allegation made by one of the Chinese members that he had received a death threat if he voted against cession. The man was refused protection and subsequently voted in favour.

Hence the atmosphere on the day of the meeting was extremely tense. That morning the *Sarawak Tribune* published a statement as to what the British government's policy in Sarawak would be if cession were approved by the Council Negri. Sarawak would not become part of the Malayan Union but would be administered 'generally on the same lines as other colonies within the British Empire' and 'in general accord' with the nine cardinal principles of the 1941 constitution. At the meeting itself, the Rajah gave a short speech before retiring from the chamber for the final time, leaving Sylvia to observe proceedings in his place, sitting alongside Bertram. Gammans, who was also present, considered the whole procedure 'most unsatisfactory', not least because the president, J. B. Archer (who appeared to Dawson to be drunk), made no attempt to maintain impartiality, and paraphrased the general statement on future policy 'in a disgraceful manner, giving the most categorical assurances that nothing in the way of ancient customs would be changed at all'.

There followed a debate consisting of speeches for and against cession, but, as Gammans noted, the English speeches were not translated into Malay, nor were the Dyak speeches into either Malay or English. Among those who spoke against were Datu Patinggi, the missionary Reverend Peter Howes, another of those who had survived internment by the Japanese and Bertram, who, as Sylvia recalled, 'made a magnificent and impassioned speech'. Sylvia wrote later that, sitting next to her brother-in-law, she had desperately wanted to tell him that she was 'as much against this thing as he was', but decided that this would be too disloyal to her husband, 'the lonely man at the Astana'.

Bertram ended his speech by saying he would rather see the line of succession come to an end than that any family differences of opinion should be the cause of quarrelling or ill-feeling among the people of Sarawak. After a final plea on behalf of cession by Archer, 'a stumbling, stuttering speech that not one of us heard or understood', as Sylvia described it, the voting began. Members had been told that only those in favour of the cession were to rise to their feet and raise their right hands, but in their excitement everyone stood up, and the courthouse became 'a turmoil of waving arms and moving bodies, so that it became virtually impossible to decide who was for the motion and who was against it'. Eventually, however, it was established that eighteen members were in favour of cession, and sixteen against.

As far as Archer and the Rajah were concerned, the matter was now settled. However, when they returned to the *Pickle*, Gammans and Rees-Williams sent for Dawson and pointed out that proper procedure demanded that there be a committee stage and a third reading of the bill. Archer at first refused to co-operate, muttering crossly about 'lawyers', and was only persuaded with difficulty to chair another session the following day, which the MPs deemed 'a little more businesslike'. The vote this time was nineteen to sixteen in favour of cession.

The deciding factor had been the vote of the Europeans, six, including the Rajah, having voted in favour and three against. When reporting the first vote to the Colonial Office, Dawson had been at pains to stress that the Europeans had not voted en bloc and knew as well as anyone what was good for the country. But there was concern in London, though, about the closeness of the vote, and Dawson was advised that unless there was a majority of at least four in the second vote he should 'mark time' until he received further instructions. On 18 May, however, he was relieved to be given the go-ahead to sign the cession document on behalf of the British government. 'A dramatic moment in history,' he recorded in his diary; 'a bit added to H.M.'s dominions.' He did not know it at the time, but Sarawak was to be Britain's last colonial acquisition.

On that same day the four postage stamps designed to celebrate the centenary of the Brooke Raj were finally issued after a five-year delay. Bearing the portraits of all three rajahs, with Vyner at the centre, the rectangular stamps appeared on the very day on which the Raj effectively ceased to exist. Two days later, on 20 May, the Supreme Council met and approved the cession of Sarawak to the King by six votes to two, and the next day the cession instrument was signed at the Astana, with portraits of the first two rajahs looking on. Dawson wrote to the Secretary of State that the result, although narrow, represented 'a victory of common sense over sentiment' in a country where 'sentiment (towards the Brookes) is a very important factor'. Everyone, he added, would feel a tinge of regret at the ending of such a romantic episode in history, but the Raj had become anachronistic. When he returned to his office after the ceremony, Dawson found a cable that had not been decoded owing to the cipher clerk having fallen ill. When he decoded it himself, he discovered that it was a last-minute instruction from Hall not to go ahead with the signing after all. 'Cold feet at the last moment,' Dawson wrote in his diary, 'not I hope a plot to fix the blame on executive officers (me) in order to side-step political bother.' He sent off a reply explaining that the cable had arrived too late and that it was impossible now to reverse what had been done. That afternoon, the Rajah and Ranee took off from Pending in a Sunderland flying boat bound for Singapore.

In Kuching, meanwhile, as Sylvia recalled, 'the storm over Cession had blown itself out; the gales of criticism and controversy were stilled, and it had never been so quiet. No drums, no gongs, no

Malay boys singing in their boats – it was just as if the little town was in mourning for the death of a dynasty.'

But the atmosphere was perhaps not quite so mournful as she made out. She omitted to mention that on the night that cession was agreed she had suggested a party at the Cathay Cabaret at which they all 'danced like anything', as Dawson recorded, and the sixty-two-year-old Ranee 'again' led a conga. In the lead-up to cession, a great many evenings had been rounded off at the Cathay, where the Ranee would invariably dragoon the revellers into a conga. 'Everybody enjoys themselves in a crude kind of a way,' wrote Dawson in his diary. 'Rather shocking for the MPs though I fear. They have gone away with a poor impression of the Sarawak European officers – a misjudgment I think very largely. They saw them at their worst. All down to Kuching from their distant places & out to have a beatup.'

The Ranee's behaviour does not appear to have perturbed Rees-Williams, who later portrayed her as 'a charming, bright and vivacious lady [who] brought the charm of Mayfair to the Tropics and some of the exotic perfume of the Tropics to Mayfair'. But Gammans was more disapproving, writing in his private memo to the Secretary of State that she was 'even more extraordinary' than her husband and

> in my opinion a bad influence in all this rather sordid family row. She has no sons, and I am convinced that she was determined, at all costs, her brother-in-law's son [Anthony] should not inherit. Some of the stories current in Kuching about the Ranee's conduct cannot even be put on paper in a private memorandum of this sort, but whilst we were there she went three times to a low-down cabaret called the Cathay Cabaret and danced the conga with professional dancing partners, all of whom were prostitutes. She has these girls to the Palace and paints their pictures. A more undignified woman it would be hard to find.

The Rajah was 'in some ways an extraordinary man', thought Gammans, but he was also 'lazy and rather stupid and for many years has preferred the fleshpots of Europe to the austerities of Sarawak. One of the reasons why he wanted the meeting of the Council Negri on 15 May was because he wanted to get home in time for the

Derby.' The Tuan Muda, Gammans liked 'very much, but I thought he was completely brainless, and is of course too old to be considered as Ruler, even if he were fit enough physically . . .' As for Anthony, Gammans had seen him 'a good few times in England and I cannot believe that he would ever be a really good ruler under the new conditions. He struck me as being a most unsatisfactory young man, and we heard stories in Sarawak of his ego-mania and his eccentricities.'

Gammans concluded that the whole cession business had been 'very badly run' and that the Rajah had misled his people by stating in his proclamation that he was coming back every year. Nor was the issue fairly put, in that the Rajah failed to make it clear that there was no question of going back to the status quo before the war. Nonetheless, he advised Stanley that the Conservatives should not oppose cession, and as a result the party raised no opposition when the Order in Council came before the House of Commons. However much he deplored the 'sloppy, unbusinesslike' manner of the proceedings, Gammans had come firmly to the opinion that on balance cession was a good thing for the people of Sarawak themselves. Everywhere he had seen 'affectionate loyalty for the Brooke rule and the Rajah whose personalised and intimate form of government they understand and appreciate'; and Bishop Hudson had told him before he left England that he knew of no part of the world where people were more happy and contented. Yet for Gammans the continued success of the Raj presupposed 'a continuation of good Brookes . . . and that is where, in fact, the whole thing has broken down'.

16

ISN'T OLD AGE AWFUL?

As the Rajah and Ranee departed from Sarawak, neither of them spoke. From the time that they boarded the plane for Singapore, Sylvia recalled, 'Vyner began to change almost before my eyes. He had carried his years lightly and borne himself nobly right up to the end; now, all at once, the fire faded and the broad shoulders were bowed. He was leaving some of his oldest and best friends . . . What could I say to soften his anguish?' Two months after they returned home, on 26 July 1946, the Privy Council ordered the annexation of Sarawak to the British Crown, and for the first time during their marriage Sylvia and Vyner found themselves redundant in her affairs, 'shorn of our glory, and faced with the necessity of adjusting to a world in which we were no longer emperors but merely two ordinary, ageing people, two misfits . . . in the changing pattern of modern times'.

Vyner, who retreated for the time being to Jewell's Farm at Stanford Dingley with 'his budgerigars and his girls', found the transition easier than Sylvia. He was, she wrote, 'basically a simple person' who had done his duty in becoming rajah. He was also able to 'close a shutter on any portion of his life that was finished', a quality that Sylvia envied but did not share. For her, the former ballroom wallflower, Sarawak had been 'like a dream come true', and when it ended she felt 'utterly lost'. 'Perhaps I had enjoyed more than I should have, seeing everyone rise to their feet as I entered a room, and the traffic drawing to one side as I went by. But that was not much consolation now.'

At the time she put a brave face on it, telling Doll: 'Of course it is sad, but it is the only thing to save Sarawak for the future. I think Sarawak will become a great little country, rich and prosperous, and progressive. The Sarawak rule was wonderful, and romantic, but the people should have more, especially the Malays. Anyway, Vyner who knows the country better than anyone made up his mind that Cession was the only answer. Peter [Anthony] Brooke is un-balanced and altogether unreliable. He was given two chances to prove his worth, and failed both times.'

She was not yet ready to let go entirely, however. Having returned to her house in Archery Close, just north of Hyde Park, she was keen that they should both return to Sarawak in the autumn, not least as a means of avoiding the winter in England. But while Vyner's promise that he would soon come back had been an important factor in reconciling native opinion to the cession, he now felt that it would only confuse the people. In order to convince Sylvia, he got MacBryan to obtain a note from the Colonial Office saying that a visit at this time would be unadvisable. Instead it was MacBryan who travelled out to Sarawak in October in order to finalise the Rajah's affairs – while there he also took the opportunity to finalise his divorce from Sylvia's former lady-in-waiting Sa'erah. Before leaving London, MacBryan had also conveyed to the Colonial Office the Rajah's view that the new governor, Sir Charles Arden-Clarke, should occupy the Astana, as it was 'the only suitable place' in Kuching, and if he did not it would again give rise to confusion. While the Rajah's palace lay empty there had been no end of speculation in Sarawak that the next occupant would be his nephew, and when Arden-Clarke arrived to take up residence, in late October, he was greeted by posters proclaiming 'God Save Anthony Brooke, Fourth Rajah of Sarawak'.

Stranded in London, Sylvia's only constant companion was her Yorkshire terrier Texas, 'the most intelligent thing I have ever seen', she told Doll, 'practically talks'. Towards the end of the war such was her devotion that she had lunched out every day at the Cumberland Grill in order to save her rations for her little dog, who 'no blame to her absolutely refuses to eat horse meat when she knows I have a bit of steak or pork in my fridge'. Sylvia found this first post-cession winter a struggle. Her house, she told Doll in February 1947, had 'no steam heating, and as this government cut down the electricity to practically nothing, and the gas is completely out, you can imagine what it is like after the heavenly warmth of Sarawak'. She did her best to keep busy, drawing dogs and Sarawak subjects on commission and writing – she went on to publish two further novels and a second autobiography – but her existence seemed 'pointless and monotonous, waking up in the morning with no definite purpose, no plan of activity, and with no future to look forward to, only the past to remember'. At night she

> still seemed to hear the Dyak gongs and the distant resonance of muffled drums; to inhale the perfume of the flowers in the little Malay girls' hair. Would I ever cease to long for that enchanted land, or to forget that I had once been part-ruler of it; or break myself of the habit of standing whenever Vyner entered a room, or walking dutifully four paces behind him? Now that we no longer had our country, we had a feeling of isolation, of not belonging. Where was the sentry presenting arms as we went in and out? Where were the Malay boys softly and gracefully waiting on our every wish? We had been spoiled and pampered and now we were two lonely people beginning the day without reason and living through it without anything to do.

Their readjustment was not made any easier by the fact that both Vyner and Sylvia knew as well as anyone that the cession had been badly handled – as was highlighted when the Rajah's loyal chief secretary Archer shot himself shortly after. There was no escaping the fact that the majority of native (i.e. non-European) members of the Council Negri had voted against the Rajah's proposal, and they were only too aware that the whole episode would deepen the rift between the two sides of the Brooke family. In February 1946 Anthony's sister Jean Halsey wrote to 'Dear Uncle Vyner' accusing him of betraying his people, who had already been hopelessly let down by the British during the war. 'It makes one ashamed to be either a Brooke or British,' she told him. Jean felt even more strongly about Aunt Sylvia, writing to Anthony after the cession that it had been the Ranee's 'life's ambition' to destroy him and their father, the only consolation being Sylvia's 'obvious discomfort' in the fact that now that she had achieved her object she found it to be 'a worthless one & with the peculiar result that our side of the family might have won on points'. Jean told Anthony that she now avoided coming face to face with her aunt, lest 'that false grin' and 'the devilment in that mind' caused her to be 'overcome with the primitive urge to slap her resoundingly – tear up her crimped hair in handfuls – wrench off and stand on her suitable little crimson monkey coat & by that time be overpowered by the police and marched off to gaol'.

Bertram, having appeared relatively calm while out in Sarawak, called a press conference on his return to London at which he rose from his chair and pounded a copy of his father's will with his open palm. 'My objection is based on that Will!' he cried. 'My brother did not consult me before giving Sarawak away. The first I knew of it was when I heard the news on the BBC.' No attempt had been made to put the facts before the 500,000 natives of Sarawak, the Tuan Muda added, while the Rajah himself was said to have described cession as 'just like a dose of castor oil – it's good for you'. Bertram predicted trouble ahead, with the possible growth of Communism, riots and house-burnings.

The strength of his feeling was more than matched by Anthony's, who, in November, announced that he was going to appeal to the Privy Council, saying he had been receiving regular messages from Sarawakians calling for a restoration of their white Raj. 'If they are held down to Whitehall by force, extremist elements are bound to get control,' he warned. In December he set off for Kuching 'to consult my friends in Sarawak about legally regaining independence'. His other purpose was to gather information to defend a libel action that had recently been brought against him by MacBryan over a note headed 'GTM MacBryan and his connection with Sarawak affairs', which he had circulated to MPs and peers on the eve of MacBryan's mission to Kuching in January 1946. However, when he reached Manila he discovered that he was barred from entering Sarawak – the governor, Arden-Clarke, having obtained the same prohibition order that the Rajah had used to get rid of MacBryan in 1936. Defending the ban in the Commons, the new Colonial Secretary, Arthur Creech Jones, said that the Rajah Muda's attempt to 'subvert existing authority' could only confuse and distract the local population from their urgent job of post-war reconstruction, and that his visit might lead to 'strife and disorder'. Anthony responded that he merely sought to ensure the indigenous people were properly consulted about the form of government in Sarawak, and among his supporters in Parliament was Winston Churchill, who branded the reasons given for excluding him as 'a very perfect declaration of tyranny'.

In Sarawak a huge rally of twenty to thirty thousand Malays and Ibans had been planned to welcome the former Rajah Muda, and the disappointment over his ban manifested itself in a rash of petitions and demonstrations. Anthony, meanwhile, eventually made his way to Singapore, where his mother Gladys had recently arrived, and together they installed themselves in a house which they named 'Sarawak Lodge' and which for the next few years served as the headquarters of the anti-cession movement.

Back in England, the retired Rajah soon began to find it difficult bending down to garden, at which point he gave up his smallholding and moved to London, to a house at 73 Albion Street, which Sylvia had found for him around the corner from hers. There he lived simply, looked after by his secretary Evelyn 'Sally' Hussey and surrounded by a few mementoes from Sarawak. At either side of the fireplace stood two Chinese brass lions which, according to Sylvia, an Indian man had brought to the Astana in a sack and sold 'in such a hurry that we were certain he had stolen them from some temple's steps'. In the drawing room bookcases housed his extensive library, and a refectory table served as his bar. A budgerigar flew freely about the room, occasionally pausing to bathe in a jug of water, from which Vyner would then pour drinks for his guests while his secretary uncomfortably looked on. According to Sylvia, Vyner was 'devoted to this little bird', but he disliked displays of affection and 'was sometimes rough and almost cruel in his handling of it. When it became old and ill and obviously dying, he turned his face away and said to his secretary, "Put it in the water jug." '

Two years after the cession Sylvia told Doll that her daily routine now consisted of working 'damned hard' on her latest novel (which she planned to call 'Now My Heart's Mended' but which eventually became *The Darlingtons*) during the early morning (5 a.m. to 10 a.m.), going over to Vyner's house for elevenses, attending to her chores and queuing for her shopping for the rest of the morning, lunch with Vyner at Grosvenor House, then 'off to a movie to get the cobwebs out of my mind, then home, back to Vyner at 6.30 pm for drinks, or else to Jack [Golden, who had recently got married and was soon to have a baby boy], then home, cook my dinner, listen to the radio during which I usually fall asleep, and then off to bed. And this goes on for day after day and so the time passes.'

From time to time, Dorothy had continued to ask both Sylvia and Oliver for money, and each of them did their best to persuade her that the other was better placed to meet her demands. During the war Oliver had pleaded that the foreign-exchange restrictions made it 'absolutely illegal' for him to send her anything, adding that 'the position of vastly rich Oriental potentates may be different, & that mean creature your sister might, if she were made differently, transfer you something from that furnace on the Equator in which she lives'. They did occasionally both stump up, however. In 1945, for example, Sylvia and Oliver sent Dorothy $1,400 and $1,000 respectively so that she could build a new house on a patch of desert property given to her by Frieda Lawrence. And in May 1947 Sylvia wrote to her sister saying that she was 'peacing out my will etc . . . and I thought perhaps you would like another thousand of yours NOW, whilst we are still young enough to enjoy it'.

She did not want to encourage more of Doll's begging letters, however, and in the autumn of 1948 she told her, 'We haven't nearly the money we had, in fact I haven't any capital at all left, only the allowance Vyner gives me.' Vyner, she said, was 'living on his capital and he figures he can last another ten years, after that we shall have to draw in our horns and see where we can live cheaply, by that I mean what country. But we don't worry as an Atom bomb might have settled the whole question by then.'

Sylvia may have exaggerated the extent of her poverty. She had, after all, eventually received £15,000 (after death duties) in 1945 from her mother's will when the Esher family's two houses on Tilney Street were sold – though she assured Doll at the time: 'I don't even see the money, it flashes by my popping eyes like an express train and vanishes into investments for the children.' But it was certainly true that she and Vyner were not nearly as rich as they had been, nor as rich as most people in Britain assumed they were.

The capital Sylvia referred to would presumably have included whatever was left of the £200,000 that Vyner had obtained in return for relinquishing his absolute powers in 1941 and the £100,000 that he had eventually agreed to accept by way of the Rajah's Dependants Order just before the cession, in lieu of the proposed pensions for him and his dependants, which would have been taxable. However, according to Sylvia, money meant little to her husband other than as something to 'hand out to those who hadn't any'. During the war she told Doll that he had financed those Sarawak government officials who had been ruined by the war, whose money was either lost or frozen. After the cession, in a gesture 'more generous than wise', he had also given his two most profligate daughters, Elizabeth and Valerie, cash settlements amounting to more than £40,000 each. He was urged by his advisers to put the money in trust, and MacBryan also tried to intervene, only to be intercepted by Sylvia. 'What a fool you are!' she wrote to him in November 1947. 'How could you be so utterly stupid as to interfere or oppose anything Vyner, the kids and myself desire? What is it to you who Vyner leaves his money to? Vyner wants to let the kids have their money now!' The money, given with no strings attached, was duly spent 'like water' and before long Elizabeth and Valerie were both back in debt. Sylvia conceded in her autobiography that she had overrated her daughters' financial responsibility. Vyner, meanwhile, when he heard what had happened 'simply sighed, shrugged his shoulders, cleared up their debts, and gave them a comfortable allowance to live on until the time of his death'.

By August 1948, with his capital fast diminishing and no other regular source of income in sight, Vyner was beginning to worry about his ability to meet the needs of his various dependants. He wrote to the Secretary of State to complain that in the absence of his adviser MacBryan he had been prevailed upon by the representatives of HM Government to sign the Rajah's Dependants Order, and that it was never explained to him that he would be 'violating a pledge already given to my own people' to set up the £1 million Sarawak State Trust Fund.

William Dale at the Colonial Office considered the Rajah's letter to be 'a most extraordinary approach, made up of misstatements & vague allegations which savour of incipient blackmail'; he concluded that it had clearly been drafted by MacBryan. But MacBryan told Dale that the driving force behind the letter had been the indignation of the Ranee (and perhaps to some extent the Rajah) due to their 'generous and public spirited act' having received next to no acknowledgement by the British government, a feeling exacerbated by the fact that most people in Britain still seemed to be under the impression that they had pocketed £1 million as a result of the deal. Sylvia was particularly annoyed when, during one of the Commons debates about Anthony's exclusion from Sarawak, the Unionist MP William Teeling said that the Rajah and his brother had received 'well over £1 million' free of income tax in return for the cession, and no one in the government corrected him.

The dispute between Vyner and the Colonial Office was further complicated by the fact that the Rajah's chief adviser was now losing his sanity. A few days after Vyner's letter to the Secretary of State, Sylvia explained that her husband had been placed in a somewhat difficult position because MacBryan had 'not been at all well and has had one or two spells of brain storms'. He had recently been arrested for stealing a peach, when he had £410 in cash in his pocket, and assaulting a policeman. This, Sylvia told the Colonial Office, was 'the conduct of a man who undoubtedly must have been suffering from a mental black out . . . but unfortunately he is the only man who knows and who holds all the important and private documents relating to the affairs the Rajah wrote to you about and that is why we are obliged in this case to make use of his services . . .' Six weeks later she telephoned the Colonial Office to warn that MacBryan was 'on the loose again' after a spell in a mental hospital, and that nothing received from him was to be regarded as written on behalf of the Rajah; when MacBryan subsequently returned to the hospital, she rang again to say that she could now speak freely without arousing his antagonism.

When Sylvia told Doll, in October 1948, that MacBryan had 'gone mad and is in a loony bin', she complained that 'they keep letting him out and he comes round here and I know one day he will just whip out a revolver and shoot me as he hates my guts'. In her autobiography she wrote that all her life she had been 'obsessed by the certainty that one day something awful will happen to me through a lunatic'. Yet, at Vyner's request, on several occasions she did go 'with the utmost trepidation' to see MacBryan in the mental hospital. On the first visit, he was 'lying quite still, staring up at the ceiling, and I could feel the tenseness of his long lean figure. I had no idea that he was strapped to his bed. I just saw the white desperate face fighting for control. When he looked at me there seemed to me no sight in his small grey eyes . . .' She was on the point of leaving when MacBryan suddenly seized her hand and pulled her diamond ring off her finger. Gazing at it with 'a fiendish glee', he kept repeating 'lovely, lovely, lovely . . .' then 'laughed that laugh of his that shook his whole body and had once been so infectious'. When the ring fell on to the bed, Sylvia grabbed it and fled.

MacBryan would be in and out of institutions for the rest of his life. The last time Sylvia went to see him, he told her that he was very much in love with Princess Margaret and that they were to be married. He had by then recently acquired a third wife, Frances, with whom he subsequently lived in South Africa, from where emanated stories of him turning up naked at parties, thinking he was invisible, or crawling across the room like a dog, barking at the top of his voice. In the spring of 1950 he reappeared in London, where Anthony (who had by then settled MacBryan's libel action out of court) told his mother that he was again under observation in a mental home, having been seized after going around with a small portable receiver slung around him, and telling everyone that he got told what to do by listening in.

By May, MacBryan was on his way to Kuching, where his bid to revive the Rajah's trust fund was turned down, and then on to Brunei, where he was appointed political adviser to the Sultan Ahmad Tajuddin, but failed to secure the succession of the Sultan's daughter (his only child) after the Sultan suddenly died from alcohol poisoning on 4 June. These setbacks seem to have precipitated yet another nervous breakdown, resulting in MacBryan's deportation to Singapore, and eventually he ended up in Hong Kong, where he put up in a cheap hotel and was arrested for directing the traffic. He died there in mysterious circumstances in 1953. Sylvia only heard of his death some years later, and had never dared ask Vyner what he thought about his downfall.

In the meantime a compromise had been reached between Vyner and the Colonial Office, whereby the Secretary of State agreed 'as an act of grace' to uphold the Rajah and Ranee's marriage settlement of 1911, which entitled them to annuities from Sarawak revenues. Although the Rajah's agreement at the time of the cession to accept the £100,000 lump sum (from a trust fund established by his father) had been 'in lieu of any other claim from the Trust Fund or Sarawak Revenue', it was recognised that he probably did not have the marriage settlement in mind when he signed, and besides he had no authority to give up the rights of his wife and daughters. So from January 1949 an annuity of £4,000 was paid to Vyner, half-yearly. On his death, Sylvia was to be entitled to an annuity of £3,000; and after the death of both of them each of their daughters would get an annuity of £500.

In the meantime, the finances of the younger Brooke daughters were not helped by the fact that their marriages kept coming unstuck, something that Oliver, for one, thought their mother had a lot to answer for. At the time of the cession, both Elizabeth and Valerie were in the process of getting divorced, Didi from Harry Roy, Vava from 'her ghastly Spanish fruit importer', Pepi Cabarro, whom she had walked out on after barely a year of marriage. Sylvia had told Doll in 1945 that she didn't think much of Vava's latest flame, 'a very la de da British Airforce Group Captain [Jimmy Addams] who wears a heavy gold bracelet and curls his moustache every morning with curling irons . . . can you imagine? He hasn't any money, is married to Arline Judge the American film star [who went on to marry seven times, reasoning, 'You gotta keep trying'], and has a grown up daughter of sixteen by his first marriage . . . He is a poop of a man, with smug good looks, and bedroom eyes. They are living together in Peterborough where he is stationed . . .' The next year Sylvia reported that he had 'just bought a Rolls-Royce, or rather she has . . . and they are contemplating buying an eleven thousand house in the country, on HER money. It is no use advising her or saying anything, she only thinks I am being unfair, and that I don't like Jimmy. Well, I don't like any man who is out of job and lives at the rate he does. He has fourteen suits of clothes and wears a gold bracelet . . . Do YOU like that?' Whether or not Sylvia's opinion counted for anything, Vava eventually turned down the group captain ('Thank God,' heaved Sylvia, 'he was an awful drip') and in 1948 married a Scottish stockbroker, Andrew McNair, 'quite a nice little man,' Sylvia told Doll, 'but a bit dull too'.

Elizabeth, after her divorce in 1947, married Richards Vidmer. 'Glorious Dick', as Sylvia described him when he first appeared on the scene, had by then become 'middle aged, and handsome in a sulky sort of way', Sylvia told Doll. 'He had his face smashed in in a plane crash when he was a pilot which hasn't helped, but he has beautiful eyes.' She later wrote that he was 'undoubtedly a fascinating man, with a certain type of American's easy charm and assurance; but I'm afraid there wasn't much underneath that handsome appearance except hot air. The trouble was, my darling daughters were, in their own individual ways, so hopelessly susceptible.'

Privately, Sylvia was no more complimentary about Leonora's new husband, whom she described variously to her sister as 'unutterably selfish', 'an old bore of a man', and 'an idle good for nothing, who goes to bed in the afternoon, and hasn't done a stroke of work since he left the Army'. She was more tactful in her autobiography, written while Tommy was still alive (he died shortly before she did), remarking that, to begin with at least, 'it looked like an excellent match. His quiet and unassuming character was the ideal counterweight to that of my highly strung eldest daughter. She was so like the old Ranee, laughter and gaiety one moment, tears rushing to her eyes the next. Tommy would take all her moods with a shrug and a smile, and help himself to another Scotch and soda.' Leonora remained devoted to him in spite of his increasing dependency on drink.

Vyner, or 'My Moppet', as Sylvia called him (he called her 'My Mip'), remained 'wonderful', she told Doll in 1948, 'hasn't altered a bit except naturally he looks a good deal older, but he is still full of beans and enjoys life . . .' A year later, he was 'as sweet as ever and as gay as ever' and 'if he ever gives up having girlfriends then I shall fear the worst'. Every now and then, he would ask Sylvia to help him get rid of one of his girls, whereupon she would go round to his house and 'play the indignant wife'. 'Some people may think my attitude towards my husband's indiscretions showed a lamentable weakness in my character,' she wrote, 'that my tolerance bordered on complicity. I suppose, in a way, it did; but you must remember that I knew and understood the limits of his affections, and his odd, compulsive need for feminine company. I never looked seriously upon his girls, and neither did he . . . They meant no more to him than, say, another man's regular visits to his local or his bookmaker: they never diminished the affection we had for one another.'

Above all, Vyner was 'fun to be with . . . he hated to be serious; and this was why his people in Sarawak loved him. We were such opposites, he and I; he with his lightness of heart, and I with my despondency and frequent tears, we made a perfect combination. He made up for all that I had missed when I was young.' Although it had been many years since they had slept together, according to Sylvia, they never felt disunited except, briefly, around the time of the cession. 'Perhaps there was more mother in me than wife; and when the sexual side of our marriage came to an end we lived our separate lives, but without severing or spoiling our relationship in any way . . . It was an arrangement that suited us, and might very well suit other married couples too.'

In Sylvia's case, it must have helped that she strove for other things besides the devotion of her husband. She still longed for success as an author, and during the late 1940s she collaborated with the young Frederick Knott (best known for his later stage thriller *Dial M for Murder*), who offered to help her with the writing of her fourth novel, *The Darlingtons*, which is the most autobiographical of her novels, the plot centring on two sisters, Susan and Henrietta, who live at White Orchard Manor and compete with each other for the hand of an eligible young man living nearby. In the background is their philandering and rather sinister 'Papa', Lord Darlington, who loiters in Hyde Park 'to wind his watch'.

Early in Susan's life there occurs an incident with the family's bailiff which, together with her father's clumsy if well-intentioned explanation of puberty and her sister's assertion that all men are beasts out for their prey and sex is an ogre about to spring at her from every corner, leads to a dread of sexual passion that Susan spends much of the book struggling to overcome.

When it came to finding a publisher, Leonora's old flame Noel Busch suggested trying America first, and he sent the manuscript to Farrar, Straus & Company in New York. When they agreed to take it, Sylvia wrote to Roger Straus to say that she was 'so goddamn excited I am not quite sure if I am sitting or standing'.

Straus asked her for some blurb to put on the jacket, whereupon Sylvia replied suggesting that her book was 'an indictment against prudery, and a condemnation upon parents who are afraid of their young, and a denunciation of sex ignorance'. He also wanted her to do a publicity tour, including a brief lecture stint and some radio appearances. She asked what clothes she should bring, 'super Oriental, or merely pseudo Eastern . . . I have my full Malay Sarong etc, which is quite effective, on the other hand maybe you don't want the Ranee element in it at all, but just want me to be a Lady (which by the by I find extremely hard).' Straus left it up to her, but hinted that, although the publicity would be primarily based around 'the novel itself, and you as a novelist . . . naturally, we would be foolish to overlook the "Ranee" aspect'.

He also requested some 'biographical material'. 'I don't know what you mean by [that],' Sylvia replied,

> but here are a few comments on my life as it is today . . . I live in a small studio Mews (alley to you) house, the windows of which look out upon an old Archery which is still in use, and the gardens of which are full of flowers and birds. No-one would believe or ever know that my street runs straight into the worst area in this City for criminals and thieves. My husband and I have been married for well on forty years. Our love is friendship which is to my mind so much finer a word. Our three daughters are all married. I have four grandchildren. My cup of contentment is well filled. I rise every morning at 5 am and write until 10 when I close down work for the day. I take my little Yorkshire terrier, by name Texas, for a walk in the park. I lunch and have lunched for the last two years at Grosvenor House. The same restaurant, the same table and at the same time every day. Every afternoon I go

> to the Pictures. I find it relaxing to live in other people's lives, and it also teaches me what NOT to write. I like to see beautiful women in beautiful clothes because I cannot wear them myself. I have neither the face nor the figure to be fashionable. I have found a good way to get slim. Do your own cooking as I do so badly that most of it is thrown down the lavatory. I have done almost everything in life except two things. I haven't had a son, and I have never come down in a parachute. Now I am too old for either of them . . . One word and one word only is written in my heart. Sarawak. That is my one nostalgia.

Despite the best efforts of Farrar, Straus, the publicity tour which she undertook in September and some reasonable reviews on both sides of the Atlantic (it was published in Britain by Boardman in 1953), *The Darlingtons* was not a runaway best-seller and, as Sylvia recalled, it died a 'slow and peaceful death'. Her next and last novel, *Headwind House*, published in 1953 by Boardman, which even Sylvia conceded was 'rather unpleasant', fared no better.

Anthony had by this time abandoned his anti-cession campaign. Still prevented from entering Sarawak, for three years he had done all he could to direct the various anti-cession organisations from Singapore. A visit to Sarawak by his wife Kathleen, in 1947–8, had helped to keep the flame alive, but the more time went on, the more frustrated and radicalised certain of the anti-cessionists became, until a terrible snapping point was reached. On 4 December 1949 Duncan Stewart, Arden-Clarke's successor as governor of Sarawak, was inspecting a guard of honour by schoolchildren on his first visit to Sibu, when a sixteen-year-old Malay youth suddenly broke from their ranks and stabbed him in the stomach with a kris. Stewart was flown to hospital in Singapore but died there a week later. The youth and his accomplice, members of the 'Thirteen Precepts', a recently formed cell committed to direct action, were sentenced to death for conspiracy to murder. Before the sentence was carried out, one of them volunteered a statement saying that Mr Stewart had had to be killed because he had obstructed the return to Sarawak of Anthony Brooke.

Anthony now came under the scrutiny of MI5, who wanted 'to get wind of any other plots which he and/or his associates in Sarawak might be hatching'. But by the spring of 1950 it was accepted that, while he had been in regular correspondence with one of the conspirators, Awang Rambli, he obviously did not know him well, was unaware of his unsavoury record and had in any case urged him to conduct his protest within the law. There was no evidence that Anthony knew of the plot to assassinate the governor.

Anthony, for his own part, was quick to distance himself publicly from what he called 'this misguided clique of extremists', and when his legal challenge to the cession was finally dismissed by the Privy Council the next year, he decided to renounce once and for all his claim to the throne of Sarawak. In early 1951 he sent a cable to Kuching appealing to the anti-cessionists to cease their agitation, citing the Cold War and the threat to the Commonwealth of 'aggressive world communism'. He urged his supporters to do all in their power to promote 'racial unity, brotherhood and solidarity among the peoples of Sarawak' so that they would be prepared to meet any emergency, inviting them to 'discontinue henceforth the practice of demonstrating on Cession Day (1 July) and to celebrate instead His Majesty the King's official birthday' on 7 July. That they rejected his advice was interpreted by one historian as 'the final indication that independence rather than the restoration of Brooke rule had become the goal of the anti-cession movement'.

The next year Anthony suffered a nervous breakdown, but he quickly recovered and embarked on a second career as a self-styled 'travelling salesman' for world peace, funded by his £2,800-a-year pension from Sarawak, which was converted into a lump sum of £70,000 in 1957. The turn of events was perhaps hardest on his only son Lionel, then aged twelve, whose childhood had been overshadowed by his father's struggle to reverse the cession, and who then had to endure five years at Eton being called 'Rajah', while all the time knowing that he would never inherit the title.

In June 1949, meanwhile, Sylvia's altered circumstances had been brought into sharp focus when she was robbed at pistol-point at her flat in London at 1 a.m. She later told reporters that one of the three intruders had worn a handkerchief round his mouth, and that another was 'good-looking, with a little Clark Gable moustache'. She was pushed into an armchair and told that she would be shot if she uttered a sound – although by her account she subsequently engaged one of them in 'a long chat'. They eventually made off with some 'worthless' Malay necklaces, a gold cigarette box and some cash, leaving behind her more valuable jewellery, including the diamond and pearl brooch given to her by King George V on her wedding. By this time, two of her daughters had moved across the Atlantic with their husbands, Leonora to Florida and Elizabeth to Barbados, and at Vyner's suggestion she had begun to spend the winter months in Barbados as a means of alleviating her increasingly acute arthritis. To begin with, it was a 'curiously empty and unhappy time', as she recalled: 'time wasted, aimlessly drifting, without real friends, sitting at bars and drinking, because other people were drinking, because there was little else to do'. She was still known as Ranee, but 'it meant nothing there. Nobody had ever heard of the Ranee . . . I was just another lonely old woman, living apart from her husband, drowning her identity in nightclubs.' She became 'consumed with self-pity', convinced that Vyner had suggested she go just so that he could be rid of her.

Each summer she would make her way back to London, and in 1953 she watched the Coronation at home there on television, 'MUCH the best way,' she told Doll. 'No crowds, no pushing and jostling, and one saw the whole crowning in the Abbey . . . Beautiful, and very very touching. The Queen looked like a little girl. Especially when she took off all her jewels and put on a pure white robe to be annointed . . . There was one beautiful moment when Prince Philip knelt before her and took the oath, and kissed her cheek. I was in floods of tears sitting here, I just couldn't help it . . . They are such a young couple, and it is all really so romantic having a young queen for a change, don't you think?' The previous year she had observed, presciently, of Queen Elizabeth II: 'There isn't one breath of a scandal or even a small wrongdoing in the whole of that blessed girl's disposition. She is the personification of perfect woman, wife and mother, so there you have it.'

Sylvia had always tended to deprecate her own appearance, and this was particularly so as she grew older. In 1949, aged sixty-four, she wrote to tell Doll that she was 'squat and square and hang in all the places I should not do, and stick out in all the places that should stick in . . . I am not really fat, but unshapely and my legs are as thin as rails. I look like Mumsey in the face, I think at least I remind myself of her.' By Coronation year, at the age of sixty-eight, she had slimmed back down to seven stone seven, 'which isn't bad for a woman of my age', but she added: 'I must say the Belgian blood in us isn't good for the figure, they ARE such an unattractive race.' Her beloved Vyner, meanwhile, was 'just about the right weight, he looks slim and has NO tummy. In fact he has a wonderful figure for a man of nearly eighty . . . Isn't old age awful,' she went on. 'I don't feel nearing seventy, but there it is . . . WE ARE, you and I and there's no getting away from the fact. All we can do is to feel young and I certainly do do that.'

Valerie had remained in England throughout this time, living at Sunningdale, where her son Stewart McNair, Sylvia's fifth grandchild, was born in 1952. Three years later Sylvia reported to Doll that Vava had abandoned her son and husband, without saying goodbye, but leaving a note, and was 'busily engaged on getting a fourth – A man who lives in Barbados, who is married and has three kids'. Didi, meanwhile, was 'in love with one of the doctors in Barbados, but I think she will probably go back to HER husband. Never a dull moment in the Brooke family we always say.'

The arrival of Valerie in Barbados was 'as if a bomb had landed in our midst', Sylvia later recalled.

> Vava, the figure of temptation and desire made quite a stir on the island's beaches. The phoney title of 'Princess' was revived. It was something that the Barbadians appreciated and understood; but it did all of us more harm than good in that unhappy time. I found myself involved in illicit love affairs, family quarrels, face-slappings and brawls – and the Brooke family were always in the wrong. It was like a madness; a touch of that same tropical fever we had all succumbed to in the Far East, and then recovered from, and now fell victim to again; a dangerous recklessness of heart that led to a dangerous recklessness of behaviour.

The experiences prompted Sylvia to write a collection of lurid short stories, which she planned to publish under the title 'Shameless Island'. 'You have never seen such free love anywhere,' she told reporters during a trip to Montreal in 1957. 'I am writing about everybody and everything. A lot of people think they are in it, and they are!'

Mercifully for all concerned, she failed to find a publisher, and the next year she told Doll that she was once again living 'a very quiet life, as my arthritis is giving me the heebee jeebies, and my feet are gradually going out of action'. She was still able to swim 'for an hour or more', but getting down to the beach was 'the hardest thing' as she could not drive a car 'and I'm far too old to learn'. In April 1959 she became a great-grandmother for the first time, when Leonora's daughter Rosemary (who had married a naval officer, Martin French) gave birth to a son, Ewan.

All this time Vyner had remained reclusively in London. He was still a devotee of the turf, and for a while he owned some racehorses, though he was overcome by shyness every time he went into the paddock to see his jockey mount. Occasionally, when Sylvia was in England, he would accompany her on visits to her family. Maurice and Zena's younger daughter Marie Cheyne remembered her aunt Sylvia as 'a pudding stirrer with a wicked sense of humour . . . the atmosphere changed when she was in the house from happy go lucky to being rather strained'. But she loved Vyner, 'a sweet, charming man. I remember once when he came to stay he dropped his watch in the bath and I found him trying to dry it on the end of a poker over the fire.'

Otherwise most of Vyner's time was spent at home, especially after he began to suffer from blackouts brought on by high blood pressure during the 1950s. Sylvia told Doll in 1958 that he seemed 'perfectly self-contained and happy with his girls. He hasn't been out of doors for eighteen months . . . He is perfectly well but nervous as he's fallen down twice in the park.' Sylvia later recalled that her husband 'would go to comical lengths to avoid the window-cleaner or the postman; yet if by mischance, he did come across them, all his shyness would vanish and he would talk quite cheerfully to them, telling Sally [Hussey, his secretary] afterwards what splendid chaps they were'.

Occasionally he would ask Sally Hussey to arrange for one of the Television Toppers dance troupe whom he had seen on television to come and see him. Like Professor Higgins, the Rajah would then take these girls under his wing and tutor them in elocution and general deportment; at least one of his 'wards' went on to marry a peer. Other celebrities whom the Rajah had first glimpsed on the BBC were also prevailed upon to come and give private performances, among them the blues protest singer and cabaret star Josh White.

By the late 1950s Sylvia was returning to London only every other year, but it was 'a comforting feeling that whenever I felt lost and adrift in Barbados, there was my Rajah in London, waiting to put me together again'. When she returned in 1961 for their golden wedding anniversary, however, 'all Vyner could talk about was his new girl . . . He was as nervous and anxious as a young man presenting his fiancée for the first time to her prospective parents-in-law.' The new girlfriend had arrived at Albion Street soon after Sylvia. She was 'pretty, and rather lush, and about nineteen, utterly unlike his usual specimens'. She had brought a rose and curtseyed as she gave it to Vyner, while Sylvia looked on stupefied. 'My old rascal was eighty-seven, and she couldn't take her eyes off him. You have to admire a man like that.' When he offered Sylvia gin and bitters rather than the champagne she had been hoping for to toast their 'fifty years of easy-going friendship', Sylvia 'gave up the idea of a romantic evening and left him with his girl'.

Sylvia returned to Barbados while Vyner again stayed in London. He was soon visited at his home by Lord Cobbold, who was chairing the commission of inquiry into the planned new independent Federation of Malaysia, which was to include Sarawak, along with North Borneo, thereafter known as Sabah. The Rajah expressed concern about how best to safeguard the unique position of the Sarawakians within the federation, and urged that their head of state should not be inferior in status to that of the present rulers of the states of Malaya, and should therefore be given the title of regent. But it was not to be, and in the event Sarawak was given another governor. In early 1963 the Rajah recorded a message to his former subjects on the eve of their joining the new country. It was his last public act. On 9 May, two months before Malaysia came into being and four months short of his eighty-ninth birthday, he died. It was later reported that when the news of the Rajah's death reached Sarawak, the spirit-worshipping Dyaks had rejoiced, for they knew that his soul would return to the land of his fathers.

The obituary in *The Times*, published the day after Vyner died, observed that his 'severe training in the art of native administration' had stood him in good stead. It drew attention to his aversion to pomp and ceremony, as well as his inscrutability, but added that 'when he mixed with the public – which was often and then always or nearly always in completely informal dress – one could not but be impressed by the innate dignity of the man. He was the Rajah.' The obituary also noted that he was overgenerous at times, and that he was sometimes taken advantage of, which was something of an understatement. A shorter piece appeared the same day in the *Daily Telegraph*, sub-headed 'Sarawak's Last White Raja', which began by saying that Vyner would 'be chiefly remembered with the anti-cession controversy' (something that *The Times* only touched on) and went on to observe mildly that although he had administered his 'primitive territory' in peace and harmony during the inter-war period and proved himself a popular ruler, 'his reign was somewhat embittered by family disputes'.

Sylvia, who had not seen Vyner since their golden wedding, learned of his death from Frank de Buono, a professional walker and the owner of the Breadfruit Club, where she was now living, and employed by wealthy elderly ladies. She remembered 'shivering with the suddenness of the shock' and catching the first available plane to London, accompanied by de Buono, whom she had recently appointed as her 'aide-de-camp'. They were met at London Airport by Leonora, Valerie and Sally Hussey, and went straight to 'the dilapidated old wreck of a house on Albion Street' where the Rajah had spent the last years of his life, refusing ever to have it repaired. 'It was even shabbier than I remembered it,' wrote Sylvia, 'patched and peeling walls, sagging curtains with tottering pelmets; even the staircase was breaking away from the wall and swayed as we climbed.' Photographs of his favourite girls stood on the mantelpiece.

A few days later Vyner was cremated and his ashes taken down to Dartmoor to be buried in the corner of the churchyard at Sheepstor given over to the White Rajahs, next to the graves of his father and great-uncle and across the fields from Burrator House, where James Brooke had lived whenever he was in England. On 27 May there was a memorial service at the Chapel of St Michael and St George at St Paul's Cathedral, with the former Bishop of Borneo, the Right Reverend Nigel Cornwall, officiating. The Reverend Philip Jones, giving the address, said that Vyner was 'one of three great men . . . men of different character . . . moulded differently by the demands of their times and purposes' but united in dedication to their subjects. Despite stories of Vyner attempting to escape from state occasions or important visitors by fleeing to his bungalow on Matang mountain, Jones went on, he 'never tried to escape from the least of his people. He loved and understood them. He was always ready to help, to advise, and to listen.'

Among the congregation were Anthony and Bertram, neither of whom had set eyes on Vyner since the cession. Bertram had retired in rather more comfort than his brother, to a large house at Weybridge, Surrey. He and Vyner had recently made their peace and planned to meet, but Vyner died before they had the chance to do so. Bertram died two years later, aged eighty-nine.

There had been no such rapprochement with Anthony, who had just turned fifty, and was now well into a new incarnation as a moral rearmer and Christian peace 'crusader'. Describing himself as a 'full-time ambassador-at-large for the people of the world', the former Rajah Muda had walked barefoot across the Punjab with the Indian 'saint' Vinoba Bhave and had audiences with Nehru, U Nu, and Chou En Lai. He later lived for a spell at Findhorn, the New Age commune in Scotland, and developed a keen interest in flying saucers.

After separating from his wife Kathleen and later asking for a divorce, Anthony explained to her in 1973 that he felt 'infused with a sense of mission' and predicted that 'within the next 18 months or two years I may be thrown into considerable publicity in connection with physical contact with extraterrestrial beings, who in Lappland areas of Norway and Finland are already quietly landing and making contact, possibly in other areas of the world too. This opens up a new phase for human history, but it is likely to be an extremely controversial one in which I certainly wouldn't want to drag you or have you pestered by the press. I need to be absolutely free in what I am doing . . .'

At the time of this letter, Anthony was staying at the Munedowk Foundation at Kiel, Wisconsin, where, he told his wife,

> there are continuous telepathic contacts with our Space Brothers, and it is all part of the overall process by which the recognition of and contact with these extraterrestrial and wiser and more civilised beings is to play its part in the establishing of peace on earth and the brotherhood of man . . . Of course they are on a higher range of evolution and have a higher technology than we do, but man is so crazy that he would try to fight them if there were any large scale landings. Anyway it would be both an intrusion and psychic shock to the consciousness of human beings which makes it necessary for the contacts to be brought about in a gentler and more gradual way. The main governments of the world are fully aware of what is going on but cannot at this stage give open recognition that there are representatives of more highly evolved civilisations in space hovering around in the earth's atmosphere, against whom there is no effective defence since they have a superior technology to ours! The fact that they are friendly would count for little if they attempted widescale landings without immigration permits! They are actually proclaiming telepathically that they are 'our brothers' and give recognition to one supreme and universal God, the father of all. The difference is that they live their spiritual convictions and understanding and we don't. Enough of this, my typewriter has run on . . .

Soon after his divorce Anthony married Gita Keiller, from Sweden, eighteen years his junior, and together they founded Operation Peace Through Unity in 1975. Although also interested in 'esoteric astrology', as Anthony recalled, Gita did not initially share his credence in flying saucers, until she saw one for herself in Sweden during the 1970s. They continued to travel around the world for another decade in furtherance of peace, lived for a time in Santa Fe, and eventually came to roost on the North Island of New Zealand, in a small clapboard villa, Te Rangi, on a hill overlooking the Maoris' sacred Wanganui river.

In the years following Vyner's death, which was followed in October 1963 by the death of her brother Oliver, Sylvia did not let up. In 1971, when she was eighty-six, she was still getting up every morning at 6 a.m. to write or paint – mainly flower pictures, which she sold to tourists for $50 or $100 a time. After 'shut down time' at noon she would rest, then entertain or visit friends – who all knew her as 'Ranee'. 'There's nothing here when you pin it down, except socially,' she admitted to a visiting reporter from the *New York Times*. She continued to wear bamboo bracelets and her royal yellow sarong, alternating with flowing calypso blouses and sneakers. Frank de Buono stayed with her as her minder, sharing a succession of houses. He was given power of attorney over her affairs. Leonora, for one, became highly suspicious of him, complaining to Vyner's executor Theodore Page that her mother never saw any letters until 'he' had opened and read them first. However, in general, Leonora had 'no beef with the way he treats Mummy, she seems to be very happy and has made new nice friends through him'.

Leonora had more beef with her mother over money. Vyner had left a relatively paltry £22,904 in his will, which in 1963 would have bought a six-bedroom house in Knightsbridge, or five second-hand Rolls-Royce motor cars. After payment of estate duty and other outgoings, this was to be divided in four equal shares between Sylvia and her three daughters, but the distribution was delayed because the Estate Duty Office took time to accept that the Rajah's domicile was Sarawak. In the meantime, Sylvia received £600 a year from an Esher family trust and also became entitled to £3,000 a year free of tax from the Sarawak government (as per the agreement of 1949 with the Colonial Office). Out of the latter she was supposed to pay her daughters £500 each, but two years after her husband's death she had still not honoured this part of the bargain. She then had the gall, as Leonora saw it, to complain about her more than generous allowance, threatening to come to England with Frank and 'expose all'. Leonora told Page that she kept a 'huge house', a boy at boarding school, a maid and a yardman on less than her mother received. But the worst of it was that her mother was blackening her father's name 'all over the place' and telling people he had left her badly off. 'Of course she is old, and has always been irrational but I do wish Daddy's name could have stayed out of it all, you know how people talk . . .'

In the meantime, Leonora was having to house Elizabeth, the former 'Princess Pearl', who was now divorced from her second husband and living 'from hand to mouth' but refused to work. 'If it was me I would scrub floors rather than live on charity,' Leonora complained, 'but she is so feeble and what makes me mad is I give her $163 a month and it is gone in a week on clothes and things she doesn't need . . . she just has no idea of money and never had.'

There remained one thing that Sylvia was determined to do before she died and that was sell her second autobiography, the manuscript of which was doing the rounds of publishers in the late 1960s. It was eventually bought by Jim Knapp-Fisher at Sidgwick & Jackson in London, edited there by William Armstrong, father of the singer Dido, and published in July 1970. Sylvia told Doll that she was 'thrilled' by this, adding disingenuously that the title, *Queen of the Headhunters* (taken from a magazine headline in America), was 'a little melodramatic'. She asked her sister to let her know what she thought of her book. Doll replied loyally that she had received it 'with great joy, and am now reading it with equal joy. You are such a very good writer, and the early part I find a bit tragic . . . The best thing for you was getting you married and out of the family. And alas now that I have proved myself Pupsy and Mumsy are no longer here to admit it. Family life seems in most cases immeasurably difficult to cope with. A bunch of totally different temperaments bandied together . . .'

Sylvia also sent a copy of her book to Sally Hussey, with whom she had been feuding over Sally's failure to send over Vyner's diaries. ('I hope for my father's sake Mrs Hussey burned these,' remarked Leonora.) Sally pronounced the book 'full of inaccuracies', to which Sylvia replied: 'I guess when one gets to eighty one's memory plays a few tricks,' adding triumphantly: 'Any mistakes I may have made didn't prevent 1,200 copies being sold in a week, & wonderful notices in most of the papers.'

For once, this was no exaggeration, Kenneth Allsop, reviewing the book for the London *Evening News*, wrote that '*Queen of the Headhunters* could be an Evelyn Waugh novel, as witty, as eccentric, as essentially English, a period piece'. The *Sunday Times* hailed it as an 'extraordinary, funny account of a life in which nothing went to plan but everything ended happily'. The *Daily Telegraph* said it was 'the candour that makes the book so enjoyable', while the *Times Literary Supplement* thought that the book had 'the improbable verisimilitude of Nancy Mitford'. Describing the book as 'mythobiography', the *TLS* reviewer said that it contained countless stories that 'one does not believe', but for all that it was 'a delightful book that one hopes will bring the Ranee of Sarawak enough money to support her in her immortality'.

The chances of it doing that were enhanced the next year when *Queen of the Headhunters* was published by William Morrow & Company in the United States, where critics sought to out-praise their counterparts across the Atlantic. 'When the enthusiastic British reviewers compared Sylvia Brooke's autobiography to novels by Evelyn Waugh or Nancy Mitford,' wrote Anatole Broyard in the *New York Times*,

> they were almost damning it with faint praise. Even Mr Waugh could not have imagined a life like hers, which resembled an antique fairy tale in a modern translation – something akin to Donald Barthelme's rewriting of Snow White and the Seven Dwarfs . . . There are many women who would not have wanted her life, who would be outraged by the submissive role she played. But it satisfied her, and that satisfaction – so deeply felt and clearly understood – has enabled her to compose one of the most remarkable autobiographies ever written by a woman.

Sylvia had at last produced a book that was a commercial as well as a critical success, and one that served briefly to reignite her celebrity. She was interviewed about her life for a television documentary in the BBC2 series *Yesterday's Witness*, with links narrated by the actress Claudette Colbert, her friend and neighbour on

Barbados. Wearing her royal yellow sarong and the pebble spectacles that had become her lot in recent years after operations for cataracts, Sylvia appeared to thoroughly relish the experience of being filmed, and with gusto impressive in a woman of eighty-five, she dutifully trotted out stories from her autobiography. Once again she staunchly defended the submissive role she had played in her marriage, declaring at the end: 'I didn't care what he did, I was a complete squaw-woman.'

In the autumn of 1971, with sales of *Queen of the Headhunters* still going strong, Sylvia again travelled to London to appear on one of the earliest *Parkinson* chat shows, sharing the billing with the actress Shirley MacLaine. She gave a sprightly and typically mischievous performance, which has sadly not been preserved on tape. Soon after returning to Barbados, Sylvia fell down at home and broke her hip. She was taken to the Queen Elizabeth Hospital at St Michael, but in the process of being treated she caught pneumonia. She clung on for a further two weeks, but on the night of Thursday, 11 November she died.

Having earlier expressed a wish to be cremated and for her ashes to be returned to Sarawak, she had subsequently decided that it would be simpler to remain on the island that had been her home for the past twenty years. So she was buried in St Peter's Cemetery at St James, near to her last house, Tuffet Cottage, Sandy Lane, with only Frank de Buono, her three daughters (who were by then all living in the United States) and a handful of friends present at the graveside.

EPILOGUE

Among the handful of obituaries that appeared, those in *The Times* and the *New York Times* were typical in portraying Ranee Sylvia as an engaging curiosity from a forgotten era, with no hint of what a stormy petrel she had been in her heyday. In Sarawak, stories of her unrestrained behaviour had circulated for a while after Vyner's abdication – so that one former colonial officer who arrived there in 1946 told me that although he never actually met the Ranee, he had occasionally dreamt of seeing her in one of Kuching's brothels. But her notoriety evidently expired before she did.

Today, the Malaysian government is not excessively keen on harping back to the days of the White Rajahs – witness the dismantling of the display devoted to their dynasty at the Kuching museum. The only obvious reminders there of Sylvia's existence are the Fort named after her at Kapit, and the discreet plaque marking the occasion in 1912 on which the newly-arrived Ranee Muda nervously opened the new dry dock in Kuching. The Sylvia Cinema was demolished to make way for a drab office block. The Astana has long been the residence of the Malay state governor, whose gaudy interior decoration makes strenuous demands on anyone trying to imagine how it might have all looked in the old days.

In Britain, too, the last White Ranee, such a favourite with the popular press during the 1930s, quickly faded from memory. Archivists at the BBC did their bit by unaccountably deciding to scrub the recording of the 86-year-old Ranee's appearance on *Parkinson*, while preserving the interview with Shirley MacLaine – who was destined to appear on the show on countless other occasions over the years. Neither were Sylvia's daughters around to keep her flame alive, having long since put down roots in America by the time of her death.

In 1986 Valerie's only son Stewart McNair travelled to Miami to meet his mother for the first time since she bolted when he was three. By then aged seventy, she had recently left her fourth husband for a new man. It was a strange, slightly farcical encounter that began with Valerie tumbling down the staircase of the Sheraton Hotel and colliding with a waitress as she hurried, arms outstetched, to greet her long lost son. She was at a loss to explain to Stewart why she had abandoned him.

Stewart, who had imagined his mother far younger and more vibrant than she now appeared, says sympathetically that Valerie and her sisters 'never stood a chance', that their mother was 'a very bad role model' and their father 'detached from reality'. 'They had a very peculiar childhood and never seem to have had any boundaries.' None more so perhaps than Valerie, who despite being the youngest of Sylvia's daughters was the first of them to die, aged seventy-seven, in 1993.

Leonora had lived in America longer than all the Brooke sisters, settling happily in Vermont with her second husband, the GI Colonel 'Tommy' Tompkins, who died in July 1971, a few months before Sylvia. She had another son, Charles, born in 1952, wrote an engaging autobiography, *My Lovely Days*, which was published in 1966, played a lot of golf and devoted any surplus energy towards rescuing stray dogs and other animals. She died aged eighty-four, in 1996.

Elizabeth, meanwhile, the most gentle-natured of the three, had divorced her second husband, Colonel 'Dick' Vidmer in 1963, but she stayed on in Barbados, later moving to Florida, where she too spent much of her time on the golf course and occasionally reminisced about the old days. Like her sisters, she had not returned to Sarawak since her first marriage in 1935, preferring to remember it 'as it was – like a wonderful dream'. She died in 2002, aged eighty-eight.

Their cousin Anthony, the disappointed heir to the Brooke Raj, survived them all, and at the time of writing he was still living, aged ninety-four, with his wife Gita at Wanganui on the north island of New Zealand. When I visited them there in 2004, Anthony struck me as saintly and serene, and though obviously a little puzzled as to why I should want to write a book about his aunt, he showed no bitterness for all the grief she had given him, and he was endlessly hospitable and patient with my enquiries, insisting I rummage wherever I liked. He was also scrupulous in working out what my stars were doing, predicting some profound though unspecified developments just ahead. 'I am so impersonal in many ways,' he told me, sitting on their verandah, 'and yet when I meet people I can feel quite a relationship; I just let love flow.' He confessed that he had 'always been a very bad manager of money', and having also been a victim of Lloyds', he had all but gone through his various inheritances; even the free biscuits from Huntley & Palmer had stopped coming. But he was not one to dwell on the past. Gita, a small dynamo of a woman, was less guarded about Sylvia, calling her 'a nasty piece of work', but she nevertheless told me that she thought her husband would have hated being Rajah, 'wouldn't have had the patience', and that all he really wanted was a crusade.

Of late, most of Anthony's crusading had been in pursuit of 'world peace and universal understanding', but in 1999 he did briefly return to the Sarawak theme, writing to Tony Blair to request 'the removal of a fifty-year-old shadow cast upon my integrity by Her Majesty's Government and which, so long as it remains unaddressed, still calls into question my status, even my loyalty, with regard to the British Crown.' Anthony was referring to the ban imposed on his entering Sarawak after it became a British colony in 1946, which had never been formerly lifted after Sarawak was incorporated into the Malaysian Federation in 1963. Instead it had simply been allowed to lapse, and despite having twice since visited Sarawak – once at the invitation of the Malaysian government at independence and once later to protest at the destruction of the rainforest – Anthony felt that 'there remains a sense of my still being persona non grata in the eyes of the British Government'. He did not receive a reply.

Anthony and Gita continue to produce a quarterly newsletter, 'Many to Many', for their charity Operation Peace Through Unity, and each September the former Rajah Muda sends his regards to the annual meeting of the Sarawak Association in London, at which a toast is raised to 'Sarawak coupled with the name of Brooke'.

NOTES

So as not to distract general readers, apart from a few footnotes I have not indicated sources and notes in the text, but they are listed below by chapter and page number. The cited fragment is usually from the beginning of the sentence or quote, but may occasionally be a more striking phrase from the middle or end. To save space, where the sender and recipient of a letter is obvious, their names are not always repeated in the source notes.

The Brooke Papers referred to are held at the Bodleian Library of Commonwealth and African Studies at Rhodes House, Oxford, as are the Boyd, Dawson, Gammans and Macaskie Papers. The Brett Papers are in the possession of the Brett family. The Esher Papers are held at the Churchill Archives Centre, Churchill College, Cambridge. The G. B. Shaw Papers cited are in the British Library, London. The abbreviations CO and WO refer to the files of the Colonial Office and War Office, which are held at the National Archives of the United Kingdom, at Kew, south London. Sylvia's letters to her sister Dorothy Brett are at the Harry Ransom Humanities Research Center (abbreviated below to HRHRC) at the University of Texas, as are other letters to Dorothy from members of her family. Her unpublished memoir is among the Dorothy Brett Papers at the Center for Southwest Research at the University of New Mexico.

I have used the following abbreviations: SB for Sylvia Brett/Brooke; DB for Dorothy Brett; MB for Maurice Brett; OB for Oliver Brett; OE for Oliver Esher, as he later became; RB for Reginald Brett; RE for Reginald Esher; VB for Vyner Brooke; BB for Bertram Brooke; AB for Anthony Brooke; GB for Gladys Brooke. Sylvia's two autobiographies, *Sylvia of Sarawak* and *Queen of the Head-Hunters*, are rendered as *Sylvia* and *Queen* respectively.

PROLOGUE

page

xvi 'tatty yellow umbrella': modelled on that used by the Sultan of Brunei, the umbrella was the only form of Oriental pageantry that the first White Rajah had allowed himself. It symbolised the origins of Sarawak as a Muslim Malay state under the overlordship of the Sultan. See R. H. W. Reece, *Masa Jepun*, p.6.

xvii '*L'État, c'est moi*': As was

remarked (quoting Louis XIV) by the governor of North Borneo, Arthur F. Richards, to the governor of the Straits Settlements, Sir Cecil Clementi, 26 August 1930, Clementi Papers, Rhodes House. Quoted by Nicholas Tarling in his article 'Sir Cecil Clementi and the Federation of British Borneo', *Journal of the Malayan Branch of the Royal Asiatic Society*, Vol.XLIV, Part 2 (1971), p.3.

xvii 'celebrate the': The centenary celebrations and speeches were chronicled in the *Sarawak Gazette*, centenary number, 20 October 1941.

xix 'kept me': Steven Runciman to Lady Halsey, 17 July 1960, Brooke Papers, Vol.40.

xix 'Of the Ranee': ibid, 5 August 1960.

CHAPTER I

page

1 'told to wave': Dorothy Brett's unpublished memoir, MSS 494 BC, Box 12, Folder 39, Center for Southwest Research, University of New Mexico; Sean Hignett, *Brett*, pp.12–13.

1 'tiresome things': James Lees-Milne, *The Enigmatic Edwardian*, p.139.

1 'nobody loved me': *Queen*, p.4.

2 'It was a curious life': *Sylvia*, p.26.

2 'crying my eyes': *Queen*, p.4.

3 'The lake and': C. H. Dudley Ward, *A Romance of the Nineteenth Century*, pp.307–8. *Queen*, p.9.

5 'I have loved': 7 August 1869, Esher Papers; Lees-Milne, p.16.

5 'be unworldly': Lees-Milne, p.12.

5 'I envy you': ibid.

6 'Floating in a': Lionel Brett, *Our Selves Unknown*, pp.27–8.

7 'Who is Lord Esher?': *Daily Chronicle*, 25 April 1910.

7 'that as against': *Our Selves Unknown*, p.28.

7 'You are a wonderful': Esher Journal, 3 March 1909, Esher Papers; Lees-Milne, p.178.

8 'intelligent enough': *Our Selves Unknown*, p.30.

8 'Mr Brett sends': Lees-Milne, p.48.

8 'She would not': *Sylvia*, p.57.

9 'Why you have': RB to Eleanor Van de Weyer, 30 July and 2 August 1879; Lees-Milne, p.49.

10 'I expected': 24 September 1889 and 24 September 1918; Lees-Milne, p.49.

10 'The better she': Lees-Milne, p.54.

10 'There was nothing': *Sylvia*, p.13.

11 'fat and phlegmatic': *Queen*, p.1.

11 'morbid child': 'Yesterday's Witness, Sylvia of Sarawak', *Listener*, 27 April 1972.

11 'not exactly ugly': DB memoir.

12 'My whole life': *Sylvia*, p.15.

12 'Who is Prime Minister?' *Sylvia*, p.26.

13 'Get along you naughty': ibid.

14 'women were only': *Queen*, p.4.

14 'I used to pray': *Queen*, p.10.

14 From James Coates's *Has W. T. Stead Returned?* (1913), cited in

A. N. Wilson's *The Victorians* (2002).
14 'For the holidays': one of the Dudley Ward boys, William, was later married to Freda (née Birkin), the long-term mistress of the Prince of Wales.
14 'a great, big': *Sylvia*, pp.33–4. Lees-Milne, p.38. Reginald Esher to OB, 18 June 1899, Brett Papers.
14 'When they built': *Queen*, p.10. *Sylvia*, p.29.
14 'It was a constant': *Sylvia*, p.15.
14 'Dorothy did not': ibid, p.14.
15 'nose twitched at dinner': Hignett, p.14.
15 'secret games': *Sylvia*, p.20.
15 'no one would volunteer': *Sylvia*, p.18.
15 'Pupsie and Mumsie': DB memoir.
15 'It was only a': *Sylvia*, p.18.
16 'smacked him': *Queen*, pp.10–12.
17 'a thing he adores': RB to Chat Williamson, 8 February 1892; Lees-Milne, p.87.
17 'so good-looking': *Sylvia*, p.27, *Queen*, p.8.
17 'simply execrable': Robert Rhodes James, *Rosebery*, p.354.
18 'very nearly pierced': Sir Frederick Ponsonby, *Recollections of Three Reigns*, p.33.
18 'grossly spoiled': *Our Selves Unknown*, p.30.
19 'listened at the': *Sylvia*, pp.22–4.
19 'black devil moods': *Queen*, p.5.
19 'My Sweet Fatty': RB to MB, 26 August 1895, Esher Papers; Lees-Milne, p.111.
19 'will you go on': ibid, 10 March 1897; Lees-Milne, p.110.
19 'I wonder whether': ibid, 24 March 1897.
19 'a walk up High St': ibid, 4 November 1897.
19 'Sometimes you have': ibid, 24 November 1897.
19 'I couldn't resist': ibid, 10 March 1898.
20 'It is many days': ibid, 26 April 1901; Lees-Milne, pp.136–7.
20 'I don't think you': MB to RE, 25 January 1899, Esher Papers.
20 'the sweetest night': ibid, 28 August 1904, Lees-Milne, p.137.
20 'a preference for': Hignett, p.21.
20 'talking to the portraits': *Sylvia*, p.44.
21 'when she set out': *Queen*, p.15; *Listener*, 27 April 1972, p.544.
21 'too much of': *Sylvia*, p.59.
21 'I pictured myself': ibid, p.62.
21 'live flamingly': ibid, p.62.

CHAPTER 2

page

22 'She had a kind of': *Toys*, p.121.
22 'all there was to know': DB memoir.
22 'reborn': *Sylvia*, p.63.
23 'The object of her ardour': in *Sylvia*, p.52, Sylvia said she was nine or ten, but she also said that Binning was in command of the Blues – which he was from 1899 – so it seems likely that it was later.
23 'an intelligent, affectionate': Lees-Milne, p.39.
23 'All that I knew': *Sylvia*, pp.53–4.

23 'final attempt to': Lees-Milne, p.227.
23 'the best if not': *Sylvia*, pp.55–6.
24 'baskets of apples': RE to OB, 6 September 1929, Esher Papers.
24 'It was a kind': *Sylvia*, pp.70–1.
24 'a sanctuary for all my sadness': ibid, p.73.
25 'no one had ever': Esher Journal, 28 December 1900, Esher Papers; Lees-Milne, p.126.
26 'they had to grope': DB memoir; Hignett p.23.
26 'brilliant success': Esher Journal, February 1901, Esher Papers.
26 'He never hesitated': RE to MB, 16 March 1902, Esher Papers.
27 'too conceited': Lees-Milne, p.139.
27 'They are like': RE to MB, 12 June 1899, Esher Papers.
27 'drew a kind of veil': *Sylvia*, pp.66–7.
27 'How dreadful at': DB memoir; Hignett, pp.25–6.
27 'There was something': *Sylvia*, pp.66–7.
28 'torn between devotion': *Sylvia*, p.68.
28 'and a nurse': Marion Mortimer, from Princess Christian's Home in Windsor, who lived permanently with the Bretts for several years after Doll got better.
28 'the vulgarest couple': DB to RE, 4 June 1902; Hignett, p.26.
28 'presented at court': *The Times*, 16 March 1903, p.8.
28 'masculine independence': *Queen*, p.18.
28 'I could hardly contain': DB memoir; Hignett, p.20.
29 'We walked along the path': ibid, Hignett, pp.30–1.
29 'He came up behind': ibid, Hignett, p.31.
30 'Here is something': 20 September 1908, Esher Papers.
30 'Reggie did not approve': Lees-Milne, pp.337–8.
30 'met anyone since': *Sylvia*, p.27.
30 'kissed me in the dark': *Queen*, p.5.
31 'give this coming out business': *Sylvia*, pp.79–80.
31 'but it was not': *Toys*, pp.141–2.
32 'It seemed unconventional': *Queen*, p.25.
33 'pioneer of freelance': Edward Banks, *Sarawak Gazette*, 20 October 1941.
34 'There isn't a lawyer': unidentified newspaper cutting, Brooke Papers, Box 16.
35 'It was all very dull': Margaret Brooke, *Good Morning and Goodnight*, pp.28–9.
36 'a queer fish!!': confidential note by Margaret Brooke to Charles Willes Johnson, 29 June 1927, Brooke Papers, Vol.18.
36 'a good cross betwixt': Charles Brooke, *Ten Years in Sarawak*, p.331.
36 'It was considered': Averil Mackenzie-Grieve, *Time and Chance*, p.111.
37 'sat by my bed': *Good Morning and Goodnight*, p.30.
37 'The only child': Margaret Brooke to Charles Willes Johnson, 25 June 1927, Brooke Papers, Vol.18; Margaret

omitted to mention Esca's presence on the ill-fated voyage in *Good Morning and Goodnight*.

37 'remember not to open': Charles Brooke to Hope Brooke, 18 October 1879, Sarawak Museum; Steven Runciman, *The White Rajahs*, p.170.

38 'he withstood': DB memoir; Hignett, p.35.

38 'what the Ranee did to you': Henry James to William Morton Fullerton, 12 March 1901, The Houghton Library, Harvard University; quoted in Marion Mainwaring, *Mysteries of Paris, The Quest for Morton Fullerton*, p.111.

38 'There was nothing very feminine': *Queen*, p.27; *Sylvia*, p.92.

39 'destroyed her pet doves': *Queen*, p.28.

39 'pillows filled with straw': Gladys Brooke, *Relations and Complications*, pp.73 and 84.

CHAPTER 3

page

41 'The last thing which occurs': transcript by Gerard Fiennes, quoted in R. H. W. Reece, *The Name of Brooke*, p.14. Another of Vyner's tutors was Walter James, grandfather of the writer P. D. James: see her memoir *Time To Be In Earnest*, p.7.

41 'His daily outing': *Relations and Complications*, p.136.

41 'that appallingly sporting': *Sylvia*, p.184.

42 'constant quarrels': *The Three White Rajas*, p.118.

43 'More than eight hundred': *Sarawak Gazette*, 1 August 1902.

44 'unscrupulous and inhuman': *The Three White Rajas*, p.127.

44 'smooth fair skin': *Queen*, pp.29–32.

45 'despotic forms': RE to OB, 17 July 1912, Esher Papers.

45 'this stranger from the Far East': *Queen*, pp.32–3.

45 'centuries if need be': ibid, p.34; *Sylvia*, p.103.

46 'Dear Mr Brooke': 4 August 1904, Brooke Papers, Vol.17.

46 'my son and successor': *Sarawak Gazette*, 4 June 1904.

47 'All the servants know': 3 August 1904, Esher Papers.

47 'squeezed through': DB memoir; Hignett, p.35.

47 'tore a portrait': *Sylvia*, p.111.

47 'accused Doll of trying to steal': DB memoir.

48 'in early summer of 1906': according to the *Sarawak Gazette*, he left Sarawak in April that year.

48 'I never had a moment': *Queen*, pp.35–6.

48 'Mrs Raj Moodah': 5 June 1906, Esher Papers.

48 'it was after this': *Sylvia*, p.113.

48 'Dear Doll, arrange': ibid, p.115.

49 'I hope you': ibid, p.117.

49 'the only man who had ever': *Queen*, p.39.

49 'the solution of what seemed to me': *Sylvia*, p.75.

49 'I wanted through my pen': *Queen*, pp.20–1.

49 'she gave it to Pupsie': DB memoir, p.63.

50 'I did so want him to admire me': *Sylvia*, p.77.

50 'Quite excellently': Esher Journal, 17 January 1908, Esher Papers.

50 'I don't think it matters': SB to RE, 15 September 1906.

50 'arranged for him': Lisa Chaney, *A Life of J. M. Barrie*, p.203.

50 'Barrie eventually rebuked her': *Sylvia*, p.87.

50 'showed his influence': see Alan L. McLeod: 'Sylvia Brooke, Ranee of Sarawak: Pioneer Feminist Writer', *Commonwealth*, Vol.22, Autumn 1999.

51 'such a chorus of praise': 18 September 1908, Esher Papers.

51 'Honourable Sylvia': *Queen*, pp.22–3. Her reply is dated 25 August 1910, 50529 GB Shaw Papers.

52 'Katie has some lace collars': Lees-Milne, p.227.

52 'The Furry Beast is awfully cocky': 3 June 1909, Brett Papers.

52 'Gilbert Cannan': Mary Barrie and Cannan were married in 1910, but divorced in 1918 after he fell for a 'radiant' 19-year-old South African, Gwen Wilson. Two years later Gwen married their lodger, Henry Mond, later the 2nd Lord Melchett, a blow from which Cannan never recovered. In 1924, by which time he had written 27 books, he was certified insane and he spent the rest of his life in mental asylums. He died at Holloway Sanatorium in 1955, leaving a barrister's wig as his only possession – Diana Farr, *Dictionary of National Biography*.

52 'among the signatories': others included Henry James, A. E. W. Mason, Beerbohm Tree and H. G. Wells.

53 'even more isolated': *Queen*, p.23.

53 'thinks he can': SB to RE, 25 May 1910, Brett Papers.

53 'a beautiful letter': ibid, 11 June 1910.

53 'the broadness of your mind': ibid, 14 June 1910.

53 'I will if I can get away': ibid, 16 June 1910.

54 'Of course we did not mention': ibid, 20 June 1910.

54 'Whenever there is a thunderstorm': ibid, 22 June 1910.

54 'dogged by the word "Honourable" ': SB to George Bernard Shaw, 25 August 1910, 50529 GB Shaw Papers.

55 'really, in her heart': RE to MB, 10 November 1910, Esher Papers.

55 'a little touched': SB to RE, 6 December 1910, Brett Papers.

56 'strange, shy luncheon': *Sylvia*, p.140; *Queen*, p.40.

56 'you must speak now': SB to RE, 1 January 1911, Brett Papers.

56 'all my gloomy thoughts': 3 January 1911, Brooke Papers, Vol.17.

56 'Vyner writes delightful letters': 4 January 1911, Brett Papers.

56 'The only thing I don't like': 24 January 1911, Brooke Papers, Vol.17.

57 'When their engagement': *Sylvia*, p.141.
57 'not at all pleased': *Sylvia*, p.143.
57 'a good natural': 2 February 1911, Esher Papers.
57 'You think Westminster': 4 January 1911, Brett Papers.
58 'Syv's official precedence': RE to OB, 15 January 1911, Esher Papers.
58 'a treacherous beast': RE to MB, 4 January 1912, Esher Papers.
58 'We have the infernal dinner': ibid, 14 January 1911.
58 'was not quite the class': undated note by Lionel Esher, 4th Viscount, Brett Papers.
58 'All now depends': RE to MB, 7 January 1910, Esher Papers.
58 'useful, I felt': ibid, 10 January 1910; Lees-Milne, pp.149–50.
59 'I have been bothered': ibid, 26 January 1911.
59 'is so absorbed': 24 April 1911, Esher Papers; Lees-Milne, p.226.
59 'The marquee': RE to OB, 25 February 1911, Esher Papers.
59 'had been dragged': *Queen*, p.48.
59 'a very quiet wedding': RE to MB, 17 February 1911, Esher Papers.
60 'rank and precedence of a duchess': according to *Burke's*, both as Ranee Muda and Ranee, Sylvia had the precedence of the daughter of a viscount. Burke, J. B.: *Genealogical & Heraldic History of the Peerage & Baronetage*. However, in Court Circular in *The Times*, she often appeared above the peerage.

CHAPTER 4

page
61 'Well, that's that then': *Queen*, p.48.
61 'It was so beautiful': ibid, p.50.
61 'bothering him': SB to RE, 9 March 1911, Brett Papers.
62 'Neither she or he': RE to Chat Williamson, 14 April 1911, Esher Papers.
62 'No two people': RE to OB, 19 April 1911, Esher Papers.
62 'so nice to everyone': *Sylvia*, pp.158–9.
62 'Ride a cock horse': ibid, p.159.
63 'The prospect of having': *Queen*, p.52.
63 'being in Stanton': Charles Brooke to GB, 7 September 1912, Brooke Papers, Vol.3.
63 'make Vyner a Highness': Court Circular in *The Times*, 24 August 1911.
63 'Oh the slap': SB to RE, 16 August 1911, Brett Papers.
63 'insolent meddling': letter from Arnold White, September 1912, Brooke Papers, Vol.4.
64 'Truly I have': 24 July 1911, 50529 GB Shaw Papers.
64 'some tremendous achievement': *Sylvia*, p.161.
64 'come and see us': 24 July 1911, 50529 GB Shaw Papers.
64 'It is possible': conversation with Michael Holroyd, 20 August 2006.
65 'considering I am': 11 November 1911, 50529 GB Shaw Papers.
65 'Sylvia, if you have': Michael

Holroyd, *Bernard Shaw*, Vol.II, pp.312–13.

66 'How is Mrs Pat?': 30 January 1913; Margot Peters, *Bernard Shaw and the Actresses*, p.339.

66 'Three weeks premature': in *Sylvia* she says three *months*, however she was already pregnant by the time she returned from honeymoon in April. Sir Henry Simson, whom she called 'Simmie', was later the surgeon present at the birth of the future Queen Elizabeth II. He was married to the actress Lena Ashwell, Bernard Shaw's original Mrs Warren and the originator of large-scale wartime troop entertainment.

66 'perched up in bed': 29 November 1911, 50529 GB Shaw Papers.

66 'in the seventh heaven': *Queen*, p.52.

67 'fatal to marital happiness': RE to Chat Williamson, 5 February 1912, Esher Papers.

67 'a great expense': Charles Brooke to F. H. M. Dallas, 1912, National Archives, PRO 30/79; R. H. W. Reece, *The White Rajahs of Sarawak*, p.75.

67 'hard to take entirely seriously': RE to OB, 24 March 1912, Esher Papers.

67 'counting the cakes': *Midway on the Waves*, p.67.

68 'secretly glad in his heart': *Sylvia*, pp.167–8.

68 'a weak-minded fool': BB to Charles Willes Johnson, 20 October 1912, Brooke Papers, Vol.4.

68 'My address is Sarawak': SB to RE, 21 March 1912, Brett Papers.

68 'tossed and tumbled': ibid, 14 April 1912.

69 'Fancy old Stead': RE to MB, 15 April 1912, Esher Papers.

69 'Poor old Stead': ibid, 17 April 1912.

69 'Poor dear': SB to RE, 12 May 1912, Brett Papers.

70 'a perfect person to travel with': ibid, 23 April 1912.

70 'To put it mildly': *Queen*, pp.54–5.

70 'better than anything': SB to RE, 12 May 1912, Brett Papers.

70 'These people': ibid.

71 'caring for Sarawak': Sir Arthur Young to Sir John Anderson, 2 June 1912, CO 531/4.

71 'Up till now': OB to RE, 13 May 1912, Brett Papers. Not everyone took such a jaundiced view of Sir Arthur Young as Oliver and Sylvia. He seems to have been regarded by most people as unpretentious, modest, solid, and impassive. One historian of Malaya described him as 'the least impressive and most successful of all the governors', content to leave the running of Singapore to his talented colonial secretary, R. J. Wilkinson. He was popular with local businessmen, many of whom had benefited from the rubber boom of 1910. He had never been near a university, but was an international footballer in his youth. His wife was the daughter of the second Marquess of Ailsa. See Robert Heussler: *British Rule in Malaya*, Clio Press, 1981.

72 'It was one of the prettiest': OB to RE, 20 May 1912, Brett Papers.
72 'the broad and winding': *Sylvia*, p.171; *Queen*, p.55.
73 'It was exactly': OB to RE, 20 May 1912, Brett Papers.
74 'I cared then': *The Three White Rajas*, p.134.
75 'It might have been Queen Mary': OB to RE, 1 June 1912, Esher Papers, 19/4.
75 'a very happy country': ibid, 15 June 1912.
76 'Elsewhere bloomed gardenias': *Good Morning and Goodnight*, p.48.
76 'ugliness and discomfort': OB to RE, 20 May 1912, Brett Papers.
76 'like a lovely cloak': *Queen*, p.56.
77 'Well, you wouldn't know': 24 May 1912, 50529 GB Shaw Papers.
78 'No one could': OB to RE, 1 June 1912, Esher Papers, 19/4.
78 'The magic of it all': *Queen*, p.57.

CHAPTER 5

page
79 'our days of freedom': *Queen*, p.58.
79 'it was the unblinking coldness': *The Three White Rajas*, p.93.
79 'previously destined': *Queen*, p.61.
80 'A subsequent chronicler': Robert Payne, *The White Rajahs of Sarawak*, p.161.
80 'in case of his': 21 April 1912, Brooke Papers, Vol.4.
80 'leave everything': note by OB, 11 June 1912, Esher Papers, 19/4.
81 'whispered words': *The Three White Rajas*, p.136.
81 'with the documents': note by OB, 11 June 1912, Esher Papers, 19/4.
81 'I, Charles Brooke': *Sylvia*, p.178.
82 'they determined to resist': note by OB, 11 June 1912, Esher Papers, 19/4.
82 'He accused Vyner': *The Three White Rajas*, p.137.
82 'fatal in a country': OB to RE, 11 June 1912, Esher Papers, 19/4.
82 'With natives': SB to RE, 26 July 1912, Esher Papers, 19/4.
83 'this new arrangement': VB to CB, 8 June 1912, Esher Papers, 19/4.
83 'I might be': VB to RE, 9 July 1912, Esher Papers, 19/4.
83 'leave it to you': 10 June 1912, quoted in *The Three White Rajas*, pp.144–5.
83 'All the sympathies': VB to RE, 9 July 1912, Esher Papers, 19/4.
84 it 'must not be thought': *The Three White Rajas*, p.145.
84 'Do you suppose': 11 June 1912, Esher Papers, 19/4.
84 'rude beyond': *Queen*, p.65.
84 'composed of just': BB to OB, 22 June 1912, Esher Papers, 19/4.
85 'If you think': BB to VB, 22 June 1912, Esher Papers, 19/4.
85 'It is entirely': 14 June 1912, Brooke Papers, Vol.4.
86 'an awful come down': SB to RE, 12 July 1912, Brett Papers.

86 'our regality': 1 August 1912, 50529 GB Shaw Papers.
86 'old and crotchety': VB to RE, 12 July 1912, Esher Papers, 19/4.
86 'with a good head': RE to Lewis Harcourt, 27 July 1912, Harcourt Papers, Bodleian Library, Oxford.
86 'This is': ibid, 25 July 1912.
87 'see bogies': RE to MB, 23 July 1912, Esher Papers.
87 'The family attempt': RE to Lewis Harcourt, 11 July 1912, Esher Papers.
87 'He cannot afford': RE to OB, 17 July 1912, Esher Papers.
87 'felt this want': RE to VB, 24 July 1912, Esher Papers.
87 'profound State secret': SB to RE, 26 July 1912, Esher Papers, 19/4.
88 'quite indefinite': Lewis Harcourt to RE, 30 July 1912, Esher Papers.
88 'Covetous eyes': *Pall Mall Gazette*, 24 August 1912.
89 'hated the City': Lees-Milne, p.136.
89 'But why she': Lewis Harcourt to RE, 26 August 1912, Esher Papers.
89 'The essence': Arnold White to Charles Willes Johnson, 19 October 1912, Brooke Papers, Vol.4.
89 'Of course he is right': 26 August 1912, Esher Papers.
89 'entirely Sylvia's doing': 25 August 1912, Brooke Papers, Vol.4.
90 'I often wished': *Sylvia*, pp.181–2.
90 'old enough': RE to MB, 7 September 1912, Esher Papers.
90 'Eventually Vyner': BB to Charles Willes Johnson, 8 October 1912, Brooke Papers, Vol.4.
90 'very persistent': Charles Brooke to Charles Willes Johnson, 30 October 1912, Brooke Papers, Vol.4.
90 'My Dear Sylvia': Charles Brooke to SB, October 1912, Esher Papers.

CHAPTER 6

page
92 'in pink jacket': 12, 14 and 15 January 1913, Esher Papers.
92 'Tell me': SB to RE, 9 August 1913, Brett Papers.
93 '*He* vigorously': ibid, 18 October 1913.
93 'The rapprochement': Runciman, p.222.
93 'off during': SB to RE, 7 October 1913, Brett Papers.
93 'perversely female infant': 16 October 1913; *Sylvia*, pp.191–2.
93 'to such a degree': RE to MB, 5 September 1913, Esher Papers.
94 'a bit commonplace': ibid, 14 October 1913.
94 'Sylvia recalled': *Sylvia*, p.185.
94 'Every meal': SB to RE, 23 August 1913, Brett Papers.
94 'a long novel': ibid, 7 October 1913.
94 'hailed by one academic': Alan L. McLeod, 'Sylvia Brooke, Ranee of Sarawak: Pioneer Malaysian Feminist Writer', *Commonwealth*, Vol.22, Autumn 1999.

94 'just to give us': SB to RE, 11 September 1913, Brett Papers.
95 'Syv will ruin': 5 August 1912, Esher Papers.
95 'a kind of courage': *Our Selves Unknown*, p.31.
96 'Remember you are': *Queen*, pp.71–2.
97 'Doll had made': Dorothy Brett memoir; Hignett, p.57.
97 'I think Doll': SB to RE, 2 August 1912, Brett Papers.
98 'bulging with babies': Hignett, p.62.
98 'Sylvia later admitted': *Sylvia*, p.190.
98 'The richness of': Mark Gertler to Dora Carrington, 9 April 1914, Noel Carrington (ed.), *Mark Gertler: Selected Letters*, pp.66–7.
98 'R was full of forebodings': Eleanor Esher journal, Esher Papers, 3/1.
98 'deeply pre-occupied': *Sylvia*, p.193.
99 'My father was': *Queen*, p.73.
99 'had to be content': Kenneth Rose, *Kings, Queens and Courtiers*, p.101.
99 'The hospital': RE to MB, 13 December 1914, Esher Papers.
99 'the arch-cat': MB to RE, 24 April 1915, Esher Papers.
100 'Out in Sarawak': the account of this expedition is taken from A. B. Ward, *Rajah's Servant*, pp.158–63; Ward was one of the officers leading the expedition.
100 'who we know': R. H. W. Reece, *The White Rajahs of Sarawak*, p.82.
101 'On the dot as usual': *Queen*, p.83.
101 'His gaze rested': *Rajah's Servant*, p.164.
101 'may want me': VB to RE, 17 August 1915, Brett Papers.
102 'Vyner in Sarawak': SB to RE, 19 August 1915, Brett Papers.
102 'From what': RE to MB, 28 August 1915, Esher Papers.
102 'A girl, of course': *Sylvia*, p.198.
103 'a criminal offence': SB to RE, 7 January 1916, Brett Papers.
103 'I am really': RE to MB, 5 January 1916, Esher Papers.
103 'I had already': *Queen*, pp.78–80; *Sylvia*, pp.200–4.
104 'not doing this': SB to RE, 24 February 1916. Brett Papers.
106 'I can't talk': ibid, 21 May 1916.
107 'You haven't flattered': SB to Donald Owen, 10 October 1916, in 'Memoirs of Donald Adrian Owen', Rhodes House Library, MSS Pac s103.
108 'He had a fine': *Sylvia*, p.208.
109 'April 23rd, Sunday': Lady Ottoline Morrell's diary, 23 April 1917, British Library.
110 'opened this new vista': SB to RE, 16 July 1917, Brett Papers.
110 'Occasionally the Rajah': *Queen*, p.89.
111 'I cannot go through': 6 January 1917, Brooke Papers, Vol.25.
111 'Ward saw': *Rajah's Servant*, p.174.
112 'coughing up': BB to Charles Willes Johnson, 29 April 1917, Brooke Papers, Vol.4.

CHAPTER 7

page

113 'I have bad news': *Rajah's Servant*, pp.174–5.
113 'the spot selected': 18 October 1917, Brett Papers.
114 'firm, strong': *Rajah's Servant*, p.176.
115 'very seedy': Eleanor Esher to Chat Williamson, 28 September 1916, Esher Papers.
116 'The days of sons': SB to RE, 26 June 1917, Brett Papers.
116 'Of course you are right': ibid, 29 May 1917.
117 'the plotting': ibid, undated.
117 'I am not quite': ibid, 8 June 1917.
118 'You only remember': ibid, 11 August 1917.
118 'vile': DB to RE, 26 September and 25 December 1917, Brett Papers.
118 'licking her boots': ibid, 8 June 1917.
119 'giggling inwardly': SB to RE, undated, Brett Papers.
119 'absolutely despondent': ibid, 5 July 1917.
119 'I have done no wrong!!': ibid,11 July 1917.
119 'So we both': Mark Gertler to SB, 16 September 1917; *Sylvia*, pp.218–19.
120 'He asks me to': SB to RE, 11 August 1917, Brett Papers.
120 'There is': ibid, 25 September 1917.
121 'I find a little of Lady Ottoline': ibid, 16 July 1917.
121 'Lady Ottoline's entourage': ibid, 11 August 1917.
121 'drastic reductions': ibid, 18 October 1917.
122 'why so much food': ibid, 8 October 1917.
122 'They cannot and must not be Miss': ibid, 18 October 1917.
122 'she has only just': DB to RE, 20 January 1918, Brett Papers.
123 'crammed full': SB to RE, 5 February 1918, Brett Papers.
123 'as if some': *Queen*, pp.97–8.
124 'a very tolerable selection': *Sarawak Gazette*, 4 June 1918.
125 'At one point': *Queen*, p.102.
125 'to be touched': *Rajah's Servant*, p.181.

CHAPTER 8

page

127 'better than he': SB to RE, 26 October 1918, Brett Papers.
128 'the best thing': ibid, 26 October 1918.
128 'the world was': *Sylvia*, p.207.
128 'depictions hurtful': SB to RE, 9 June 1919, Brett Papers.
128 'It is better to be': RE to OB, 28 October 1920, Esher Papers.
128 'I think Maurice': OB to RE, 26 October 1920, Brett Papers.
128 'shadows in his life': *Toys*, p.117.
129 'Deborah was everything': *Toys*, p.116.
129 'When Doll sent': Hignett, p.114.
129 'almost unreadable': RE to Chat Williamson, 28 September 1920, Esher Papers.
129 'She is a clever': ibid, 12 March 1921.
129 'could not lay' and 'a consistent study': *Sylvia*, p.239.

129 'The idea is not': *Times Literary Supplement*, 18 October 1923.
130 'doing the things': handwritten fragment of memoir by Elizabeth Brooke Vidmer, 'The Reluctant Princesses' (1976), in the possession of her son, David Roy.
130 'It was one of': in 1923, the Rajah took on the former curator of the Kuching museum, J. C. Moulton, as his first chief secretary, and directed that all the residents' reports should go to him. 'The officers who had grown up with the Rajah were furious,' recalled one officer. 'They disliked Moulton intensely, called him "God" and expressed their feelings on their annual visit to the races in Kuching.' None of the Rajah's old friends, so skilled in practical administration, in fact proved that suited to the paper and committee work in the office of the chief secretary, and they came and went in quick succession – eight in twelve years. Undated note by E. Banks, Brooke Papers, Vol.17A.
130 'In the evening': Charles Allen, *Tales from the South China Seas*, p.142.
130 'a most terrible ordeal': *Queen*, p.106.
131 'At one time': Payne, p.169.
131 'Travelling with him': note by E. Banks, Brooke Papers, Vol.17A.
131 'chill unsuitable familiarity': Runciman, p.232.
131 'If the officer': Allen, pp.138–9.
131 'He never sought': Note by E. Banks, supra.
131 'strapped to his': SB to RE, 26 October 1918, Brett Papers.
132 'With small loss of life': *Sarawak Gazette*, 16 May 1919.
132 'lost no opportunity': Juliette Huxley, *Leaves of the Tulip Tree*, pp.67–8.
133 'entertaining your': Eleanor Esher to DB, 11 April 1919; Hignett, p.98.
133 'hereby not to': SB to RE, 13 April 1919, Brett Papers.
134 'to the ravings': ibid, 15 August 1919.
134 'swallowed whole': DB to Eleanor Esher, 15 April 1919, Brett Papers.
135 'to be dragged round': *Sylvia*, p.243.
135 'Doll would never': VB to RE, 3 August 1919, Brett Papers.
136 'no one could': Somerset Maugham, 'The Yellow Streak', *The Casuarina Tree*.
137 'Gifford yelled at him': In *A Writer's Notebook*, Maugham identified the only other white man in the boat apart from himself and Haxton as 'R', but the *Sarawak Gazette* confirms that it was Captain Barry Gifford, 2 May 1921, p.70.
137 'so that we': letter to a friend, reprinted in the *Sarawak Gazette*, 1 August 1921.
137 'Before leaving for Singapore': Somerset Maugham, *Writer's Notebook*, p.199.
139 'We woke at': *Queen*, pp.112–13.
140 'hardly true to': 8 May 1928,

Boyd Papers, Box 2/1, Rhodes House.

141 'formal and elaborate': *Time and Chance*, pp.88–9.

141 'part of his': *Queen*, pp.126–7.

142 'madly good-looking': Elizabeth Brooke Vidmer memoir.

142 'made love': *Queen*, p.135.

142 'I was curious': *Queen*, p.113.

143 'Finally she made me': Edward James, *Swans Reflecting Elephants*, pp.26–7.

143 'a dreadful affair': RE to OB, 26 February 1922, Esher Papers.

143 'an irreparable injury': 7 September 1921, Brett Papers.

143 'It is not easy': RE to MB, 8 June 1922, Esher Papers.

143 'she seemed much': MB to RE, 6 June 1922, Esher Papers.

144 'a perfect loony': Lees-Milne, p.328.

144 'It is now scotched': RE to MB, 26 and 31 October 1922, Esher Papers.

144 'If it comes off': ibid, 1 November 1922.

144 'Again Sylvia was unwell': ibid, 22 November 1923.

144 'must have been': Leonora Brooke Tompkins, *My Lovely Days*, p.13.

144 'I would try': ibid, pp.21–2.

145 'knew no harm': ibid, p.18. Sylvia could be similarly spartan in her treatment of her daughters, and Leonora once suffered a burst abscess in her ear after her mother sent her swimming 'with a raging earache', ibid, p.8.

145 'To start the ball rolling': ibid, p.18.

CHAPTER 9

page

147 'a mass of nerves': extracts from Nellie Boult's diary, in her letter to Anne Bryant, 2 January 1938, Brooke Papers, Box 11/1; *The Name of Brooke*, pp.20–2.

147 'shooting wildly': *Queen*, p.125.

148 'hurling his bedroom furniture': BB to Undersecretary of State for the Colonies, 13 November 1941, Brooke Papers, Box 20, file 1, ff20–5.

148 'his elder brother Jack': J. C. W. MacBryan topped the batting averages for Somerset for several seasons in the early 1920s, and in 1924 he was selected for England in the Test Match at Old Trafford against South Africa. Due to rain, only 66 overs were possible on the first day, with South Africa batting, after which the match was completely rained off. Jack MacBryan was dropped for the next match and never got another chance, despite being one of Wisden's Five Cricketers of the Year in 1925. Thus he earned the dubious distinction of being the only Test player never to have bowled, batted or made a catch. Previously, in 1920, he had won an Olympic gold medal playing hockey for Great Britain.

149 This account of Gerard MacBryan's early years is mostly based on letters from J. C. W. MacBryan to Margaret Noble, copies of which were lent to the author by Professor Nicholas Tarling.

149 'quite unaware': *Queen*, p.123.
149 'extraordinarily efficient': BB to Undersecretary of State for the Colonies, 13 November 1941, supra.
150 'amazing muscles': *Queen*, pp.115–16.
150 'the sprinkling of blood': *Sarawak Gazette*, 1 December 1924.
151 'asked Reggie Esher': VB to RE, 22 November 1918, Brett Papers.
151 'a sum which': Walter Ellis to Sir Lawrence Guillemard, 24 June 1927, CO 531/20 [31728].
151 'Let's all go': Elizabeth Brooke Vidmer memoir.
152 'God-like beings': *My Lovely Days*, p.8.
152 'We were often': ibid, p.9.
152 'It is no exaggeration': unidentified newspaper cutting in Sylvia's scrapbook, Brooke Papers, Box 16.
153 'Bohemian parties': *Sylvia*, p.245.
153 'It looks better': *Queen*, p.111.
153 'Syv came to': MB to RE, 8 October 1924, Esher Papers.
154 'Of course': RE to MB, 24 March 1925, Esher Papers.
154 'Poor little Syv's': ibid, 7 and 10 October 1927.
154 'in the Provinces': ibid, 18 October 1927.
155 'Her "plans" are bound': ibid, 8 April 1925.
155 'I suppose it is a "duty" visit': ibid, 3 November 1925.
155 'Syv's adventure': ibid, 19 May 1927.
155 'a very dull': ibid, 7 October 1927.
156 'shown marvellous vitality': RE to OB; 15 August 1925, Esher Papers.
156 'a brilliant book': *Sylvia*, p.254.
156 'ingeniously macabre': *Times Literary Supplement*, 17 September 1925, p.601.
156 'These shell-shocked men': *Sylvia*, p.212.
157 'Barry soaks whisky': 7–13 October 1927, Esher Papers.
157 'Here, look after': *Sylvia*, p.253.
157 'marry Ivy Duke': *Sarawak Gazette*, 1 October 1930.
158 'impressed everyone': *Rajah's Servant*, p.182.
158 'terribly changeable': Stirling Boyd to his father, 29 August 1928, Boyd Papers, Box 2/1.
158 'one of the most superficial': Stirling Boyd to his mother, 4 March 1929, Boyd Papers, Box 2/1.
158 'He had a method': *Sarawak Gazette*, 2 January 1931, p.9.
159 'dabbled in journalism': *Daily Express*, 22 March 1929; *Sunday Graphic*, 7 April 1929.
159 'clumsily constructed': *Sylvia*, p.262.
159 'They are': Stirling Boyd to his mother, 31 July 1929, Boyd Papers, Box 2/1.
159 'sparing both of': *Times Literary Supplement*, 26 June 1930.
159 'My Dear Ranee': Sir Frederick Ponsonby to Margaret Brooke, 7 November 1928, Brooke Papers, Vol.16, p.46. Ponsonby's wife Ria was Ranee Margaret's closest friend; however, as Treasurer and

Keeper of the King's Privy Purse, Ponsonby himself was a great admirer of Reggie Esher, which may explain why he makes general remarks about the 'younger generation', rather than criticising Sylvia directly.

160 'It really is': 7 November 1928, Brooke Papers, Vol.16, p.62.

160 'no intention whatsoever': *Sarawak Gazette*, 1 December 1928.

160 'She rules over': unidentified newspaper cutting from Sylvia's scrapbook, Brooke Papers, Box 16.

160 'I have my finger': SB to DB, 'Feb 11th', no year, HRHRC.

161 'Your uncle was monarch': 10 August 1927, Brooke Papers, Vol.18A.

161 'persuaded to give up his claim': *The Name of Brooke*, p.19; Esca renewed his claim again after the cession – see CO 537/1632, ff 142–76.

162 'No, no babies': *Queen*, p.102.

162 'Women make the': 16 October 1913, quoted in *Sylvia*, p.192.

162 'appointed him GCMG': Knight Grand Cross, Order of St Michael and St George.

162 'Only daughters, sir': Margaret Brooke to Sir Frederick Ponsonby, 21 February 1934, Brooke Papers, Vol.40, file 1; *The Name of Brooke* p.29.

162 'I see Sylvia': *Relations and Complications*, pp.134–5.

163 'appeared to protest': SB to BB, 8 July 1940, Brooke Papers, Vol.36, file 1, pp.3–4.

163 'MacBryan's rise': J. C. W. MacBryan to Margaret Noble, supra.

163 'Police Constables': Gerard MacBryan to Stirling Boyd, 28 November 1928, Boyd Papers, Box 3/1.

163 'both ambitious and': *Queen*, p.138.

163 'I know MacBryan': notes by Margaret Noble for Cedric Drewe, MP, in confidence, Brooke Papers, Vol.41; Margaret Noble was the wife of the general manager of Sarawak Oilfields Ltd and a good friend of Vyner and Sylvia until she fell out with them over the cession in 1946. The notes were prepared in connection with the cession, which was debated at Westminster.

164 'MacBryan had already': BB to Undersecretary of State for the Colonies, 13 November 1941, Brooke Papers, Box 20, file 1, ff20–5.

164 'as was alleged': *The Name of Brooke*, p.24.

164 'making violent love': SB to BB, 8 July 1940, Brooke Papers, Vol.36, file 1.

165 'When Elizabeth': notes by Margaret Noble for Cedric Drewe, supra.

165 'But MacBryan subsequently': memorandum by Eva MacBryan, 1947; *The Name of Brooke*, p.26n.

165 'One can't help': Stirling Boyd to his mother, 18 February 1929, Boyd Papers, Box 2/1.

165 'I don't suppose': ibid, 22 January 1929.

166 'he understood the undertow':

conversation with Lord Tanlaw, 20 September 2005.

166 'Hatred and resentment': note by Edward Banks, Brooke Papers, Vol.17A.

166 'a cleverer man': notes by Margaret Noble for Drewe in confidence, Brooke Papers, Vol.41, supra.

167 'Vyner later maintained': VB to Sir Shenton Thomas, 19 February 1937, Brooke Papers, Vol.36, file 1, fol. 11.

CHAPTER 10

page

168 'I had never': *Queen*, p.119; Lees-Milne, p.352.

168 'It is really only': SB to DB, 11 February 1930, HRHRC.

169 'transferred his worship': Lees-Milne, p.351.

169 'No man has ever': Lees-Milne, p.355.

169 'Dignity does not enter': RE to Chat Williamson, 12 March 1921, Esher Papers.

170 'They had all': *Queen*, p.126.

170 'everything the three Princesses': *Queen*, p.119.

170 'cheapened and ridiculed': *The Three White Rajas*, p.296.

171 'Everything in this obscure': see *Sarawak Gazette*, 2 January 1931. Mjöberg book.

171 'is a very important': Sir Lawrence Guillemard 1927/28, CO 531/20.

171 'entirely impossible': SB to RE, 20 May 1912, Brett Papers.

171 'The idea of an adviser': Nicholas Tarling, 'Britain and Sarawak in the Twentieth Century', *Journal of the Malayan Branch of the Royal Asiatic Society*, Vol.XLIII, Part 2, December 1970.

171 'Nor, to begin with': Nicholas Tarling, 'Sir Cecil Clementi and the Federation of British Borneo', *Journal of the Malayan Branch of the Royal Asiatic Society*, Vol.XLIV, Part 2, December 1971.

172 'no longer a': *The Three White Rajas*, p.161.

172 'a marble-slabbed': *Time and Chance*, p.88.

172 'because there was a cake': Stirling Boyd to Thomson, 24 January 1932, Boyd Papers, Box 2/5, fol. 26.

173 'I don't imagine': Stirling Boyd to his mother, 3 October 1929, Boyd Papers, Box 2.

173 'Asun eventually': Runciman, p.240.

173 'though he had earlier': Stirling Boyd to Geoffrey Hope, 26 December 1936, Boyd Papers, Box 2/7.

173 'Masses of Europeans': VB to Anne Brooke, 28 December 1932, Brooke Papers, Vol.37, fol. 2.

173 'knock off the stengahs': Boyd Papers, Box 2/5, fol. 26.

174 'threatening to paint': 20 March 1932, Boyd Papers, Box 2/5.

174 'half-encircled by': Richard Halliburton, *The Flying Carpet*.

175 'I hadn't time to protest': *Sarawak Gazette*.

176 'asking new recruits': R. H. W. Reece, *The White Rajahs of Sarawak*, p.98.

176 'being run by': Stirling Boyd to A. W. Cockburn, 1 March 1932, Boyd Papers, Box 2/5.

176 'charming and kind': *Sylvia*, pp.259–60.
176 'most prodigiously plain': SB to DB, undated (1932), HRHRC.
176 'With regard to': T. Morand to Margaret Brooke, Brooke Papers, Vol.16, fol. 36.
177 'Ranee Margaret was visited': Margaret Brooke to Frederick Ponsonby, 21 February 1934, Brooke Papers, Vol.40.
177 'After his resignation': see Jack MacByran's letters to Margaret Noble (supra) and wartime intelligence report on MacBryan, written by B. J. C. Spurway, Brooke Papers, Box 2/3.
177 'the claims of his wife': memorandum by Edward Gent, 27 January 1937, National Archives, CO 531/27/6.
178 'with the smartness': *Sarawak Gazette*, 1 March 1935.
179 'this long journey': *Sylvia*, p.271.
179 'dull little girl': *Sylvia*, pp.209 and 250.
179 'He had been born': *Dictionary of National Biography*, 2004.
179 'London's loudest-blowing': *Time*, 26 August 1935.
180 'an uncertain and uneven': *Sylvia*, pp.266–7.
180 'Quite OK Eliza': *Time*, 26 August 1935. Stirling Boyd assumed it was the Ranee who had leaked the Rajah's cable to the press: 'Who else could have done so?' he wrote to A. W. Cockburn. 'She seems to have a mania for publicity in cheapest and sloppiest form.' 16 June 1935, Boyd papers, Box 2/7, fol. 14.
180 'letting the blue blood': *Sylvia*, p.267.
180 'all rather awkward': BB to Anne Brooke, 26 July 1935, Brooke Papers, Box 28, file 2.
180 'She's a dear': ibid, 12 August 1935.
181 'His Highness the Rajah's': *Sarawak Gazette*, 2 September 1935; *The Name of Brooke*, p.96.
181 'Seldom has a': *Daily Mail*, 7 August 1935.
182 'It did become': Charles Allen, *Tales from the South China Seas*, p.138.
182 'she photographs marvellously': *Sunday Graphic*, 8 December 1935.
182 'He was told firmly': VB to Sir Shenton Thomas, 19 February 1937, CO 531/27/6.
183 'discarded by': Boyd to Cockburn, 5 December 1937, Boyd Papers, Box 2/7, fol.135.
183 'given the name': *Sarawak Gazette*, 2 December 1935.
183 'almost megalomaniac' *Queen*, pp.138–9.
184 'MacBryan was warned': Boyd to Noel Hudson, 17 May 1936, Boyd Papers, Box 2/7.
184 'lodged a complaint': MacBryan invoked Article V of the Protectorate Agreement (1888) between Sarawak and Britain which stipulated: 'British subjects, commerce and shipping shall enjoy the same rights and privileges and advantages as the subjects, commerce and shipping of the most favoured nation, as

well as any other rights, privileges and advantages which may be enjoyed by the subjects, commerce and shipping of the State of Sarawak.'

184 'exposé of Brooke rule': note by BB on MacBryan, Brooke Papers, Box 20, file 1, ff3–4; and BB to Undersecretary of State for the Colonies, 13 November 1941, Box 20/1, ff20–5.

184 'quite impossible': VB to Sir Shenton Thomas, 19 February 1937, CO 531/27/6.

184 'he would be pleased': Gerard MacBryan to Permanent Under-secretary of State, Colonial Office, 6 January 1937, CO 531/27/6.

184 'solemn word': Gerard MacBryan to VB, 24 June 1936, CO 531/27/6.

184 'Dear Baron': VB to Gerard MacBryan, 26 June 1936, CO 531/27/6.

185 'adaptability': *Times Literary Supplement*, 10 October 1936, p.807.

185 'superintending': DB to Una Jeffers, 28 September 1936, University of California, Berkeley.

186 'one of the last': *The Times*, 2 December 1936.

186 'passing of a': *Sunday Times*, 6 December 1936.

186 'Another newspaper': *Evening News*, 1 December 1936.

186 'My Dear Baron': 29 December 1936, CO 531/27/6.

187 'clear the stigma': 6 January 1937, CO 531/27/6.

187 'in order to give': Gerard MacBryan to H. R. Cowell, 25 January 1937, CO 531/27/6.

188 'theatrically-worded': memorandum by H. R. Cowell, 23 March 1937, CO 531/27/6.

188 'and that he': BB to Under-secretary of State for the Colonies, 13 November 1941, Brooke Papers, Box 20/1, ff 20–5.

188 'Sylvia's unspecified': *The Name of Brooke*, p.28.

CHAPTER 11

page

189 'treated like royalty': *Sarawak Gazette*, 1 May 1937.

190 'ability to bluff': see Lionel Godfrey, *The Life and Crimes of Errol Flynn*.

190 'an absurdity': *Queen*, pp.133–4.

190 'stilled his sexual passions': there is still debate about the nature of the first Rajah's wound. The modern consensus seems to be that he was shot through the lung, and that the story about the wound to his groin had been put about to hide the fact that he was homosexual – or at least bisexual. In support of this is the fact that James Brooke acknowledged a natural son, Reuben George Brooke, who was born in 1834, well after his wounding, the result – so it was alleged – of a liaison with a maid at his father's house. He seemed to genuinely believe himself to be the father, although some of his contemporaries suspected Reuben was simply a new protégé and James wanted an

excuse to show an interest in him. See Nigel Barley, *White Rajah*, pp.12–13; Runciman, p.136.

191 Flynn was paid: *Errol Flynn* by Michael Freedland (1978), p.80.

191 'technical advisor': *Port Arthur News*, Texas, 5 December 1937.

191 'But she never': Hignett, p.217.

191 'odder than ever': Aldous Huxley to Julian Huxley, 3 June 1937; Hignett, p.229.

191 'My sister tells me': DB to Una Jeffers, 4 March 1937, University of California, Berkeley; Hignett, p.230.

192 'Like most of my friends': Harry Richman, *A Hell of a Life*, p.197.

192 'my beloved boy': SB to DB, undated, late December 1939; SB to DB, 22 January 1941, HRHRC.

193 'whispered to be Cuban': Stirling Boyd to Wilson, 12 December 1937, Boyd Papers, Box 2/7; Boyd hazarded that Gregory had changed his name.

193 'like tarts': Boyd to Ruth Waterhouse, 9 January 1938, Boyd Papers, Box 2/7.

193 'moral training': Boyd to Hugh-Jones, 9 February 1938, Boyd Papers, Box 2/7.

193 'The Siren of Sarawak': *Oakland Tribune*, 5 January 1939.

194 'by her account': *Sunday Pictorial*, 7 January 1940.

194 'Babaland': *Time*, 5 February 1940.

195 'strangely uncurious': interview with AB, 2004.

195 'Everyone is bewilderingly embarrassing': AB to Jean Halsey, 28 June 1934, Brooke Papers, Vol.36, file 2.

196 'The sooner Vyner': 16 October 1913, quoted in *Sylvia*, p.192.

196 'desirous of divesting': 'secret' minute by Gent, 20 July 1938, CO/531/28/6.

196 'figure of £5 million': Thackwell Lewis to AB, 27 February 1946, Brooke Papers, Box 2/3; *The Name of Brooke*, p.102.

197 'The Rajah did not': note by Edward Gent, 21 July 1938, National Archives, CO 531/28/6.

198 'sang their farewell': *Sarawak Gazette*, 1 February 1939.

198 'the appeal of': *The Times*, 10 February 1939, p.20.

198 'appeal to the': *Times Literary Supplement*, 11 February 1939, p.83.

198 'still Princess Baba': *Time*, 1 May 1939.

198 'doing physical jerks': *Queen*, pp.130–1.

198 'The previous autumn': *San Franscisco Chronicle*, 27 October 1938.

199 'She had something': *Queen*, p.131.

199 'Mussolini and Hitler': AB to Jean Halsey, 24 April 1939, Brooke Papers, Box 12/11; *The Name of Brooke*, p.66.

199 'not exactly a model': when Boyd's successor, Thackwell Lewis, read the file of the investigation, he was appalled by the 'shocking irregularity of the proceedings and the improper treatment which was meted out to the most senior officers in the service who were quite

obviously being forced to tender resignations'; apart from that 'there was the apparent moral obliquy of the Rajah himself as shown in the correspondence'. It was perfectly clear to Thackwell Lewis that the Rajah was shirking his responsibility and getting Anthony Brooke to do the dirty work. See note by H. Thackwell Lewis, 3 March 1942, Brooke Papers, Vol.33, file 1, item 15.

200 'He has a Japanese wife': Sir Shenton Thomas to Malcolm Macdonald, 19 April 1939, CO 531/29/3.

200 'Breen's report': CO 531/27/4.

201 'the father of his people': CO 537/1631.

201 'Sarawak is a territory': note by Edward Gent, 23 May 1939 and 3 May 1939, CO 531/29/3.

201 'The Ranee is a dangerous woman': minute by Dufferin, 26 May 1939, CO 531/29.

202 'longing to be back with': SB to DB, 24 September 1939, HRHRC.

202 'I think all the': ibid, 30 September 1939.

202 'debts of $7,000': R. A. B. Mynors to A. E. Forrest, 11 March 1942, CO 531/30/1; *The Name of Brooke*, p.73.

202 'it would break': SB to DB, 21 November 1939, HRHRC.

203 'out every night': ibid, 3 November 1939.

203 'I hope to God': ibid, 18 December 1939.

203 'together like Scrooges': ibid, undated.

204 'Why the heck': *Queen*, p.136.

204 'Rajah left in a huff': Stirling Boyd to Sir John Kerr, 15 February 1940, Boyd Papers, Box 3/6.

204 'disturbing reports': BB to GB, 31 January 1940, Brooke Papers, Box 2/2.

204 'another man': Stirling Boyd to Sir John Kerr, 15 February 1940, supra.

204 'flavour of the day': correspondence with author, 27 March 2006.

205 'symptoms of': *Queen*, p.140.

205 'Master Peter': Stirling Boyd to Sir John Kerr, 15 February 1940, supra.

205 'No one could have': BB to GB, 31 January 1940, Brooke Papers, Vol.26, file 2.

206 'extraordinarily generous': VB to AB, 29 and 30 October 1939, Brooke Papers, Vol.26, file 2; *The Name of Brooke*, p.29.

CHAPTER 12

page

207 'I knew the nephew': Associated Press, 23 January 1940.

207 'pretty sure': *Daily Express*, 24 January 1940.

207 'Good Gad!': minute by Edward Gent, 24 January 1940, CO 531/29/3.

207 'this rotten cheap': AB to Jean Halsey, 7 February 1940, Brooke Papers, Vol.36, file 3.

208 'If you would': AB to R. N. Greenwood, 3 February 1940, Brooke Papers, Vol.36, file 5.

209 'in the interests': AB to BB, 20 February 1940, Brooke Papers, Vol.26, file 2.

209 'my views on': OE to DB, 16 January 1940, HRHRC.
209 'one of the last': *The Times*, 8 February 1940.
209 'I must say': SB to DB, 22 March 1940, HRHRC.
210 'yelling for me': ibid, 22 March 1940.
210 'branded for life': BB to GB 31 January 1940, Brooke Papers, Vol.26, file 2.
210 VB to AB, 4 March 1940, Brooke Papers, Vol.26, file 2.
210 'There's an Indian': BB to Margaret Noble, 21 August 1940, Brooke Papers, Vol.26, file 2.
210 'quite politely': note by BB, 23 October 1941, Brooke Papers, Vol.36.
211 'I am so glad': SB to BB, 8 July 1940, Brooke Papers, Vol.36.
212 'MacBryan then applied': unsigned Colonial Office note, 6 April 1941, CO 531/30/10 (folio 39).
212 'accidentally': note by BB on Lane's report about MacBryan, Brooke Papers, Vol.37, file 2.
213 'reached a settlement': BB to Undersecretary of State for the Colonies, 15 November 1941, CO 513/30/10.
213 'a cloak to conceal': AB to Edward Gent, 4 August 1942, CO 531/30/13; *The Name of Brooke*, p.35. Having convinced himself that there was nothing in Brunei custom or Mohammedan law that precluded the enthronement of female issue, the Sultan had anointed his daughter as heir-apparent and in 1937 he had his wazirs sign a document recognising her succession. However, this was overridden when he died in 1950, and he was succeeded by Sir Omar Ali Saiffuddin Saadul Khairi Waddien, whereupon MacBryan wrote a letter of protest to *The Times*. See 'Funeral of the Sultan of Brunei', by A. M. Grier, Rhodes House, MSS Pac s77, and letter from MacBryan to *The Times*, 26 October 1950.
213 'If this was the case': VB to BB, 4 July 1950, Brooke Papers, Box 5, cited by Crisswell, *The End of the Brooke Raj in Sarawak*, p.73.
213 'rumoured to have': *Masa Jepun*, p.16; report on G. T. M. MacBryan by Colonel Lane, Brooke Papers, Vol.37, file 2.
214 'Vyner was able': See BB's note on above report, Brooke Papers, Vol.37, file 2.
214 'hopeless way that': SB to DB, 17 August 1940, HRHRC.
214 'I really think': ibid, 29 September 1940.
215 'a definite job': SB to Anthony Eden, 11 December 1940, FO 954/29A.
215 'her blue blood' *Time*, 7 October 1940.
215 'my old prim': SB to DB, 2 January 1941, HRHRC.
215 'In February': ibid, 10 April 1941.
215 'walked the streets': Associated Press, 4 August 1941.
215 'one of the most': *Queen*, p.137.
217 'The acting treasurer': Thackwell Lewis to AB, 27

February 1946, Brooke Papers, Box 10/1, ff32–6. See also enclosure 14 of 'The First Constitution of Sarawak', Brooke Papers, Vol.26, file 1.

217 'Dear Pitt': personal communication from C. Pitt-Hardacre to R. H. W. Reece, 3 October 1976; see *The Name of Brooke*, p.74. See also enclosure 14 of 'The First Constitution . . .', supra.

217 'who no doubt': note by Thackwell Lewis, 3 March 1942, Brooke Papers, Box 6/1, item 15.

217 'pension for life': *The Name of Brooke*, p.74.

218 'exceedingly gratified': enclosures 1–5 of 'The First Constitution . . .', supra.

218 'any advice': AB to J. B. Archer, 19 March 1941, enclosure 6 of 'The First Constitution . . .', supra.

219 'In return for all this': AB, *Facts About Sarawak*, pp.30–2.

219 'After the royal': note by H. Thackwell Lewis, supra.

219 'I have always': *Sarawak Gazette*, 1 April 1941.

219 'invested the officers': note by H. Thackwell Lewis, supra.

220 'It was rumoured': Thackwell Lewis to AB, 27 February 1946, Brooke Papers, Vol.26, file 3; *The Name of Brooke*, p.77.

220 'undue haste': note by Thackwell Lewis, 3 March 1942, Brooke Papers, Vol.33, file 1, item 15.

220 'paid £10,000': report on MacBryan by Colonel Lane, Brooke Papers, Vol.37, file 2, ff 25–8, and notes thereon by Bertram Brooke; see also Pepys's report after visit to Sarawak, 28 June 1941, CO 531/30/10.

220 'as the Government': Shenton Thomas to Lord Moyne, 1 April 1941, CO 531/129/23; *The Name of Brooke*, p.117.

220 'might be wiser': ibid, 20 May 1941, CO 531/29/23; *The Name of Brooke*, p.118.

220 'pitchforked into': report by W. E. Pepys after visit to Sarawak, 28 June 1941, CO 531/30/10.

221 'It has just about': G. E. Bettison, Sarawak Diary 1939–41, Rhodes House, MSS Pac s56; *The Name of Brooke*, p.82.

221 'could not help': *Queen*, p.142.

221 'Rajah James cannot': 2 May 1941, Brooke Papers, Vol.37, file 2, f4.

222 'Because the present system': BB, 'Self Government for Sarawak', 10 May 1941, Brooke Papers, Box 11/2; *The Name of Brooke*, p.83.

222 'in a small': AB to BB, 19 August 1941, 'The First Constitution of Sarawak', enclosure 46, Brooke Papers, Vol.26, file 1.

223 'merely a junior': J. B. Archer to AB, 21 April 1941, ibid, enclosure 25.

223 'this impersonal': AB to Cyril Le Gros Clark, 8 July 1941, ibid, enclosure 29.

223 'He even admitted': note by Thackwell Lewis, 3 March 1942, Brooke Papers, Vol.33, and

report by W. E. Pepys, 28 June 1941, supra.
223 'seeing death': K. H. Digby to A. R. Thomas, 14 May 1941, CO 531/30/4; *The Name of Brooke*, p.81.
223 'a background of intrigue': enclosure 56 of 'The First Constitution . . .', Vol.26, file 1.
224 'in a green-gold': Associated Press, 4 August 1941.
224 'looking very fit': VB to BB, 26 August 1941, Brooke Papers, Box 19, file 8.
224 'telegraphed': VB to BB, 19 September 1941 and BB to VB, 22 September 1941, Brooke Papers, Vol.26, file 3.
225 'my nephew': minutes of Supreme Council meeting, 25 September 1941, Brooke Papers, Box 10/4.
225 'ridiculous': BB to VB, 8 June 1943, Brooke Papers, Box 19, file 8.
225 'wonderful simplicity': SB to DB, 29 September 1941, HRHRC.
226 'in view of': memorandum by Thackwell Lewis, sent to AB on 27 February 1946, Brooke Papers, Vol.26, file 1, ff32–6.
226 'badly needed': VB to Sir Ronald Cross, 31 January 1942, CO 531/30/21.

CHAPTER 13

page
228 'expected Britain': *The Name of Brooke*, p.123.
229 'totally inadequate': J. L. Noakes, 'Report on Defence Measures adopted in Sarawak from June 1941 to the Occupation in December 1941 . . .' quoted in *The Name of Brooke*, p.123 (typescript in possession of Professor Bob Reece).
229 'There have been too many retreats': ibid.
230 'returning to Sarawak': SB to DB, 3 November 1941, HRHRC.
230 'everything the Japs': Associated Press, 19 December 1941.
230 'Nine-Year-Old Boy': *Daily Mirror*, 3 December 1941, *The Name of Brooke*, p.93.
230 'ridiculous': BB to VB, 8 June 1943, Brooke Papers, Box 19, file 8.
230 'just reached Sydney': VB to BB, 31 December 1941, Brooke Papers, Box 19, file 8.
230 'I deeply regret': VB to Cyril Le Gros Clark, 16 December 1941, Australian Archives, A 981, quoted in *The Name of Brooke*, p.164.
231 'a spitfire of a man': VB to BB, 31 December 1941, Brooke Papers, Box 19, file 8.
231 'the most skilled jungle men': VB to Sir Ronald Cross, 31 January 1942, CO 531/30/21.
231 'I think natives': VB to BB, 31 December 1941, supra.
232 'letter of credence': VB to G. T. M. MacBryan and 'Whom It May Concern', 30 December 1941, Brooke Papers, Box 5, file 1.
232 'in no uncertain': account of the Japanese invasion of Sarawak, by John Gilbert, Brooke Papers, Vol.27.

232 'Further tension': secret report by B. A. Trechman, 23 December 1941 to 18 January 1942, Brooke Papers, Box 5, file 1.
232 'Quisling on his way': report on G. T. M. MacBryan, Brooke Papers, Vol.27.
232 'confiscated': VB to Sir Ronald Cross, 31 January 1942, supra.
232 'shot on the spot': account of the invasion of Japanese Sarawak, by John Gilbert, supra.
233 'On 11 January': VB to Sir Ronald Cross, 31 January 1942, supra.
233 'It is possible': minute by Gent, 9 May 1941, CO 531/30/4; *The Name of Brooke*, pp.165–6.
233 'refuted by Lord Moyne': Ronald Cross to VB, 13 February 1942, CO 531/30/21.
233 'my special messages': telegram from H. C. (High Commission) Australia to D. O. (Dominions Office), 2 February 1942, CO 531/30/21.
234 'bemused the Colonial Office': minute by Monson, 25 December 1941, CO 531/30/1.
234 'titled fools': *People*, 7 December 1941.
234 'We all knew': *Evening News*, 19 February 1942, *The Times*, 20 February 1942. Edward Gent at the Colonial Office observed that the exaggerated remarks were 'a good example of the Ranee's style'. 'In fact a number of the British officers in the Sarawak Service made their way to Dutch territory, and indeed a quorum of the Supreme Council has collected in Australia with the Rajah. The Rajah has not been missing since he left the State early in October last. The Kuching airfield was being used by reconnaissance aeroplanes of the RAF until the Japanese arrived.' Minute by Gent, 20 February 1942, National Archives, CO 531/30/1.
235 'Neither of them': OE to DB, 22 January 1942, HRHRC.
235 'I hope to goodness': ibid, 28 August 1944.
235 'no chance of Mop': SB to DB, 27 June 1942, HRHRC.
235 'driving was something': *My Lovely Days*, p.83.
235 'hanged himself': *My Lovely Days*, p.96.
235 'fell over a cliff': *My Lovely Days*, pp.101–2.
235 'free and lonely': *My Lovely Days*, p.104.
236 'they all brought us presents': conversation with Lady Rosemary French, 12 May 2006.
236 'standing in a confusion': *Queen*, p.147.
236 'the Ranee': minute by Edward Gent, 3 February 1942, CO 531/30/1.
236 'Shortly afterwards': R. A. B. Mynors to A. E. Forrest, 11 March 1942, CO 531/30/1.
236 'it seems to be': minute by W. B. L. Monson, 3 March 1942, CO 531/30/1.
237 thwarted ambition: *Queen*, p.145.
237 'I have it with two pals': quoted in *Time* magazine, 11 May 1942.
237 'cut away entirely': SB to Jack Golden, 4 July 1942, CO 531/30/1.

237 'doing my own chores': VB to Jean Halsey, 31 July 1942, Brooke Papers, Box 10.
238 'the winding up': note by H. Thackwell Lewis, 3 March 1942, Brooke Papers, Vol.33, file 1, item 15.
238 'wish me back': VB to BB, 24 March 1942, Brooke Papers, Box 19.
238 'In April': memorandum signed by VB, Brooke Papers, Box 5, file 1.
238 'would fall in': VB to Cecil Pitt-Hardacre, 3 April 1942, Brooke Papers. Vol.36, file 1, item 17.
239 'Bertram suspected': note by BB on letter from VB to Pitt-Hardacre, 3 April 1942, Brooke Papers, Vol.36, file 1.
239 'prevailed upon the': AB to Edward Gent, 28 April 1942, Brooke Papers, Box 19.
239 'I wish': SB to Jack Golden, 15 June 1942, CO 531/30/1.
239 'It may so happen': ibid, 4 July 1942.
240 'why I feel': ibid, 17 July 1942.
240 'some crack-brained': minute by Leslie Monson, 21 July 1942, CO 531/30/1.
240 'like mystery': minute by J. L. Lloyd, 21 July 1942, CO 531/30/1.
240 'she is a neurotic': minute by Gent, date illegible, CO 531/30/1; see also Information Sheet on G. T. M. MacBryan, Brooke Papers, Vol.30; and *The Name of Brooke*, pp.100 and 168–9.
240 'presumed to be Pitt-Hardacre': minute by Monson, 30 July 1942, CO 531/30/1; VB to Lord Cranborne, 24 October 1942, Brooke Papers, Vol.30.
241 'a kind of evil genius': undated 'secret' note by AB, following lunch with Ranee in summer 1945, Brooke Papers, Vol.30, f 186.
241 'cruel and unjust': SB to Lord Cranborne, 25 September 1942, CO 531/30/1.
241 'Once again': Colonial Office note, 19 October 1942, CO 531/30/1.
241 'Americans DO like': SB to Anthony Eden, 11 December 1940, FO 954/29A.
241 'I get on with Americans': SB to DB, 27 June 1942, HRHRC.
241 'a dither of excitement': *My Lovely Days*, p.110.
242 'very sweet': SB to DB, 12 April 1943, HRHRC.
242 'knew his way': *Queen*, p.151.
242 'their two children': Sylvia already had high hopes for her granddaughter Roberta: 'a slim graceful little girl,' Sylvia told Doll, 'with enormous black eyes' and 'a fascinating speaking voice and will I think when trained make a wonderful Film Star. She acts all the time. She doesn't live on earth at all but in a world of her own.'
242 'he doesn't seem': SB to DB, 27 June 1942, HRHRC.
242 'I thank God': ibid, 12 April 1943; *Queen*, p.151.
243 'If I were you': OE to DB; 21 July 1943, HRHRC.
243 'I could see nothing': *Queen*, p.148.
244 'prevented from using': VB to

General Douglas MacArthur, 28 September 1942, Brooke Papers, Vol.30.
244 'confidential agent': VB to Roy Kendall, 12 October 1942, Brooke Papers, Vol.27, file 3.
244 'A plenipotentiary': BB to VB, 26 January 1943, Brooke Papers, Box 19.
245 'I must say': SB to DB, 12 April 1943, HRHRC.
245 'painting BOMBERS': DB to OE, 3 March 1943, quoted in Hignett, p.237.
245 'I paint in the mornings': DB to Dorothy Norman, 10 March 1943, quoted in Hignett, p.237.
245 'wangle': DB to OE, 5 July 1943, quoted in Hignett, p.238.
245 'jolly good care': OE to DB, 19 September 1942, HRHRC.
246 'much amused': OE to DB, 1 November 1942, HRHRC.
246 'poor silly pompous': SB to DB, 12 April 1943, HRHRC.
246 'Nothing will': ibid, 27 June 1942.
246 'thrilled to death': ibid, 12 April 1943.
247 'I like her': ibid, 16 May 1944.
247 'too good an': ibid, 12 April 1943.
247 'made a glorious': ibid, 1 June 1945.
247 'gave it to him': VB to BB, 2 July 1943, Brooke Papers, Vol.30.
247 'convince you of': Gerard MacBryan to BB, 14 July 1943, Brooke Papers, Vol.30.
248 'I think I can': SB to Oliver Stanley, undated, CO 531/30/1.
248 'had no hesitation': minute by Monson, 10 December 1943, CO 531/30/1.
248 'The war is': SB to DB, 16 May 1944, HRHRC.

CHAPTER 14

page
249 'If I elected': VB to BB, 23 November 1943, Brooke Papers, Vol.30.
249 VB to BB, undated, Brooke Papers, Box 19, file 8.
250 'not too soon': Oliver Stanley to VB, 19 June 1944, Brooke Papers, Vol.30; *Facts About Sarawak*, pp.65–6.
250 'Aplin reported': résumé of relations between His Majesty's Government and the Government of Sarawak since June 1944, Brooke Papers, Vol.30; Aplin to VB, 25 July 1944, Brooke Papers, Vol.21A.
250 'I should be': VB to Oliver Stanley, 3 August 1944, Brooke Papers, Vol.30; *Facts About Sarawak*, pp.66–7.
251 'no septuagenarian's': BB to AB, 21 May 1944, WO 203/3973.
251 'the old boy': AB to Kathleen Brooke, 29 June 1944, quoted in *The Name of Brooke*, p.179.
251 'In November': ibid, 7 November 1944.
251 're-educating the': ibid, *The Name of Brooke*, pp.180–1.
251 'Soon after': *Facts About Sarawak*, pp.5–6.
252 'in the hour': 26 November 1944, WO 203/3973.
252 'almost insurmountable': minute by Paskin, 3 January 1945, CO 531/31 [2344].

252 'Letters went': *Facts About Sarawak*, p.6.
252 'raising': Oliver Stanley to AB, 7 March 1945, Brooke Papers, Vol.30.
253 'unfortunately': 19 July 1945, Brooke Papers, Vol.30.
253 'exceedingly friendly': undated 'secret' note by AB following lunch with the Ranee in summer 1945, Brooke Papers, Vol.30, f186.
254 'I am genuinely': undated letter from SB to AB, Brooke Papers, Vol.30.
254 'By the end of August': Gerard MacBryan to VB, 31 August 1945, Brooke Papers, Vol.30.
254 'in our formal': note headed 'Previous Cabinet Policy Towards Sarawak', National Archives, CO 537/1632, ff297–8.
255 'questioned him closely': *Queen*, p.150.
255 'We could of course': SB to DB, 4 July 1946, HRHRC.
255 'However, his eventual': VB to Secretary of State, 1 November 1945, CO 537/1634.
255 'It isn't an': 8 September 1945, Brooke Papers, Box 19, file 3.
256 'Two days after': VB to Provisional Government, 10 September 1945, Brooke Papers, Box 21/1.
256 'Such plans as': minutes of Sixty Fourth meeting of the Sarawak Commission, 22 September 1945, Box 21/2.
256 'a direct affront': 4 October 1945, Brooke Papers, Vol.21A.
256 'deeply shocked': VB to AB, 12 October 1945, quoted in *Queen*, pp.149–50.
256 'our lunches': SB to AB, 23 October 1945, Box 19, file 3, ff 17–18.
257 'interfere in the': *Daily Telegraph*, 3 January 1947.
257 'petty and stupid': BB to VB, 29 January 1946, Brooke Papers, Vol.21A.
257 'very influential friends': Arthur Bryant to AB, 15 January 1945, Brooke Papers, Box 19, file 3.
257 'almost religious reverence': note by J. J. Paskin after visit to Labuan, December 1945, CO 537/1631.
258 'offered a knighthood': Gerard MacBryan to Smith, 4 December 1947, cited in *The Name of Brooke*, p.187.
258 'found [MacBryan's] suave': minute by Kenneth Roberts-Wray, 21 January 1946, National Archives, CO 537/1638.
258 'Besides his helping': *The Name of Brooke*, p.187.
258 'sheds more light': see Smith to Gent, 14 December 1945, and minute by Galsworthy, 14 December 1945, National Archives, CO 537/1637.
258 'MacBryan was to be': War Office to Brigadier E. C. Gibbons, 19 December 1945, WO 203/3973.
258 'They arrived': report by W. C. S. Corry on his visit to Sarawak, CO 537/1631, ff358–61.
259 'In addition': *The Name of Brooke*, pp.199–201. It appears that MacBryan had also used money to obtain the signatures of

leading members of the Chinese community on a statement supporting a new agreement with the British government; Ong Tiang Swee, the most prominent of the Sarawak Chinese, later thanked the Rajah for the $42,500 that his people had been given.

259 'fulfil in every sense': 7 January 1946, CO 537/1631, f382.

259 'perfectly fair to': Corry to Gent, 7 January 1946, WO 203/3974.

259 'in accordance': report by W. C. S. Corry on his visit to Sarawak, CO 537/1631, ff358–61.

260 'more direct protection': *Sarawak Tribune*, 8 February 1946.

260 'Its egotistical': Brooke Papers, Box 2/3; *The Name of Brooke*, p.203n.

260 'indulging his lust': *Queen*, pp.155–6.

261 'a real desire': *Hansard*, Fifth Series, Vol.418, pp.1726–31.

261 'Britain Buys Sarawak': *Evening Standard*, 6 February 1946.

261 '£1,000,000 compensation': *Daily Express*, 7 February 1946.

261 'put too much trust': *Queen*, pp.156–60.

262 'crude Imperialism': *Manchester Guardian*, 7 February 1946.

262 'You ask me': OE to DB, 22 April 1946, HRHRC.

262 'Of the British newspapers': *The Times*, 7 February 1946; *Manchester Guardian*, 8 February 1946; *Sunday Times*, 10 February 1946.

263 'In Sarawak': *Sarawak Tribune*, 8 February 1946; CO 537/1640.

263 'Wake up!': Goss to Macaskie, 14 January 1946, Macaskie Papers.

263 'pay annual visits': *Sarawak Tribune*, 22 and 23 February 1946, quoted in *The Name of Brooke*, p.206.

263 'The Malay National': Malay National Union to Datu Patinggi, 12 March 1946, Brooke Papers, Box 11/2, quoted in *The Name of Brooke*, p.206.

263 'more favourable response from the Chinese': *The Name of Brooke*, pp.208–9.

263 'The Ibans will lose': *Sarawak Tribune*, 23 and 26 February 1946, quoted in *The Name of Brooke*, pp.209–10.

264 'under some improved': *The Times*, 14 February 1946.

264 'those peculiar girls': *The Name of Brooke*, p.213.

264 'out of the world': Shenton Thomas to George Hall, 17 February 1946, National Archives, CO 537/1632.

265 'incompetent and corrupt': note of interview with Bishop of Newcastle [late February 1946], CO 537/1632.

265 'parliamentary mission': *Hansard*, 27 March 1946.

CHAPTER 15

page

267 'one last desperate': *Queen*, p.156.

267 'He recalls that': conversation with Lord Tanlaw, 20 October 2005.

268 'buxom blonde': note by BB, 3

March 1946, Brooke Papers, Box 2, file 3, f65.
268 'got me into': *My Lovely Days*, pp.113–14.
268 'By Bertram's account': note by BB, 3 March 1946, supra.
268 'the most wonderful': *My Lovely Days*, pp.113–14.
268 'dull little American': SB to DB, 16 May 1944, HRHRC.
268 'They reported back': *The Name of Brooke*, p.213.
268 'understood by no one': Banks to Macaskie, 23 March 1946, Macaskie Papers, file 3.
268 'no room for doubts': Creech Jones to VB, 12 March 1946, Brooke Papers, Box 6/1.
269 'Vyner initially': G. H. Hall to BB, 2 April 1946, quoted in *Facts About Sarawak*, p.55.
269 'greater prosperity': Datus Menteri, Hakim, Amar and Pahlawan to BB, 11 April 1946, Brooke Papers, Vol.21.
269 'immense moral': BB to Datus Menteri, Hakim, Amar and Pahlawan, 12 April 1946, Brooke Papers, Vol.21; *The Name of Brooke*, p.216.
269 'simply vanished': *Queen*, p.159.
269 'a difference of': VB to Secretary of State, 6 August 1948, CO 938/5/1.
269 'some camouflage': BB to Margaret Noble, 5 April 1946, Brooke Papers, Box 12/3.
270 'others who did not': *The Name of Brooke*, p.218.
270 'a good deal of gin': Dawson Diary, Rhodes House Library.
270 'Never before': *Queen*, pp.158–9.
271 'The next morning': Dawson Diary, 15 April 1946, supra.
271 'What! No cession?': Kuek Seow Hiang to BB, 17 May 1946, quoted in *The Name of Brooke*, p.219.
271 'We have not': *Daily Telegraph*, 18 April 1946.
272 'played a part': Macaskie to Lloyd, 4 April 1946, CO 537/1637, f26.
272 'nice round heads': Dawson Diary, 16 April 1946.
272 'It was as if': *Queen*, p.161.
274 'with true Oriental': Philip Ziegler (ed.): *Personal Diary of Admiral The Lord Louis Mountbatten, 1943–46*, pp.321–2.
275 'and the true': *Queen*, p.160.
275 'I have given': *Sarawak Tribune*, 26 April 1946.
276 'giving the impression': Dawson report, 20 May 1946, CO 537/1633.
276 'not very good': Dawson Diary, 27 April 1946.
276 'he was amongst': *Queen*, pp.162–3.
277 'they had simply': *Queen*, p.166.
277 'making a beeline for': Gammans: Parliamentary Mission to Sarawak, 1946, Gammans Papers, Rhodes House Library, MSS Pac r10; many Sarawakian girls, mainly Chinese and Iban, were conscripted into Japanese military brothels, supplemented by more girls from Taiwan, Korea and Java. The main military brothel in Kuching was the former home of the manager of the Borneo Company; two schools were also

used for the same purpose. The establishments were run by madams, the women given regular health checks, and charges levied according to rank. Local women of a higher class were recruited for the senior officers' club. See *Masa Jepun*, pp.93–6.

277 'really quite pretty': Dawson Diary, 21 May 1946.

277 'polite request': Dawson Diary, 1 May 1946.

277 'simple Dayaks': Dawson Diary, 1 May 1946.

278 'R & R': Dawson Diary, 3 May 1946.

278 'infested with': Gammans: Parliamentary Mission, supra, p.11.

278 'No Cession': ibid, pp.13–14.

278 'establish a suitable': Dawson's report to Hall, 20 May 1946, CO 537/1633, f216.

279 'in our view': Gammans and Rees-Williams to Hall, 10 May 1946, Gammans Papers.

279 'they lopped off': Gammans: Parliamentary Mission, supra, p.26.

279 'look silly': VB to BB, undated, Brooke Papers, Box 19, file 8, ff 43–4.

280 'In that case': F. H. Pollard report, p.6, Brooke Papers, Vol.21, quoted in *The Name of Brooke*, p.232.

280 'to become the': BB to VB, 7 May 1946, Brooke Papers, Box 2/3, quoted in *The Name of Brooke*, p.229.

280 'secrecy and': BB to VB, 13 May 1946, Gammans Papers, quoted in *The Name of Brooke*, p.230.

280 'shaken his fist': Dawson Diary.

280 'received a death threat': Pollard report, supra, p.5.

280 'generally on the same lines': *Sarawak Tribune*, 15 May 1946.

280 'most unsatisfactory': Gammans: Parliamentary Mission, supra, p.19.

281 'made a magnificent': *Queen*, p.169.

281 'When reporting': Dawson Diary, 16 May 1946; *The Name of Brooke*, p.237.

282 'four postage stamps': the stamps had been designed and printed in 1941 and as a war precaution were originally despatched to Sarawak that September in two consignments. The first consignment was diverted to Australia due to the invasion of Sarawak by the Japanese, while the second ended up in South Africa. It was the Australian consignment that the Rajah took with him out to Sarawak in 1946. See W. Batty-Smith, 'Sarawak – the Bradbury Wilkinson issues, 1934–1947', *Gibbons Stamp Monthly*, Vol.34, No.2 (July 2003), p.395.

282 'a victory of': Dawson's report to Hall, 20 May 1946, CO 981/1 [58501], quoted in *The Name of Brooke*, p.238.

282 'Cold feet': Dawson Diary, 18 May 1946.

282 'the storm over': *Queen*, p.170.

283 'a charming, bright': Lord Ogmore: 'A Voyage in HMS *Pickle*', *Contemporary Review*, Vol.206 (May 1965), p.239.

283 'even more extraordinary':

Gammans: Parliamentary Mission, supra, pp.18–21.

CHAPTER 16

page

285 'Vyner began': *Queen*, pp.171–5.
286 'Of course it is sad': SB to DB; 4 July 1946, HRHRC.
286 'the only suitable place': CO 539/1639.
286 'the most intelligent': SB to DB, 1 June 1945, HRHRC.
287 'no steam heating': ibid, 4 February 1947.
287 'pointless and monotonous': *Queen*, pp.173–4.
287 'Dear Uncle Vyner': 6 February 1946, Brooke Papers, Box 19, file 4.
288 'life's ambition': undated, Brooke Papers, Box 19, file 5.
288 'to consult my friends': *Evening Standard*, 5 December 1946.
288 'His other purpose': AB to Colonial Secretary (Creech Jones), 6 November 1946, *Daily Telegraph*, 21 December 1946.
289 'Anthony responded': *Daily Telegraph*, 21 December 1946.
289 'In Sarawak': *The Name of Brooke*, pp.266–7.
289 'in such a hurry': *Queen*, pp.174–5.
290 'damned hard': SB to DB, 18 October 1948, HRHRC.
290 'absolutely illegal': OE to DB, 21 October 1941, supra, quoted in Hignett, pp.236–7.
290 'They did occasionally': Hignett, pp.242–3.
290 'peacing out my will': SB to DB, 30 May 1947, supra.
290 'We haven't nearly': ibid, 18 October 1948.
290 'received £15,000': A. F. Pollard to J. A. Smith, 30 January 1945, Brooke Papers. Vol.19.
290 'I don't even see': SB to DB, 1 June 1945, supra.
291 'hand out to those': *Queen*, p.182.
291 'During the war': SB to DB, 16 May 1944, supra.
291 'What a fool': SB to Gerard MacBryan, 2 November 1947, CO 938/5/7.
291 'like water': *Queen*, pp.182–3.
291 'violating a pledge': VB to Secretary of State, 6 August 1948, CO 938/5/1.
292 'a most extraordinary': minute by W. L. Dale, 27 August 1948, CO 938/5/1.
292 'not been at all': SB to A. Creech Jones, 11 August 1948, CO 938/5/1.
292 'gone mad': SB to DB, 18 October 1948, HRHRC.
293 'obsessed by' *Queen*, pp.177–8.
293 'turning up naked': Payne, p.167.
293 'small portable': AB to GB, May 1950, Brooke Papers, Box 34, file 11, f98.
294 'Sylvia only heard': *Queen*, p.179.
294 'in lieu of': minute by Sir G. Whiteley, 14 August 1948, CO 938/5/1.
294 'a very la de da': SB to DB, 1 June 1945, HRHRC.
294 'just bought': ibid, 4 July 1946.
295 'middle aged': ibid, 4 July 1946.
295 'it looked like': *Queen*, p.173.

295 'hasn't altered': SB to DB, undated, HRHRC.
295 'as sweet as': ibid, 7 December 1949.
296 'play the indignant': *Queen*, p.173.
296 'fun to be': ibid, p.176.
297 'an indictment': SB to Roger W. Straus, 15 April 1950, Farrar, Straus & Giroux, Inc. Records, New York Public Library.
297 'the novel itself': Roger Straus to SB, 20 April 1950, ibid.
297 'I don't know': undated note, ibid.
298 'slow and peaceful': *Queen*, p.177.
299 'to get wind': Security Services to C. J. J. T. Barton, Colonial Office, 9 February 1950, National Archives, KV2/1855.
299 'no evidence': report on AB by Security Intelligence Far East, 24 March 1950, National Archives, KV2/1855.
299 'the final indication': *The Name of Brooke*, p.277.
300 'curiously empty': *Queen*, p.180.
300 'MUCH the best': SB to DB, 1 August 1953, HRHRC.
300 'There isn't': ibid, 20 October 1952.
301 'squat and square': ibid, 7 December 1949.
301 'which isn't bad': ibid, 1 August 1953.
301 'busily engaged': ibid, 5 April 1955.
301 'as if a bomb': *Queen*, p.181.
302 'You have never': *Gazette*, Montreal, 2 July 1957.
302 'a pudding stirrer': conversation with Marie Cheyne, April 2004.
302 'perfectly self-contained': SB to DB, 3 February 1958, HRHRC.
302 'would go to': *Queen*, p.190.
303 'Occasionally, he would': conversation with Lord Tanlaw, 20 September 2005.
303 'a comforting feeling': *Queen*, p.184.
303 'all Vyner': ibid, p.186.
304 'It was later reported': *Time*, 17 May 1963.
304 'severe training': *The Times*, 10 May 1963.
304 'be chiefly': *Daily Telegraph*, 10 May 1963.
304 'shivering with': *Queen*, p.189.
305 'one of three': ibid, 191.
305 'full-time ambassador': *Scotsman*, 19 March 1960.
305 'infused with a': AB to Kathleen Brooke, 10 March 1973, Brooke Papers, Box 35, file 7.
307 'Leonora for one': Leonora Tompkins to Theodore Page, undated, Brooke Papers, Vol.19.
307 'no beef with': ibid, 24 August 1964.
307 'Leonora had more beef': ibid, 24 August 1964 and 7 August 1965.
308 'published in July 1970': all the correspondence relating to its publication seems to have been lost during the takeover of Sidgwick & Jackson by Macmillan.
308 'a little melodramatic': SB to DB, 12 August 1970, HRHRC.
308 'with great joy': DB to SB, 14 November 1970, Brooke Papers, Box 16, file 5.
308 'I guess when one': SB to Evelyn

Hussey, undated, Brooke Papers, Vol. 19.

309 'no exaggeration': the reviews appeared on the dust jacket of the American edition (William Morrow, 1972).

309 'the improbable': *Times Literary Supplement*, 4 September 1970.

309 'When the enthusiastic': *New York Times*, 14 April 1972, p. 37.

310 'I didn't care': See *Listener*, 27 April 1972, p. 544.

SELECT BIBLIOGRAPHY

Books by Sylvia Brooke (Sylvia Brett before her marriage in 1911)

NON-FICTION

Sylvia of Sarawak, Hutchinson, 1936
The Three White Rajas, Cassell, 1939
Queen of the Head-Hunters, Sidgwick & Jackson, 1970

FICTION

Pan and the Little Green Gate, Hodder & Stoughton, 1908
The Street With Seven Houses, Hodder & Stoughton, 1909
Toys, John Murray, 1923
The Cauldron, Eveleigh Nash & Co., 1925
Lost Property, Eveleigh Nash & Co., 1930
A Star Fell, Harrison-Hilton (US), 1940; T. Werner Laurie, 1941
The Darlingtons, Farrar, Straus & Giroux (US), 1950; Boardman 1953
Headwind House, Boardman, 1953

OTHER BOOKS

Allen, Charles: *Tales from the South China Seas*, André Deutsch, 1983
Banks, E. H.: *The Green Desert*, privately published
Barley, Nigel; *White Rajah*, Little, Brown, 2002
Barrow, Andrew: *Gossip: A History of High Society from 1920 to 1970*, Hamish Hamilton, 1978
Birkin, Andrew: *J. M. Barrie and The Lost Boys*, Yale University Press, 2003
Brett, Lionel: *Our Selves Unknown*, Victor Gollancz, 1985
Brooke, Anthony: *The Facts About Sarawak*, Balding and Mansell, 1946
Brooke, Charles: *Ten Years in Sarawak*, Tinsley Brothers, 1866; Oxford University Press, 1990
Brooke, Gladys: *Relations and Complications*, Bodley Head, 1929
Brooke, Margaret: *Good Morning and Goodnight*, Constable & Co., 1934
Brooke, Margaret: *My Life in Sarawak*, Methuen & Co., 1913
Brooke Tompkins, Leonora: *My Lovely Days*, Carlton Press, New York, 1966

Buruma, Ian: *Inventing Japan*, Weidenfeld & Nicolson, 2003
Carrington, Noel (ed.): *Mark Gertler: Selected Letters*, Rupert Hart-Davis, 1965
Chaney, Lisa: *A Life of J. M. Barrie*, Hutchinson, 2005
Crisswell, Colin N.: *Rajah Charles Brooke, Monarch of All He Surveyed*, Oxford University Press, 1978
Crisswell, Colin N.: *The End of the Brooke Raj in Sarawak*, Kiscadale, 1994
De Windt, Harry: *My Restless Life*, Grant Richards, 1909
Digby, K. H.: *Lawyer in the Wilderness*, Cornell, 1980
Dunbar, Jane: *J. M. Barrie: The Man Behind the Image*, Collins, 1970
Dudley Ward, C. H.: *A Romance of the Nineteenth Century*, John Murray, 1923
Esher, Reginald: *Cloud-capp'd Towers*, John Murray, 1927
Floyd, Barry: *The White Rajahs of Sarawak: a Philatelic and Historical Study*, Travellers Tree, 2003
Fraser, George MacDonald: *Flashman's Lady*, Barrie & Jenkins, 1977
Fraser, Peter: *Lord Esher: a Political Biography*, Hart-Davis MacGibbon, 1973
Glyn, Elinor: *The Career of Katherine Bush*, Duckworth, 1917
Glyn, Elinor: *Three Weeks*, Duckworth, 1907
Halliburton, Richard: *The Flying Carpet*, Garden City, New York, 1932
Harrisson, Tom: *World Within*, The Cresset Press, 1959
Hignett, Sean: *Brett, From Bloomsbury to New Mexico*, Hodder and Stoughton, 1984
Holroyd, Michael: *Bernard Shaw*, Vol.II, Chatto & Windus, 1989
Hose and MacDougall: *Pagan Tribes of Borneo*, Macmillan, 1912
Howes, Peter H. H.: *In a Fair Ground*, Excalibur, 1995
Huxley, Julian: *Memories*, Allen and Unwin, 1970
Huxley, Juliette: *Leaves of the Tulip Tree*, John Murray, 1986
James, Edward: *Swans Reflecting Elephants, My Early Years*, Weidenfeld & Nicolson, 1982
Lees-Milne, James: *The Enigmatic Edwardian*, Sidgwick & Jackson, 1986
Lees-Milne, James: *Midway on the Waves*, Sidgwick & Jackson, 1985
McLeod, Alan L.: 'Sylvia Brooke, Ranee of Sarawak: Pioneer Feminist Writer', *Commonwealth*, Vol.22, N1, Autumn 1999
Mackenzie-Grieve, Averil: *Time and Chance*, Geoffrey Bles, 1970
McKinstry, Leo: *Rosebery, Statesman in Turmoil*, John Murray, 2005
Mainwaring, Marion: *Mysteries of Paris: the Quest for Morton Fullerton*, University Press of New England, 2001
Martine, Roddy: *Scorpion on the Ceiling*, Librario, 2006
Maugham, W. Somerset: *The Casuarina Tree*, Heinemann, 1926
Maugham, W. Somerset: *A Writer's Notebook*, Heinemann, 1949
Mjöberg, E.: *Borneo: Durch die Insel der Kopfjäger: Abenteuer im Innern von Borneo*, Brockhaus/Leipzig, 1929; translated from the original German as *L'ile des Chasseurs de Têtes*, Paris, 1934
Morgan, Tom: *Somerset Maugham*, Jonathan Cape, 1980
Morris, James: *Farewell the Trumpets*, Faber & Faber, 1978
Morris, James: *Pax Britannica*, Faber & Faber, 1968

Ogmore, Lord: 'A Voyage in HMS *Pickle*', *Contemporary Review*, Vol. 206 (Jan-Jun 1965), pp.239–46 and 300–4.
O'Hanlon, Redmond: *Into the Heart of Borneo*, Salamander Press, 1984
Parris, Matthew: *Great Parliamentary Scandals*, Robson Books, 1995
Parry-Jones, William: *The Trade in Lunacy*, Routledge & Kegan Paul, 1972
Payne, Robert: *The White Rajahs of Sarawak*, Robert Hale, 1960
Peters, Margot: *Bernard Shaw and the Actresses*, Doubleday, 1980
Pollard, Elizabeth: *Kuching Past and Present*, Borneo Literature Bureau, 1972
Ponsonby, Sir Frederick, *Recollections of Three Reigns*, Eyre & Spottiswoode, 1951
Pringle, Robert: *Rajahs and Rebels*, Macmillan, 1970
Pybus, Cassandra: *White Rajah: a Dynastic Intrigue*, University of Queensland Press, St Lucia, 1996.
Reece, R. H. W.: *The Name of Brooke*, Oxford University Press, 1982
Reece, R. H. W.: *Masa Jepun*, Sarawak Literary Society, 1998
Reece, R. H. W.: *The White Rajahs of Sarawak: a Borneo Dynasty*, Archipelago Press, 2004
Richman, Harry: *A Hell of a Life*, Duell, Sloan and Pearce, 1966
Rhodes James, Robert: *Rosebery*, Weidenfeld & Nicolson, 1963
Rose, Kenneth, *King George V*, Weidenfeld & Nicolson, 1983
Rose, Kenneth, *Kings, Queens and Courtiers*, Weidenfeld & Nicolson, 1985
Runciman, Steven: *The White Rajahs*, Cambridge, 1960
Rutter, Owen: *Triumphant Pilgrimage*, Harrap & Co., 1937
Seymour, Miranda: *Ottoline Morrell: Life on a Grand Scale*, Hodder and Stoughton, 1992
Smith, Grover: *Letters of Aldous Huxley*, Chatto & Windus, 1969
Tarling, Nicholas: *Britain, the Brookes and Brunei*, Oxford University Press, 1971
Tarling, Nicholas: 'Sir Cecil Clementi and the Federation of British Borneo', *Journal of the Malayan Branch of the Royal Asiatic Society*, Vol. XLIV, Part 2 (1971), pp.1–34
Tarling, Nicholas: 'Britain and Sarawak in the Twentieth Century: Raja Charles, Raja Vyner and the Colonial Office', *Journal of the Malayan Branch of the Royal Asiatic Society*, Vol. XLIII, Part 2 (December 1970), pp.25–52
Ward, A. B.: *Rajah's Servant*, Cornell University, 1966
Ziegler, Philip (ed.): *Personal Diary of Admiral The Lord Louis Mountbatten, 1943–1946*, Collins, 1988

INDEX